DONALD M. LEWIS

A SHORT
HISTORY OF
CHRISTIAN
ZIONISM

FROM THE REFORMATION TO
THE TWENTY-FIRST CENTURY

An imprint of InterVarsity Press
Downers Grove, Illinois

InterVarsity Press
P.O. Box 1400, Downers Grove, IL 60515-1426
ivpress.com
email@ivpress.com

InterVarsity Press® is the book-publishing division of InterVarsity Christian Fellowship/USA®, a movement of students and faculty active on campus at hundreds of universities, colleges, and schools of nursing in the United States of America, and a member movement of the International Fellowship of Evangelical Students. For information about local and regional activities, visit intervarsity.org.

Cover design and image composite: David Fassett
Interior design: Daniel van Loon
Images: antique map of Israel © Hemera Technologies / AbleStock.com / Getty Images Plus
    Star of David © Issaurinko / iStock / Getty Images Plus
    silver paint stroke © jayk7 / Moment / Getty Images
    bright blue grungy texture © R.Tsubin / Moment / Getty Images

ISBN 978-0-8308-4697-9 (print)
ISBN 978-0-8308-4698-6 (digital)

Printed in the United States of America ♾

InterVarsity Press is committed to ecological stewardship and to the conservation of natural resources in all our operations. This book was printed using sustainably sourced paper.

Library of Congress Cataloging-in-Publication Data
Names: Lewis, Donald M., author.
Title: A short history of Christian Zionism : from the Reformation to the
  twenty-first century / Donald M. Lewis.
Description: Downers Grove, IL : IVP Academic, [2021] | Includes
  bibliographical references and indexes.
Identifiers: LCCN 2021013506 (print) | LCCN 2021013507 (ebook) | ISBN
  9780830846979 (paperback) | ISBN 9780830846986 (ebook)
Subjects: LCSH: Christian Zionism. | Christianity and other
  religions—Judaism—History. |
  Judaism—Relations—Christianity—History. | Jews—Restoration. |
  Religion and politics—History. | Israel—History.
Classification: LCC DS150.5 .L493 2021 (print) | LCC DS150.5 (ebook) |
  DDC 231.7/6—dc23
LC record available at https://lccn.loc.gov/2021013506
LC ebook record available at https://lccn.loc.gov/2021013507

P	25	24	23	22	21	20	19	18	17	16	15	14	13	12	11	10	9	8	7	6	5	4	3	2	1
Y	42	41	40	39	38	37	36	35	34	33	32	31	30	29	28	27	26	25	24	23	22	21			

CONTENTS

Acknowledgments | *ix*

Introduction | *1*

1   From the Early Church to the Reformation | *17*

2   Geneva and the Jews: Tectonic Shifts in the Landscape of Jewish-Christian Relations | *44*

3   English Puritanism and the Jews | *57*

4   The German Pietists and the Jews: Philo-Semitism and the New Evangelistic Imperative | *78*

5   Restorationism in America: From the Early American Puritans to the American Revolution | *86*

6   The Jews and Nineteenth-Century British Evangelicalism: Restorationism Morphs into Christian Zionism | *92*

7   Preparing the Ground for the Balfour Declaration | *118*

8   Restorationism and Christian Zionism in America from the Revolution to 1914 | *132*

9   The Balfour Declaration of 1917 | *164*

10 American Christian Zionism from 1914 to 1948: World War I and the Vindication of Premillennialism | *186*

11 Christian Zionism and Developments in Palestine: From the Balfour Declaration to Israeli Independence | *216*

12 American Christian Zionism Since 1948 | *243*

13 American Christian Zionist Activities and Organizations | *289*

14 Christian Zionism in Renewalist and Global Movements | *316*

15 Christian Zionism Today: A "New" Christian Zionism | *344*

General Index | *363*

Scripture Index | *373*

ACKNOWLEDGMENTS

I WOULD LIKE TO EXPRESS my appreciation to those who have enabled this work. First and foremost, I would like to express my gratitude to my wife, Lindi, whose loving support is deeply appreciated. Second, I want to thank the Regent College board of governors, who have generously funded my teaching and research over many years as a full-time faculty member. The board has enabled me to undertake the sort of sustained, serious scholarship that can only be done with the leisure of time and the funding necessary to travel, attend conferences, and do archival research. I am deeply indebted to the college's generosity in all these matters.

I would also like to thank Dr. Cindy Aalders, the Regent College librarian, and her staff, who have been unfailingly helpful and considerate. I also want to express my appreciation to the librarians of the University of British Columbia and of the Bodleian Library, Oxford, for their excellent professional services, which have enabled me to access their superb theological and historical collections. I also want to express my appreciation to the Rev. David Pileggi, rector of Christ Church, Jerusalem, who warmly welcomed me to Jerusalem, entertained me in his own home, and allowed me to consult Christ Church's archives dealing with the London Jews Society's work in nineteenth-century Palestine. I also want to acknowledge the kind hospitality of Gary Hedrick of CFJ Ministries based in San Antonio, Texas, who allowed me to stay at the CFJ's Halff House in Jerusalem during a period of research, and to the International Christian Embassy Jerusalem, and especially Jehu Ketola, for their warm welcome to their celebration of the Feast of Tabernacles in October 2017. I am also grateful to Johannes Gerloff, a journalist and author based in Jerusalem who graciously welcomed me on my visit, providing insight and helpful background.

I want to express my appreciation to Jon Boyd, the editorial director for IVP Academic, whose professionalism and kindness have characterized all our communications.

A number of remarkably capable teaching assistants have worked with me on the book over several years, and I wish to thank them by name: Erica Bowler, James Hooks, Tim Opperman, Yehuda Mansell, and Jacob Samuel Raju. Three of these are now in doctoral programs, and a fourth is hoping to undertake doctoral studies in the near future.

There are a number of scholars who have read and commented on part or the whole manuscript, and I am especially grateful for their advice: Yaakov Ariel, Philip Church, Andrew Crome, Rodney Curtis, Paul Freston, Daniel Hummel, Daniel Nessim, Eric Newberg, Martin Spence, and Matthew Westbrook. And there are those whose advice I have sought on particular sections of the manuscript: Darrell Bock, George Carras, Gershon Greenberg, Gerald Hobbes, Paul C. Merkley, Stephen Pattee, Matthew Avery Sutton, Bruce K. Waltke, Steve Watts, Paul Wilkinson, and N. T. Wright. I am also grateful for helpful conversations with David Bebbington, whose encyclopedic knowledge of evangelical history never ceases to amaze. I also want to thank the three anonymous reviewers of the first draft of this book who were commissioned by IVP Academic. Their feedback has been invaluable. To all of these scholars I want to express my gratitude and appreciation.

While I am indebted to many academic colleagues who have assisted me in writing this book, I know not all of them will feel that they can agree with my conclusions. None of them is responsible for the use that I have made of their help, and needless to say, responsibility for any errors of fact or peculiarities of interpretation is to be laid at my feet.

INTRODUCTION

Virtually no histories of Zionism, Israel, and the Arab-Israeli conflict have paid much attention to evangelical support of the advancement of the Zionist plan and the Israeli state.[1]

YAAKOV ARIEL, 2013

THIS BOOK SEEKS TO PROVIDE an overview of the history of Christian Zionism by charting the genesis of the movement and tracing its lineage. Although it is an important contemporary phenomenon whose significance is now being widely acknowledged, its long history is little understood.[2] As Shalom Goldman has observed regarding Zionist historiography, "For the most part Christians do not feature in this narrative except as antagonists."[3] This book seeks to understand the movement's lineage, and how and why it has developed as it has. It is not a polemical work, either for or against Christian Zionism. It seeks more to understand than to persuade, in the hope that a fair-minded evaluation of the movement's history will promote understanding.

THE POLITICIZED NATURE OF THE TOPIC

Christian Zionism is usually examined solely through a political lens. This approach often fails to take the role of theology seriously, which as Faydra Shapiro has argued, "misses a great deal about the culture of Christian

---

[1]Yaakov Ariel, *An Unusual Relationship: Evangelical Christians and Jews* (New York: New York University Press, 2013), 9.
[2]On the history of the study of Christian Zionism to 2009, see Shalom Goldman, *Zeal for Zion: Christians, Jews, & the Idea of the Promised Land* (Chapel Hill: University of North Carolina Press, 2009), 15-16.
[3]Goldman, *Zeal for Zion*, 1.

Zionism. Focusing overly much on the political does a disservice to the complex and powerful motives and implications of this world view."[4] Christian Zionism has a political dimension, but its implications are complex and rarely straightforward. It is, as Matthew Westbrook has argued, "a long-developing and complex phenomenon that requires careful delineation and study in its various iterations and contexts."[5] There have been, and are still, differing "Christian Zionist streams from versions both historical and con-temporaneous [that] take various positions on theological issues, each with their own (often significant) social effects."[6] The theological basis of the un-derlying Christian Zionist beliefs has kept on shifting over time, which makes tracking its history more difficult.

Definitions

Historically, the term *restorationism* was used to designate the belief that the Jews would one day be physically restored to their homeland in the Middle East. It was generally understood that this physical restoration would occur after the mass conversion of the Jewish people to the Christian faith. How that prophetic belief morphed into the political movement that I am de-fining as "Christian Zionism" is the central narrative of this book. This shift from a prophetic restorationism that envisioned the eventual return of the Jews to a political movement that promoted such a return in the here and now occurred in the nineteenth century.

Defining Christian Zionism is fraught with difficulty. I begin by defining what I mean by *Zionism*. The term was first used only in 1890; the Merriam-Webster dictionary definition is: "an international movement originally for the establishment of a Jewish national or religious community in Palestine and later for the support of modern Israel."[7] The term *Christian Zionist* can be found as early as 1896, when the Jewish Zionist leader Theodor Herzl referred to William Hechler, the Anglican chaplain to the British Embassy

---

[4]Faydra Shapiro, *Christian Zionism: Navigating the Jewish-Christian Border* (Eugene, OR: Cascade, 2015), 44.

[5]Matthew C. Westbrook, "The International Christian Embassy, Jerusalem, and Renewalist Zion-ism: Emerging Jewish-Christian Ethnonationalism" (PhD diss., Drew University, 2014), 25.

[6]Westbrook, "Christian Embassy," 25.

[7]Merriam-Webster, "Zionism," www.merriam-webster.com/dictionary/Zionism#h1. This point is important to distinguish traditional Jewish longings for a return to Zion from the new movement that emerged among Jews in the late nineteenth century intent on making this happen.

in Vienna, as a "Christian Zionist" and the following year Herzl again used that term to describe Jean-Henri Dunant, a Swiss banker and founder of the Red Cross, and an observer at the First Zionist Conference.[8] In 1899 Richard Gottheil, professor of Semitic languages at Columbia University, published a Zionist article in which he quoted "a Christian Zionist" (George Eliot) who many years before had written, "The sons of Judah have to choose, in order that God may again choose them."[9] The *New York Times* used the term *Christian Zionist* in obituaries, and it appears in letters to the editor from about 1903. Nahum Sokolow in his 1919 *History of Zionism: 1600–1918* refers to Lawrence Gawler as a "Christian Zionist."[10] The earliest use of the term *Christian Zionism* (rather than *Christian Zionist*) appears to have been in 1899, but it was used very infrequently between 1899 and 1905 and then not again until 1939. It became more frequent in the 1980s and 1990s, and much more frequent after the year 2000.[11]

Matthew Westbrook has observed that "no research has posited an ideal type of Christian Zionism from which iterations of the movement can be contrasted and compared."[12] My definition seeks to take his observation seriously. Thus, I define Christian Zionism across time as *a Christian movement which holds to the belief that the Jewish people have a biblically mandated claim to their ancient homeland in the Middle East.* Today the term *Christian Zionism* is widely used of Christians who hold that the state of Israel's right to exist is based on biblical teachings. (I qualify this because before the twentieth century many "restorationists" envisioned a "Jewish return" and a Jewish "homeland" but not necessarily a Jewish state.)

Of course, many Christians have believed in Israel's right to exist without being "Christian Zionists" in the way thus defined. In 1948 many Christians supported the establishment of the state of Israel without a specifically

---

[8]Paul Richard Wilkinson, *For Zion's Sake: Christian Zionism and the Role of John Nelson Darby*, Studies in Evangelical History and Thought (Milton Keynes, UK; Paternoster, 2007), 16. Dunant had a strong Calvinist upbringing, but he based his support on his humanitarian and moral concerns, not on the basis of biblical prophecy.

[9]Richard Gottheil, "Zionism," *Century Illustrated Magazine*, December 1899, 299. I am indebted to Andrew Crome for this reference. Gottheil does not identify the author, but the passage is from George Eliot's novel *Daniel Deronda* (1876), chap. 42, 1354.

[10]Nahum Sokolow, *History of Zionism, 1600–1918* (London: Longmans, Green, 1919), 2:410.

[11]The Google Books search engine enables one to track the use of the term over the past two hundred years in millions of printed works.

[12]Westbrook, "Christian Embassy," 62.

Christian Zionist motivation. One can be a Christian and favorable toward the notion of a Jewish homeland without being a "Christian Zionist"—that is, not all Christians who are Zionists are necessarily motivated by a biblical-theological concern. Yet, to date, there exists no comprehensive history of Christian Zionism that demonstrates a close acquaintance with the nuances of Christian theology.[13] This work hopes to fill this gap and is directed in the first instance to those who are puzzled by Christian Zionism.

Robert O. Smith defines the term in a similar way, only applying it to Christians who have been politically engaged in supporting the idea of a Jewish homeland.[14] Smith is reluctant to use the term of someone like John Nelson Darby, the father of dispensational premillennial theology, because he was apolitical. I agree with Smith's point. While Darby and the Plymouth Brethren believed theologically in the eventual establishment of a Jewish homeland, Darby did not teach that it would happen in this age but only after the "Rapture," and was unwilling to lift a finger to help accomplish it.

My use of the term *movement* in speaking of Christian Zionism is deliberate because it captures a sense of its momentum, in that Christian Zionism has always been like the Amazon, starting small with its headwaters in the Reformation but moving more quickly at different times and places—even cascading through pivotal events like the Balfour Declaration, Israeli Independence, and the 1967 Six-Day War—as it moved forward. But it has always been "on the move," adapting to changing circumstances and new events, morphing to adjust to various theologies and prophetic understandings. Christian Zionists, however, tend to view it as unchanging, forever true, and fixed. Sean Durbin's observation is appropriate here: "While Christian Zionism and what it means to support Israel has varied (and continues to vary)

---

[13] A British rabbi has written a helpful overview. See Dan Cohn-Sherbok, *The Politics of Apocalypse: The History and Influence of Christian Zionism* (Oxford: Oneworld, 2006).

[14] Robert O. Smith defines Christian Zionism as "political action, informed by specifically Christian commitments, to promote or preserve Jewish control over the geographic area now comprising Israel and Palestine." Göran Gunner and Robert O. Smith, *Comprehending Christian Zionism: Perspectives in Comparison* (Minneapolis: Fortress, 2014), 293. See also Carl F. Ehle, "Prolegomena to Christian Zionism in America: The Views of Increase Mather and William E. Blackstone Concerning the Doctrine of the Restoration of Israel" (PhD diss., New York University, 1977), 399. Samuel Goldman follows Spector's definition of the term *Christian Zionist* "to describe supporters of a Jewish state in some portion of the biblical Promised Land who draw their main inspiration from Christian beliefs, doctrines, or texts." Samuel Goldman, *God's Country: Christian Zionism in America* (Philadelphia: University of Pennsylvania Press, 2018), 4.

throughout history, this form of Christian identity must be continuously enacted in a given context, as though it were a static thing—in this case a static form of authentic, and hence original, Christian identity."[15] Within the claim by contemporary Christian Zionists, like John Hagee, that their Christian Zionism is simply "an essential component of authentic Christianity is the further implication that they are the purveyors of a rarefied form of knowledge of the world about which others remain ignorant."[16]

PROTESTANT SUPPORT AND TRADITIONAL CATHOLIC OPPOSITION TO CHRISTIAN ZIONISM

Until the twentieth century, Christian Zionism was an overwhelmingly Protestant movement and, as will be argued, was closely related both to anti-Catholic and anti-Muslim sentiments.[17] Some well-known Roman Catholics supported Zionism prior to Vatican II, notably the British diplomat Sir Mark Sykes and a few Catholic theologians and writers: Jacques Maritain, the French philosopher who helped draft the International Declaration of Human Rights; and the English writer G. K. Chesterton. (Perhaps it is significant that Sykes, Maritain, and Chesterton were all born into Protestant homes.) More will be said of recent changes in Catholic attitudes in the final chapters of this book, but suffice it to say that until the 1960s the Roman Catholic Church was not part of the story of Christian Zionism. From the time of the First Zionist Congress in 1897, the Vatican had fairly consistently opposed Zionism. Jewish scholars have generally followed the lead of Sergio Minerbi, the Italian Jewish historian who believed "that the Holy See harbored an implacable theological animus against the very idea of a Jewish state in the Holy Land because of the ancient teaching of contempt which held that the temple was destroyed and the Jews exiled from their homeland because of their alleged collective guilt for the death of Jesus."[18] Even Eugene

---

[15]Sean Durbin, *Righteous Gentiles: Religion, Identity, and Myth in John Hagee's Christians United for Israel*, Studies in Critical Research on Religion 9 (Leiden: Brill, 2019), 5.

[16]Durbin, *Righteous Gentiles*, 16.

[17]It has been very rare for an Eastern Orthodox theologian or writer to be supportive of Zionism, although it has been suggested that Lev Gillet (1893–1980), a French Roman Catholic convert to Orthodoxy, was such an exception.

[18]Eugene J. Fisher, review of *Cross on the Star of David: The Christian World in Israel's Foreign Policy, 1948–1967* by Uri Bialer, *Catholic Historical Review* 92, no. 3 (July 2006): 343, accessed January 20, 2021.

Fisher, of the Secretariat of Ecumenical and Interreligious Relations of the US Conference of Catholic Bishops, concedes that "this idea was commonly held among [Catholic] Christians before the Second Vatican Council's declaration *Nostra Aetate* in 1965."[19] The anti-Muslim impulse will be explored in chapter two, when dealing with the rise of Calvinism, and then in the final chapters of the book, when this concern reemerged.

RECENT WORKS

I want to acknowledge my debt to a number of historians whose works have appeared since my *Origins of Christian Zionism* was published in 2009. Yaakov Ariel, the leading scholar on Jewish-evangelical relations, published his *An Unusual Relationship: Evangelical Christians and Jews* in 2013 and continues to produce important writings. Shalom Goldman's book *Zeal for Zion: Christians, Jews, and the Idea of the Promised Land* (University of North Carolina Press, 2009) was published at the same time as my book, and thus I was not able to benefit from his excellent work. On the American side of things, Samuel Goldman's *God's Country: Christian Zionism in America* (University of Pennsylvania Press, 2018) has been especially helpful. Daniel G. Hummel's *Covenant Brothers* (University of Pennsylvania, 2019) is also excellent, based as it is on extensive archival resources in both the United States and Israel. Sean Durbin's study *Righteous Gentiles: Religion, Identity, and Myth in John Hagee's Christians United for Israel* (Brill, 2019) is a fascinating assessment of the theology and culture of the most important Christian Zionist group working to "bless" Israel.

CHRISTIAN ZIONISM AND IDENTITY FORMATION

Robert O. Smith's work *More Desired Than Our Owne Salvation: The Roots of Christian Zionism* (Oxford University Press, 2013) and Andrew Crome's *Christian Zionism and English National Identity, 1600–1850* (Palgrave-Macmillan, 2018) have been especially helpful in understanding the British context and its impact on national identity formation. Crome's observation that "projects to restore the Jews to their ancient homeland, whether expressed as eschatological hopes, utopian schemes, or in practical political

---

[19]Fisher, review of *Cross on the Star of David*, 343.

terms, have consistently served as means of national identity construction"[20] is particularly important in understanding both the past history of Christian Zionism, and its many new expressions in the twenty-first century. Crome's work develops "a model of national identity formation fueled by prophecy, oriented towards the fulfillment of national mission."[21] It is applicable across the centuries as restorationists and Christian Zionists have often understood their particular nation as an "elect" nation, but not finally *the* elect nation. As Crome has argued, Gentile nations can only ever experience "a form of secondary election," and they often understand "national identity primarily in relation to their nation's service to the Jewish people."[22] In doing so Christian Zionism employs "a form of othering in which identity developed by comparison with an outside group."[23] The "other" is positively construed. "In fact, the Jews when restored would be superior to the nation aiding them and would return to their place as God's first nation."[24] Chosen Christian nations never replace Israel as *the elect nation,* thus complicating the way one thinks about prophecy and national identity.

The central thesis of my earlier book *The Origins of Christian Zionism* was that "evangelical interest in the Jews was part and parcel of a wider process of evangelical identity construction that took a decisive turn in the nineteenth century."[25] The thread that holds this book together is a further development of this thesis, both backward and forward in time. Restorationism/Christian Zionism has been an important aspect of Protestant identity formation from the time of the second generation of the Reformation up until this present day, a concern that has had profound implications for Christian nations and the Jews.

The "restoration of Israel," then, has never been simply about the Jews, or "the land," or even Christian understandings of prophecy; it has been in large measure about how some Protestants have framed and acted out their own identity. Since the Reformation, this identity formation has been hammered

---

[20]Andrew Crome, *Christian Zionism and English National Identity, 1600–1850* (Cham, Switzerland: Palgrave Macmillan, 2018), 2.

[21]Crome, *Christian Zionism*, 2-3.

[22]Crome, *Christian Zionism*, 3.

[23]Crome, *Christian Zionism*, 3.

[24]Crome, *Christian Zionism*, 3.

[25]Donald M. Lewis, *The Origins of Christian Zionism: Lord Shaftesbury and Evangelical Support for a Jewish Homeland* (Cambridge: Cambridge University Press, 2009), 12.

out on the anvil of their relationship with the Jews. The ethno-nationalism that Christian restorationists fostered in England in the seventeenth century was largely focused on Protestant England's duties toward the Jews, and from there this ethno-nationalism spread to America and in the last few decades has flowed to the ends of the earth. Now any and all nations can be "elect nations" as they choose to "bless Israel." Christian Zionism today is an ever-widening stream and is expanding rapidly in many directions; it is a river that has burst its banks and is flooding new territory. Understanding its genesis and mapping its genealogy are the concerns of this book.

This book questions the significance often given to dispensational premillennialism in the standard narratives of Christian Zionism. While John Nelson Darby (the key formulator of dispensationalism) and his successors have been important, especially in America, this book argues that the influence of this movement is fairly recent in Christian Zionism's long history. While Darby himself cannot be considered a Christian Zionist, it will be argued in chapter eight that others who drew inspiration from Darby and/or dispensationalism became politically active Christian Zionists by significantly modifying Darby's teaching to insist that the restoration of the Jews would happen before the rapture, and they organized politically to enable this to happen. Ironically politically engaged American liberal Protestant supporters were more important to the American Zionist movement up to the 1970s than were the dispensationalists.[26]

This book thus attempts to achieve a comprehensive understanding of the phenomenon of Christian Zionism, which takes seriously its history, theology, and politics. It does so by examining its rise in the wake of the Protestant Reformation, tracing its development and changes over time, and assessing its influence in the modern world. The approach employed is chronological—it begins with the biblical material, the early church, moves on to the Middle Ages and then the Reformation, but then focuses on developments in Puritan England, colonial America, and nineteenth-century British evangelicalism, with particular attention given to the influence of German Pietism. The last section deals with the ways in which the movement has morphed in the twentieth and twenty-first centuries and now is rapidly

---

[26]In this I am echoing similar points made by Goldman, *God's Country*, 6-7.

expanding in the non-Western world as Christianity's center has moved from the North Atlantic world to the Global South.

AN OVERVIEW OF JEWISH ATTITUDES TO ZIONISM

It is profoundly ironic that the first modern Zionists were Christians, but this is understandable given that the talmudic tradition had long opposed any Zionist impulse. Following the fall of the temple in Jerusalem in AD 70, the Babylonian Talmud (Ketubbot 111A) had interpreted the first two of the three abjurations of the daughters of Jerusalem (Song of Songs 2:7; 3:5; 5:8) as involving two tasks given to the Jewish people. The first forbade Jews to return to *'erets* Israel (the land of Israel) "as a wall" meaning "en masse"; the second forbade them from rebelling against the nations in which they were dispersed. The long-standing rabbinic tradition focused on the messianic hope and the expectation of an eventual Jewish return to Zion accomplished by the Messiah alone. As Michael Stanislawski has observed, the rabbis had long opposed apocalyptic speculation: "Jews were forbidden to 'advance the end' or even calculate it. The messiah would be chosen by God in God's good time, and any activism among human beings to intervene in this process was heresy, to be condemned and punished."[27] Shalom Goldman comments, "Most, but not all, European Orthodox rabbinical authorities opposed Zionist plans for a Jewish political entity in Palestine. Individual or small group settlements were acceptable to these Orthodox rabbis, but any larger political plans contravened the idea that Jewish redemption would only come through divine intervention."[28]

In keeping with the second abjuration of the daughters of Zion, rabbinic Judaism had adopted a policy of "passive resistance" in the face of anti-Semitism, maintaining that Jews should keep a low profile and not challenge political authorities wherever they lived. This strategy of passivity was reinforced by Jewish religious law (halakah). The approach, writes Milton Viorst, "contained a vow on the part of the Jews—for reasons that were not clear—never to organize to return to their ancient home in Palestine. This vow, too,

---

[27]Michael Stanislawski, *Zionism: A Very Short Introduction* (New York: Oxford University Press, 2017), 3. For further details of rabbinic Judaism's traditional opposition to Zionism, see Goldman, *Zeal for Zion*, 4-5.

[28]Goldman, *Zeal for Zion*, 10.

became a fundamental tenet of rabbinic Judaism."[29] As Shalom Goldman has observed, "Until the late nineteenth century, most plans for a Jewish entity in Palestine were Christian."[30]

The political quietism of rabbinic Judaism was rejected out of hand by the early secular Jewish Zionist leaders. With the rise of ethnic nationalism in the nineteenth century, some Jews began to insist that Jews constituted not a religious group but rather a nation, and this implied a common history, a common language, and a geographically defined homeland. The Zionists stood in stark opposition to the traditional Jewish religious consensus. In 1806 the Great Sanhedrin of European rabbis had declared that the Jews were not a nation but rather a transnational religious group awaiting its messianic hope for transformation at the hands of God, not of humans.[31]

Jewish nationalism predated the widespread outbreaks of persecution in the early 1880s in Russia and the rising tide of anti-Semitism in France and Germany. Zionists applied ideas of Jewish nationalism on their own; they were not simply responding to persecution.[32] By the late nineteenth century, Jewish nationalists were prepared to turn their backs on the rabbinic consensus and take things into their own hands.[33] Although the Russian pogroms in the 1880s aimed against the Jews and growing anti-Semitism throughout Europe undoubtedly led more Jews to support Zionism, these factors facilitated but did not create the movement.

Most German Jews at the beginning of the nineteenth century were religious traditionalists, but by its end most were not. This shift, however, did not bring with it a groundswell of support for Zionism.[34] In the mid-nineteenth century, Zionism was rarely entertained, even by liberal rabbis. The avant-garde minority of rabbis who met in 1845 in Frankfurt-am-Main hoping to adapt Jewish ritual and beliefs to the modern age were willing to

---

[29]Milton Viorst, *Zionism: The Birth and Transformation of an Ideal* (New York: Thomas Dunne Books; St. Martin's Press, 2016), 2.

[30]Goldman, *Zeal for Zion*, 3.

[31]Isaiah Friedman, *The Question of Palestine, 1914–1918: British-Jewish-Arab Relations*, 2nd ed. (New Brunswick, NJ: Transaction, 1992), 32.

[32]Stanislawski, *Zionism*, 9.

[33]Viorst, *Zionism*, 3.

[34]Yaakov Ariel, "Wissenschaft des Judentums Comes to America: Kaufmann Kohler's Scholarly Projects and Jewish-Christian Relations," in *Die Entdeckung des Christentums in der Wissenschaft des Judentums*, ed. Görge K. Hasselhoff (Berlin: de Gruyter, 2010), 166.

give up on the traditional hopes of a personal Messiah; for them, "the Jews, instead of waiting to be redeemed by a Messiah, should themselves redeem the world."[35] They did not think redemption would be accomplished by resorting to a Jewish ghetto in Palestine; Jews should seek to be dispersed "still further into every land in the world till every nation should acknowledge one God alone, in the pure terms of the Jewish tradition."[36] As Christopher Sykes has observed of the mid-nineteenth century, "In Germany the influence of Moses Mendelssohn and his followers remained strong: the passion to be part of the civilization of the West was more powerful among German Jews than any sense of anger or embitterment."[37]

Even in the early twentieth century, Zionism was a tiny minority opinion within Judaism, rigorously opposed theologically by both Reform and Orthodox rabbis as well as by many more secular Jews who believed Jewish political emancipation required the integration of Jews into the political life of Western democracies, not identification with a Middle Eastern homeland. Furthermore, there was the pragmatic argument: in the nineteenth century the area known as Palestine had been an integral part of the Ottoman Empire, and the sultan was not disposed to cede territory to Jews. To do so was unthinkable, for he was the acknowledged defender of Islam and its holy sites. The Qur'an forbade the ceding of land taken by Islam. Even after the Balfour Declaration of November 1917 pledging British support for a "Jewish homeland," most Jews regarded the Zionist ideal as profoundly impractical given the violent opposition of Palestinians to Zionism.[38] In the period between the 1880s and 1945 Zionism was a minority view among Jews throughout the world; most rabbis and lay leaders were unsympathetic.[39]

The secular Jews who gathered in 1897 at the first World Zionist conference were also eager to abandon the messianic hope, but rather than advocate for assimilation they sought a Jewish restoration to Palestine accomplished by secular Jews like themselves. There were a handful of deeply religious Jews in the late nineteenth and early twentieth centuries who were

---

[35]Christopher Sykes, *Two Studies in Virtue* (London: Collins, 1951), 122.
[36]Sykes, *Two Studies in Virtue*, 123.
[37]Sykes, *Two Studies in Virtue*, 122.
[38]Stanislawski, *Zionism*, 54.
[39]Stanislawski, *Zionism*, 9. See also Goldman, *Zeal for Zion*, 68.

in favor of the Zionist cause, but they were a tiny minority.[40] The early Zionist pioneers Theodor Herzl and Israel Zangwill, and the key founders of the state of Israel—David Ben-Gurion, Menachem Begin, and Golda Meir—were resolutely secular Jews who received far more opposition to Zionism from rabbis than they did support.

It is important to acknowledge that in the late nineteenth and early twentieth centuries there were a few pioneering rabbis who argued that the secular Zionists were unwittingly doing God's will in promoting a return of Jews to Palestine. The key figure who emerged in the messianic Zionist movement was Rabbi Abraham Isaac Kook (1865–1935), the chief rabbi in the British Mandate period. There was also a small number of Orthodox Jews who were neither secular nor messianic, but rather were seeking a pragmatic solution to the threats of assimilation and anti-Semitism. In 1902 they formed a small party, Mizrahi, within the larger Zionist movement under the leadership of Rabbi Isaac Joseph Reines.[41] But such religious Zionists were very much the exception to the general rule. In fact, before 1945 most religious Jews regarded Zionism with deep hostility, believing that only the Messiah would return the Jews to their ancestral homeland.[42] Thomas Kolsky maintains that even after World War II "Zionism remained a minority movement among Jews."[43] After 1945 Jewish anti-Zionism was overwhelmed, and opposition to Zionism from religious Jews went into decline; even many pragmatists who had balked at the idea of a Jewish state changed their minds. In all this, it was the Holocaust that persuaded many Jews to embrace Zionism.[44]

The Holocaust brought about a significant change of heart on the part of many religious Jews, and their traditional anti-Zionist sentiments dissipated (but have not disappeared). Many previously hostile Jewish religious leaders came to embrace the establishment of the state of Israel. In view of the revelations of the extent of Hitler's implementation of his "final solution," a Jewish homeland came to be seen as the only way of safeguarding world

---

[40]Most prominent was Joseph Herman Hertz, the chief rabbi of the United Kingdom. Sykes, *Two Studies in Virtue*, 222.

[41]On Reines see Joshua Hovsha, "Clashing Worlds: Religion and State Dualism in Jewish Political Thought" (master's thesis, the University of the Witwatersrand, Johannesburg, South Africa, 2015), 44-45.

[42]Goldman, *Zeal for Zion*, 5.

[43]Thomas A. Kolsky, *Jews Against Zionism: The American Council for Judaism, 1942–1948* (Philadelphia: Temple University Press, 1990), 16.

[44]Stanislawski, *Zionism*, 54.

Jewry. It is important to appreciate that this was perhaps the greatest U-turn in the history of Judaism, simply breathtaking in its significance but obscured by the narrative recently spun by many that the Zionist achievement was the expected fulfillment of traditional Jewish religious hopes. This abandonment of the traditional expectations of the Messiah led to profound disillusionment and questioning of the whole religious tradition by some Jews and led some to abandon any belief in God. The American Yiddish writer Kadya Molodowsky, who had been raised as a Zionist in Eastern Europe, expressed the profound disillusionment felt by some Jews in the opening stanzas of her poem titled "Merciful God":

> Merciful God,
> Choose another people,
> Elect another.
> We are tired of death and dying,
> We have no more prayers.
> Choose another people,
> Elect another.
> We have no more blood
> To be a sacrifice.
> Our house has become a desert.
> The earth is insufficient for our graves,
> No more laments for us,
> No more dirges
> In the old, holy books.
>
> Merciful God,
> Sanctify another country,
> Another mountain.
> We have strewn all the fields and every stone
> With ash, with holy ash.
> With the aged,
> With the youthful,
> And with babies, we have paid
> For every letter of your Ten Commandments.[45]

---

[45]Kadya Molodowsky, "Merciful God," in *Paper Bridges: Selected Poems of Kadya Molodowsky,* trans., introduced, and ed. Kathryn Hellerstein (Detroit: Wayne State University Press, 1999). Used by permission.

It is important to realize that Israel's secular founders envisioned Israel as a secular state and a secularizing state. As Shalom Goldman has observed, "Political Zionism was founded and led by secular Jews, and . . . Israel's ruling elites are to this day secular."[46] Israel's founders wanted a home for Jews, not a homeland for Judaism. As Stanislavski comments, "Ben-Gurion and his minions were tied to a view of Jewish history based on the experience of the Jews in Europe, an expectation that once Jews were exposed to 'modernity,' they would undergo a fundamental transformation: First, they would shed their antiquated religious views and practices in favor of a new, secular worldview and style of life."[47]

Thus the 1948 Declaration of Independence made no mention of Israel as the divinely promised land for the Jews, although it closes with the words "With trust in Almighty God. . . ." The founders hoped the Israeli army and the government school system would work together to ensure that religious Jews coming to Israel would become like themselves—*Haskalah* Jews (or Enlightenment-oriented Jews.) This vision is captured in Naphtali Herz Imber's rousing song, a favorite of the early Zionist movement known as *Hatikvah* (Our hope), first published in 1886. In 2004 it was adopted as Israel's national anthem. *Hatikvah* projects a secular Zionist vision with no mention of God or Judaism, yet it claims the age-old longing for Jerusalem fostered by Judaism as an ethnic and cultural memory, but not as a religious one. A translation of the first stanza illustrates this:

> As long as deep within the heart of a Jewish soul beats,
> And to the far reaches of the East the eye yearns for Zion,
> Our hope, the hope of two thousand years, is not lost,
> To be a free people in our land,
> The Land of Zion, Jerusalem.[48]

Ultra-Orthodox Jews, the Haredim, still strongly object to it. American Christian Zionists often sing it at their pro-Israel rallies, and some have incorporated it into the liturgies of their churches. Imber often acknowledged that *Hatikvah* would not have been written, except for the influence

---

[46]Goldman, *Zeal for Zion*, 3.
[47]Stanislawski, *Zionism*, 68.
[48]Goldman, *Zeal for Zion*, 42.

of Laurence and Alice Oliphant, wealthy and eccentric Gentile Zionists who shared his enthusiasm.[49]

But the Jewish secularists' hope for Israel was not realized, for while a loss of faith happened among some Jews (especially in the West), it was not characteristic of many others. As the prophets of secularization theory have had to revise their prognostications about the eventual disappearance of religion in the modern world, so too have those secular Jews who expected that Israel would become an increasingly secular society and turn its back on traditional Jewish belief and practice. In the immediate wake of independence, Israel encouraged unlimited Jewish immigration. The immigrants from places like Iraq and Romania and from other countries that were either communist or Arab were often very devout. By and large, the wealthy (and often much more secular) Jews from North and South America, Western Europe, and Australia did not emigrate to Israel.

The influx of deeply religious Jews displaced from areas of the Arab world in the wake of the Six-Day War in 1967 and the immigration of Russian Jews since the fall of the Berlin Wall in 1989 have contributed to a steady growth of conservative forms of Judaism in Israel (although not, ironically, of the liberal movement known incongruously as Conservative or Masorti Judaism). Concessions made by Ben-Gurion (perhaps as early as 1947) allowing the ultra-Orthodox (the Haredim) to maintain their own schools (apart from the state secular and the Orthodox Zionist systems), exempting their young men who were studying in the talmudic academies from conscription into the Israel Defense Forces, and provision of government subsidies and allowances for Jewish religious groups have set precedents that the ultra-Orthodox have capitalized on. The Chief Rabbinate, an Orthodox Jewish institution, was given great power and considerable financial resources by the government. It regulates issues of personal status such as Jewish marriage, divorce, and adoption. Its religious courts for Israeli Jews are run exclusively by Orthodox rabbis. The Chief Rabbinate has "a monopoly over *kashrut* certification for businesses dealing with food, and a monopoly over conversion to Judaism (which in Israel is also the gateway to full citizenship for immigrants.)"[50] The official days of rest were to be

---

[49]On the Oliphants see Goldman, *Zeal for Zion*, chap. 1.

[50]Tomer Persico, "The End Point of Zionism: Ethnocentrism and the Temple Mount," *Israel Studies Review* 32, no. 1 (2017): 115.

Saturday and Jewish high holy days; food in the army and eventually in all state institutions was to be kosher.[51] Tensions today between secular Israeli Jews and the ultra-religious are deep and are a cause of great concern to Israeli policymakers.

Many of the early historians of Zionism were either unaware or dismissive of any significant role for Christians in Zionist history. Ironically, the established Zionist historiography has been dominated by historians who chaffed at the suggestion that religion—whether Jewish or Christian—was in any way helpful in the founding of Israel. That has changed. Benjamin Netanyahu has repeatedly stated that Christian Zionist support was critical in founding the state of Israel in 1948. Netanyahu's view would have been tantamount to heresy to the early historians of Zionism. This book hopes to make sense of the role, the motivations, and the impact of this little-understood movement.

---

[51]Stanislawski, *Zionism*, 71.

1

FROM THE EARLY CHURCH
TO THE REFORMATION

THIS CHAPTER IS INTENDED as background for readers with little knowledge of Jewish-Christian relations from biblical times to the sixteenth-century Reformation. Such an overview is hopelessly inadequate as there have been many more books written on these matters than there are words in the chapter! On first reading the matters discussed may seem disparate and unconnected, but each of them is important for Christian Zionism's emergence as a movement in the sixteenth century.

In the first century AD, ethnic Jewish believers in Jesus considered themselves to be faithful Israelites and not as the followers of a new religion. But as the Gentile mission expanded, the question of how to describe non-Jewish believers in Jesus became problematic. While not Jews, they had as the central figure of their faith a Jew, and his Jewish context and self-understanding are essential to understanding Christianity.[1] While remaining Gentiles they have historically understood themselves as "the Israel of God," a phrase Saint Paul uses to describe Christians in Galatians 3:29 and Galatians 6:16. How this "Israel of God" relates to the Jews is the central question underlying Christian identity making, and in turn, Christian Zionism.

Gentile Christians have a new adoptive identity. Their forebears may have worshiped Odin, Zeus, Thor, or Vishnu, or no god at all, but they now have

---

[1]I am careful about using the terms *Christianity* and *Judaism* in this period, as the early Jewish believers did not think of two different religions, one "Judaism" and the other "Christianity." I am indebted to Philip Church for his advice on this matter. See John M. G. Barclay, *Jews in the Mediterranean Diaspora: From Alexander to Trajan (323 BCE–117 CE)* (Edinburgh: T&T Clark, 1996), 410; Steve Mason and Philip F. Esler, "Judaean and Christ-Follower Identities: Grounds for a Distinction," *New Testament Studies* 63 (2017): 493-515; and John H. Elliott, "Jesus the Israelite Was Neither a 'Jew' Nor a 'Christian': On Correcting Misleading Nomenclature," *Journal for the Study of the Historical Jesus* 5 (2007): 119-54.

an adoptive ancestry as the spiritual descendants of Abraham, Isaac, and Jacob, a lineage that is not a natural part of their cultural or spiritual history. Central to Christian self-understanding is the idea that Gentiles have been grafted into the Jewish family tree—an image that Paul develops in Romans 11:17-18: "You [Gentile Christians], though a wild olive shoot, have been grafted in among the others and now share in the nourishing sap from the olive root." Christian identity making invariably involves Christians coming to grips with their Jewish roots. But how are Christians to relate to the Jews? How are they to understand the ongoing role of Jews as a people?

Related to these questions is the issue of "the land," a key concept repeatedly referenced throughout the Jewish Scriptures. Are the land promises to the Jews still in effect? Does the idea of a Jewish restoration remain valid? How does it fit in the history of Jewish and Christian thinking? The question of how Christians should regard the notion of Jews returning to a "Jewish homeland" is both complex and problematic given the nature of the Jewish and Christian Scriptures. Christian uncertainty in these matters has been paralleled by Judaism's own ambivalence about how and when such a "return" might take place. Certainly the concept of "the land" is central to Jewish history and longing. For over a millennium and a half Jews have longed for such a restoration, have prayed daily for the rebuilding of the temple, but have believed that the return of the Jews would be accomplished by God's Messiah, an exceptionally holy human, for whom Jews should patiently wait.

Biblical Backgrounds

The Abrahamic promise regarding the land—Genesis 12. The starting place for these theological questions for both Jews and Christians is the call of Abram in Genesis 12:1-8:

Now the LORD said to Abram,

"Go forth from your country,
And from your relatives
And from your father's house,
To the land which I will show you;
And I will make you a great nation,
And I will bless you,
And make your name great;

And so you shall be a blessing;

And I will bless those who bless you,

And the one who curses you I will curse.

And in you all the families of the earth will be blessed."

So Abram went forth as the LORD had spoken to him; and Lot went with him. . . . Thus they came to the land of Canaan. . . . The LORD appeared to Abram and said, "To your descendants I will give this land." (NASB)

According to Joshua 21:43-45 this promise regarding the land was at one point fulfilled:

So the Lord gave Israel all the land which He had sworn to give to their fathers, and they possessed it and lived in it. And the Lord gave them rest on every side, according to all that He had sworn to their fathers, and no one of all their enemies stood before them; the Lord gave all their enemies into their hand. Not one of the good promises which the Lord had made to the house of Israel failed; all came to pass. (NASB)

For Christians a key point of debate is whether this Abrahamic covenant is still in force or whether, like the Mosaic covenant and the Mosaic law, it was superseded by the coming of Christ.

In the Hebrew Scriptures, the possession of the "land" was understood to be contingent on Israel's faithfulness to the commandments (Deuteronomy 28:8-9). Gerald McDermott has observed, "The Torah never guaranteed eternal possession of the land. It made possession conditional on faithfulness to God and justice to the residents of the land."[2] Many modern Christian Zionists distinguish between "ownership" of the land by the Jews, which is understood to be eternal, and "possession" of the land, which is conditional. They argue that the land given to Abraham and his descendants will always be owned by the Jews, while they have at times not been able to actually possess it.

THE NEW TESTAMENT AND THE QUESTION OF TWO ISRAELS

Early Christian writers grappled with the New Testament's attitude toward Judaism. On the one hand, many regarded the church now as the "Israel of God," picking up on Paul's language in Galatians 3:29 and Galatians 6:15-16.

---

[2]Gerald R. McDermott, "A History of Christian Zionism: Is Christian Zionism Rooted Primarily in Premillennial Dispensationalism?," in *The New Christian Zionism: Fresh Perspectives on Israel and the Land*, ed. Gerald R. McDermott (Downers Grove, IL: IVP Academic, 2016), 51.

A strand of thinking emerged that the church has superseded the religion of the Jews—"completed" or "fulfilled" perhaps would be a way some Christians framed this. Here is the origin of "supersessionism," or what is often called "replacement theology" or "transference theology"—which advocates that the church has superseded the Israel "according to the flesh" (the Jewish people) and the church has now inherited the promises made to Israel in the Hebrew Scriptures. The position was put succinctly by Augustine in his commentary on Psalm 114:3:

> Let us therefore consider what we are taught here; since both those deeds were typical of us, and these words exhort us to recognize ourselves. For if we hold with a firm heart the grace of God which hath been given us, we are Israel, the seed of Abraham: unto us the Apostle saith, "Therefore are ye the seed of Abraham." . . . [Gal 3:29] Let therefore no Christian consider himself alien to the name of Israel. For we are joined in the corner stone with those among the Jews who believed, among whom we find the Apostles chief. Hence our Lord in another passage saith, "And other sheep I have, which are not of this fold; them also I must bring, that there may be one fold and one Shepherd." [John 10:16] The Christian people then is rather Israel, and the same is preferably the house of Jacob; for Israel and Jacob are the same. But that multitude of Jews, which was deservedly reprobated for its perfidy, for the pleasures of the flesh sold their birthright, so that they belonged not to Jacob, but rather to Esau. For ye know that it was said with this hidden meaning, "That the elder shall serve the younger."[3]

Another important passage that is often pointed to is Paul's dealing with circumcision in Romans 2:28-29: "A person is not a Jew who is one only outwardly, nor is circumcision merely outward and physical. No, a person is a Jew who is one inwardly; and circumcision is circumcision of the heart, by the Spirit, not by the written code. Such a person's praise is not from other people, but from God." These passages raise the vexed question: Who is a Jew?

This position tends toward the view that Israel is now entirely irrelevant and obsolete, no longer having an ongoing part in God's redemptive plan.

---

[3]Augustine of Hippo, *Expositions on the Book of Psalms*, in *A Select Library of the Nicene and Post-Nicene Fathers of the Christian Church*, ed. Philip Schaff, trans. A. Cleveland Coxe, First Series (New York: Christian Literature Company, 1888), 8:550.

Supersessionists, however, would disagree with being told that they have a "replacement theology." In their view the church has not replaced Israel, but it "has always been the true Israel by faith" (cf. Romans 9:6).[4] As Andrew Crome points out, "The difference rests in the way the church is used (as a spiritual, rather than a national body) as God's prime instrument, and the access now available to the gentiles. Supersessionists would therefore argue that their theology promotes continuity: the prophets and patriarchs are therefore as much a part of the church as the contemporary believer."[5]

On the other hand, Paul writing in Romans 11:1 argues from Jewish history: "I say then, God has not rejected His people, has He? May it never be! For I too am an Israelite, a descendant of Abraham, of the tribe of Benjamin" (NASB). As noted above, it is here that he speaks of the Gentiles being wild olive branches grafted into Israel but hopes that the "natural olive branch" might be grafted back in again at some point in the future (see Romans 11:17-24). Paul concludes his argument toward the end of the chapter with some of his most perplexing and disputed statements:

> For I do not want you, brethren, to be uninformed of this mystery—so that you will not be wise in your own estimation—that a partial hardening has happened to Israel until the fullness of the Gentiles has come in; and so all Israel will be saved; just as it is written,
>
> "The Deliverer will come from Zion,
> He will remove ungodliness from Jacob."
> "This is My covenant with them, When I take away their sins."
>
> From the standpoint of the gospel they are enemies for your sake, but from the standpoint of God's choice they are beloved for the sake of the fathers; for the gifts and the calling of God are irrevocable. For just as you once were disobedient to God, but now have been shown mercy because of their disobedience, so these also now have been disobedient, that because of the mercy shown to you they also may now be shown mercy. For God has shut up all in disobedience so that He may show mercy to all. (Romans 11:25-32 NASB)

This passage is central in the history of Christian-Jewish relations. But it is not clear to all that when Paul uses the term "Israel" in this passage that

---

[4] Andrew Crome, *Christian Zionism and English National Identity, 1600–1850* (Cham, Switzerland: Palgrave Macmillan, 2018), 3n4.
[5] Crome, *English National Identity*, 3n4.

he is using it in the same way each time. Does he mean when he says "all Israel shall be saved" that at some point "all Jews will be saved"? Or does he use "Israel" speaking of the unbelieving Jews in the first instance, "Israel has become hardened in part," but then intend in the second reference to Israel, the new Israel of God made up of both Jews and Gentiles? Those who favor the second explanation maintain that Paul is not promising the salvation of all Jews at some point in the future, but means that when the formerly excluded Gentiles are brought into the newly constituted people of God, then the new Israel will be complete and thus all of the new Israel ("the Israel of God") will be saved. Whichever interpretation one takes, Paul clearly expects a continuing religious Jewish existence apart from Christianity while at the same time insisting that the church should never conceive itself as disconnected from its Jewish roots. How Christians are to relate to the ongoing "Israel according to the flesh" is one of the most complex and difficult matters in the history of Christianity.

JEWISH HISTORY AND THE LOSS OF THE LAND

Jewish history has been ruptured by conquests, massacres, and exile. Yet remarkably, Jews have retained a distinct identity in spite of their widespread scattering throughout the world. History knows of no other people whose faith and identity has survived repeated devastations and the trauma of exile, and that not once but twice. In 722 BC the Assyrians conquered the northern kingdom of Israel and scattered its Jews; the search for whatever became of the "Ten Lost Tribes of Israel" dates from this period. The second Jewish Diaspora (dispersion or scattering) dates from 597 BC, with Nebuchadnezzar's deporting Jews from the southern kingdom of Judah. After his conquest of Judah in 586 he allowed some to create a distinct exile community in Babylon. In 538 BC, Cyrus the Persian ruler permitted Babylonian Jews to return to Palestine, although many declined. Nehemiah (d. ca. 413 BC) ascribed the exile to God's punishment of the unfaithfulness of Israel.

At the time of Christ the great majority of Jews were dispersed throughout the Roman Empire, with many in Egypt and other parts of the Middle East. When the newly constituted Roman protectorate of Judaea revolted in AD 70, the Romans destroyed Jerusalem, annexed Judaea as a Roman province, and drove many Jews out of the city. Palestine's Jews were devastated following the

Bar Kokhba revolt of AD 132–136, following which the Romans banned Jews from living in Jerusalem. The Roman historian Dio Cassius claimed that the Romans had killed 580,000 Jewish men and more died from famine and disease.[6] Another Jewish revolt in AD 350–351 was quickly crushed, and several thousand more Jews died. Following the permanent division of the Roman Empire in AD 395, the Byzantine rulers kept up the pressure on Palestine's Jews, and by AD 500 Jews were a minority in the area.[7]

Yet many religious Jews hoped the Messiah would eventually secure the settlement of the Jews back in Palestine and Jerusalem would again be the religious and cultural center of their faith. This hope still lingers among some ultra-Orthodox Jews who insist that only the Messiah can bring about this restoration and look with disfavor on the idea of a Jewish state established in large measure by people whom they regard as secular Jews. (In Hebrew the religious Jews refer to them as *heeloni*, "the profane.")

THE EARLY CHURCH FATHERS: UNDERSTANDINGS OF THE BIBLICAL BACKGROUND VIS-À-VIS THE JEWS

> *The errors of Judaism are in fact central to the truth claims of Christianity. In the Christian view, it was precisely the errors of Judaism and the Jews that paved the way for the emergence of Christianity. Jewish error and Christian truth are thus intrinsically linked to one another. The Jews necessarily loom large in the Christian scheme of things, whether or not Jews are actually present.*[8]
>
> ROBERT CHAZAN

Among Christians a deep ambivalence toward the Jews developed in the post–New Testament period with the ongoing clash between church and synagogue being worked out in the first centuries of the Christian era. The New Testament writers were all Jews, as were the early leaders of the Jerusalem church, but by the second century virtually all the Christian

---

[6]David Brog, *Reclaiming Israel's History Roots, Rights, and the Struggle for Peace* (Washington, DC: Regnery, 2017), 18.

[7]Brog, *Reclaiming Israel's History*, 21.

[8]Robert Chazan, "The Prior Church Legacy," in *The Middle Ages: The Christian World* (Cambridge: Cambridge University Press, 2018), 9.

leaders were Gentiles. The writings of the apostle Paul contained different emphases that proved difficult for the Gentile leaders of the Christian church to hold in tension. For them the biblical stories of sibling rivalry between Isaac and Ishmael, and between Jacob and Esau were representative of the Jewish-Christian conflict with primacy shifting from the older to the younger and the elder reduced to insignificance. The physical law had been superseded by the spiritual faith and, as Robert Chazan has argued, Paul's "projection of the Jews as the elder brother passed over for primacy, created a negative view of Judaism and Jews in the gentile Christian community and constituted a powerful legacy for all subsequent Christian thinking about Judaism and Jews."[9] At the same time, in the book of Romans, Paul speaks with high praise of the Jews' roles in divine revelation while castigating his fellow Jews for their stubbornness, and yet he expresses his deep love for them and his hope for their eventual restoration to God given that they are and remain the root of the olive tree into which gentile Christians have been grafted. As Chazan observes, "For subsequent Christian thinking, the Pauline oscillation between castigation and mitigation came to play a decisive role, especially for major Christian thinkers who sought to ascertain the normative Christian stance on Judaism and Jews. These thinkers regularly reinforced the complex Pauline message."[10] The Gospel accounts and the book of Acts have perhaps been even more important than Paul's epistles in influencing Christian thinking about the Jews, particularly as they relate to assessments of Jewish culpability in the death of Christ.[11]

A debate emerged in the early Christian church between those who were so intensely hostile to Judaism that they rejected the Hebrew Bible and the mainstream, which insisted that these books were also Christian Scriptures. The Old Testament was to be embraced as the "precursor and the predictor of the succeeding [Christian] phase of divine outreach to humanity."[12] This was an important part of defining the limits and nature of Christian identity. As Chazan observes,

---

[9]Chazan, "Prior Church Legacy," 10.
[10]Chazan, "Prior Church Legacy," 15.
[11]For an extended discussion of this see Chazan, "Prior Church Legacy," 15-23.
[12]Chazan, "Prior Church Legacy," 24.

The process of absorbing the Hebrew Bible and the Israelites into the core of Christianity had to include pejorative contrasts between Christianity and Judaism, and it did. The Church Fathers of the early Christian centuries fashioned an extensive *contra Judaeos* literature, intended to portray Judaism and Jews in a way that would diminish any potential appeal they might have for unsuspecting Christians, who might be attracted to a more literal reading of the Hebrew Bible or might be swayed by Jewish views of it.[13]

Central to this Christian apologetic literature was Paul's contrast of physicality and spirituality. The unspiritual Jews had failed to embrace the arrival of a new spiritual era and clung to their ritual laws, which the Christian writers sharply critiqued:

> Ongoing Jewish observance of the ritual laws subsequent to the advent of Jesus was stridently criticized, condemned as an embrace of the physical; these practices were contrasted with Christian capacity to extract the spiritual —i.e., true—meaning of religious ritual originating with the Hebrew Bible. Jewish literal reading of the biblical record was a further aspect of Jewish failure and indeed the key to the quarrel between the two faith communities. Both communities saw their foundations in the Hebrew Bible, which Jews read incorrectly and Christians understood properly.[14]

A new development in the anti-Judaic polemic arose from the political events that saw the Roman destruction of the temple in Jerusalem in AD 70. The hostility of the Jews toward Christians intensified with its destruction because Christians understood it to be the fulfillment of a prophecy by Christ ("not one of stone here will be left on another"), which is repeated in each of the Synoptic Gospels (Matthew 24:2; Mark 13:2; Luke 19:44). Origen of Alexandria (ca. 184–ca. 253) and Eusebius of Caesarea (260/265–339/340) both made explicit their view that the destruction of the temple was divine judgment for the crucifixion.[15] The subsequent Jewish defeat in the Bar Kokhba rebellion in the 130s only reinforced the polemic. As Chazan points out, "The Church Fathers could and did interpret Jewish defeats as divine interventions intended to prove the errors of the Jews." This assessment

---

[13]Chazan, "Prior Church Legacy," 25.
[14]Chazan, "Prior Church Legacy," 25.
[15]Shalom Goldman, *Zeal for Zion: Christians, Jews, & the Idea of the Promised Land* (Chapel Hill: University of North Carolina Press, 2009), 6.

"became part of the standard Christian view of Judaism and Jews in late Antiquity and thereafter."[16] This fierce competition between the church and the synagogue in the succeeding centuries is entirely understandable given that the synagogue felt that it had lost many adherents to what they regarded as a new faith and wanted to emphasize the discontinuities between synagogue and the church, arguing that for all their similarities, they were in effect two different faiths.

The idea of the millennium among the church fathers. Another factor influencing early Christian attitudes was the matter of eschatology (from the Greek word *eschaton*, which means "last," hence the doctrine of the last things or end times). Christians of the Eastern (Orthodox) and Western (Roman Catholic and Protestant) Churches have commonly subscribed to the Apostles' and Nicene-Constantinopolitan Creeds, which both state that Jesus Christ "will come to judge the living and the dead," and affirm "the resurrection of the body, and the life everlasting" but are otherwise silent on issues of eschatology (the future). But one of the most important issues dividing Christians when it comes to interpreting apocalyptic biblical passages is the interpretation of the "thousand" (Latin = *mille*) years mentioned in Revelation 20. This is the only passage in the whole of the Old and New Testaments that speaks of this prophetic period of a "thousand years" (*millennium* in Latin). These mysterious words appear six times in six consecutive verses (Revelation 20:2-7) and yet nowhere else in Scripture. Ernest Lee Tuveson has observed that "surely no other passage of comparable length has ever had such great and long-lasting influence on human attitudes and beliefs."[17] These six verses have probably engendered more controversy over their meaning than any other passage in the Hebrew and Christian Scriptures.

The early Christian theologians were divided in their understanding of the "end times," with some of them taking a literal interpretation of Revelation 20:1-7, which speaks of Christ reigning on earth for a thousand years. The English word *millenarian* refers to those who believe in a literal thousand-year reign of Christ. Those who expect Christ's return before

---

[16]Chazan, "Prior Church Legacy," 25.
[17]Ernest Lee Tuveson, *Redeemer Nation: The Idea of America's Millennial Role* (Chicago: University of Chicago Press, 1968), 9.

(pre-) the thousand-year reign of Christ on earth are known as premillennialists. This early form of patristic premillennialism is often claimed as the forerunner of modern expressions of premillennialism, but this claim is both inaccurate and misleading. Modern exponents of what is often termed "historic/historical/covenantal" premillennialism have tried to find historical precedents for their views in patristic premillennialism, but this is not supported by the evidence. As Stanley Grenz has observed,

> A comparison of the view espoused today [by "historic premillennialists"] with that of Irenaeus and Justin, however, indicates that contemporary [historic/covenantal/historical] premillennialism is quite different from the ancient variety. In fact, as sympathetic a historian as D. H. Kromminga concludes that they constitute two distinct views of the end of the age.[18]

Grenz summarizes, "Patristic premillennialism interpreted the Apocalypse in a preterist fashion, that is, as primarily referring to events transpiring in the first centuries of the church."[19]

Patristic premillennialists believed that the church would experience the period of tribulation before Christ's return and thus are now often referred to as posttribulation premillennialists—that is, Christ will return *after* (= *post*) the tribulation.[20] To confuse matters even further, there is a view called "historicist premillennialism," which is often confused with "historic/historical/covenantal premillennialism." These differing views will be discussed at length below as these different understandings were to profoundly affect Jewish-Christian relations.

Preterism views the prophetic passages as concerned with events that happened in the first and second centuries. It is important to differentiate "full" and "partial" preterism or "classical preterism." Partial preterists believe that while some events such as the destruction of Jerusalem and the great tribulation were fulfilled in the early centuries, they would not agree that the second coming or the final judgement have already occurred. "Classical" or

---

[18]Stanley J. Grenz, *The Millennial Maze: Sorting Out Evangelical Options* (Downers Grove, IL: InterVarsity Press, 1992), 144-45.

[19]Grenz, *Millennial Maze*, 145.

[20]Among the church fathers who advocated premillennialism are Bishop Papias of Hierapolis (ca. 70–163), Irenaeus of Lyons (130–202), Bishop Polycarp of Smyrna (ca. 70–155), and Justin Martyr (100–165). J. N. D. Kelly, *Early Christian Doctrines*, 5th ed. (London: A. C. Black, 1977), 465-69.

"partial" preterism was embraced by Eusebius of Caesarea in the early fourth century and came to characterize the position of the Roman Catholic Church. Classical preterism fit well with both the premillennial and amillennial approaches to these issues.

The premillennial view, however, while it did gain a significant following, did not become dominant in the broader church; in particular Origen of Alexandria rejected this approach and argued that the words should be understood as an allegory. Origen denied a literal understanding of the thousand-year reign of Christ, seeing the thousand years as referring to the age of the church (hence amillennialism or literally "no thousand"-year reign).[21] In the fourth century the greatest of the church fathers, Augustine (354–430), while at first embracing premillennialism, came to reject it and argued against a literal millennium; the millennium was henceforth understood as the age of the flourishing and triumph of the Christian church. Augustine's mature view came to represent the consensus of the church, both of the Eastern Orthodox Church in the eastern Mediterranean and the Roman Catholic Church in the West. His view was that Christ's victory was being worked out now on the earth. Any form of millennialism thus came to be viewed as unacceptable and was condemned in 431 as superstition by the ecumenical church council at Ephesus.[22] From the fifth to the sixteenth century the Roman Church was committed to the suppression of millenarianism. The emergence of new forms of premillennialism in the seventeenth century will be dealt with below, as will a third view that emerged—which held that Christ would return at the end of the millennial age spoken of in Revelation 20—hence, postmillennialism.

The early church fathers and the idea of a Jewish return. Whether an incipient form of Christian restorationism was an understanding held by some church fathers, or indeed by any Christian theologian in the first millennium

---

[21]Among the church fathers in this group were Clement of Rome (d. ca. 99), Ignatius of Antioch (ca. 35–108), Polycarp of Smyrna (69–155), Tatian (d. ca. 185), Athenagoras (ca. 133–190), Cyprian (ca. 200–258), Clement of Alexandria (ca. 150–ca. 215), Origen of Alexandria (ca. 184/185–ca. 253/254), and Dionysius of Alexandria (d. 264). Louis Berkhof, *The History of Christian Doctrines*, Twin Brooks Series (Grand Rapids: Baker, 1975), 262.

[22]Peter Toon, introduction to *Puritans, the Millennium and the Future of Israel: Puritan Eschatology 1600 to 1660*, ed. Peter Toon (Cambridge: James Clarke, 1970), 14.

of the Christian era, has recently been disputed.[23] Nabil Matar has argued that there is no evidence that it was and his view appears to be the general scholarly consensus.[24] It is difficult to find anyone in the early church who held the view that Christians should be working to enable the Jews to return to Palestine and be re-established there as a nation before the return of Christ. Some of the premillennialists like Tertullian, held to an eventual "restoration of Israel," and Justin Martyr and Irenaeus agreed upon a re-building of Jerusalem in the distant future. In the nineteenth century the Scottish theologian David Brown carefully examined the church fathers and demonstrated that while they were divided on the interpretation of the millennium, none of them taught a literal restoration of the Jews to Palestine. Brown was a postmillennialist who believed that the Scriptures taught the future restoration of the Jews to their homeland. So, while he was a strong "restorationist," as a scholar, however, he concluded that none of the early Fathers held this position; none expected the Jews to be so restored. (For Brown, this was of little consequence because he did not highly value the Fathers' opinions on theology.) He concludes in his *The Restoration of the Jews:* "It is a curious fact, and one that will probably startle my readers, that the national and territorial restoration of the Jews not only never entered into the controversy at all, but seems not to have been believed in by either of the parties."[25]

All of the early Fathers, Brown observed, considered that "the distinction between Jew and Gentile to have been utterly and to all effects done away in Christ, [thus] they understood those predictions which relate to the restored condition of 'Israel,' 'Judah,' 'Jacob,' 'Zion'—in short, the covenant people— simply of the Christian Church, or believers in Christ."[26] In commenting on Justin Martyr (AD 100-165), an early premillennialist, he writes, "With all the

---

[23]Gerald McDermott has claimed that "Christian Zionism goes back two thousand years to the New Testament, and has been sustained with varying intensity ever since." Gerald R. McDermott, "Introduction: What Is the New Christian Zionism?," in McDermott, *New Christian Zionism,* 15.

[24]Nabil I. Matar, "The Idea of the Restoration of the Jews in English Protestant Thought: Between the Reformation and 1660," *Durham University Journal* 78, no. 1 (December 1985): 23. I have not found any support for the idea in the many Jewish scholars whom I have read.

[25]David Brown, *The Restoration of the Jews: The History, Principles, and Bearings of the Question* (Edinburgh: A. Strahan, 1861), 13.

[26]Brown, *Restoration of the Jews,* 14.

fathers, he understood the prophecies of Israel's restoration simply of the Christian Church; and, with Irenaeus [ca. AD 120/140—ca. 200/203] [another early premillennialist] and other millenarians, he applies them generally to the resurrection state, though in a higher style of conception than Irenaeus."[27] Brown's view is corroborated by a contemporary Christian Zionist apologist, Thomas D. Ice, who concedes that the ante-Nicene fathers "did not really look for a restoration of the Jews to the land of Israel, even though premillennialism was widespread."[28] And another scholar, Carl Ehle, also supportive of Christian Zionism, acknowledges, "One might expect to find a long tradition of commentary on the restoration doctrine stemming from the early church; however, one gains the impression from reviewing the equivocal or noncommittal statements of the New Testament and of the Church Fathers that the doctrine of restoration is an innovation of the second generation of the Protestant Reformers."[29]

The early church fathers and the idea of rebuilding the temple. Some have reasoned that among the early church fathers there was the expectation that the Jewish temple would be rebuilt and that this hope indicates a belief in a Jewish return. The Epistle of Barnabas (ca. 130 AD) speaks of the rebuilding of the temple, but on a close reading it is clear that the author is speaking allegorically: the temple is going to be rebuilt in the hearts of Christian believers.[30] The premise that the hope for the rebuilding of the physical temple necessarily required a belief in the physical return of the Jews is further shown to be faulty in that there were those in the fourth century who envisioned the rebuilding of the temple without the return of the Jews. In the early 360s AD, Emperor Julian (known as "The Apostate" for his rejection of his Christian upbringing and his attempt to re-establish paganism) sought to encourage Palestinian Jews to rebuild the Jewish temple

---

[27]Brown, *Restoration of the Jews*, 25.

[28]Thomas D. Ice, "Lovers of Zion: A History of Christian Zionism," *Article Archives*, paper 29 (2009): 2, http://digitalcommons.liberty.edu/pretrib_arch/29.

[29]Carl Frederick Ehle Jr., "Prolegomena to Christian Zionism in America: The Views of Increase Mather and William E. Blackstone Concerning the Doctrine of the Restoration of Israel" (PhD diss., New York University, 1977), 1. See also his statement, "What is singularly absent from early millenarian schemes is the motif of the Restoration of Israel, a doctrine that was commonplace in post-reformation thought." Ehle, "Prolegomena," 31.

[30]Brown, *Restoration of the Jews*, 17. See also John J. Gunther, "The Epistle of Barnabas and the Final Rebuilding of the Temple," *Journal for the Study of Judaism* 7, no. 2 (1976): 143-51. I am indebted to Jacob Samuel Raju for this reference.

in Jerusalem and to re-institute temple sacrifices because he understood that this would discredit the Gospel account in which it was understood that Christ had prophesied that the temple would never be rebuilt. Christians thought the rebuilding of the temple was blasphemous, thus the idea that early Christians must have hoped for a return of the Jews in order to rebuild the temple is hard to credit.

THE MIDDLE AGES

The Augustinian legacy. Emperor Constantine's conversion in 312 and the legal toleration of Christians soon led to a sea change in the life and theology of the Christian church. From being a marginalized and persecuted minority, Christians were being courted and promoted by the emperor. The patristic premillennial teachings that had characterized some of the early fathers went into rapid decline, and Augustine's formulation of his version of the amillennial view won the day.

Augustine's attitudes toward the Jews were enormously important in shaping Western Christian attitudes. Two of his leading episcopal contemporaries, Ambrose of Milan and John Chrysostom, were virulently anti-Jewish, and their verbal assaults on the Jews were matched by encouragements of violent assaults on synagogues, Jewish property, and individual Jews. In contrast, Augustine's views can be considered moderate: he argued that Jews should not be persecuted by Christians but rather protected. He understood the exile of the Jews from Palestine as divine punishment for Israel's unfaithfulness; specifically, he believed their expulsion was God's judgement on them for their role in the death of Christ. They had to remain a people separate and dispersed to show the justice of divine punishment for their deicide. The idea of Christians working to return them to their homeland would have been anathema.

In his commentary on Psalm 59:11, Augustine identified David's enemies as the contemporary Jews, and he interpreted David's prayer—"Do not kill them; otherwise, my people will forget. By Your power make them homeless wanderers" (HCSB)—as a prophetic injunction as to how Christians should treat the Jews: they were not to be killed but protected and scattered. Their status as wandering Jews was to be a reminder of God's judgment on them. In his *City of God*, he observed,

Therefore God has shown the Church in her enemies the Jews the grace of His compassion, since, as saith the apostle, "their offence is the salvation of the Gentiles." [Rom 11:11] And therefore He has not slain them, that is, He has not let the knowledge that they are Jews be lost in them, although they have been conquered by the Romans, lest they should forget the law of God, and their testimony should be of no avail in this matter of which we treat. But it was not enough that he should say, "Slay them not, lest they should at last forget Thy law," unless he had also added, "Disperse them;" because if they had only been in their own land with that testimony of the Scriptures, and not everywhere, certainly the Church which is everywhere could not have had them as witnesses among all nations to the prophecies which were sent before concerning Christ.[31]

The continued dispersion of the Jews "as witnesses among all nations," not any sympathy for their return to their homeland, was central to Augustine's thinking in regard to the Jews. Jeremy Cohen in his *Living Letters of the Law* has traced how the Augustinian characterization of the Jew as "witness" influenced the canonical legislation of Gregory the Great (pope from 590 to 604).[32] Gregory's letter of 598 instructing the bishop of Palermo not to destroy a synagogue is known as *Sicut Iudeis* and was frequently cited in the Middle Ages in church documents relating to the Jews.[33] In the Middle Ages the general attitude toward the Jews was thus ultimately indebted to Augustine, who held that Jews served as witnesses in two senses: positively in preserving the Old Testament Scriptures for the Christian church while negatively their dispersal throughout the world testified to God's judgment on them for their role in the death of Christ. As he put it, the Jews are "in their books our supporters, in their hearts our enemies, in their copies [scrolls] our witnesses."[34] Augustine's legacy thus gave the Jews a protected place in the Latin Christian world so that they could carry the Hebrew Bible, which Christians believed contained the prophecies concerning Jesus Christ.

---

[31] Augustine, *City of God* in *A Select Library of the Nicene and Post-Nicene Fathers*, trans. Marcus Dods (Buffalo: Christian Literature Company, 1886), 2:389.

[32] On Augustine see Jeremy Cohen, *Living Letters of the Law: Ideas of the Jews in Medieval Christianity* (Berkeley: University of California Press, 1999), 23-71.

[33] For a discussion of *Sicut Iudeis*, see Anna Sapir Abulafia, "Medieval Church Doctrines and Policies," in *The Cambridge History of Judaism*, vol. 6, *The Middle Ages: The Christian World*, ed. Robert Chazan (Cambridge: Cambridge University Press, 2018), 37.

[34] Augustine, *Concerning Faith of Things Not Seen* 9, New Advent, https://www.newadvent.org/fathers/1305.htm.

Jews were to serve Christians by being object lessons whose circumstances were living proof that those who denied Christ would lose their homeland and yet survive, dispersed in Christian lands where they would prove useful as servants of their new lords.

Another aspect of Augustine's view needs to be appreciated, as Robert Chazan has pointed out: while Augustine emphasized God's judgment on the Jews, "nonetheless, the merciful God always holds out love and hope, even for those whom he severely chastises. The Jews must be preserved within and by Christian society, because in the fullness of time they will yet return in repentance and win once more divine love and grace."[35] Augustine and his successors could thus hold together the idea of replacement while holding to the belief that the Jews would eventually, as a people, turn to Christianity. "'If the Jews were utterly wiped out,' Bernard of Clairvaux asked [in the twelfth century]: 'what will become of our hope for their promised salvation, their eventual conversion?'"[36] This view reinforced the Augustinian injunction to protect the Jews in view of this eventuality. Christian theologians have often held that "old" Israel has not permanently been superseded. They have not generally, however, embraced the idea that the Jews would physically return to establish a homeland in Palestine.

In the year 1000, European Jews were only a tiny portion of the world's Jews. The overwhelming majority of Jews lived under Islamic rule, and the largest European Jewish communities were to be found in those regions of southern Europe ruled by Muslims.[37] The second largest grouping of Jews was in Byzantium, the Eastern Christian empire, which was shrinking under Muslim pressure. While in 1000 Latin Christendom was the weakest of the three religio-political blocks (alongside Islam and Byzantium), in the five centuries between the turn of the millennium and the sixteenth century, Europe began to expand economically and politically; its military successes pushed back Muslim forces in Spain and the Italian peninsulas with most Jews opting to accept the enticements on offer from Christian rulers to stay in place when Muslim rule ended. Jewish settlers were also attracted from

---

[35]Robert Chazan, *The Jews of Medieval Western Christendom, 1000–1500* (Cambridge: Cambridge University Press, 2018), 37.

[36]Todd M. Endelman, introduction to *Jewish Apostasy in the Modern World*, ed. Todd Endelman (New York: Holmes & Meier, 1987), 3.

[37]Chazan, *Jews of Medieval Western Christendom*, 2.

Muslim territories and many new European Jewish communities were formed. By the early modern era, the European Jewish community was the largest in the world. For a time, many Jews in Europe were able to thrive in spite of restrictions, sometimes supported by civil rulers such as Henry IV, the Holy Roman emperor, who favored them in his ongoing disputes with the papacy. At the same time popular outbursts of anti-Semitism erupted as early as 1062, when Pope Alexander II had to intervene to protect Spanish Jews during the Spanish Reconquista.[38] Again in 1096, when crusaders went off-script and decided to slaughter German Jews, they did so in spite of the pope's admonitions to the contrary. But "attacks upon Jews during the Crusades, although not within the official mandate of the crusaders, undoubtedly awakened Christian society to the anomaly of the Jews' position: enemies/ killers of Christ whose lives and errant religion God had protected for the greater good of Christendom."[39] A huge change took place between roughly 1200 and 1500 that drove most Jews out of Western Europe to the east. In 1290 England expelled its Jews, as did France in the 1306 and Spain and Portugal in the late fifteenth century. The same occurred in some cities in the German territories after about 1400, but the dispersion of political power in that region enabled some Jews to remain in place and thrive.

Shifts away from Augustine. Cohen argues that this decisive shift began in the twelfth century with the Augustinian characterization of the Jew as "witness" giving way to that of heretic and enemy. The church's historic commitment since Augustine had been to allow Jews to live safely and securely within Christian society, but fears were also growing that Jewish influence might inflict damage. The decisions of the Fourth Lateran Council in 1215 need to be understood in light of this shift. The council declared that Jews were to wear distinctive dress in public to signal their social exclusion; it changed the status of Jews both politically and theologically as "servants of sin"; it banned them from public office; it forbade them from appearing in public in Holy Week; and it imposed a tax on them to be paid to Christian clergy.[40] Yet, as Anna Sapir Abulafia has shown, the Christian rulers of

---

[38]Cohen, *Living Letters of the Law*, 150.

[39]Cohen, *Living Letters of the Law*, 51.

[40]These were only some of the restrictions. For an extended discussion of the Fourth Lateran Council's canons related to the Jews, see Anna Sapir Abulafia, "Medieval Church Doctrines and Policies," in Chazan, *Christian World*, 32-53.

Europe were often protective of "their Jews" who served them well, which made uniform enforcement of the council's decrees (including the wearing of distinguishing dress)[41] impossible in Latin Christendom. Further, some princes and even clergy were happy to put Jews in positions of authority if it suited their purposes. As she notes, "This was especially the case in Iberia where Christian lords needed Jews with their mastery of Arabic to help them govern over the lands which they had newly conquered from the Muslims."[42] At a popular level anti-Semitism was undoubtedly stoked by the influx of Jewish immigrants that evoked fear of competition and change, which often issued in anti-Jewish rioting and outright persecution. Such violence had been specifically prohibited in ecclesiastical law by Pope Alexander II in 1063. Christian bishops generally sought to restrain such attacks, and even at times the attackers of Jews were severely punished, as occurred in the city of Speyer, where the bishop was strong enough to effect this.[43]

Cohen has argued that the marked shift away from the Augustinian legacy of toleration and protection of the Jews was largely brought about by the new medicant orders—particularly the Dominicans and the Franciscans —in the period from the Fourth Lateran Council of 1215 through to the mid-fourteenth century. The friars "developed, refined, and sought to implement a new Christian ideology with regard to the Jews, one that allotted the Jews no legitimate right to exist within European Society."[44] Their attack was primarily on rabbinic Judaism and its talmudic tradition, which did not reflect the sort of Judaism rooted in the defunct Sadducean tradition, which was the lens through which Christians understood Judaism. Talmudic Judaism was not the biblical Judaism that Augustine had envisioned deserved protecting. Surprisingly, before "the twelfth century, there is almost no evidence of Christian awareness of the central role played by the Talmud in Jewish life."[45] But the Christian "discovery" of the Talmud changed perceptions of Judaism. As Cohen puts it, "When Christian theologians

---

[41]As Abulafia notes, "The introduction of any kind of distinguishing dress or badge depended entirely on the wishes of individual Christian princes *and* their ability to enforce their will in matters such as these." Abulafia, "Medieval Church Doctrines," 42.

[42]Abulafia, "Medieval Church Doctrines," 36.

[43]See Abulafia, "Medieval Church Doctrines," 34, and Chazan, *Jews of Medieval Western Christendom*, 3-4.

[44]Jeremy Cohen, *The Friars and the Jews: The Evolution of Medieval Anti-Judaism* (Ithaca, NY: Cornell University Press, 1982), 13.

[45]Chazan, *Jews of Medieval Western Christendom*, 48.

awakened to the disparity between the Jew they had constructed and the
real Jew of history, they could construe the latter's failure to serve the purposes allotted him as an abandonment of his Judaism."[46] In the view of the
mendicants the Talmud had "distorted the true biblical Judaism whose observance theoretically entitled the Jews to remain in Christendom. Other
friars subsequently concluded that if rabbinic Judaism had no legitimate
place in a properly ordered Christian society, neither did the Jews who subscribed to its teachings, and they employed every available means of harassment to undermine the security of Jewish existence."[47]

Attention was drawn to the Talmud by a dispute in the early 1230s within
the Jewish community over the teachings of Moses Maimonides, with one
faction appealing to Christian clergy to adjudicate the matter.[48] Following an
examination, Pope Gregory IX condemned the Talmud in 1239 as "a heretical
deviation from the Jews' biblical heritage."[49] The following year he wrote
letters to the kings of France, England, and Spain, asking them to have their
medicants investigate allegations that the Talmud contained blasphemies
against Christ and the Virgin Mary. In 1242 the Talmud was duly condemned
by the king's court and "carloads of Talmudic and other Jewish manuscripts
were publicly burnt, to the horror of the Jewish communities of Christendom."[50]
The *Sicut Iudeis* tradition was being clearly being undermined. The prohibition of the Talmud, however, was short-lived as in 1247 Pope Innocent III
responded to Jewish protests by adopting a policy of tolerating it "with ex-
cision of sections deemed offensive," which became the standard policy for
most of Christendom in the West.[51] Joel Rembaum notes that following the
Talmud dispute "there is no indication that the papacy sought to intervene
in other aspects of Jewish religious or institutional affairs" and that later
medieval popes had little to say about the Talmud's significance.[52]

Cohen maintains that by the early fourteenth century the friars were
openly advocating "that Latin Christendom rid itself of its Jewish population,

---

[46]Cohen, *Living Letters of the Law*, 2.

[47]Cohen, *Friars and the Jews*, 16.

[48]See Cohen, *Friars*, chap. 2.

[49]Cohen, *Friars and the Jews*, 242. On the trial see Joel Rembaum, "The Talmud and the Popes:
   Reflections on the Talmud Trails of the 1240s," *Viator* 23 (1982): 203-23.

[50]Abulafia, "Medieval Church Doctrines," 47.

[51]Chazan, *Jews of Medieval Western Christendom*, 58.

[52]Rembaum, "Talmud and the Popes," 211.

whether through missionizing, forced expulsions, or physical harassment that would induce conversion or flight."[53] From the scholarly pushback on Cohen's revisionist thesis, it is clear that medieval scholars are very cautious about his generalizations about what the friars did or did not do, or what they thought.[54] The major orders, the Franciscans and Dominicans, were very different in their mentalities and approaches, often disagreeing with each other on many topics, and were often directly opposed to each other.[55] There were anti-Semitic friars, but it was just such a Cistercian friar, Ralph, with whom Bernard of Clairvaux intervened, first to warn and then to personally silence, going to the Rhineland to stop his anti-Semitic sermons and order him back to his cloister.[56]

In spite of popular expressions of anti-Semitism, the Augustinian tradition of toleration was not entirely snuffed out and, as Cohen acknowledges, "the medieval papacy never officially called for the expulsion or physical persecution of European Jewry."[57] The church hierarchy tended to retain the Augustinian perspective at least in theory. From about 1200 anti-Jewish violence increased across Europe and Christian art became noticeably more demeaning and hostile toward the Jews. In the mid-fourteenth century Jews were being blamed for the Black Death, and thousands died at the hand of anti-Semitic mobs, with entire Jewish populations of some cities being massacred. The expulsion of Jews from Western Europe was largely achieved by the mid-1500s.

Accounting for changing attitudes toward the Jews. In trying to account for this shift from the Augustinian focus on witness to enemy and heretic, Cohen asks the question, "What led to the theological attack on rabbinic Judaism by the mendicants in the thirteenth century?" What could possibly account for "the ideational substance" of the alleged mendicant attack on

---

[53]Cohen, *Friars and the Jews*, 14.

[54]See Gordon Leff's review in the *Times Literary Supplement*, November 5, 1982, 1208. Leff suggests Cohen has "a tendency to treat premises as conclusions." See also Anna Sapir Abulafia, "The Evolution of Medieval Anti-Judaism," *Theoretische Geschiedenis* 2 (1984): 77-81; Robert I. Burns, "Anti-Semitism and Anti-Judaism in Christian History: A Revisionist Thesis," *Catholic Historical Review* 70 (1984): 90-93.

[55]I am indebted to Steve Watts for his advice on this matter.

[56]Chazan, *Jews of Medieval Western Christendom*, 53.

[57]Cohen, *Friars and the Jews*, 243.

the Jews?[58] He has proposed three underlying reasons. His first is the influence of the eschatology of Joachim of Fiore (1134–1202), an Italian abbot, and its emphasis on the imminent transition to "the final, perfect age of the spirit."[59] Apocalyptic speculation was widespread in the Middle Ages and flourished at all levels of society. While amillennialism was the official view of the Roman Church, in practice many ignored this position. The study of prophecy was not a preoccupation of social outcasts and political revolutionaries alone, but attracted the sustained attention of serious theologians, historians, and politicians.[60] In spite of the church's rejection of millennialism in the fifth century, the idea of a future millennial age did not disappear.

As Cohen acknowledges, it received a huge boost in the twelfth century through the writings of Joachim of Fiore, who believed he had been given a divine revelation enabling him to understand the book of Revelation. Joachim divided history into three overlapping eras, each of which he associated with a member of the Trinity. The Age of the Law (the Old Testament) had been overseen by the Father, the Age of Grace (New Testament) was begun by the Son, and the final era, the Age of the Spirit, was about to dawn—a period that he believed would be ushered in by a new monastic order. The messianic expectations "naturally contributed to the general conversionist spirit exhibited by the friars during the thirteenth century. Since of all the infidels the Jews were supposed to convert first, many probably viewed their conversion en masse—one means of ridding Christendom of Judaism—as a pressing task to be performed in order to pave the way for final redemption."[61] Joachim wrote his own polemical treatise against the Jews, *Adversus Iudeos*. For a time Joachim received the avid support of three successive popes, but eventually some of his teachings were deemed heretical by the church and a rather ineffective clampdown began on his apocalyptic views. However, the Spiritual Franciscans, a group within the Franciscan movement that held closely to his millennial teachings and developed a number of pseudo-Joachian prophecies of their own, made the case that

---

[58]Cohen, *Friars and the Jews*, 246.

[59]Cohen, *Friars and the Jews*, 246.

[60]Paul Boyer, *When Time Shall Be No More: Prophecy Belief in Modern American Culture* (Cambridge, MA: Belknap Press of Harvard University Press, 1992), 50.

[61]Cohen, *Friars and the Jews*, 247.

the monastic movement Joachim had foreseen was the Franciscan order. Cohen is convinced that this shift in eschatology contributed to this massive sea change in Christian attitudes to Judaism.

Cohen's other two reasons can only be described briefly. His second is the new emphasis on the organic unity and universality of Christendom under papal direction under Innocent III in the early thirteenth century whereby the papacy became a monarchy claiming authority over all earthly rulers, a totalizing force in medieval Christendom that could no longer tolerate dissent in any form, either of wayward Christians or recalcitrant Jews. The support for the papacy from the mendicant orders did much to augment its power. Cohen's third reason is the leadership role of the mendicant orders who spearheaded the anti-Jewish offensive. Cohen argues that they faced strong opponents within the church who accused them of theological innovations that mirrored the errors of the Jews, inventing new doctrines such as that of absolute poverty (just as the Jews had been innovative in creating the Talmud) and of Pharisaism in styling themselves as the true Christians within the church. The campaign against the Jews in the Latin Christian world was a means of the friars demonstrating their zeal for the true faith in seeking to pursue Jewish conversion—by incentives, by their inflammatory conversionist sermons that Christian princes were expected to require their Jewish subjects to listen to, and by the negative restrictions on European Jewry enumerated at the Fourth Lateran Council. Cohen's concluding sentences of his book on the friars puts all of this in context: "The attack of these friars on the Jews might well be understood, therefore, as deriving from the overriding concern for Christian unity during the thirteenth and early fourteenth centuries and from their active roles in trying to realize it—whether as inquisitor, missionary, Semitist, poet, or itinerant preacher."[62]

The Augustinian hope for the Jews' eventual conversion was strong in the thirteenth and fourteenth centuries, and intense missionizing efforts were undertaken with some notable successes.[63] Their return to Palestine, however, was not canvassed except, perhaps, by proto-Protestants like John Wycliffe and Jan Hus, both of whom Christopher Hill maintains had

---

[62]Cohen, *Friars and the Jews*, 264.

[63]For a study of these efforts see Robert Chazan, *Daggers of Faith: Thirteenth-Century Christian Missionizing and Jewish Response* (Berkeley: University of California Press, 1989).

"interpreted literally the Biblical texts relating to the return of the Jews to Palestine."[64] Up until the late Middle Ages one is hard-pressed to find historical precedent in Christian history for the notion that Christians should expect the Jewish people to return to Palestine and reestablish their presence there as a nation.

The Holy Land in Christian thinking during the Middle Ages. Although the notion of a Jewish return was not discussed by Christians in the Middle Ages, the Holy Land itself was at the forefront of the medieval European Christian imagination and of European politics, and this was a factor that would loom large in centuries to come. Up to the early seventh century, the Eastern Mediterranean had been under Christian domination and was part and parcel of Byzantium, which continued on for centuries after the collapse of the Roman Empire in the West. Most of the inhabitants of the region were in some sense Christian. All this changed abruptly and dramatically between 632 and 710 with the rise of Islam. Muhammad united many of the Arab tribes, and soon Muslim armies conquered Egypt and then spread quickly across North Africa, up into Spain and Portugal, vanquishing lands that had been under nominal Christian rule. The Muslim forces were only stopped at the Battle of Tours in central France when they were finally defeated by a Frankish army in 732. Beaten back out of France, the next several centuries were characterized by Christian resistance to the Muslim presence in the Iberian Peninsula.

The conflict with Islam escalated sharply in the 1070s with the rise of the Seljuk Turks, a Tartar tribe from central Asia that established an empire in Persia; the stalemate between Christian and Muslim forces was soon broken, and the remaining Christian empire in the East experienced severe and prolonged pressure from Islam. This change came on the heels of the Great Schism of 1054, when, because of theological differences, the pope excommunicated the Eastern Orthodox patriarch and with him the Eastern Orthodox Church, thus driving a religious and political wedge between the Eastern and Western Christian churches. The Eastern Christians trembled before the power of militant Islam, and attacks on Christian pilgrims rose and atrocities against Christians at the hands of the Seljuks

---

[64]Christopher Hill, "Till the Conversion of the Jews," in *Millenarianism and Messianism in English Literature and Thought, 1650–1800*, ed. Richard H. Popkin (Leiden: Brill, 1988), 14.

occurred—particularly massacres of Christians in Antioch and Jerusalem. The beleaguered Eastern Christians soon appealed to the West for help, and a response was forthcoming: in 1095 Pope Urban II preached the First Crusade with the goal of reclaiming Palestine for Christ, drawing on an already established link between penance and military activity. Those who fought on behalf of the church were promised remission of sin and release from the heavy burden imposed on sinners by the church's penitential system. Others drew on Augustine's "just war" concept, Old Testament precedents, and the well-established warlike tendencies of the Germanic tribes to urge the recapture of the Holy Land and to guarantee Christian pilgrims safe access to the holy sites.

For our purposes it is striking that throughout this time, medieval Christians never thought of the "Holy Land" as a place properly belonging to the Jews. It was a territory special to God; he was the supreme Lord, and his honor had been diminished by the land being taken from Christians and occupied by hostile forces. Once it had been enriched by the blood of the Son of God, but now it was occupied by cruel and evil people. It was incumbent on Christians to reclaim the land for its rightful owner, Christ, not to secure it for the Jews. The European feudal mentality was built on social obligations of inferiors to their superiors—vassals to their temporal lords, the temporal lords to their kings, kings to the Lord of all. It was the duty of all Christians to see that what belonged properly to the Lord of all be restored to him, thereby vindicating God's honor, something that made sense to people inhabiting an honor-shame culture.

The Holy Land occupied a central place in the Western Christian imagination for several centuries before the Reformation. The struggle with Islam in Europe and in the Middle East was at center stage throughout the High and late Middle Ages; resistance to militant Islam was symbolized by the control of Palestine. The Christian West abandoned its attempts to recapture Palestine when the Seventh (and last) Crusade ended in 1395, but the loss was never fully accepted in Europe. Byzantium eventually capitulated to Muslim pressure in 1454, when Constantinople, its last remaining stronghold, fell to Islamic forces. The idea of the Holy Land belonging properly to the Jews never entered into Christian thinking. This background is important for appreciating the changes in thinking that occurred in the sixteenth century and for understanding the attitude of Islam to any perceived European intrusion into the Middle East. It also helps one to appreciate why the modern state of Israel is regarded by many Muslims as a new form of a crusader state, an intrusion into an area long controlled by Islam. In the minds of radical Muslims, the teaching of the Qur'an and the Hadith (the received tradition that has grown up around the Qur'an) is that Islam is destined to dominate the whole world; thus no Muslim is ever to sell land to "infidels," and no land that has come under the domination of Islam is ever to be conceded to the control of the infidel. The implications of such views for the notion of a Jewish state in the heart of what had been Muslim territory are obvious.

Perceptions of the Holy Land remained closely tied to Christian eschatology even at the end of the Middle Ages. Christopher Columbus was strongly influenced by Joachim of Fiore and perceived his conquest of the Indies as part of the fulfillment of prophecy that included the global spread of the Catholic faith, the defeat of Islam by a pincer movement from the east, leading to the reconquest of Jerusalem. So in spite of the church's official rejection of millennialism, medieval Catholicism in general, and late fifteenth-century Spanish Catholicism in particular, exuded a "messianic milieu"[65] affecting not only Columbus but also his patrons, King Ferdinand and Queen Isabella of Spain.

TWO ONGOING QUESTIONS

Two key questions emerge from our study of this period: What is a Jew? And what is Judaism? From the time of Christ to the 1500s Christians and Jews developed quite different answers to these questions. To Jews the answers were self-evident: a Jew was defined by faith and ethnicity and by association with the Jewish community. By the High Middle Ages Judaism was defined largely by adherence to the rabbinic tradition and its devotion to the Old Testament and the Talmud. For Christians, their tradition insisted that they were the new people of God, the true Jews by faith in the Jewish Messiah. Judaism, which they had understood to be rooted primarily in the Old Testament, had been traditionally protected in Christendom, but

---

[65]Leonard I. Sweet, "Christopher Columbus and the Millennial Vision of the New World," *Catholic Historical Review* 72, no. 3 (1986): 373.

whether rabbinic Judaism should be became an open question. With the Christian discovery of the talmudic tradition, the older understanding largely gave way to a hostility to the talmudic innovations and to a subsequent Christian denigration of Judaism as it had evolved. Armed with an understanding of this background, we turn to the new developments in prophetic understanding and new wrestling with questions of religious identity that emerged among sixteenth-century Protestants, where we find the genesis of the movement known as "restorationism," which eventually morphed into Christian Zionism.

2

GENEVA AND THE JEWS

Tectonic Shifts in the Landscape of Jewish-Christian Relations

This chapter tracks the ideation behind restorationism—examining how ideas emerged and evolved in the sixteenth century that were eventually to germinate in a movement that would work to return the Jews to the Holy Land. These ideas developed slowly, beginning with the idea of a "spiritual return," followed by a "physical return." Those who advocated a physical restoration of the Jews were known as "restorationists," but they cannot at this point be classified as "Christian Zionists" because they often envisioned the "Restoration" as an apocalyptic event far off in the future, not something to be worked for in the here and now, although there might possibly be small steps (such as Jewish readmission to England) that could be taken to prepare for the ultimate end. For most restorationists the "return" was something God would accomplish, just as the devout Jews believed that the Messiah would bring about the "return" when he appeared.

As has been seen, during the late Middle Ages Latin Christendom had developed what is often referred to as a "teaching of contempt" toward the Jews. From about the twelfth century an increasingly hostile attitude toward the Jews and Judaism emerged, which turned its back on the Augustinian emphasis on the Jews as "witnesses" to Christian truth, and began to view the Jews as heretics and enemies. In broad terms, Martin Luther early in his ministry tended in the Augustinian direction. In 1523 he wrote an essay, *That Jesus Christ Was Born a Jew*, which urged kind treatment toward Jews in the hopes that they would convert. But by the late 1530s, when he realized that this was not happening, he did a complete about-face and fully embraced the late medieval hostility to the Jews in all its ugliness, campaigned against their presence in Saxony, and became incredibly hostile toward them and their religion. In 1543 he produced two works—*On the Jews and Their Lies* and *The Whole Jewish Belief*—both of which are shockingly violent in their attitudes. Now no mercy is to be shown them: their synagogues and schools are to be destroyed, their prayer books seized, their rabbis prohibited from preaching, their property and assets seized, and their expulsion from Christendom mandated. Many books have been written examining Luther's views and actions, often distinguishing between his theological anti-Judaism and racial anti-Semitism.[1] For our purposes it is significant that Luther's attitude differed sharply from the pro-Jewish views that emerged in Calvinism. The ideation behind Christian restorationism found no support in the Lutheran world in the sixteenth century.

Luther's Historicist Turn

Apart from Luther's reversal of his attitude toward the Jews, another significant move he made had a long-term impact well beyond Lutheranism. Luther retained Augustine's amillennialism, but shifted in his approach to the church age.[2] While he agreed with Augustine that the church age was the millennium, he understood prophetic passages in Scripture to be referring to different events in the past and present history of the church. His general approach is called "historicism." His "historicist amillennialism" began a tradition within Protestantism of mapping the symbols of the apocalyptic passages onto church history and current events. If the symbols were meant to be clues as to what God was doing in history, then surely his people were meant to decipher them and have a good sense of when Christ would return. Setting a crucial trajectory for Protestant interpreters for centuries, Luther in 1530 identified "the Turk" (Islam) and the papacy as

---

[1]See William Nicholls, *Christian Antisemitism: A History of Hate* (London: Jason Aronson, 1998), 268-71; Edward H. Flannery, *The Anguish of the Jews: Twenty-Three Centuries of Antisemitism* (New York: Paulist Press, 1985), 152-53; and James Carroll, *Constantine's Sword: The Church and the Jews* (New York: Houghton Mifflin, 2001), 366-68.

[2]Peter Toon, introduction to *Puritans, the Millennium and the Future of Israel: Puritan Eschatology, 1600 to 1660*, ed. Peter Toon (Cambridge: James Clarke, 1970), 6.

antichrist, the two-headed beast of Revelation.[3] In his commentary on
Ezekiel he identified "Gog" and "Magog" as the Ottoman Empire.[4] As
Bernard McGinn comments,

> This identification [of the papacy with the antichrist] was made within the
> context of a historically progressive reading of the text. Earlier interpreters,
> such as Joachim (but not Augustine), had also claimed to find a consonance
> between Revelation's prophecies and the events of Church history, but they
> had begun with Scripture and used it as the key to unlock history. Paradoxi-
> cally, Luther, the great champion of the biblical word, claimed that history
> enabled him to make sense of Revelation.[5]

Luther's historicist turn was pivotal. Many of his Protestant successors
embraced it, even if they believed in a real millennium. As Peter Toon observes, "Henceforth most Protestant writers who commented on the Apoc-
alypses of John and Daniel followed his lead and saw in their highly symbolic visions and dreams 'prophecies' of the downfall of the Turks, of the
destruction of the city of Rome, of the demise of the Papacy, and of the ultimate triumph of the Protestant cause."[6] McGinn comments,

> [Luther's] insistence that history enabled him to make sense of Revelation
> introduced a tension into Reformation commentary that is evident in the
> following centuries. . . . The Protestants' need to demonstrate the evan-
> gelical claim that the papacy itself (along with the dreaded Turk) consti-
> tuted the institutional embodiment of the Antichrist was at the heart of the
> new historicization.[7]

Thus the Protestant experience of Catholic persecution was explained in
apocalyptic terms. Following Luther the classic Protestant commentators
agreed that "Revelation, correctly understood, showed how the papacy
throughout history had functioned as the persecuting Antichrist."[8]

---

[3]Robert O. Smith, *More Desired Than Our Owne Salvation: The Roots of Christian Zionism* (New
York: Oxford University Press, 2013), 29.
[4]Smith, *More Desired*, 49-50.
[5]Bernard McGinn, "Revelation," in *The Literary Guide to the Bible*, ed. Robert Alter and Frank
Kermode (Cambridge, MA: Harvard University Press, 1987), 529.
[6]Toon, introduction, 6.
[7]McGinn, "Revelation," 534.
[8]McGinn, "Revelation," 535.

PROTESTANT INDIVIDUALISM

The Reformation's emphasis on the individual fueled popular interest in biblical apocalyptic passages. The reformers wanted everyone to have access to Scripture in the vernacular and taught that Scripture, while complex, was clear as regards its central message about salvation; the phrase used was "the perspicuity of the Scriptures." Protestants saw this as a core tenet of their worldview, and believed that Scripture would bring about the needed correctives and the impetus for renewal to liberate Christianity from the shackles imposed by the medieval theologians, moving the church away from its preoccupation with Greek and Roman thought and philosophy, to a more robustly biblical worldview. Thus theological positions established by the tradition of the church had to be reexamined to establish their congruence with Scripture.

Issues of identity thus became crucial at the time of the Reformation: Who are we? And where do we fit in relation to the long centuries of the Christian tradition? In Protestant minds, an enormous revolution had occurred within Western Christianity, one of world-historical importance. Constructing a Protestant identity involved identifying their spiritual forebears. Which aspects of Christian tradition could they embrace? Where had it gone wrong, and how could it be fixed? What were they to endorse? And what were they to oppose?

This "reexamination" occurred in a particular historical setting. Two key points need to be appreciated. First, Reformation Protestants operated in a world shaped by late medieval apocalyptic thinking, which was influenced by the catastrophic debacle of the Crusades; late medieval European Christendom was preoccupied with the threat of Islam and the return of Christ. The reexamination involved a reshaping of apocalyptic expectations in relation to the event of the Protestant Reformation itself, which was seen in apocalyptic terms. Second, this reexamination was being carried out in a dangerous and hostile environment. Sixteenth-century Protestants operated in a world dominated by two major enemies: the Roman Catholic Church ("the pope"), which was persecuting Protestants throughout Europe, and "the Turk"—that is, Islam, the centuries-old enemy of Western and Eastern Christianity that for two centuries had been pressing on Europe's eastern flank, coming within striking distance of Vienna in the 1520s. Protestant identity was thus hammered out both apocalyptically and politically on the twin anvils of "the pope" and "the Turk." Anti-Catholic and anti-Muslim attitudes became deeply rooted in the process of Protestant identity formation, which was closely entwined with Protestant attitudes to Catholicism, Islam, and the Jews.

For many Calvinists, the particular and unique relationship of Protestantism to the Jews became a way of distinguishing Protestantism from Catholicism. There were, in effect, two different ways of understanding restorationism (the "restoration of the Jews"). The first was that the Jews would be "spiritually restored"—that is, there would be a mass conversion of Jews to Christianity at some point in the future, which as we have seen was a common view in medieval Christianity. The idea was embraced by the young Luther, although he later despaired of this. Belief in a widespread Jewish conversion, however, continued as a tenet of the mainstream "orthodox" Lutheran party until about 1650; thereafter it came under criticism and became associated with the more radical spiritualist writers.[9] The idea was accepted relatively quickly by many Protestants in the Reformed (Calvinistic) tradition. As early as 1590 English biblical scholars were teaching that Romans 11:25-26, especially the phrase "all Israel shall be saved," promised a mass Jewish conversion to Christianity. By contrast, both Martin Luther's mature view and John Calvin's consistent position was to accept an Augustinian interpretation that denied any continuing significance to Jews and Judaism.[10]

Johannes Wollebius (1586–1629), a Reformed theologian in Basel, pointed out that it was these two verses in Romans 11 that became the "chief authority" for the early seventeenth-century view—common among English Puritans and later with New England Puritans such as Cotton Mather and Jonathan Edwards—that a "national conversion" of Jews was to be expected.[11] Jean de Labadie, the influential French Reformed pastor, expressed a similar view in his L'Ideé d'un bon Pasteur et d'une bonne Eglise (1667), in which he

---

[9]Christopher M. Clark, The Politics of Conversion: Missionary Protestantism and the Jews in Prussia, 1728–1941 (Oxford: Clarendon, 1995), 18.

[10]Mayir Vereté, "The Restoration of the Jews in English Protestant Thought, 1790–1840," Middle Eastern Studies 8, no. 1 (January 1972): 15.

[11]Iain H. Murray, The Puritan Hope: A Study in Revival and the Interpretation of Prophecy (London: Banner of Truth Trust, 1971), 61.

maintained that Israel's conversion would usher in the church's golden age.[12] Thus by the middle of the seventeenth century the interpretation of prophecies concerning a spiritual "return" of the Jews to Christianity was widely—although not universally—accepted, especially in English Calvinist circles. The two Reformation figures most responsible for the new identification of "Israel" in Romans 11 as "the Jews" instead of the church were Theodore Beza, who succeeded Calvin as the chief pastor in Geneva following the reformer's death, and Calvin's close associate Martin Bucer.

A second idea came to be associated with a spiritual Jewish restoration: that it would (perhaps simultaneously) be accompanied by a literal return of the Jews to their ancestral "homeland" in Palestine. None of the leading Protestant Reformers (Martin Luther, Philip Melanchthon, Huldrych Zwingli, and John Calvin) expected such a return. While Luther had hoped for their conversion, he had denied their return "for, there is no prophet, nor promise, which foretells its [Jerusalem's] restoration, as happened in Babylon and Egypt."[13] The early Protestant Reformers, both Lutheran and Reformed, followed in the amillennial footsteps of Augustine and rejected the radical millenarianism of the early church fathers, and similar millenarian views expressed by some contemporary Anabaptists (who apparently drew on the work of Joachim of Fiore), which they strongly deplored.[14]

This new understanding, however, insisted that the Old Testament promises about the physical return of the Jews to their homeland remained to be accomplished. The earliest proponents of this emerged in Strasbourg in 1526 with Martin Borrhaus, a German Hebraic scholar, who then convinced Wolfgang Capito, the respected provost of St. Thomas Church (another Hebrew scholar), of this interpretation. Capito incorporated it in his Latin commentary on Hosea, published in 1528.[15] Borrhaus and Capito,

---

[12]Jean de Labadie, *L'Ideé d'un bon Pasteur et d'une bonne Eglise* (Amsterdam, 1667) cited in Christopher M. Clark, "'The Hope for Better Times': Pietism and the Jews," in *Pietism in Germany and North America, 1680–1820*, ed. Jonathan Strom, Hartmut Lehmann, and James Van Horn Melton (Farnham, UK: Ashgate, 2009), 2.

[13]Martin Luther, *Against the Sabbatarians: Letter to a Good Friend* (1538), in *Luther's Works* [American ed.], ed. Helmut T. Lehman (Philadelphia: Fortress, 1971), 47:84.

[14]Toon, introduction, 6. It is thought that Melchior Hoffman, a leading Anabaptist figure, was influenced by Joachim.

[15]Capito built his argument from Hosea 1:11 and Hosea 3:5. See Wolfgang Capito, *In Hoseam Prophetam* (Strasbourg: Joannem Hervagium, 1528).

however, found their ideas firmly rejected by the Reformed leaders closest to them—Bucer and Zwingli.[16] This position did not gain traction until it was taken up by English Protestants and became entwined with English nationalism in the early seventeenth century. Not all who embraced the "spiritual restoration" necessarily embraced the idea of a "physical restoration."[17] But the idea of the "physical restoration" emerged as the Protestant prophetic imagination discerned this interpretation in the biblical symbols that had long mystified Christian theologians. Here we find the genesis of what would eventuate in the modern movement of Christian Zionism. This is where the genealogy begins.

The Reformers' Approach to Scripture

Luther, Zwingli, and Calvin struggled with what systematic approach (or in technical terms, what "hermeneutic") to adopt in reading Scripture. Roman Catholics were taught that Scripture was to be read in accordance with church tradition, but Protestants, while not rejecting tradition outright, thought it unreliable. Even those traditions enshrined in councils of the church could be wrong. They were sure that Jan Hus in the early fifteenth century had been correct in arguing that the Roman Church had erred in the matter of the withholding of the wine from the laity in Communion decreed by the Council of Constance in 1415.

Calvin and the Reformed tradition emphasized the Bible as God's Word written and valued all of Scripture as equally authoritative (if not as equally important), as all Scripture had been inspired by the same God. While the young Luther had for a time doubted the value of the book of James, no such uncertainty plagued John Calvin or others in the Reformed movement. There arose an emphasis on the "plain literal sense" of Scripture among Reformed Protestants, while they also made room for various literary forms such as allegory and metaphor. While none of these early Reformation

---

[16]I am indebted to Gerald Hobbes for the information on the Strasbourg developments. Gerald Hobbes, "Will the Jews Return to Palestine? A 16th Century Reformation Debate" (paper presented at the Vancouver School of Theology Theological Forum, December 5, 2005).

[17]The following writers accepted the spiritual conversion but denied a physical return: Luther, Andrew Willet, William Perkins, Hugh Broughton, Thomas Draxe, and a number of Scottish theologians. See Nabil I. Matar, "The Idea of the Restoration of the Jews in English Protestant Thought: Between the Reformation and 1660," *Durham University Journal* 78, no. 1 (December 1985): 29-30.

leaders employed a literal approach when interpreting Old Testament passages regarding the return of the Jews to Palestine, many of their successors did, and a few of their contemporaries did as well.

THE REFORMATION AND THE APOCALYPTIC TRADITION

The cataclysms of the 1520s brought eschatology to the fore. Without intending to do so, an obscure monk in the backwaters of northern Europe had inaugurated a movement that was changing the course of history. Luther feared the wrath of both the pope and the Holy Roman emperor and for a time had to go into hiding. Similarly, John Calvin and his family lived daily with the threat of assassination by agents of the king of France. At the same time Muslim armies that had been threatening Eastern Europe since about 1300 were encroaching from the east and remained a threat through to the middle of the seventeenth century. Luther thought that he was living in the last days and expected the imminent return of Christ.

Other events soon cast a long shadow over Protestant discussions of eschatology. In 1524 a sometime associate of Luther, Thomas Müntzer, became obsessed with prophetic speculation and was convinced that with the apocalypse at hand, God would use him to exterminate the godless. In the same year German peasants revolted against their landlords and the territorial princes who supported them with many believing that Christ would return to vindicate their cause. Peasant revolts were common in the previous century, but in this case the widespread movement was combined with apocalyptic elements. Luther was aghast and rashly encouraged the territorial princes to suppress the rebellion harshly, which they did. Müntzer was beheaded and the peasants' cause discredited, doing great damage to the popularity of Lutheranism among the lower classes. Upward of one hundred thousand rebels are believed to have died in the Peasants' War of 1524–1525. In 1525 the Anabaptist movement began in Zurich—a radical movement that rejected infant baptism and insisted on the (re)baptism of believers as adults, breaking decisively with the idea of a state church. The Anabaptists were fascinated with apocalypticism and were convinced of the imminent return of Christ. Both Luther and Calvin reacted strongly against these trends, and the extremists in the German city of Münster who overthrew the local government and instituted a radical millenarian regime in the early 1530s did long-term damage to the Anabaptist cause.

Beza's Shift: the Spiritual Restoration of the Jews

Calvin had been cautious of prophetic speculation, but his successor in Geneva, Theodore Beza, was not. Beza adopted Luther's modified historicist approach, but taught what neither Augustine nor Calvin had explicitly taught, that "near the end of the age large numbers of Jews, or perhaps the whole Jewish people would be converted to Christianity from Judaism, and by their conversion bring great spiritual blessing to the Church on earth."[18] Once again, the key passage in the whole debate was Romans 11:25-32. The key words are "and so all Israel shall be saved" (Romans 11:26). Luther and Calvin had understood the words "all Israel" to be a reference to the Christian church composed of Jews and Gentiles—the "Israel of God" that Paul refers to in Galatians 6:16—whereas Beza interpreted it to mean Jews whose religion was Judaism. Beza influenced the English exiles in Geneva in the 1550s on this matter. Known as the "Marian exiles," these Protestant leaders had fled Queen Mary I's persecution of Protestants after she came to the throne in 1553.

The Marian Exiles and the Geneva Bible

In the 1550s these exiles together produced the Geneva Bible, an English translation that was the most popular version of the Bible for generations. Its strongly Calvinistic slant influenced both British and American Protestants and popularized specific prophetic understandings across the English-speaking world.[19] It was, in effect, the first "study Bible." Its short notes in the 1557 and 1560 editions instructed readers—following Beza—that the "Israel" referred to in Romans 11:26 was "the nation of the Jews." The marginal note on Romans 11 in the 1560 edition reads, "He sheweth that the time shall come that the whole nation of the Jews, though not every one particularly, shall be joined to the church of Christ."[20] Through the work of Beza, the Geneva Bible and its notes, as well as a host of English Puritan writers "the doctrine of the conversion of the Jewish people was widely diffused in England, Scotland and New England."[21] Peter Toon argues that

---

[18]Toon, introduction, 6.
[19]For an extended discussion of the various editions of the Geneva Bible see Crawford Gribben, *The Puritan Millennium: Literature and Theology, 1550-1682*, rev. ed. (Milton Keynes, UK: Paternoster, 2008), 71-86.
[20]Murray, *Puritan Hope*, 41.
[21]Peter Toon, "The Latter-Day Glory," in Toon, *The Puritans, the Millennium and the Future of Israel*, 24.

most Puritans (using this term in its widest sense) believed that Paul in Romans 11:25ff was speaking of some kind of large-scale conversion of Jews to Christ before the Second Coming of Christ. Yet there were still a few who denied that such an event would take place, since, in their view, "Israel" in Romans 11:25ff. referred to the whole New Testament Church of Gentile and Jew.[22]

THE "NATION" OF THE JEWS AND THE FORGING OF ENGLISH NATIONALISM

Another crucial idea that became popular in English Protestantism was that the Jews constitute a distinct nation. The Geneva Bible speaks of the Jews not as a people, but as a "nation." James Shapiro points out that its English editors had in view the Jews as a distinct ethnic group, one that was entitled to its own homeland. The term *nation* had been used of groups sharing common fraternal and genealogical bonds, but "when combined with a sense of the importance of territoriality in early modern England, a concept that placed particular nations within distinct territories, the idea of the Jews as a separate 'nation' led towards a belief that they would possess their own land."[23] England in the mid-sixteenth century experienced both expansion (in its union with Wales in 1545) and retraction (with the loss in 1558 of Calais) and was becoming more conscious of its own delineation as a territorial unit.[24] During this period "a distinct sense of the English nation began to emerge through an imagined conjunction of the state, church and land,"[25] something that was heightened by England's full break with Rome in 1558. "This concept of nations mapped to firmly bounded physical territories resonated with the Old Testament promises to the Jews to establish them in a land with firm territorial boundaries."[26] As England was becoming more aware of its own boundedness, Jewish "restoration to Palestine seemed like an understandable wish for this landless nation."[27] The idea that the "wandering Jew" would find his way home in the apocalyptic

---

[22]Peter Toon, conclusion to Toon, *Puritans, the Millennium and the Future of Israel*, 126.

[23]Andrew Crome, *Christian Zionism and English National Identity, 1600–1850* (Cham, Switzerland: Palgrave Macmillan, 2018), 65.

[24]Crome, *English National Identity*, 64.

[25]Crome, *English National Identity*, 64.

[26]Crome, *English National Identity*, 64-65.

[27]Crome, *English National Identity*, 65.

future was beginning to take hold. How and when that would happen was much debated, but the stage was being set for English Protestants to ask whether God might be calling their nation to take part in the stage-managing of that history.

Linking the Jews to English Nationalism: John Bale and John Foxe

This linking of the Jews to English nationalism was developed by two Marian exiles: John Bale and John Foxe. Beza's position regarding the conversion of the Jews was at the forefront of the writings of John Bale (1495–1563), whose *The Image of Both Churches* (1545) was the first full-length English commentary on the book of Revelation and contrasted the false Babylonish (Roman) church and the true, apostolic one (the evangelical church) as it had developed over seven ages of history. Like Luther and Calvin, Bale specified the papacy and the Turk as the great enemies of true religion. However, he introduced "a new field of thought concerning Jews and their place within Christian apocalyptic hope,"[28] arguing for the national conversion of the Jews to Protestantism.

Important for our purposes, Bale also began to link the conversion of the Jews with English nationalism as he developed the idea of England as an "elect nation," chosen by God to perform his will in the world. Bale constructed a new historiographical narrative of the English church, which found its origin in the work of Joseph of Arimathea, establishing thereby the apostolic claims of the Church of England, before the rise of the papacy.[29] Bale in turn influenced John Foxe (1517–1587), whose *Actes and Monuments* popularized many of his emphases.[30] English national identity was thus apocalyptically constructed by Bale and Foxe. Robert O. Smith comments, "John Bale's project of constructing Protestant meaning, with its anti-Catholic, Judeo-centric and historiographic elements, shaped both the trajectory of English nationalism and the history of the theopolitical prophecy interpretation."[31] As Nabil Matar has observed,

---

[28]Smith, *More Desired*, 57.
[29]Smith, *More Desired*, 61-62.
[30]Smith, *More Desired*, 62-63.
[31]Smith, *More Desired*, 63.

Indeed, the more the English theologian was anti-Catholic—and after 1588 and 1605 there would be ample reasons—the higher was the position in which he held the Jew. For there was to the Protestant a triangle of peoples with whom he was dealing: the Jew, the Turk, and the Catholic. Invariably, of these three, the Jew was viewed with the highest sympathy, because, understandably, he posed the least danger.[32]

While English Protestants were influenced by Lutheran readings,[33] English interpretations of the book of Revelation differed from those on the Continent, and crucially "these differences spring from the relationship of English Protestant faith to particular developments in English nationalism."[34] English national identity and the Reformation cause became closely linked in the minds of many. In the hands of their Protestant interpreters, Jews came to be invested with apocalyptic meaning and significance, but they were to play a role that was clearly constructed by a Christian imagination toward Protestant ends. It is ironic that this happened at a time when England had no Jews, as they had been expelled in 1290, over two centuries before the famous Spanish and Portuguese expulsions in 1492. In the evolving construction of Protestant apocalypticism both the pope and the Turk would be thwarted by the Jews returning to Palestine, aided by their best friend, Protestant England.

Although a clear instance of restorationist thinking had emerged in the 1520s in Strasbourg in the writings of Borrhaus and Capito, it had then been firmly rejected by key Protestant leaders. It did not gain much traction on the Continent in the rest of the century and was not initially advocated by those who adopted the view that the Jews would convert en masse in the end times. Significantly, Beza's modified historicist position, which promoted the idea of the future conversion of the Jews to Christ, was widely adopted by key English-speaking Protestants, notably William Perkins, Elnathan Parr, and Robert Baillie. It was one thing to believe in the conversion of the Jews; it was another to believe in their return to Palestine. Yet, as will be seen, the view of a physical restoration that had been mooted in the sixteenth century came into its own in the next century. In our pursuit of the ideation

---

[32]Matar, "Idea of the Restoration," 26.
[33]Smith, *More Desired*, 55.
[34]Smith, *More Desired*, 55.

behind Christian Zionism, we have found that it emerged as Calvinists came to emphasize a spiritual restoration of the Jews, and then their eventual physical restoration to Palestine, followed by English Puritans viewing the Jews as a distinct nation, yet one without a land. The idea began to emerge that the Jewish nation was to be aided by the English nation in the fulfillment of the Old Testament land promises. The alliance of English nationalism with the Jewish nation, over against the pope and the Turk, was slowly being forged in the minds of Calvinistic Protestants.

3

ENGLISH PURITANISM
AND THE JEWS

Internal needs along with foreign threats made English politicians, theologians and evangelists turn toward the Jew, and assign him functions that served first, in the confrontation with the Turks and the Catholics; secondly, in the millenarian expectations of the Civil Wars; and thirdly, in the moral responsibility of proselytizing. The Jew became a victim of English aspirations, and was completely perceived through these three perspectives.[1]

NABIL I. MATAR

THE EARLY CHURCH WAS CHARACTERIZED by an eager expectation of Christ's return, the final victory of good over evil, and the end of sorrow and pain. Augustine had dampened down such expectations, insisting that millennial perfection will not be achieved in this world. While Augustine believed in the personal return of Christ to judge the world at the end of time, he was certain that humans were not given to know anything about how the end would come, when it would happen, or who would be saved. In the meantime, Christians were not to forsake their daily responsibilities. Augustine had toned down apocalyptic hopes and introduced a heavy dose of pessimism as to the possibility of real progress on earth. English Protestantism, while deeply indebted to Augustine in much of its theology, sought to reverse his pessimistic expectations as to what could be accomplished in

---

[1]Nabil I. Matar, "The Idea of the Restoration of the Jews in English Protestant Thought: Between the Reformation and 1660," *Durham University Journal* 78, no. 1 (December 1985): 24.

the church age. New hope sprang up among English Puritans about the future nurtured by apocalyptic writers. The ancient Jewish tradition of the apocalyptic was taken over, revised, and transformed. In Ernest Lee Tuveson's words, in the seventeenth century the fires that were kindled from the book of the Revelation of Saint John "became a beacon of hope for mankind, and this change has been one of the most momentous events in the intellectual history of the West since the Reformation."[2]

Although many Englishmen including Royalists, Baptists, Anglicans, and Fifth Monarchists addressed the issue of Jewish restoration in the seventeenth century, those most responsible for its emergence in early modern England belonged to the Puritan grouping within the Church of England until 1662, with many joining Nonconformist churches thereafter.[3] The Puritans were a powerful group of clergy and laity within the Church of England who first acquired the name Puritan in the 1550s because they believed that the Anglican Church had only been partially reformed along Calvinistic lines. It was not adequately "purified," hence the nickname Puritan.

ENGLAND AS A "CHOSEN NATION" WITH TASKS TO PERFORM

The Puritans were convinced that God not only chose (or "elected") individuals to do his will but also chose particular nations, such as the Jews. They also believed God had chosen Protestant England and given it tasks to perform. Being chosen or "elected' involved particular obligations, and in the wake of the Reformation, English Puritans believed that England had been entrusted with a special leadership role in the international Protestant cause, reflecting the fact that "internationalism and cooperation have often been a part of conceptions of national chosenness."[4] Its government was to defend the faith from (Catholic) foes, both without and within. A nation that failed in fulfilling its divine calling would be judged by God in history. Just as the Hebrew prophets had warned the Jews that they would suffer

---

[2] Ernest Lee Tuveson, *Redeemer Nation: The Idea of America's Millennial Role* (Chicago: University of Chicago Press, 1968), 2.

[3] Andrew Crome, *Christian Zionism and English National Identity, 1600–1850* (Cham, Switzerland: Palgrave Macmillan, 2018), 71. The term *Puritan* has been applied to numerous groups outside of the Church of England including some Baptists. I am using it to refer to those moderate Puritans who remained within the Church of England until 1662.

[4] Crome, *English National Identity*, 6.

God's displeasure as a nation for their disobedience, so too would Protestant England. Chosenness had conditions attached. England could not act as it pleased and was called to higher standards (and greater blessings or greater judgments) than other nations. In Todd Gitlin and Liel Leibovitz's words, chosenness could at times "feel like a sentence" as much as a blessing.[5]

Such views helped to shape England's national identity. Beyond leading the international Protestant cause, many Puritans became convinced that God was specifically calling England to aid the Jewish people to return to the Holy Land. This involved England's embracing "a form of secondary election, in which they understood national identity primarily in relation to their nation's service to the Jewish people."[6] Often national identities are constructed by "othering" outside groups, but in this instance the "other" was viewed positively. "In fact, the Jews when restored would be superior to the nation aiding them, and would return to their place as God's first nation."[7] This approach is hardly unique and runs through the subsequent five-century history of Christian restorationism/Zionism. As Andrew Crome observes, "Projects to restore the Jews to their ancient homeland, whether expressed as eschatological hopes, utopian schemes, or in practical political terms, have consistently served as means of national identity construction."[8] England might be a "chosen" nation to fulfill God's purposes, but the Jews would remain God's unique and sole "elect nation."

PURITANISM, THE POPE, AND THE ENGLISH STATE

The Puritans were remarkably tenacious and persistent, and gained parliamentary support for church reform and the Protestant nature of England's calling, which put them on a collision course with successive monarchs. Elizabeth I (1558–1603), as the head of the state church, sought to keep them in check and prevented their discontent from disrupting both church and state with their calls for further reform. After her death, the Puritans encountered the Stuart monarchs, who were far more hostile to them than Elizabeth had been, and far more sympathetic to Roman Catholicism.

---

[5]Crome, *English National Identity*, 56.
[6]Crome, *English National Identity*, 3.
[7]Crome, *English National Identity*, 3.
[8]Crome, *English National Identity*, 2.

In the wider European context the Puritans were facing a resurgent Roman Catholicism. The Reformation had reduced the number of European Catholics, but it also strengthened the devotion of many Catholics to the papacy.[9] The Counter Reformation grew in strength in the 1550s, and leading the Catholic resurgence were monarchs who sought to crush the Protestant states and re-impose papal rule by force. This struggle played out dramatically in England and shaped English history and (more broadly) British national identity in the succeeding centuries. When Queen Mary died in 1558 and was succeeded by Elizabeth I, Roman Catholicism was displaced by an English Protestant state church under Elizabeth. The Catholics long sought to return England to the Roman fold. In 1570 Pope Pius V endeavored to destabilize Elizabeth I's governance by excommunicating her and releasing English Catholics from their oaths of obedience to her as monarch; furthermore, he encouraged her overthrow and even connived in her assassination in the Ridolfi plot of 1571. Protestants regarded continued loyalty to Rome as disloyalty to the English Crown and resisted ongoing attempts to overthrow the Protestant Ascendancy. In 1572 the Saint Bartholomew's Day Massacre of French Protestants reinforced English Protestant fears. The defeat of the Spanish Armada in 1588 was interpreted as England's providential deliverance from its foe. In 1605, Guy Fawkes, a Catholic plotter, sought to blow up the houses of Parliament, hoping to kill the king and many legislators. All of these events naturally strengthened English fears of Catholicism.

The British historian Linda Colley has argued in *Britons: Forging the Nation, 1707–1837* that Protestant belief in England's identity as a chosen nation was a key factor in the formation of the modern British state.[10] The idea that Protestant England was God's chosen nation was at the core of the Puritan understanding of England's calling and was disseminated most effectively through John Foxe's *Actes and Monuments*[11] (1563), which, after the Bible and John Bunyan's *Pilgrim's Progress*, was the most widely read book in the English language for several centuries. Thus, in the sixteenth and

---

[9]Peter Toon, introduction to *The Puritans, the Millennium and the Future of Israel: Puritan Eschatology 1600 to 1660*, ed. Peter Toon (Cambridge: James Clarke, 1970), 22.

[10]Linda Colley, *Britons: Forging the Nation, 1707–1837* (New Haven, CT: Yale University Press, 1994).

[11]Commonly referred to as Foxe's *Book of Martyrs*.

seventeenth centuries, English national identity was hammered out on the anvil of Catholic-Protestant rivalry. By the end of the seventeenth century, the result was a resolutely Protestant royal family. The Puritans by then had been vanquished, but their identification of England as essentially Protestant had won the day. These political events are important in understanding the emergence of Christian restorationism.

Millenarians Suppressed

The Stuart monarchs (James I and Charles I) viewed millenarian authors (mainly Puritans) with alarm, and in the first four decades of the seventeenth century suppressed their publications, seeing them as potentially subversive. Once Charles I was deposed in 1642, however, during the Puritan revolutionary period (ca. 1642–1660) millenarian authors whose writings had long been suppressed, such as Thomas Brightman (1562–1607), Sir Henry Finch (ca. 1558–1625), and Joseph Mede (1586–1639) (all postmillennialists), became widely popular, and the idea gained traction among the people that the end was near (probably in 1656): the Jews would convert, the Turk be overthrown, and the pope brought low. At a time of widespread confusion, the newfound liberty of the press "helped to open up the space to discuss different concepts of nationhood."[12] Chief among them was England's role in Jewish conversion and restoration to their ancestral homeland.

From the seventeenth century and forward through to the nineteenth century much of Christian restorationism would be framed in terms of Britain's responsibility to help the Jews, on the one hand, and to oppose Catholicism, on the other. For many Puritans, England as an "elect nation" had to defend the realm against Catholic intrigue, and bore a peculiar responsibility toward the Jews, God's elect nation "according to the flesh." Their restoration was both England's calling and opportunity, for "indeed, restored and converted Jews would be the ideal allies in the battle against the papacy."[13] These ideas, of course, were closely tied into Puritan understandings of eschatology.

---

[12]Crome, *English National Identity*, 68.
[13]Crome, *English National Identity*, 64.

THE PURITAN HOPE: LATTER-DAY GLORY

In spite of their difficult surroundings in the first few decades of the seventeenth century—the continuing Catholic threat from the Continent, the setbacks for the Protestant cause in Europe in light of an aggressive Catholic resurgence, the steadfast opposition from James I and open persecution by Charles I in the 1630s—the Puritans remained remarkably positive about the future. This optimism was grounded in the Puritan historicist understanding that Revelation 6–20 was a description of the history of the church from Saint Paul to the time of Elizabeth I. They strongly believed that the Reformation was a decisive and powerful work of God, which because of its divine origin was bound to triumph—and their reading of the book of Revelation seemed "explicitly to promise that triumph."[14]

From the 1550s through to 1660 there was widespread unanimity among Puritan writers that the triumph of the gospel foreseen in the books of Daniel and Revelation would be manifested in the imminent collapse of Rome. As Peter Toon has written,

> It was heartily believed that soon the cry would be heard, "Fallen, fallen is Babylon the great" [Rev 14:8], and the chorus would follow, "Salvation and glory and power belong to our God for he had judged the great harlot which did corrupt the earth with her fornication and He hath avenged the blood of His servants at His hand" [Rev 19:1-2].

They discerned the collapse of Catholicism in their readings of Daniel and Revelation, and their interpretation fit well with their experience of Rome. Toon elaborates when he observes that sympathetic readers

> can well see how they were so sure that the seers, Daniel and John, had spoken of the Papacy. That which seemed to John, the prisoner on Patmos, as an ugly beast (Rev 13) had its headquarters in the city of Rome and that which appeared to Luther, and all Protestants, as the persecuting Antichrist also had its headquarters in Rome. And the persecuting nature of the Roman Empire under Diocletian was similar to the persecuting nature of the Papacy and its agents; for example, both claimed divine powers.[15]

---

[14]Peter Toon, "The Latter-Day Glory," in Toon, *Puritans, The Millennium and the Future of Israel*, 25.
[15]Toon, "Latter-Day Glory," 126.

The "persecuting nature" of Rome they had experienced firsthand, and the memory of past persecution was kept immediately before them in the writings of John Foxe and in reports of the ongoing Catholic persecution of Protestants.

But both major eschatological options they embraced (postmillennialism and premillennialism) were remarkably hopeful. Christ as King had won the decisive victory over Satan. The Puritans were confident that this triumph would soon be manifested in the world. A period of "latter-day glory" was just around the corner. The papacy would soon collapse, Islam would be overthrown, and the Jews would be converted. Whether this "glory" would be manifest before or after Christ's return was a point of difference, but either way, the Puritans were persuaded that a glorious future awaited them. Not yet heaven, but certainly a utopia, was soon to be revealed.

Puritanism, the Holy Land, and Islam

The Holy Land loomed large in the Christian imagination throughout the Middle Ages. With the presence of Muslim forces on the eastern flank of Europe, the Islamic threat was real and greatly feared across Christian Europe. The identification of the Ottoman Empire ("the Turk") with Islam had a long history, predating the rise of the Puritans; it was a commonplace among European Christians, Protestant and Catholic.[16] With the historicist turn in Protestant understandings of prophecy, the Puritan prophetic writers consistently dealt with this fear of "the Turk" and invariably linked it to their anti-Catholicism. As Nabil Matar has observed, "There is scarcely a mention of the Turks and Islam in early modern English eschatology without an immediate mention of the Pope and Catholicism."[17] Because the Ottoman Turks were followers of Muhammad, whom the Puritans regarded as a false prophet, they identified "the Turk" as an agent of Satan intent on destroying the true church. It was not a great stretch, therefore, for them to deduce that "God had given to John on Patmos a vision of this great enemy of the elect of God, who would one day be destroyed by the power of Christ."[18] The

---

[16]Robert O. Smith, *More Desired Than Our Owne Salvation: The Roots of Christian Zionism* (New York: Oxford University Press, 2013), 47.

[17]Nabil I. Matar, *Islam in Britain, 1558–1685* (Cambridge: Cambridge University Press, 1999), 154.

[18]Toon, introduction, 20.

Turks were understood as the sixth vial of judgment from Revelation. The "kings of the east" of Revelation 16:12 were the Jews who would ultimately fight the Turk and destroy him.[19]

Brightman's Historicist Postmillennialism

Building on the historicist turn of Luther and Beza (both amillennialists), some of the English Puritans developed a form of historicist postmillennialism (although the term *postmillennialism* was not used by them). Its key formulator was Thomas Brightman (1562–1607), whose works were all published after his death and only first published on the Continent. Brightman's view that the Church of England was Laodicea would not have endeared him to James I or Charles I, although it is unclear whether they were personally aware of Brightman.[20] In 1644, during the English Civil War, Parliament ordered all his long-suppressed works to be reprinted.

Brightman assured fellow Protestants that the Reformation was a great act of God and that Christ would act to vindicate their sufferings, a peculiarly attractive message to Protestants experiencing major reverses to Roman Catholicism. Robert O. Smith observes, "Brightman's correlation of history and prophecy led him to a critical nationalism, which in turn produced an unprecedented interpretation of England's role in God's eschatological plan."[21] Brightman worked out a scheme whereby the historicist view—that the history of the church is predicted in Scripture—could be elaborated in detail. In Crome's words, Brightman achieved "a dramatic reimagining of the English prophetic tradition."[22]

In the early 1600s Brightman warned that Europe's Protestants were about to face great wars and troubles—and in this he was very astute, as the Thirty Years' War (1618–1648) proved to be devastating, particularly to the German territories. He assured his readers that Rome would soon be destroyed, the pope overthrown, and the Turks defeated. This would require a time of great trial; in the succeeding decades Brightman's writings gained

---

[19]Matar, "Idea of the Restoration," 24.
[20]Brightman's *A Revelation of the Revelation. A Most Comfortable Exposition of the Last and Most Difficult Pages of the Prophecies of Daniel* was first published in Latin in Frankfurt am Main in 1609, and the first English version was printed in Amsterdam in 1611.
[21]Smith, *More Desired*, 73.
[22]Crome, *English National Identity*, 51.

a wide following, as many of his predictions were accurate. But Brightman had great hopes for the future: he was convinced that the latter-day glory of the saints would far outshine their earlier suffering.

A crucial passage that Brightman cites is Ezekiel 37, which begins with the vision of the valley of dry bones but then promises a future restoration. Ezekiel's idyllic picture is not to be realized without much struggle and suffering. Brightman sees the Jewish people in the future engaged in the great battle with Gog and Magog (Revelation 20:8)—that is, the Turks and their allies. The Jewish people, now converted, will be returned to their native homeland but will be surrounded by the Turks (Revelation 20:9). God will then miraculously intervene on behalf of his ancient people and destroy their enemies; the full conversion and restoration of the Jewish nation will constitute a great resurrection (Revelation 20:11-12). Revelation 21–22 then becomes a description of the new kingdom, refounded in a renewed Jerusalem, which will become the center of the earth "in which all men confess Jesus as Lord." But while he envisioned a unity of Jews and Gentiles in the millennial age, he believed that "God had separate earthly plans for each. Even in the millennial period, they would remain radically different. Indeed, the millennium would be a period of Jewish dominion over the earth."[23] At the end of this period the second coming of Christ will occur and be followed by the final judgment.[24]

Brightman developed a historicist postmillennial understanding that is quite different from Augustine's amillennial position. His thousand years does not refer to the whole of the church age; Brightman posits two millennia, one beginning in the fourth century and ending about 1300, and then a second millennium. He maps the history of the church onto this framework. And while Augustine had believed that the age would end with a brief time of tribulation for the church, Brightman saw this coinciding with the defeat of the pope and the Turk, which preceded the latter-day glory that was to be manifested toward the end of the second millennium. "The fact that the millennium was currently ongoing," writes Crome, "meant that all signs pointed to a continued improvement in earthly conditions."[25] Only at the

---

[23]Crome, *English National Identity*, 53.
[24]Toon, "Latter-Day Glory," 29-30.
[25]Crome, *English National Identity*, 47.

end of the age would Christ personally return to raise the dead and judge the world.[26]

For our purposes, it is crucial that Brightman expected a physical restoration of the converted Jews as they participate with God in setting up Christ's kingdom. It is also important to note that in Brightman's scheme, the Jews will be converted first to Christianity before their "restoration." Brightman's view accords England a key role in the end of days, and in which the Jews are at center stage and, once converted en masse, will return to their homeland. Crucially, Brightman puts the return of the Jews far off in the prophetic future.

SIR HENRY FINCH, WILLIAM GOUGE, AND JOHN OWEN

Sir Henry Finch's *The Worlds Great Restauration, or, The Calling of the Jewes* (1621), edited by William Gouge (1575–1653), was clearly indebted to Brightman. It argued for the national conversion of the Jewish people and their "restoration" to their ancient homeland thereafter. So unpopular was this work with King James I that Finch and Gouge were both arrested and imprisoned because the king understood Finch to be arguing the subjection of Christian kings to Jews. Only after apologizing for the work and providing satisfactory explanations for their views were they released, but the book was suppressed by the English government, albeit not very effectively.

Significantly, Finch argued that when scriptural passages speak of "Israel," "Judah," "Zion," and "Jerusalem" they are referring to the Jews as a group or to the places where the Jews lived. They were not to be understood allegorically as referring to the Christian church, and thus scriptural references to their return to their land, the defeat of their enemies, and their rule of the nations are to be understood literally. So too are references to "Gog and Magog," "King of the north," and "Leviathan," which are to be taken as references to the Turks, again a cipher for Islam.[27]

The conversion of the Jews will include the ten lost tribes of the northern kingdom of Israel as well as the two tribes of the southern kingdom (Ezekiel 37:16, 19; Hosea 1:11; Jeremiah 3:12-14; Isaiah 11:12-13)[28] and will begin to take

---

[26]Toon, "Latter-Day Glory, 30-31.
[27]Toon, "Latter-Day Glory, 32.
[28]Toon, "Latter-Day Glory," 33.

place when the Turkish rule in Europe (posited at 1300) has lasted 350 years. Thus they expected the mass Jewish conversion to begin around 1650. Shortly thereafter the power of Rome would be broken. In the following forty-five years Jews from the north and east would travel toward Palestine and cross the Euphrates on dry land, recalling the Israelites' miraculous crossing of the Red Sea in a similar manner. This will arouse fear among the Turks, which will lead their armies to attack the Jews only to be destroyed by another divine intervention at a battle by the Sea of Galilee, some 395 years after the rise of the Ottoman Empire. Finch and Gouge clearly depended heavily on Brightman's *Commentary.* This historicist approach enabled them to date-set the final Jewish-Turkish battle on the shores of Galilee in 1695.

Finch, Gouge, and the greatest of the Puritan theologians, John Owen (1616–1683), built on the work of Brightman. They taught that the end of the current age would be characterized by what they termed as a period of "Latter-Day Glory for the church," which would come after the downfall of the papacy and the conversion of the Jewish people. A great revival of Christianity was to be expected, which would be inaugurated through the preaching of Spirit-filled men, both Jews and Gentiles. In their view, this current age would soon end, and a thousand-year period would ensue, with Christ returning personally at the end of the thousand years to judge the world. Again, these writers put the Jewish return in the future, but not the distant future (as Brightman had), but rather as an event that was expected to happen by the end of the seventeenth century.

Key Themes Common to Puritan Writers

By the 1640s such views were widely accepted in England. Clearly the social conditions and the general upheaval of the 1640s contributed to the reception of philo-Semitic views, but many of the leading advocates were learned scholars. Elsewhere I have discussed themes prominent in Puritan prophetic writers, so here I will only summarize their emphases.[29] Five words come to mind: *esteem, gratitude, love, longing,* and *realism.* First, *esteem.* Rejecting the medieval "teaching of contempt" toward the Jews as "Christ killers," Puritans advanced a "teaching of esteem" rather than of

---

[29]Donald M. Lewis, *The Origins of Christian Zionism: Lord Shaftesbury and Evangelical Support for a Jewish Homeland* (Cambridge: Cambridge University Press, 2009), 26-36.

contempt toward the Jews. In Thomas Draxe's words, the Jews remain a "chosen nation, the particular people, and a royall Priesthood."[30] Jews were to be celebrated for their many accomplishments and the great gifts they had given to the world. This emphasis on esteeming the Jews and celebrating the ways in which they have been a blessing to the nations runs through Puritan writings and resurfaces often in nineteenth-century British evangelical writings, and is often repeated in twenty-first-century Christian Zionist circles.

Second, *gratitude*. The Puritans were aware that Paul in Romans 11:28a had said that the Jews were loved "on account of the patriarchs" (NIV). Thus another important theme developed by Draxe is that of Christian gratitude and indebtedness to the Jews—that is, the rich inheritance of Judaism had prepared the way for the Christian faith, and the Jews were chosen and beloved of God because of their role in guarding that inheritance (echoing Augustine's arguments). Christians should nurture a sense of gratitude for the inheritance that the Jews had received which had so enriched the world.

Third, Christians were to be taught to *love* the Jews rather than to despise them. Repeatedly the Puritans castigated the medieval Catholic treatment of the Jews, a theme that runs down the centuries in Christian Zionist writings (although, as will be seen, it has largely disappeared in the twenty-first century and the blame placed on supersessionism, whether Catholic or Protestant).[31] Fourth, this love was to lead to a *longing* for their conversion. Jews, of course, did not view the Puritans' desire for their conversion in a positive light, but it was logically consistent from the Puritans' point of view that they saw such efforts as a means of blessing the Jews. Fifth and finally, there was a degree of *realism* urged on them by Paul. The other half of the same verse that says they are loved "on account of the patriarchs" reads "As far as the gospel is concerned, they are enemies for your sake" (Romans 11:28). So, on the one hand, Christians were urged to be grateful for the contributions of the Jews, but on the other, they are not to be naïve and realize that the unbelieving Jews regard the Christian gospel as nonsense and disavow the fundamental Christian claim about the salvific work of Christ and his cross. These five aspects of the Puritans' attitudes have to be

---

[30]Thomas Draxe, *The Worldes Resurrection, or The Generall Calling of the Iewes* (London: G. Eld and John Wright, 1608), 3, 63-64, quoted in Smith, *More Desired*, 71.
[31]See the discussion of Derek Prince in chap. 14.

appreciated if one is to understand their attitudes to the Jews and how they play out in the history of Christian Zionism: esteem, gratitude, love, longing, and realism.

POSTMILLENNIALISM AND CHRISTIAN RESTORATIONISM

The postmillennial position was always strongest in Reformed circles—in Scotland, England, and New England—and in its seventeenth-century form was often strongly restorationist. It is important to underline this point, because the strong link between postmillennialism and what developed into Christian Zionism has not necessarily endured. A leading contemporary postmillennial proponent, Loraine Boettner, has argued that "since the Messiah has come and has fully performed his work of atonement, this special role assigned to the Jews has been fulfilled." By the rending of the temple veil at the time of the crucifixion "the old order of ritual and incense . . . and of the Jews as a separate people and Palestine as a separate land—all of that as a unit had fulfilled its purpose and was abolished forever."[32] As has been seen, this view is known as "supersessionism." The new emphasis in much of Puritan thinking on England as a chosen nation tasked to protect and "restore" the Jews was a way of resolving the challenge, but "it moved away from the emphasis on similarity that viewed Christians and Old Testament Jews as part of one long story."[33]

YET ANOTHER PURITAN OPTION: HISTORICIST PREMILLENNIALISM

In the early 1600s Joseph Mede (1586–1638), professor of Greek at Cambridge, pioneered a version of historicist premillennialism. He was indebted to Johann Heinrich Alsted (1588–1638), a German Calvinist thinker enormously respected among Protestant theologians. According to Alsted, careful exegesis required that the thousand-year period described in Revelation 20

---

[32]Loraine Boettner, "A Postmillennial Response," in *The Meaning of the Millennium: Four Views,* ed. Robert G. Clouse (Downers Grove, IL: InterVarsity Press, 1977), 53-54.

[33]Crome, *English National Identity,* 37. Postmillennialism attracted some of Reformed Christianity's most brilliant minds, including the seventeenth-century New England Puritan John Cotton, and Jonathan Edwards in the eighteenth century, and in the nineteenth, the American Presbyterian theologians at Princeton Seminary Charles Hodge and Augustus Strong, and the Free Church of Scotland theologian Patrick Fairbairn. So popular was this eschatology among English Congregationalists that it was adopted in 1658 as the standard interpretation endorsed by the Savoy Declaration of Faith and Order, which modified the Westminster Confession of Faith (1646).

should be understood as a description of the future, which was eagerly anticipated. While he fervently believed that such a period was to come, he expected that Christ would personally inaugurate this time by his personal return. This view was never as popular as the postmillennialist position among English Puritans, but it did maintain a significant minority following. Yet Mede, along with other Puritan premillennialists, Thomas Goodwin and Nathaniel Holmes, "expected that the return of the Jews to the true Messiah, Jesus of Nazareth, and to the land promised to Abraham by God, would usher in the millennium, or, at least, be one of the first things accomplished in the millennium."[34]

As the seventeenth century wore on, the premillennial option seemed more realistic. The hopes nurtured in the early seventeenth century that had anticipated the imminent overthrow of Catholicism and Islam were disappointed. Rome was not in decline, but was consolidating its position in Europe and expanding overseas. Protestantism seemed embattled, and its gradual triumph appeared less reasonable. Only the personal and dramatic intervention of Christ posited by the premillennialist authors would reverse the situation. And by the 1630s the Puritans were experiencing the wrath of Charles I. While some Puritans fled to Holland, and some to the American colonies, the great reversal they longed for could only be envisioned in the emerging millenarian options.

The new interest in the early church before the rise of the papacy had revealed the millenarianism of Tertullian and Irenaeus, and "the view that the millennium had ended in either 1070 or 1300 and was followed by a 'short season' (Rev 20:3) was wearing thin."[35] Many English Puritans were therefore moving toward the idea of a future millennium. These writers were probably unaware of the political and social factors, but premillennial writers like Mede and Alsted "would probably have argued that they arrived at their premillennial doctrine of the second coming of the Lord Jesus Christ wholly on the basis of sound exegesis."[36] None of their contemporary critics suggested that "the doctrine of the future millennium, and the ideas

---

[34]Toon, introduction, 127.

[35]R. G. Clouse, "The Rebirth of Millenarianism," in Toon, *Puritans, the Millennium and the Future of Israel*, 54.

[36]Clouse, "Rebirth of Millenarianism," 55.

associated with it, were either produced or sustained by social, economic or political factors." Rather they critiqued millennialism because they regarded it "as a theological heresy which came into being through a mistaken exegesis of Scripture and the application of a false hermeneutical principle . . . for them the primary cause was theological in nature."[37]

Date-Setting the Return of Christ: the Day-Year Theory

The historicist turn in the understanding of prophecy (whether by premillennialists or postmillennialists) employed a theory that had been developed many centuries earlier that a "day" spoken of in the Old Testament prophecies represented a year. This "day-year theory" found a basis in Ezekiel 4:4-6, where Ezekiel is instructed to lie on his side for 390 days, then for 40 days, the first to represent 390 years, and the latter 40 years. While the Jewish rabbis had used this formula in their interpreting the book of Daniel, Protestants used it as a way of making sense of the days spoken of in the book of Revelation. As Toon observes, "For many Puritans this theory became an unquestioned premise."[38] Writers on prophecy used it to understand references to forty-two months in Revelation 11:2 and Revelation 13:5. Assuming that each month represents 30 days, the 42 months were interpreted as 1260 days (30 × 42), which was taken to mean 1260 years and seemed to be corroborated by Revelation 11:1-3.

Jewish Readmission to England

In 1649 Ebenezer and Joanna Cartwright, two English Puritans residing in Amsterdam, petitioned the English government to allow the readmission of Jews to England as follows: "That this Nation of England, with the inhabitants of the Netherlands, shall be the first and the readiest to transport Israell's sons and daughters in their ships to the Land promised to their forefathers, Abraham, Isaac and Jacob for an everlasting Inheritance."[39] The Cartwrights wanted Jewish readmission to England, seeking the reversal of

---

[37] A. R. Dallison, "Contemporary Criticism of Millenarianism," in Toon, *Puritans, the Millennium and the Future of Israel*, 112.

[38] Toon, "Latter-Day Glory," 23.

[39] Quoted in Barbara W. Tuchman, *Bible and Sword: England and Palestine from the Bronze Age to Balfour* (New York: New York University Press, 1956), 120. For further discussion see Lewis, *Origins*, 31-32.

King Edward I's 1290 banishment of the Jews from England. In 1655 an important conference was held at Whitehall to discuss readmission. Crome has undertaken a careful study of this gathering and has summarized the consensus of the conference in five points:

> First, God chose England to restore Israel, but not as her replacement. Second, the duty that England had towards the Jews was both missionary and cove-nantal—her fate was tethered to that of the Jews, and God required the nation to take the lead in their restoration (of which readmission was the first step). Third, this provided a providential explanation for England's trials during the civil wars, and a way of understanding the confusing patterns of providence. As per the Abrahamic covenant, England faced punishment for the nation's ongoing sins towards the Jewish people [especially the expulsion of Jews in 1290]. Readmission therefore offered a tangible way of reversing this, and a readable vision of providence. Fourth, this readability combined with anxiety about England's eschatological role. This, in turn, encouraged proponents to active political involvement in order to benefit the Jews. Finally, this whole scheme meant that engagement with Jews offered to legitimate the nation. The Jews' survival as a separate group demonstrated the way in which God worked through nations, providing further confidence in God's work through England. Although England was inferior to Israel, advocates at Whitehall nevertheless believed that their nation could offer benefits to the Jews.[40]

Jewish readmission was ultimately achieved by a legal decision that declared there was no legal barrier to the Jews' reentry. When the Puritans lost their influence with the return of Charles II in 1660, the readmission of the Jews was based on a legal decision and was not part of the legislation enacted during the Commonwealth era. In 1664 the residence of Jews in England was authorized; in 1673 their religious status was legally secured.

After the expulsion of the Puritans from the Church of England in 1662 most moved into English Nonconformity. Yet Puritanism had done much to strengthen interest in the study of Hebrew in English universities, and Hebrew became central to the curriculum of all ten colleges founded in colonial America prior to the Revolution.[41] Millennialism, however, was

---

[40]Crome, *English National Identity*, 103.

[41]See Christopher M. Clark, *The Politics of Conversion: Missionary Protestantism and the Jews in Prussia, 1728–1941* (Oxford: Clarendon, 1995), 9. On the impact of Hebrew in America see Shalom Goldman, *Zeal for Zion: Christians, Jews, & the Idea of the Promised Land* (Chapel Hill: University of North Carolina Press, 2009), 9.

now associated with the instability of the Puritan Commonwealth period; the restoration of Charles II to the British throne brought with it a reaction against Puritan millenarianism, and after 1660 there was "a decline in an expectation of the imminent coming of Christ's kingdom."[42] As Crome has shown, however, Jewish restorationism did not disappear. The late Puritan Richard Baxter (1615–1691) considered it still so prevalent in 1690 that he attacked the restorationist theology in *The Glorious Kingdom of Christ Described and Clearly Vindicated: Against the Bold Asserters of a Future Calling and Reign of the Jews. . . .* Crome has demonstrated that over the next century its advocates moderated its character, and the expectation shifted to England's facilitating Jewish conversion "rather than physically carrying them back to Palestine."[43]

RESTORATIONISM IN THE WAKE OF PURITANISM'S DECLINE

Restorationism declined in England as the Puritan hopes for a Jewish spiritual return and their physical return to the Holy Land were put off into the distant future. The great Puritan hope for the Jews became muted. Sarah Hutton has noted that in the late seventeenth and early eighteenth centuries a group of academic theologians on both sides of the Atlantic continued to speculate on the role of the Jews in England's national calling and identity. Included among the "Cambridge school" of millennial speculation were Henry More (1614–1687), Isaac Newton (1642–1727), William Whiston (1667–1752), and Samuel Clarke (1675–1729). They did not represent a specific school of thought, as they disagreed on important issues.[44] Henry More doubted Jewish restoration, while Isaac Newton "saw a restored Jewish state in Palestine as a key element of God's plans for the world."[45] As the supreme importance of reason came to the fore in English theological discussion in the early eighteenth century, the millennium became for some a spiritually transforming process, to be achieved through the growth of knowledge and the application of reason. But many of the leading thinkers of the new century continued to be interested in biblical prophecy.[46]

---

[42]Crome, *English National Identity*, 125.
[43]Crome, *English National Identity*, 128.
[44]For a discussion of these scholars see Crome, *English National Identity*, 110-12.
[45]Crome, *English National Identity*, 118.
[46]See Lewis, *Origins*, 33-37.

THE "JEW BILL" OF 1753

Jewish matters came to public prominence in the debate aroused by the Jewish Naturalization Bill of 1753, popularly known as the "Jew Bill," which sought to address the legal situation facing foreign-born Jews who constituted the majority of the eight thousand Jews living in England. As such they were unable to participate in the colonial trade and were liable to port fees, and they were discriminated against in the customs rates. Like Roman Catholic aliens (against whom the laws had been designed), they also could not own land and could not become naturalized citizens without receiving Anglican Communion. The Whig government passed the measure in 1753, only for it to be repealed by Parliament later in the same year. It generated a heated, vicious debate in Parliament and in the popular press, which was complex, but both sides shared many concerns that arose out of the Judeocentric prophetic tradition but took them in different directions. Some opponents of the bill argued that the measure was inspired by deists seeking to discredit Christianity by proving Old Testament prophecies false. "If Jews could be naturalized, worried some of the Bill's opponents, this would disprove the curses against them in the Old Testament, demonstrating the Bible's inaccuracy."[47] Other opponents appealed to theories of Jewish militarism and a Jewish takeover of England reminiscent of James I's response to Sir Henry Finch's writings observed earlier. Many supporters of the bill believed that naturalized Jews would more easily convert to Christianity and fulfill their prophetic destiny, arguing "for the centrality of the restoration of the Jews and England's role within it."[48] In Crome's words, "The idea that England would face blessing or curse dependent on her treatment of the Jews was still clearly an important part of the debate."[49]

PRIOR TO THE FRENCH REVOLUTION

From 1753 through to the French Revolution in 1789 apocalyptic speculation continued in England by both scholarly and popular writers. "As Neil Hitchin has noted, it would be a mistake to see apocalyptic speculation

[47]Crome, *English National Identity*, 143.
[48]Crome, *English National Identity*, 161.
[49]Crome, *English National Identity*, 161. See Crome's discussion of this complex debate in *English National Identity*, 153-62.

suddenly emerging from hibernation in the 1790s."[50] Although the writers were not particularly creative, the most popular was Bishop Thomas Newton, whose *Dissertations on the Prophecies Which Have Remarkably Been Fulfilled, and at This Time Are Fulfilling in the World* (3 vols., 1754–1758) went into at least nine editions in the forty years following its first appearance and appears to have been particularly important in shaping the views of English evangelicals, although the bishop himself was not an evangelical. Significantly, he rehearses a polemic developed in the seventeenth century and that would be reinvigorated in the nineteenth: "God had decreed that only 'wicked nations' persecute the Jews; 'persecution is the spirit of Popery . . . the spirit of Protestantism is toleration."[51] Newton was immensely influential and "remained one of the most frequently cited sources by later commentators, and his hearty commendation of restorationism helped to ensure its respectability into the nineteenth century."[52] One of the few evangelicals who wrote extensively on prophecy in the eighteenth century was the high Calvinist Baptist theologian John Gill (1697–1771), a respected Hebrew scholar. One of the most important Nonconformists of the time, he reflected the strong restorationist consensus of his Puritan forebears.[53] Scholars have debated whether there was a sudden increase in restorationist belief or a stable continuity of interest. Crome has argued that the latter seems the most likely. As he observes, "The treatment of the theme in this period provides evidence for the same pattern seen earlier in the century: espousing Jewish restoration was a respectable (but always contested) position."[54]

Thus by the early 1600s, the English Puritans had emerged as the main champions of restorationist readings of prophecy in the English-speaking world. In closely identifying with the Jews, Puritans hoped to demonstrate that they were the true Christians, the rightful heirs to the mainstream of

---

[50]Crome, *English National Identity*, 165, citing Neil Hitchin, "The Evidence of Things Seen: Georgian Churchmen and Biblical Prophecy," in *Prophecy: The Power of Inspired Language in History, 1300–2000*, ed. Bertrand Taithe and Tim Thornton (Thrupp, UK: Sutton, 1997), 134.

[51]Crome, *English National Identity*, 167.

[52]Crome, *English National Identity*, 168.

[53]Crome, *English National Identity*, 171. For an extended treatment of Gill, see Crawford Gribben, *Evangelical Millennialism in the Transatlantic World* (Basingstoke, UK: Palgrave Macmillan, 2011), 62-67. For discussion of other eighteenth-century prophetic writers, see Lewis, *Origins*, 35-36.

[54]Crome, *English National Identity*, 169.

the Christian tradition, which they believed had lost its way in the Middle Ages regarding central Christian doctrines and practice. And just as late medieval Catholicism had embraced a "teaching of contempt" toward the Jews, the Puritans wanted to promote a very different attitude, a "teaching of love of and esteem for" the Jews, one that respected Jewish learning and the Hebrew language and honored the Jewish people who are to be "loved on account of the patriarchs" (Romans 11:28). Further, they wanted to facilitate the eventual conversion of the Jewish people to the true Christian faith (although this was something that they would await and not do much to bring about). By the mid-1640s, hopes for the eventual conversion of the Jews and their "Restoration" to Palestine were central for the Protestant movement in England and Scotland—the Puritans in the Church of England and in Dissent, and later the Quakers did the most to promote this view. Despite widespread persecution by the Stuart monarchs, the Puritans in the first half of the seventeenth century were generally enormously confident and optimistic about the prospects for Protestantism because the pope would soon be overthrown, and Islam would collapse as the inevitable triumph of the gospel was realized. The Jews would turn to Protestant Christianity en masse, and Islam would be thwarted by the eventual return of converted Jews to Palestine. The timetable for all these events might have been vague, but that did not shake the confidence of Puritans writers like John Milton, who, even after the political failure of English Puritanism in 1660, could write in his *Paradise Regained* (1671),

> Yet He at length, time to himself best known,
> Remembering Abraham, by some wondrous call
> May bring them back, repentant and sincere,
> And at their passing cleave the Assyrian flood,
> While to their native land with joy they haste,
> As the Red Sea and Jordan once he cleft,
> When to the Promised Land their fathers passed.
> To his due time and providence I leave them.[55]

---

[55]John Milton, *Paradise Regained* (London: John Starkey at the Mittre in Fleetstreet, near Temple Bar, 1671), chap. 3.

The seeds of these restorationist ideas had been sown deep in the English Protestant mind and as we will see, continued to be nurtured in the new soil of American Puritanism.

In tracing the genealogy of this movement, our attention will now shift from old England to New England, as in the last quarter of the seventeenth century the baton of restorationism was effectively passed from England to the Puritans in colonial America. Before we turn our attention to the developments in colonial America we will consider a movement that was emerging in the German territories at the very time that English Puritanism went into decline, and consider how German Pietism was to profoundly influence Protestant interest in the Jews in both England and America.

4

THE GERMAN PIETISTS
AND THE JEWS

PHILO-SEMITISM AND THE NEW
EVANGELISTIC IMPERATIVE

Whoever touches you touches the apple of his eye.

ZECHARIAH 2:8

Pietists were essential to the rise of both Christian and Jewish Zionism, influencing evangelical opinions and actions and often cooperating with evangelical Christian Zionists on mutual projects.[1]

YAAKOV ARIEL

IF ONE IS TO UNDERSTAND the convoluted lineage of Christian Zionism, one must consider the influence of German Pietism, which was revolutionary in terms of its impact on Christian-Jewish relations. While claiming to be loyal Lutherans, they rejected Martin Luther's later anti-Judaic attitudes. They could point to his early friendly overtures toward the Jews but clearly and decisively broke with his later attitudes toward the Jews, seeking to promote a "teaching of love and esteem" toward them, and not one of contempt.

The original German Pietists were not Christian restorationists, but they profoundly influenced Christian-Jewish relations in the English-speaking

---

[1]Yaakov Ariel, "From the Institutum Judaicum to the International Christian Embassy," in *Comprehending Christian Zionism: Perspectives in Comparison*, ed. Goran Gunner and Robert O. Smith (Minneapolis: Fortress, 2014), 200.

world in the nineteenth century because they were the first Protestants to make the proselytization of Jews central to their mission in the world and they endeavored to promote a love for God's people "according to the flesh." The duty to love and esteem the Jew was central to their promotion of philo-Semitism. In the nineteenth century Christian Zionists in Britain embraced the active evangelization of Jews in Britain, Europe, and the Middle East— something they learned from the German Pietists. The unique role of the Jews in salvation history was central in their thinking, and the German Pietists and British evangelicals often cited the Old Testament phrase that speaks of the Jews as "the apple of his eye" (see Deuteronomy 32:10; Psalm 17:8; Proverbs 7:2; Zechariah 2:8).

THE ORIGINS OF GERMAN PIETISM

German Pietism was a movement of spiritual renewal within German Lutheranism. Its rise is associated with the publication by Philipp Jakob Spener of *Pia Desideria* (Pious longings) in 1675. In Spener's thinking, the renewal of the church depends on its accomplishing the tasks given to it by Christ. The most important is the duty to evangelize the Jewish people. Had not the apostle Paul emphasized the duty of proclaiming the gospel "to the Jew first" (Romans 1:16; 2:10), even though Paul's own ministry was focused on Gentile conversion?

The evangelization of European Jewry became a critical task in the unfolding of the "Last Days" for the German Pietists. Informing this was an optimistic postmillennial vision: as the church began to take this responsibility seriously, the prospect of the Christ's return would be enhanced.

English-speaking historians have tended to overlook the vast influence that developments on the Continent—especially in the German-speaking world—had on British and American evangelicalism, and this is true especially with regard to the impact of the Pietists' views of the Jews and their pioneering initiatives in Jewish evangelism. One British historian has titled his book on the international evangelical community that existed in the mid-nineteenth century *No North Sea: The Anglo-German Evangelical Network in the Middle of the Nineteenth Century*.[2] The rise of

---

[2]Nicholas M. Railton, *No North Sea: The Anglo-German Evangelical Network in the Nineteenth Century* (Leiden: Brill, 2000).

German nationalism that accompanied the Franco-Prussian War of 1870–1871 and the unification of German states as the German Empire in 1871 no doubt contributed to the gulf that subsequently grew between Britain and Germany. Prior to that date, English-German relations were much closer, and their shared Protestant identities were an important factor facilitating such ties.

Halle Pietism and Its Relationship to the Prussian State

Pietism's organizational center was at the University of Halle in southern Prussia, where Spener, through the patronage of King Frederick of Prussia, was invited in 1692 to establish a Pietist faculty of theology. Often aided by the patronage of the rulers of Brandenburg-Prussia in the late seventeenth and early eighteenth centuries, Pietism established itself as a major influence within the Lutheran Church and within the Prussian state, which looked to Halle for teachers in the emerging state school system. Halle sought to train pastors who would imbue the German Lutheran state church with its theology and practices. Modern German historians have created a "growth industry" in Pietist studies, seeking to study its relationship to the emergence of the German state and the rise of German capitalism, its influence on education (especially in Prussia but also throughout Protestant and Catholic Europe and even in Orthodox Russia), and on the development of modern science.[3]

Halle itself was a beehive of Pietist activity and generated a vast religious publishing network, impressive educational initiatives, an enterprising pharmaceutical industry (to provide cheap drugs for the masses and to finance Halle's many charities) and Protestantism's first missionary-sending community. Its press quickly became one of the most prolific in Germany, producing works not only in German, Greek, and Russian Cyrillic type but also in a host of languages that had never known mass publishing before.

---

[3]James Van Horn Melton, *Absolutism and the Eighteenth Century Origins of Compulsory Schooling in Prussia and Austria* (Cambridge: Cambridge University Press, 1988), 23. On its impact on modern science, see Martin Schmidt, "Der Pietismus und das moderne Denken," in *Pietismus und Modern Welt*, ed. Kurt Aland (Wittenberg: Luther-Verlag, 1974), 9-74.

The Centrality of Jewish Evangelism to the Pietist Vision

Both Spener and his successor, August Hermann Francke (1663–1727), conceived of their mission as a world mission, and the Jews were a central aspect of that mission. In *Pia Desideria*, Spener outlined the Pietists' program for the renewal of the Lutheran Church from within. The book anticipates a mass conversion of the Jews to Christianity. In Spener's view the unwillingness of the Jews to convert to Christianity was understandable given the blatant immorality and unchristian actions of professing Christians. It was the young Luther himself who had famously asserted that "if he were a Jew, and could see how immoral and divided the Christians were, he would rather be a pig than a Christian."[4] Significantly—even crucially—Spener linked improvement in the life of the church with Jewish conversion. The evangelization of the Jews was in Spener's mind an essential duty of Christians. He argued, "It is incumbent on all of us to see to it that as much as possible is done, on the one hand, to convert the Jews and weaken the spiritual power of the papacy and, on the other hand, to reform our church."[5] Although the mainstream "Orthodox" Lutheran party had by that time moved away from belief in a mass conversion of Jews (as the later Luther had), Spener was able to cite numerous Lutheran authorities, including the young Luther, who had endorsed such a position.

Spener was aware that the prospect of a future mass conversion of Jews could lead to inaction on the part of Christians: if their conversion was prophesied and bound to happen, then why should the church bother now to evangelize unresponsive Jews? Spener would have none of this reasoning; in his view God used means to accomplish his purposes, and the means were human agents. Failure to respond to God's command to evangelize the Jews was a real possibility, but it would incur the judgment of God on faithless Christians. Evangelistic work among Jews would require highly skilled workers with specialized knowledge and appropriate financial and communal support. The very future of the Protestant cause depended on it. Its success required a new way of Christians approaching the Jews based on an

---

[4]Christopher M. Clark, *The Politics of Conversion: Missionary Protestantism and the Jews in Prussia, 1728–1941* (Oxford: Clarendon, 1995), 24.

[5]Philipp Jacob Spener, *Pia Desideria*, trans. and ed. Theodore G. Tappert (Philadelphia: Fortress, 1964), 78.

appreciation of Jewish traditions and sympathy for their plight in a hostile culture. In Spener's view the Pietist mission to the Jews was at the very heart of Protestant identity. As Christopher Clark has put it, "The mission was urgent because God's honour was at stake. It was a question of making amends for the history of human ingratitude in the face of God's grace and favour. In this way, Spener made the conversion of the Jews the keystone in the arch of revealed Christian truth."[6] Spener linked the success of Protestantism to its mission to the Jews.

Now, for the first time in the history of Protestantism, the Jews were being focused on as a group to be proselytized by voluntary agency and not by state initiative. For centuries it had been the policy of Continental governments to use more or less nefarious means to induce Jewish conversions. The new mission to the Jews was a voluntary one, a key element of the impressive international outreach of the Pietist institutions in Halle, which the philosopher Leibniz predicted would become the world center for a general reformation. Two of Pietism's novel emphases were the engagement of Lutherans in cross-cultural missionary work and, flowing out of Spener's new eschatological view, the need to establish missions to the Jewish people whom Spener regarded as integral to God's sovereign plan for the end of history. Other Protestant theologians of his day, like the English Puritans and Jonathan Edwards in colonial America, shared Spener's conviction about the strategic role of the conversion of the Jews in the unfolding of history, but it was Spener who operationalized this in practical ways to reach out to the Jews evangelistically.

In 1702 Spener developed his ideas on Jewish conversion further in his *Theologische Bedencken* arguing for noncoercive missions that were sensitive to the economic and social problems of the Jewish community. In a tone and manner markedly different from Luther's proposal that the Jews be forced to till the land, Spener reasoned that agricultural labor was inherently moral and educative, and would prepare Jews for divine influence. Agricultural work was part of the Jewish biblical tradition, and it would restore them to a harmony both with their ancient traditions and with nature. As Christopher Clark has observed, "Through work they could be restored to the

---

[6]Clark, *Politics of Conversion*, 24.

Christian image of an original Jewish identity." Halle Pietism was thus characterized by a mixture of self-improvement and "the mercantilist social awareness of the early Enlightenment."[7] The Pietists were convinced, from their experience with the famous Halle orphanage system, of the importance of virtuous and productive labor in matters spiritual. The aim of the Pietist mission to the Jews was far larger than securing a profession of Christian beliefs; it aimed to restructure the lives of the converts, and this change involved the occupational retraining of converts, thus enabling them to forsake what the Pietists were convinced were the morally enervating occupations of peddling and small-scale trade. Interestingly the Pietist agricultural program in many ways anticipated emphases of the early Zionist initiatives of the 1880s and 1890s. As Nahum Sokolow wrote in his *History of Zionism*, "There it will win through agriculture that attachment to the soil which preserves a country to a nation, and it will find that bodily and moral welfare which must be the proper aim of all Jewish aspirations."[8]

Spener's concerns were operationalized by Francke, who in 1702 established the Collegium Orientale Theologicum, a center for the advanced study of the East. Here students learned Arabic, Persian, and Ottoman Turkish in order to prepare for missionary encounters with those of other faiths. At Halle, the Pietists also developed a whole range of conversionary techniques to commend Christianity to the Jews. It was one of this college's students, Johann Heinrich Callenberg (1694–1760), who gave concrete expression to Francke's concern for the Jews in 1728 by establishing the Institutum Judaicum, where students could study Yiddish as well as Hebrew[9] as they prepared to become missionaries to evangelize Europe's Jews. It also produced an enormous amount of printed material—especially editions of the New Testament in Hebrew.

The institute sought to study the variegated expressions of Jewish culture and the daily life and living conditions of Jews, dispelling the notion that the Jews were a "people frozen in time, practicing a uniformed and static tradition

---

[7]Clark, *Politics of Conversion*, 28.

[8]Nahum Sokolow, *History of Zionism: 1600–1914* (London: Longmans, Green, 1919), 423.

[9]For a detailed history of the Institutum see Yaakov Ariel, "A New Model of Christian Interaction with the Jews: The Institutum Judaicum and Missions to the Jews in the Atlantic World," *Journal of Early Modern History* 21 (2017): 116-36.

all around the globe."[10] Their encounters with the desperate poverty of many Jews in Germany and Poland challenged the widely held image of Jews as wealthy. They sought to engage in welfare and charitable work not only as a means of accessing the Jews but also as a way of offering Christian charity. In all of this the Pietists emphasized the need for this work to be done in love and with great esteem for God's chosen people. The Pietists were as strong as the English Puritans had been on esteeming the Jews, but the Pietists took the concern for Jewish evangelism much further and made it an important aspect of their apocalyptic hope. The Pietists of the eighteenth century, however, did not focus on the Puritan concern for the return of the Jews to Palestine and thus cannot be considered "restorationists," or proto-Christian Zionists, but their eventual long-term impact on Jewish-Christian relations played a key role in interesting English-speaking evangelicals in the evangelization of the Jewish people and, in turn, on Christian Zionism.

Potential converts to Christianity who were drawn to the institute faced a rigorous screening before they were baptized. They were advised how to find gainful employment, and it became routine for converts to be retrained in manual crafts or in agricultural labor as an integral part of the institute's approach. In this way the Pietists' theology took seriously the social environment and in particular its poverty, its occupational realities, and the sense of social isolation experienced by Jews. Highly innovative in "its attention to proselyte care, occupational rehabilitation and broader questions of identity and assimilation," it created "a uniquely energetic missionary programme whose legacy can be discerned in the missionary revivals of London, Basel and Berlin after the turn of the nineteenth century."[11]

Another German influence was the Pietist theologian and biblical scholar Johann Albrecht Bengel (1687–1752), who made much of the role of the Jews. Bengel's *Gnomon novi testamenti* (1742) was drawn on by John Wesley in his *Notes Upon the New Testament*, which appeared in 1755.[12] Bengel had even

---

[10]Yaakov Ariel, *An Unusual Relationship: Evangelical Christians and Jews* (New York: New York University Press, 2013), 25.

[11]Christopher M. Clark, "'The Hope for Better Times': Pietism and the Jews," in *Pietism in Germany and North America 1680–1820*, ed. Jonathan Strom, Hartmut Lehmann, and James Van Horn Melton (Farnham, UK: Ashgate, 2009), 22.

[12]On Bengel's influence on Wesley see W. Reginald Ward, *Early Evangelicalism: A Global Intellectual History, 1670–1789* (Cambridge: Cambridge University Press, 2006), 135-39.

speculated that the millennial age would begin in 1836, although it would not end for two millennia after that.[13] Very much the same sentiments were expressed by one of the chief heralds of German Pietism, Count Nicholas von Zinzendorf, the leader of a breakaway group, the Moravian Brethren.

JEWISH EVANGELISM BUT NOT RESTORATIONISM

Significantly, Spener's discussion of the conversion of the Jews never mentions their restoration in Palestine, either in the immediate future or in the "last days." As Naomi Shepherd has observed, the issue of the Jews' return to Jerusalem "was confined to Evangelical circles in England and Protestant groups in America."[14] The fascination with the physical restoration of the Jews to Palestine was not a Pietist distinctive; it was a distinctly Calvinist idea that had been popular with the English Puritans and was kept alive in eighteenth-century colonial America by preachers like Jonathan Edwards, who stood in the Puritan tradition, even as it seems to have somewhat fallen out of favor in Britain.

As we shall see, restorationism became popular again in Britain in the 1790s and then in the first half of the nineteenth century was taken up by German Pietists. But it was the Pietists' new concern with Jewish evangelism that was to be one of the key factors in the emergence of evangelical preoccupation with the Jews that developed in Britain in the early nineteenth century. In turn, it would be the renewed British interest in restorationism and, in turn, Christian Zionism as it emerged that would influence the Continent. As Franz Foerster has argued, in the nineteenth century "the connection between the Holy Land and the mission to the Jews was imported to the Continent from England."[15]

---

[13]I am indebted to W. R. Ward for this observation.

[14]Naomi Shepherd, *The Zealous Intruders: The Western Rediscovery of Palestine* (London: Collins, 1987), 229.

[15]Franz Foerster, "German Missions in the Holy Land," in *Jerusalem in the Mind of the Western World, 1800–1948*, ed. Y. Ben-Arieh and M. Davis (Westport, CT: Praeger, 1997), 185.

5

RESTORATIONISM IN AMERICA

From the Early American Puritans
to the American Revolution

THE AMERICAN FASCINATION with the Jews and America's role in the physical restoration of the Jews to Palestine did not begin—as is often assumed—with the emergence of dispensational premillennialism in the nineteenth century. It is much older and is indebted to the English Puritan tradition that flourished in colonial America after it had gone into decline in England. As English Puritans began to move to America in the 1620s, they brought with them the assumptions of their religious culture, and although the colonists came to understand themselves as distinctly American, up until the 1760s they continued to think of themselves as thoroughly British. Their imaginations and vocabulary were shaped by the biblical narrative, and they understood their experiences in terms of their covenantal relationship with God, a God who continued to act in history to both bless and judge nations. While not seeking to distance themselves from the English Puritans, they developed a belief that God had called America to a distinct and unique destiny. From the early years of Puritan settlement, it had been acknowledged that God was doing a new thing in America and that here Puritanism could flourish relatively unhindered by a hostile English monarch.

John Winthrop, the first governor of the Massachusetts Bay Colony, famously characterized the new project in biblical terms: the Puritans in America were to understand themselves as a "city built on a hill that cannot be hid" (Matthew 5:14). American Puritans understood themselves bound by a covenant with God that was both biblical and flexible; it was also outward looking—involving the Puritans as a community—and upward looking—it was a covenant with God himself. It was a covenant with promises of blessing for a people who kept faithfulness, and curses for unfaithfulness. This understanding was shaped by the Puritan apocalyptic tradition that focused on the Jews and included the Protestant tradition's hostility to Catholicism and Islam ("the pope" and "the Turk"). In spite of the relatively small size of the Puritan community, its influence on American history was disproportionally large because of the Puritan penchant for writing so much, and for grappling with issues of life and death with such intensity. As Mark Noll has observed, "Puritanism is the only colonial religious system that modern historians take seriously as a major religious influence on the Revolution."[1] Their writings influenced fellow colonists to think of America as an "elect nation," a new Israel.

The millenarian perspectives of the American Puritans can be traced back to John Cotton (1585–1652), and in him are to be found the anti-Catholic and anti-Islamic themes common to the English Puritans. Cotton was a historicist postmillennialist following the lead of Thomas Brightman, which was the dominant Puritan view in England. It was a form of historicist premillennialism, however, that was to become the dominant prophetic view among American Congregationalists, at least up to the time of Jonathan Edwards. It was Increase Mather (1639–1723) who played the leading role in "the first salient school of thought in American history that advocated the national restoration of the Jews."[2] He published his *The Mystery of Israel's Salvation* in 1669, and forty years later his *A Dissertation Concerning the Future Conversion of the Jewish Nation* (1709) outlined his historicist premillennial position. Mather expected the Jews would return to Palestine before their mass conversion to the Christian faith (an option that some English Puritans had embraced),[3] which would lead to the destruction of the pope and the Turk. Interestingly, he also speculated on the "rapture of

---

[1] Mark Noll, *America's God: From Jonathan Edwards to Abraham Lincoln* (New York: Oxford University Press, 2002), 32-33, quoted in Robert O. Smith, *More Desired Than Our Owne Salvation: The Roots of Christian Zionism* (New York: Oxford University Press, 2013), 119.

[2] Carl Frederick Ehle Jr., "Prolegomena to Christian Zionism in America: The Views of Increase Mather and William E. Blackstone Concerning the Doctrine of the Restoration of Israel" (PhD diss., New York University, 1977), 331.

[3] Mel Scult, *Millennial Expectations and Jewish Liberties* (Leiden: Brill, 1978), 32.

the Saints into the air to meet Christ."[4] Increase Mather and his son Cotton Mather (1663–1728) were key figures in what Stephen Stein has called the "Americanization of the apocalyptic tradition."[5] Rejecting the conjectures of English writers like Joseph Mede that America might be part of a demonic army that would join in rebellion against Christ at the end of the millennium, colonial Puritans outlined a special role for America in their historicist readings of the apocalyptic Scriptures.

From the early eighteenth century through well into the nineteenth century, the anti-Islamic theme was reinforced in America by contemporary events. American sailors in the Mediterranean had ample reasons to fear Muslim pirates from the Barbary Coast of North Africa who regularly seized American ships and held their crews hostage or simply sold them into slavery. Cotton Mather published his *Pastoral Letter to the English Captives in Africa* in 1698 and sought to encourage those so captured not to forsake their Christian faith. The Barbary pirates attacked American ships repeatedly during the American Revolutionary War, and by the 1790s these persistent attacks led the American government to pay tribute to the Barbary states and eventually forced the new republic to develop its own navy. In the early nineteenth century America fought two Barbary wars (1801–1805 and 1815). Such encounters, in tandem with prophetic discourse, kept anti-Muslim sentiment alive and well in America.

JONATHAN EDWARDS

The key theologian who developed American restorationist thinking in the eighteenth century was Jonathan Edwards, the pastor of a Congregationalist church in Northampton, Massachusetts, whose congregation was at the center of the Great Awakening, which began about 1735 in New England. By the early 1740s with the revival sweeping the colonies, end-time speculation became common. Perry Miller has called Edwards "the greatest artist of the apocalypse."[6] Edwards was hesitant about publicly setting dates for specific

---

[4]Smith, *More Desired*, 126.
[5]Paul Boyer, *When Time Shall Be No More: Prophecy Belief in Modern American Culture* (Cambridge, MA: Belknap Press of Harvard University Press, 1992), 68.
[6]Boyer, *When Time*, 71.

events[7] but did believe that the church was now in a period preceding the millennium that would be marked by conflict and struggle as well as periods of intermittent revival.[8] But unlike the earlier American Congregationalist mainstream, Edwards was a postmillennialist, apparently drawing on the work of Daniel Whitby (1638–1726), an Anglican Bible commentator with whom Edwards clashed on other doctrines.

Edwards embraced the teaching received from his English Puritan forebears that the Jews would convert en masse to Christianity and that they would be returned to Ottoman Palestine. Central to his understanding was the idea that the Jews had been rejected, but would eventually be restored as God's people. Thus he wrote, "Nothing is more certainly foretold than this national conversion of the Jews."[9] The two old foes of Protestantism were included in his analysis: "This conversion would follow the time in which 'Antichrist shall be utterly overthrown' with the destruction of 'the spiritual Babylon, that great city of Rome' and 'that other great kingdom that Satan has set up in opposition to the Christian church, viz. his Mahommedan kingdom.'" As Robert O. Smith has written,

> The cosmic redemption Edwards imagined was predicated on the future conversion of the Jews to Christian faith and their literal, physical restoration to Palestine. As a pivotal figure in the development of distinctly American Protestant modes of thought, Edwards carried forward the tradition inherited from England and bequeathed them to subsequent generations of American Protestants intent on discovering (and in some cases manufacturing) their place in God's cosmic drama.[10]

By the middle of the eighteenth century, for many colonial interpreters of prophecy, America's political and military history was also to be understood

---

[7]In his *Humble Attempt* he acknowledges the suggestion of a certain Mr. Lowman that Christ would return in 250 years but argues that such date-setting is unwarranted by Scripture. Jonathan Edwards, *An humble attempt to promote explicit agreement and visible union of God's people in extraordinary prayer for the revival of religion and the advancement of Christ's Kingdom on earth, pursuant to Scripture-promises and prophecies concerning the last time* (Boston: Henchamn, 1747), 127 and 129.

[8]Gerald McDermott argues that Edwards consistently saw this as a period of perhaps up to three hundred years. Gerald R. McDermott, *One Holy and Happy Society: The Public Theology of Jonathan Edwards* (University Park: Pennsylvania University Press, 1992), 50-52.

[9]Quoted in Smith, *More Desired*, 130.

[10]Smith, *More Desired*, 135.

apocalyptically, laying the groundwork for what Nathan Hatch has described as "civil millenarianism,"[11] producing a "civil religion" that saw America and its role in the world in apocalyptic terms. Noll has noted that ironically the impact of Jonathan Edwards was in a secularizing direction: he weakened the emphasis on a national covenant and opened American "thought to a subtle, yet powerful, move from theology to politics, and intellectual leadership to a shift from the clergy to men of state."[12] The American project became linked to the millennial hopes, but American civil religion came to be more about America than about America's Christian identity.

A second subtle shift occurred in the understanding of America's calling to be a light to the nations. Rather than America's role as a redeemer nation being that of spreading the Christian faith, it came to be understood as the defender and purveyor of liberty, particularly over and against Catholic France. Following the precedents set by English Puritans a century earlier, British interests in North America were seen as part of a battle between Protestant England and Catholic France. But by the 1760s, the focus changed, and in the eyes of many colonists, the new tyranny was that of being ruled by an English king. Yet at the same time, as Hatch has observed, "the religious patriotism that animated the Revolution had intellectual roots far more British than American."[13] It was in the revolutionary period that "millennialism fully merged with American secular republican ideology and became an essential ingredient of national culture."[14]

By the time of the Revolution, George III had come to be viewed as the antichrist and America became the place where Christ would build his kingdom on earth in the last days.[15] Edwards's own grandson, Timothy Dwight, a key figure in the Second Evangelical Awakening and president of Yale College, promoted the view of America as the center of God's work on earth. Ruth Bloch has argued that such apocalypticism was "basic to the formation of American revolutionary ideology."[16] The American colonies were identified with Old Testament Israel; America was now God's favored Gentile nation in the last days, an object of his special care.

---

[11]Boyer, *When Time*, 75.
[12]Mark Noll, *America's God*, 50, quoted in Smith, *More Desired*, 136.
[13]Smith, *More Desired*, 135.
[14]Ruth Bloch quoted in Smith, *More Desired*, 142.
[15]Boyer, *When Time*, 73.
[16]Boyer, *When Time*, 74.

Robert O. Smith in commenting on the intertwining of American national identity at the time of the Revolution has observed, "Just as Christian Judeocentrism is grounded in the understanding that Jews have a central role to play in Christian apocalyptic hope, Jews (understood literally or figuratively) are central to the narrative of American national identity."[17] In a similar vein, Robert K. Whalen has observed that "in the early national period, religious literature abounded that foresaw the conversion of the Jews and the restoration of Israel as the ordained task of the millennial nation—the United States."[18] Puritan ethno-nationalism both in England and America was thus configured around a proto-Zionist agenda focused on "the restoration of Israel."

In his book *God's Country: Christian Zionism in America* Samuel Goldman has a chapter titled "On Eagle's Wings: Jewish Restoration and the American Republic," in which he tracks the centrality of America's role in restoring the Jews in the early years of the republic. Many Americans understood that the history of Israel was being reprised in their day. And while the eagle, the symbol of the new nation, had signified for many God's provision in bringing his people to America, "the flight of the eagle was not one-way. After depositing the church in America, it might depart for a second journey to bear Israel home. God's finger pointed from the West back to the East, retracing the journey of the Puritan fathers."[19]

The seeds of English Puritan thinking had taken deep roots in American soil; the notion that America would aid the Jews in their restoration was widely accepted, and by the late eighteenth century it continued to influence America's self-understanding of its national responsibilities. How this return would be accomplished was unclear, and no political actions were advocated that would lead to the attaining of this goal. So while restorationism was embraced in theory, there were no practical steps open to American restorationists to promote the cause. Thus Christian Zionism was not a live option, even if one were a restorationist. The shift to an active political Christian Zionism would happen, but it would occur first in old England, not in America. We turn now to look at how restorationism morphed into Christian Zionism.

[17]Smith, *More Desired*, 138.

[18]Robert K. Whalen, "'Christians Love the Jews!' The Development of American Philo-Semitism, 1790–1860," *Religion and American Culture* 6, no. 2 (Summer 1996): 225.

[19]Samuel Goldman, *God's Country: Christian Zionism in America* (Philadelphia: University of Pennsylvania Press, 2018), 63.

6

THE JEWS AND NINETEENTH-CENTURY BRITISH EVANGELICALISM

RESTORATIONISM MORPHS INTO CHRISTIAN ZIONISM

MANY OF THE MOST INFLUENTIAL WRITERS in the nineteenth century who shaped restorationism and what became Christian Zionism were British rather than American. This chapter's five sections examine distinct but closely related developments in Britain: first, the emergence of forms of "adventism,"[1] particularly historicist premillennialism; second, the growing interest in Jewish evangelism among English-speaking evangelicals; third, the emergence of a distinct expression of Christian Zionism; fourth, the development of evangelical philo-Semitism and its effects on evangelical-Jewish relations; and fifth, the impact of these developments on Palestine.

HISTORICIST PREMILLENNIALISM

> [The French Revolution] undermined the progressive and rationalist cosmology of the eighteenth century, but its most important contribution to the millenarian revival was the spur it provided to further prophetic study.[2]
>
> ERNEST SANDEEN

---

[1]I am using the term *adventism* to apply to any group that emphasizes the immediate return of Christ. The term applies particularly to advocates of historicist premillennialism, but can also be used to describe other groups, such as the futurist dispensationalists.

[2]Ernest Sandeen, *The Roots of Fundamentalism: British and American Millenarianism 1800–1930* (Chicago: University of Chicago Press, 1970), 7.

The French Revolution stimulated a renewed interest in biblical prophecy in the 1790s. The three key prophetic interpreters in the period from 1789 to the 1820s were postmillennialists: Thomas Scott, George Stanley Faber, and James Bicheno.[3] Three features distinguished these writers: first, they believed that the French Revolution should be understood prophetically; second, they achieved a wider popular following than previous authors; and third, evangelicals came to dominate prophecy interpretation.[4] These authors gave the conversion of the Jews and their restoration to Palestine a prominent place in their schemes, picking up on emphases that had been common in Puritan writers.

In the 1820s the postmillennial consensus was under attack by advocates of historicist premillennialism, which offered a hopeful future and a way of identifying themselves as the best friends of the Jews, working both to protect them and to return them to their ancestral homeland. Two adventist writers prepared the way for the shift in prophetic thinking: James Hatley Frere (1779–1869), an Anglican layman, and James Haldane Stewart, whose *Thoughts on the Importance of Special Prayer for the General Outpouring of the Holy Spirit* was published in 1821.

HISTORICIST PREMILLENNIALISM AND THE JEWS

The Jews and their restoration to Palestine were center stage in historicist premillennialism. The early public spokesman was the controversial Edward Irving, who built much of his teaching on the writings of Frere.[5] In the long run the most important popularizer was Edward Bickersteth, the leading evangelical Anglican clergyman after Charles Simeon, who went through a conversion from postmillennialism to adventism in the early 1830s. His books were widely read not only in Britain but also in America well into the later nineteenth century. (Bickersteth was the close friend and spiritual advisor to Lord Shaftesbury, whose social reforms and Christian Zionism were

---

[3]Oliver characterizes Bicheno as "a postmillennialist with pre-millennial hesitations." W. H. Oliver, *Prophets and Millennialists: The Uses of Biblical Prophecy in England from the 1790s to the 1840s* (Oxford: Oxford University Press, 1978), 49.

[4]Donald M. Lewis, *The Origins of Christian Zionism: Lord Shaftesbury and Evangelical Support for a Jewish Homeland* (Cambridge: Cambridge University Press, 2009), 40.

[5]For a summary of the historiography on Irving see Nicholas J. C. Tucker, "In Search of the Romantic Christ: The Origins of Edward Irving's Theology of Incarnation" (PhD diss., University of Stirling, 2018), 14-48.

deeply informed by historicist premillennialism.) A second influential popularizer was E. B. Elliott, whose *Horae Apocalypticae* (London, 1843) was
widely read.[6] This approach came to dominate English evangelical Anglicanism between the 1820s and the 1860s. By 1855 it was reckoned that a
majority of the evangelical clergy in the Church of England had embraced
this interpretation, and its popularity appears to have grown until the 1860s
but then went into a rapid decline.[7] The Achilles's heel of the historicist
position was that it was falsifiable because it was given to date-setting the
return of Christ. The most frequently agreed on dates for Christ's Advent
were 1866 or 1868, which helps to explain its precipitous decline.[8]

In this understanding, postmillennialism's belief in the gradual improvement of the world's situation with the slow dawning of the kingdom of
God was rejected: Christ's return would be dramatic, visible, and cataclysmic; his kingdom would arrive suddenly, not gradually. Given the momentous changes in church and state that occurred in the late 1820s and
early 1830s, the time appeared ripe for a rethinking of prophecy. The approach drew in many of the wealthiest and best educated in British society.[9]

The British millenarian revival in the 1820s was characterized by a new
passion for a prophetic interpretation of Scripture; a renewed interest in the
Jews and the concomitant belief in their physical return to Palestine; and the
insistence on the return of Christ before the coming of the millennium.[10] In
the summer of 1826, Lewis Way, Edward Irving, and Frere founded the Society
for the Investigation of Prophecy. About twenty invited guests (a who's who
of the prophetic writers) soon gathered for the first Albury Conference on
prophecy, held on Henry Drummond's sprawling Albury Park estate in Surrey.

The Albury conference reconvened annually for several years. In 1829
Henry Drummond published the points on which attendees had agreed:

---

[6]W. T. Gidney, *The History of the London Society for Promoting Christianity Amongst the Jews* (London: London Society, 1908), 211.

[7]David Bebbington, *Evangelicalism in Modern Britain: A History from the 1730s to the 1980s* (London: Unwin Hyman, 1989), 85, 191.

[8]Elliott, a fellow of Trinity College, Cambridge, placed the occurrence in 1866. His *Horae Apocalypticae* (1843) was the basis for much of John Cumming's preaching. Sandeen, *Roots*, 82, and Nicholas M. Railton, *No North Sea: The Anglo-German Evangelical Network in the Nineteenth Century* (Leiden: Brill, 2000), 205.

[9]For a detailed treatment of this see Lewis, *Origins*, 36-48.

[10]Sandeen, *Roots*, 8-13.

1. This "dispensation" or age will not end "insensibly" but cataclysmically in judgment and destruction of the church in the same manner in which the Jewish dispensation ended.

2. The Jews will be restored to Palestine during the time of judgment.

3. The judgement to come will fall principally upon Christendom.

4. When the judgement is passed, the millennium will begin.

5. The second advent of Christ will occur before the millennium.

6. The 1260 years of Daniel 7 and Revelation 13 ought to be measured from the reign of Justinian to the French Revolution. The vials of wrath (Revelation 16) are now being poured out and the second advent is imminent.[11]

The final point indicates that the Albury people were historicist premillennialists, for they see the prophetic passages of the Old and New Testament as describing the past and present history of the church rather than a description of its future history. Here the Albury participants are reflecting a traditional Protestant interpretation that links the passage in Daniel 7:15-28 with Revelation 13 with its description of the beast out of the sea, which is said to rule for forty-two months. The two prophetic passages were understood to be referring to the same event: the tyranny of the Roman Catholic Church, which they believed ended in 1798 with Napoleon's troops marching into Rome, and the pope's banishment. Calculating the 1260 years retrospectively, the consensus was that the papacy had arisen in AD 538 with the rule of Justinian and its power broken in 1798.[12] As Ernest Sandeen comments, "The identification of the events of the 1790s with those prophesied in Daniel 7 and Revelation 13 provided biblical commentators with a prophetic Rosetta stone. At last a key had been found with which to crack the code."[13] By the late 1820s the prophetic message of impending judgment and Jewish restoration was being spread far and wide by new millenarian periodicals as well as by a plethora of books devoted to explaining how the mysterious biblical symbols related to contemporary events, usually starting with the French Revolution.

---

[11]Henry Drummond, *Dialogues on Prophecy* (London: Nisbet, 1827) 1:ii-iii, quoted in Sandeen, *Roots*, 21-22.

[12]Sandeen, *Roots*, 6.

[13]Sandeen, *Roots*, 7.

This form of adventism was fueled in part by the crises of the French Revolution and the Napoleonic Wars and the important political changes threatening Britain's Protestant established state churches; yet it also fed on the failure of the established postmillennialist tradition to achieve the evangelization of the world by gradual, ordinary means. Irving and his followers agreed that the kingdom of Christ would come, but it would not be realized by human efforts, but rather be achieved only (in Irving's words) by Christ's "own personal appearance in flaming fire."[14] The French Revolution was interpreted as God breaking into history—as a judgment and as a warning of further judgment to come. The second coming, foreshadowed by the French Revolution, would be a similar cataclysmic event.

David Bebbington has suggested that the blending of evangelicalism with Romantic taste accounts for the rise of adventism at this time.[15] Irving and Lewis Way illustrate the appeal of Romanticism to the evangelicals of their generation. Way was an admirer of Lord Byron and wrote a sonnet on Byron's death, which he published in an appendix on his work *Palingenesia—The World to Come.*[16] It was Irving's friendship with Samuel Taylor Coleridge, the Romantic poet, that influenced Irving to despair of a gradual process toward the millennial age and exchange the postmillennial hope for a much more dramatic, immanent hope and to threaten his listeners with the overthrow and destruction of society unless divine intervention occurred.[17] Given this new perspective, Irving mounted his relentless attacks on what he termed the "Religious World." The reaction to Irving was predictably hostile; one writer in the *Eclectic Review* referred to him as the "accuser-general of the religious world."[18] In the late 1820s Irving's leadership of the radicals disintegrated as he moved in a sectarian direction, but the new adventist hope had won many followers.

---

[14]Edward Irving, "Preliminary Discourse," in *Coming Messiah in Glory and Majesty*, by Juan Josafat Ben Ezra (London, 1827), vi, quoted in D. Bebbington, "The Advent Hope in British Evangelicalism Since 1800," *Scottish Journal of Religious Studies* 9, no. 2 (1988): 103.

[15]Bebbington, foreword to *Heaven on Earth: Reimagining Time and Eternity in Nineteenth-Century British Evangelicalism*, by Martin Spence (Eugene, OR: Pickwick, 2015), ix.

[16]Geoffrey Henderson, *Lewis Way—a Biography* (London, HTS Media, 2014), 144.

[17]Tim Grass, "Edward Irving: Eschatology, Ecclesiology and Spiritual Gifts," in *Prisoners of Hope? Aspects of Evangelical Millennialism in Britain and Ireland, 1800–1880*, ed. T. Stunt and C. Gribben (Milton Keynes, UK: Paternoster, 2004), 97.

[18]*Eclectic Review*, 3rd ser. i (1829): 10, quoted in David Hempton, "Evangelicalism and Eschatology," *Journal of Ecclesiastical History* 31, no. 2 (April 1980): 90.

The historiography concerning British evangelicalism in the first half of the nineteenth century has often misunderstood the nature of the changing currents within the movement in the first half of the century. Historians have written the story through the lens of dispensational (futurist) premillennialism—reading back a profound pessimism into the spirit of the movement—not understanding the hopeful nature of the historicists' vision.[19] In part this has been due to the fact that there has been a concentration on two of the early articulators of the position mentioned above—Irving and Way—both of whom through their denunciatory preaching gave the impression that the movement was world-denying and always threatening judgment. But both of them were unstable visionaries and not representative of the movement as it developed in the 1830s and beyond: Irving moved out of the Church of Scotland to found his own denomination, the Catholic Apostolic Church, but died soon thereafter; and the wealthy, talented, but unfortunate Way died in an asylum for the insane in 1840.

Because they warned about judgment, the impression has been that the historicists were profoundly pessimistic and negative. But Martin Spence has demonstrated that they were enormously optimistic and world-affirming. They were strong advocates of social engagement and of social reform; they called for social action to improve the world, not for withdrawal into sects and secession from the state churches. In all of this, they drank deeply from the wells of English Romanticism and shared the spirit of the age.

This helps us understand two important developments, one at the beginning of the movement in the 1820s and 1830s, and the other after the movement went into decline in the late 1860s. In the early period, it accounts for the tremendous appeal of historicist premillennialism to postmillennialists. Both were profoundly optimistic about the future although they had different timetables. The shift from postmillennialism to historicist premillennialism was from one optimistic eschatology to another. Many leading evangelicals made this shift in the 1830s, including two of British evangelicalism's most influential clergy: the Anglican Edward Bickersteth and the Presbyterian Thomas Chalmers, the most important evangelical in the

---

[19]For a discussion of the charge of pessimism characterizing dispensational premillennialism, see B. M. Pietsch, *Dispensational Modernism* (New York: Oxford University Press, 2015), 154-65.

Church of Scotland. Charles Haddon Spurgeon, the great Baptist preacher of the second half of the nineteenth century, was also a historicist premillennialist and restorationist.[20]

It also helps us understand what happened in the late 1860s to these optimistic, socially involved historicists when their expectation of the return of Christ was disappointed. Many undoubtedly continued in their optimism and activism, but it would seem that in the 1870s this vision enabled some to coalesce around the "social gospel"—a world-affirming movement often associated with postmillennialism that sought to bring in the kingdom through divinely assisted efforts. As Bebbington has observed, the historicist premillennialists "anticipated some of the policies of a later social gospel generation, showing distinctly progressive characteristics."[21] In this they could join with other optimistic evangelicals—those who still embraced postmillennialism. In their disappointment some apparently began to embrace dispensational premillennialism, mixed with Keswick Holiness teaching as it gained strength in the 1870s.

What is crucial is the historicists' attitude to the physical restoration of the Jews at the time. The historicists understood themselves as "literalists" when it came to their reading of Scripture—but one has to be careful because both the historicists and the dispensationalists used such language to describe themselves but arrived at very different understandings of what the Scripture "literally" meant. The historicists used the term to distance themselves from Catholic readings of the text—as Protestants they were seeking its "plain meaning," which was available to all. No mystical revelation or insight was needed; the quadriga, the fourfold method of Catholic exegesis, was rejected. The influence of Scottish commonsense realism is clearly evident in this hermeneutical approach.

It was their "plain reading" of talk of a kingdom and a king that was at the core of their approach. The Old Testament talked about the establishment of a kingdom, and the historicists took this literally—a real kingdom would be established physically in Jerusalem, ruled over by a real king, Christ. Their thinking started with the physical restoration of the Jews

---

[20]Yaakov Ariel, *An Unusual Relationship: Evangelical Christians and Jews* (New York: New York University Press, 2013), 36-37.
[21]Bebbington, foreword to *Heaven on Earth*, x.

and then went on to insist that such a material fulfillment necessitated a personal physical return of Christ. Central to all of this was the restoration of the Jews. The historicists made the physical return of the Jews the event that must happen in order that Christ might be king over his people.

Spence in his recent work *Heaven on Earth* has produced a study that challenges the stereotypes associated with historicist premillennialism as it emerged in England in the 1820s. As Bebbington has observed of historicist premillennialism, "What might seem to subsequent generations an obscurantist preoccupation was in the mid-nineteenth century an enormously influential way of thinking that colored all the opinions of its advocates and molded their priorities for action."[22] Surprisingly, while the overall theological stance was "literalist," it was not a conservative one. Bebbington argues that "far from being arch-conservatives, the historicists held broad views showing affinities with those of contemporary liberal theologians, actually looking at the prospects of the world with as much optimism as their secular contemporaries who embraced the idea of progress. Historicist premillennialists were part of the theological and intellectual mainstream."[23] In his study, Spence shows that the historicist premillennialists shared a number of affinities with Protestant liberalism as it developed in the mid-nineteenth century.

The historicists were Calvinists, committed to state-church establishments, believing "that God had not only acted in history, but also in the magisterial churches of Great Britain and Ireland,"[24] thus accounting for its popularity with Anglicans and Presbyterians (in the Church of Scotland). "Nor was it a coincidence that a willingness to endorse the materialism of Christian hope was found among those who valued Christian faith expressed through a visible national church that held out grace through the ministry of Word and Sacrament."[25] As Edward Bickersteth put it, "The outward ordinances, and the union of Church and State, and the right enjoyment of God's creation, and the restoration of Israel, are as real a part of God's design of love to men, as the invisible and spiritual glories of his church."[26]

---

[22]Bebbington, foreword to *Heaven on Earth*, ix.

[23]Bebbington, foreword to *Heaven on Earth*, x.

[24]Spence, *Heaven on Earth*, 122.

[25]Spence, *Heaven on Earth*, 123.

[26]Edward Bickersteth, *The Restoration of the Jews to Their Own Land: In Connection with Their Future Conversion and the Final Blessedness of Our Earth*, rev. ed. (London: Seeley and Burnside, 1841), 97, cited in Spence, *Heaven On Earth*, 123.

Historicists were convinced that history was moving toward a comprehensive restitution, the climax of a recovery process that had been in operation since creation itself. They were hopeful about the long-term trajectory of God's oversight and orchestration of history: the current situation was soon going to be changed by Christ's personal appearing, which would bring not the withdrawal of the saints in the rapture but purging fire and the coming of heaven to earth and the restoration of all things—a view compatible with the optimism of postmillennialism—only the timetable was much shorter and Christ's return was personal and immanent. So there was much to warn about, but much more to be hopeful about. Even, for some, hope for a universal salvation. Despite their threats of judgment, these historicists shared the hopeful optimism of the postmillennialists, and they agreed with them that there was work to do, society to be reformed (in keeping with the Reformed "creation mandate"), mission work to be done, the Jews to be returned, and their salvation sought.

They did not hope they would "go to heaven" when they died, but that Christ would return and reign with his saints on earth. Instead of focusing on a spiritual heaven, they believed that Christ would bring heaven to earth. The *Christian Observer*, the organ of traditional Claphamite evangelicals, commented of the adventists in 1828, "[They] find nothing in Scripture of what we old-fashioned Christians call heaven."[27] Spence comments,

> These premillennialists instead devoted much time to describing the world that would dawn when Christ returned, a world that they believed would be full of physical people living within communities alive with science, art, and technological progress. They claimed biblical warrant for their vision, but their vision for the future was also shaped profoundly by the society and culture in which they lived.[28]

Taking the phrase "the restitution of all things" from Peter's sermon in Acts 3:20, they believed that this involved the restoration of creation as first created. For some in the subsequent generations, this led them on to not only a physical restoration but also a moral restoration (either conditional immortality or full-blown universalism).

---

[27] *Christian Observer*, 1st ser., 28 (1828): 400, quoted in Spence, *Heaven on Earth*, 102.
[28] Spence, *Heaven on Earth*, 103.

Christ would come before the millennium of Revelation 20 to establish a physical kingdom in which this "restitution of all things" would take place. Crucial for their theology was the linking of what the "restitution of all things" looked like with the millennium. Because Peter in Acts 3 was preaching to Jews and referred to the notion of a predicted divine "restitution," this "allowed the nineteenth-century premillennialists to extrapolate that this passage linked the return of Christ to the promise in the Old Testament of the restoration of the Jewish people from captivity."[29]

At the heart of the historicists' approach was their understanding of a "literal reading" of Scripture. As Spence argues,

> What premillennialists specifically meant by a desire to interpret the Bible "literally" was that it must be interpreted in a way that affirmed the physical reconstitution of God's chosen people as promised in the Old Testament. It was this *particular* theological point (which also included the physical return of the Messiah as the ruling King of this kingdom) that premillennialists believed an appeal to a more *general* common sense reading of scripture would support.[30]

Thus for Lewis Way "the nub of the link between literalism and material restitution, [was] his assertion of the literal restoration of a territorial nation of Israel."[31]

Yet as Spence points out,

> An appeal to literalism was not, then, an *a priori* method for interpreting Scripture, but was itself a theological doctrine, a belief in the materiality—that is, the literality—of God's prophetic promises; a belief that God had promised redemption on earth, not heaven; that Christ would come down, rather than the soul go up, and that God would enact redemption within time, not eternity. . . . The historicist appeal to literalism really had nothing to do with a general method of treatment of prophetic texts . . . but was actually another way of underscoring the type of eschatological materialism that was the pervasive theme of all premillennial theology.[32]

Beza and the English Puritans had rejected Luther and Calvin's view that the Jews had no continuing role in the Christian future and that the Jews

---

[29]Spence, *Heaven on Earth*, 106.
[30]Spence, *Heaven on Earth*, 112.
[31]Spence, *Heaven on Earth*, 112.
[32]Spence, *Heaven on Earth*, 111.

had been replaced by the church. According to Luther's and Calvin's view, the Old Testament promises to Israel were fulfilled in Christ and the Jews as a distinctly chosen people had no national or ethnic identity with which Christians should be concerned. Matthew Henry, the seventeenth-century Bible commentator whose work was widely followed, had argued a similar anti-adventist line: "Christ came to set up his own kingdom, and that a kingdom of heaven, not to *restore the kingdom to Israel*, an earthly kingdom . . . we are bid to expect *the cross* in this world, and to wait for *the kingdom* in the other world. . . . How apt we are to misunderstand scripture, and to understand *that* literally, which is spoken *figuratively*."[33]

The historicists were thus following the line of argument that we have seen was developed by Theodore Beza and Martin Bucer, which was the mainstream Puritan view, widely popularized through the means of the Geneva Bible. What had been a hope of Puritans and many eighteenth-century evangelicals—the conversion of the Jews in the last days—now "became inextricably linked with hopes for the physical reconstitution of dispersed European Jews into a geopolitical entity in the Eastern Mediterranean."[34] By the 1860s many British evangelicals believed that their religious identity was wrapped up with the notion that the unfolding of God's millennial kingdom here on earth would soon bring about the restoration of the Jews to Palestine. In their understanding, Britain's role as an "elect" nation under God included working to facilitate this.

Evangelizing the Chosen People

In the early 1800s the renewed interest in biblical prophecy made British evangelicals receptive to the Pietist emphasis on Jewish evangelization as a means of seeing prophecy fulfilled. But the British interest in evangelizing Jews included a restorationist vision of the return of the Jews to Palestine, something that had not been part of the Pietist agenda. Yet Anglo-German Protestant cooperation worked both ways: because of the British enthusiasm for a Jewish "return," many nineteenth-century German Pietists came to embrace Christian restorationism.

---

[33]Matthew Henry, *An Exposition of the Old and New Testament* (Edinburgh: Bell, Bradfute, Dickson and M'Cliesch, 1791), 6:8.
[34]Spence, *Heaven on Earth*, 114.

It was German-speaking Jewish converts who signaled to British evangelicals the significance of the Jews in their various prophetic scenarios—replaying and popularizing ideas that had been commonplace in the Puritan era. In 1801 Joseph Frey (1771–1850), a German Jewish convert to Christianity, arrived in London from Germany to prepare for missionary service abroad. However, he developed a significant ministry among Jews in London and in 1809 established the London Society for Promoting Christianity Amongst the Jews (LSJ). (It was known in the nineteenth century as the "Jews' Society" and is now The Church's Ministry among the Jewish People.) Frey was the bridge that brought the German Pietist concern for the evangelization of Jews to the English-speaking world.[35] Matthew Westbrook writes, "It seems clear that figures like Frey, assisted by organizations like the London Jews' Society, were forerunners of the modern Messianic Jewish movement, path-breaking in their emphasis on a distinctly Jewish interpretation of the scriptures, especially of biblical prophecy."[36]

The LSJ owed much to Pietism and to workers recruited from Germany. With Frey, the long-held Pietist concern was transplanted in the English-speaking soil by a Jewish convert. In the late 1810s, the LSJ turned its attention from attempts to evangelize English Jews to those in Europe, North Africa, and the Near East. Of the first fifteen missionaries sent abroad by the LSJ, eleven of them were Germans. Just as the inspiration for Jewish evangelism had come from the German Pietist world, so too did the missionaries to carry out the task. The LSJ quickly became the leading British organization concerned with the evangelization of Jews and set the pattern for Jewish evangelism for such efforts throughout the English-speaking world.[37] A recognition of Jewish distinctiveness was crucial in arguing for the necessity of a missionary society uniquely geared toward Jews. From the Pietists the English evangelicals learned that a particular mission required workers attuned to Jewish culture, its languages and sensitivities.[38]

---

[35]For details see Lewis, *Origins*, 57-58.

[36]Matthew C. Westbrook, "The International Christian Embassy, Jerusalem, and Renewalist Zionism: Emerging Jewish-Christian Ethnonationalism" (PhD diss., Drew University, 2014), 95.

[37]For details on the Pietist influence and the origins of the LSJ see Lewis, *Origins*, 55-56.

[38]Andrew Crome, *Christian Zionism and English National Identity, 1600–1850* (Cham, Switzerland: Palgrave Macmillan, 2018), 259.

British evangelicals were being told the injunction that the Christian gospel should be preached "first to the Jew" (Romans 1:16) was still operative. Prior to 1789 there had been virtually no interest in Jewish evangelism among British evangelicals, but by 1850 it seemed that the British evangelicals were obsessed with this evangelistic concern, with evangelical Anglicans spending about a third of their considerable missionary giving on Jewish evangelism (on the roughly six million Jews throughout the world) and about two-thirds on the whole Gentile world (about roughly a billion non-Christian Gentiles in 1850).[39]

The LSJ attracted wealthy and powerful support from key lay figures, among them some of the wealthiest figures in British society. This interest was particularly strong among those on "the Celtic fringe"—particularly in Scotland and Ireland.[40] In the early 1800s two important works promoting Jewish evangelism were written by Scottish Calvinists: David Bogue's *The Duty of Christians to Seek the Salvation of the Jews* and Greville Ewing's *Essays for the Jews* (commissioned by the London Missionary Society). Scots and Irish evangelicals were strong supporters and promoters of Jewish missions.[41]

The most important theological leader in the LSJ was the Irish-born Alexander McCaul (1799–1863), who became interested in Jewish missions through contact with the ubiquitous Lewis Way.[42] Way persuaded him to work for the LSJ, which in 1821 sent him to work for ten years in Warsaw, in the heart of a traditional Jewish society. A brilliant scholar, McCaul became deeply immersed in Jewish literature and learning, achieving fluency in Hebrew and Yiddish. The anti-Talmud debate, which we have seen preoccupied the thirteenth-century Latin church, was thus revived by McCaul. David Ruderman notes that McCaul "was deeply committed to Jewish learning while openly critical of the Talmud, Jewish law, and the rabbis. His long career and writings present a remarkable case study of a dialectical relationship with Jews and Judaism, one of sincere affection but also bitter criticism; intense devotion to his subjects while displaying contempt for the

---

[39]Lewis, *Origins*, 119.

[40]The "Celtic fringe" refers to five areas associated with the Celts: Brittany in France, Ireland, Scotland, Cornwall in southwestern England, and Wales.

[41]Notable among the Celts would be Robert Haldane, Greville Ewing, Horatius Bonar, and David Bogue.

[42]David B. Ruderman, "Towards a Preliminary Portrait of an Evangelical Missionary to the Jews: The Many Faces of Alexander McCaul," *Jewish Historical Studies* 47 (2015): 56.

very core of their beliefs, especially repudiation of their rabbinic leadership."[43] That repudiation was most carefully elaborated in *The Old Paths; or, A Comparison of the Principles and Doctrines of Modern Judaism with the Religion of Moses and the Prophets* (1837). His daughter, Elizabeth Finn, posthumously explained his intent:

> Father began writing a series of papers to show how the rabbis had departed from the Mosaic law and that the Christian religion was the proper outcome of that of Moses and the prophets. . . . These subjects had been deeply impressed upon him while in Poland. He had learnt to love and admire the Jewish people there, and to deplore the manner in which their fine intellects were being enslaved by Rabbinical teaching, and he longed to set them free, and now at last he had the opportunity of attempting to do so. These papers he called "The Old Paths" and used as a motto the words of the prophet Jeremiah, exhorting his people to look back to "the old paths."[44]

In particular McCaul critiqued the rabbis for their treatment of three groups: "the non-Jew, especially those who profess a monotheistic faith; the poor and indigent Jews whose horrendous economic conditions are exacerbated by an uncompassionate and uncompromising rabbinate; and Jewish women whose nobility and dignity are diminished by their inferior status under rabbinic law."[45] McCaul's depth of learning and his careful argumentation from Jewish sources aroused a great deal of debate among European Jews, eliciting "an intense transnational response from Jewish leaders and intellectuals across the continent."[46] Later in life he expressed his opinion that the emergence of Reform Judaism in Britain and on the Continent was to some extent influenced by his critique of rabbinism.[47] McCaul became the most influential clerical figure in the LSJ and profoundly affected its strategy and its training of missionaries. He eventually became professor of Hebrew and rabbinical literature at King's College, London.[48]

---

[43]Ruderman, "Portrait," 50.

[44]Elizabeth Ann Finn, *Reminiscences of Mrs. Finn, Member of the Royal Asiatic Society* (London: Marshall, Morgan and Scott, 1929), 23, quoted in Ruderman, "Portrait," 57.

[45]Ruderman, "Portrait," 60. Ruderman elaborates on these critiques on 60-63.

[46]Ruderman, "Portrait," 66.

[47]Ruderman, "Portrait," 63. Ruderman points out how Jewish critics of traditional Judaism had to walk a fine line in agreeing with some of McCaul's observations in defending Judaism while at the same time seeking to reform it. Ruderman, "Portrait," 66.

[48]On McCaul, see also David Feldman, "Evangelicals, Jews, and Anti-Catholicism in Britain, c. 1840–1900," *Jewish Historical Studies* 47 (2015): 101-2.

THE CONVERSION OF THE JEWS: "THE MOST IMPORTANT OBJECT IN THE WORLD"

[I am] a friend of the Jews, whose restoration to God shall be
the redemption of the whole world.[49]

CHARLES SIMEON, 1835

The leadership of Anglican evangelicalism represented by William Wilberforce and his associates in the "Clapham sect" was sympathetic to the new profile being given to Jewish evangelism. The major clerical promoter of Jewish evangelism was Charles Simeon (1759–1836), the most influential Anglican minister in the first third of the nineteenth century. Although Simeon never embraced the new adventist interpretation, he did much to raise evangelical interest in Jewish evangelism. Simeon was a stalwart LSJ supporter and for years attended and spoke at its annual meeting.[50] In 1818 he published a sermon in which he had reminded his hearers that "it is a Jew who is at this moment interceding for us at the right hand of God." In the words of Bishop Daniel Wilson of Calcutta, Simeon was the society's "chief stay."[51] It was Simeon who interested Bickersteth in Jewish evangelism. Once, while sitting on the platform for the LSJ, Bickersteth was taken aback when Simeon asserted that the conversion of the Jews was the most important object in the world. Bickersteth handed Simeon a slip of paper with the following question: "Six millions of Jews, and six hundred millions of Gentiles—which is the most important?" Simeon wrote back, "But if the conversion of the six, is to be life from the dead to the six hundred millions—what then?"[52] In his final appearance at the LSJ's annual meeting in 1835 Simeon put forward his own understanding of Jeremiah 33:7-9:

> God shall glorify himself in Israel in a manner in which he has not yet glorified himself. . . . God intends to glorify his people. . . . Jehovah declares that his honour, and his own happiness, so to speak, is connected with the

---

[49]*Jewish Intelligence, and Monthly Accounts of the Proceedings of the LSPCJ* 1 (June 1835): 132.
[50]*Jewish Intelligence* 3 (June 1837): 138.
[51]Gidney, *History,* 148.
[52]T. R. Birks, *Memoir of the Rev. Edward Bickersteth, Late Rector of Watton, Herts.* (London: Seeleys, 1852), 61. Gidney retells the story but quotes eight hundred millions, and eight millions. Gidney, *History,* 273.

restoration of Israel . . . an event which compasses no less than the salvation of the whole world. Do not conceive me as speaking too strongly when I say, the salvation of the whole world is dependent and arising out of this important consequence. Am I a friend to the Gentiles? I am known to be so, and therefore am I a friend of the Jews, whose restoration to God shall be the redemption of the whole world.[53]

Here Simeon is picking up on the idea that in the "last days" converted Jews will become the evangelists who will bring large numbers of Gentiles into the Christian fold. Their evangelization therefore had to be prioritized because of their strategic importance in the end of days.

Along the same lines Bickersteth cites Romans 11:12: "If such blessings were connected with the fall of the Jews, what with their fulness? If their casting away was the reconciling of the world, what shall the recovery of them be but *life from the dead?*"[54] In the minds of many evangelicals the evangelization of the Jews and the cause of their physical restoration to Palestine were closely linked. In 1836 Bickersteth published *The Restoration of the Jews to Their Own Land*. Bickersteth was well acquainted with all that the Puritans had to say about Jewish conversion and return.[55] He outlines his view that the Jews are the key to understanding the divine unfolding of history.

For Bickersteth, Jewish conversion would be not facilitated by the removal of "Jewish disabilities"[56]—that is, the extension of full civil rights to the Jews at the cost of the renunciation of Britain's identity as a Christian nation—but by the removal of the "great stumbling-blocks that Christians had placed in their way by their own inconsistencies," echoing a theme that can be traced back to Spener, the Puritans, and even Luther. The position is rooted in the notion that there is a permanent distinction among nations, one that is not dissolved by conversion. (In this he is echoing the sentiments of Thomas Brightman, discussed in chapter three, on the radical and ongoing differences between Jews and Christians, even in the millennium.) Many restorationists followed Bickersteth's argument and opposed the extension of Jewish political rights in England because on the one hand it would signal the death

---

[53]*Jewish Intelligence*, 1:132.
[54]Bickersteth, *Restoration*, 118.
[55]Douglas J. Culver, *Albion and Ariel: British Puritanism and the Birth of Political Zionism*, American University Studies 7, Theology and Religion 166 (New York: Lang, 1995), 4.
[56]Bickersteth, *Restoration*, 89.

of England's claim to be a Christian nation and thereby invite divine judgment for its apostasy, and on the other, it would affirm the unique calling of the Jews to return to the country where, in William Fremantle's words, they "had unsurpassed glories to look forward to in Palestine."[57] This has sometimes been interpreted as an indication of anti-Semitism, and while at times their attitudes were not entirely free from anti-Semitism, this hardly characterizes their general attitude.[58] As Andrew Crome puts it, "Restorationists projected their glory into another geographical and chronological horizon," which could become "a justification for denying them political rights in the present. The allosemitic impulse, in which Jews were always other, meant that restorationists were able to swing towards supporting Jewish rights in some areas, while denying them in others."[59]

THE SHIFT FROM RESTORATIONISM TO AN EARLY FORM OF CHRISTIAN ZIONISM

Thus far I have not identified restorationists as "Christian Zionists." It is at this point that we can begin doing so, for Bickersteth (like Increase Mather discussed above) believed a mass conversion of Jews to Christianity would occur after their return to Palestine, rather than before, and in this matter he differs from the general Puritan consensus. Once "restoration" could conceivably occur before conversion, then it could happen whenever the political circumstances allowed for the possibility—there was no need for Christians to wait for the mass conversion of the Jews. Christian restorationists could now become "Christian Zionists" and work for the goal of a Jewish return "in unbelief," although—it should be noted again—the term *Christian Zionist* was not invented until the 1890s.

As Bickersteth was writing his book in the 1830s, the political circumstances in the Middle East were changing. Britain was becoming more involved in propping up the Ottoman Empire in the face of Russia's desire to expand its influence at Ottoman expense. This is the critical turning point at which restorationism begins to morph into a politically active Christian Zionism. As will be seen, the political leadership of the Christian Zionist

---

[57]Crome, *English National Identity*, 261.
[58]Crome, *English National Identity*, 261-62.
[59]Crome, *English National Identity*, 262.

cause in Britain came from Bickersteth's spiritual mentee, Anthony Ashley Cooper, the seventh Earl of Shaftesbury.

In practical terms, Bickersteth outlines what he saw was the duty of British Christians:

> . . . to remove our own causes of offence. Any aid too that we can nationally render to their peaceful return (without sanctioning their impenitence or any injustice to others), will be graciously accepted by the God of Abraham, of Isaac and of Jacob, and will bring down blessings on the country rendering such aid. (Ps. cxxii.6 Gen xii:3) Indeed mercy and kindness shewn to them are bright tokens of future good and preservation to the nations or the individuals shewing this mercy. Isaiah lx.12. Jeremiah xxxviii. 7-12; xxxix. 15-18. Would to God that our country might be favoured among the nations of the earth in aiding the restoration of Israel! May the Lord of all dispose our rulers to this course![60]

In making this political agenda explicit, Bickersteth is clearly setting forth an active Christian Zionist agenda. It is also significant in that he reflects two important preconceptions that were common to the evangelicals' understanding of Palestine (and especially his friend Lord Shaftesbury): first, that Palestine is "almost emptied of its inhabitants;"[61] and second, that current events were providentially helping "to prepare the way for their quiet, gradual, and safe return to their own country, and their protracted residence there."[62] Bickersteth's understanding of the Jews' return to Palestine was set within his historicist premillennial framework and was closely linked with the necessity of Jewish evangelism. The significance of the LSJ in evangelism was thus underlined by Bickersteth:

> This makes the establishment of a distinct society, for their spiritual welfare, a matter of real importance. It answers one of the most plausible objections against the formation of the Jews' Society,—that other Missionary Societies might undertake this work. No! their case is peculiar; it lies at the root of all other good. It demands the magnitude of its consequences, a distinct effort and an undivided attention.[63]

---

[60]Bickersteth, *Restoration*, 91.
[61]Bickersteth, *Restoration*, 81.
[62]Bickersteth, *Restoration*, 81.
[63]Bickersteth, *Restoration*, 229.

The LSJ at Palestine Place in Bethnal Green, its home base in London, developed and refined the techniques used by German Pietists in their mission efforts among the Jews: a Jewish chapel for Hebrew services, a home for persecuted converts, a training school for missionaries, a Bible depot. But it soon started sending missionaries abroad and by the end of the nine-teenth century had several hundred missionaries spread across Europe, North Africa, and the Middle East.[64]

Bickersteth did not claim any ability to set a precise date as to the second coming of Christ, but made the argument common among prophetic inter-preters that there were signs indicating its imminence. The next great event to be anticipated was the personal return of Christ, and this return was in-timately linked to the fate of the Jews and their restoration to Palestine.

For many historicists the evangelization of the Jews was central to God's plans, just as it had been for the German Pietists. Jewish distinctiveness would not end with their conversion, or even with Christ's return. In Crome's words,

> Far from trying to eradicate Jewishness, Jews were the original nation, des-tined to be predominant, and always marked out by national and cultural distinctiveness. For restorationists, conversion was therefore not an eradi-cation of Jewish culture replaced by gentile norms, but an embracing of the full covenantal, messianic promises of the Old Testament. While nineteenth century Jews strongly disagreed with this position, restorationists were far from seeking their cultural annihilation.[65]

A criticism made of these restorationists is that their efforts were imperial-istic, aimed at benefiting England and its wider empire.[66] They clearly be-lieved that aiding Jewish restoration would benefit England as it fulfilled its designated prophetic role. But this benefit would not be primary, because they believed that Jewish restoration would lead to a diminishment of the

---

[64]For a detailed recent study of the work of the LSJ's work in London see Rodney Curtis, "Evan-gelical Anglican Missionaries and the London Jews Society: Palestine Place at Bethnal Green and Related Developments, 1813–1895," *Jewish Historical Studies* 50, no. 1 (2018): 5, 69-100. For a summary of the LSJ's expansion beyond England see Yaron Perry, *British Mission to the Jews in Nineteenth-Century Palestine* (London: Frank Cass, 2003), 7-11.

[65]Crome, *English National Identity*, 259.

[66]Nabil I. Matar, "The Controversy over the Restoration of the Jews: From 1754 Until the London Society for Promoting Christianity Among the Jews," *Durham University Journal* 82, no. 1 (1990): 42-43.

British Empire, which would be eclipsed by the restored Israel.[67] The Christian Zionists' goal was not to secure the British Empire, but to establish the Jewish one:

> Palestine was Israel's land, not England's, and English rule in Jerusalem was ultimately as unacceptable as Turkish dominance. . . . For restorationists, prophecy, not imperial glory was their main concern. Finally, this led them to see in the Jews the legitimation of their own nation and understand their own current prominence in world affairs. If God had exalted the nation above all others, and established her as the dominant maritime power, he had done so for a reason: in order that she may fulfill her appointed role and restore the Jews to Palestine.[68]

Crome further observes that "prophecies of Jewish restoration acted as a legitimization of an 'informal' empire of civilization. This was not Britain ruling the world, but a political ascendance preparatory to the renovation of the world in the Jewish millennium."[69]

Scholars who question the motivation of the evangelicals often dismiss their professed concern for the Jews as merely a façade designed to mask proselytizing designs. For some, it seems to be an article of faith that the professed love of Jews by these Christians is in some way a form of anti-Semitism, in spite of any and all evidence to the contrary. In his seminal work, *The Balfour Declaration*, published in 1961, the late Leonard Stein argued that because Shaftesbury sought the conversion of Jews, he desired that Jews would lose their identity by becoming Christians, and therefore could neither be a friend of the Jews nor considered a forerunner of Zionism.[70] Stein later conceded that he was mistaken in this.[71] As Isaiah Friedman has written, "Far from wishing the Jews to lose their identity, Shaftesbury hoped England would play a leading role in fostering their nationality and in restoring them to the Land of their Ancestors."[72] While the evangelical hope for the conversion of individual Jews is not to be ignored,

---

[67]Crome, *English National Identity*, 262.

[68]Crome, *English National Identity*, 258.

[69]Crome, *English National Identity*, 258.

[70]Leonard Stein, *The Balfour Declaration* (London: Jewish Chronicle Publications, 1961), 7.

[71]Isaiah Friedman, *The Question of Palestine, 1914–1918: British-Jewish-Arab Relations*, 2nd ed. (New Brunswick, NJ: Transaction, 1992), li n. 75.

[72]Friedman, *Question of Palestine*, xxvii.

it is perhaps the case that scholars (including those hostile to proselytizing by the evangelicals) are asking the wrong questions. It is, after all, intrinsic to evangelicalism to seek the conversion of all people to the Christian faith, whether Jew or Gentile. For evangelicals to exclude offering Jews salvation through the one whom they believe to be the Jewish Messiah would be an act of anti-Semitism.

Loving, Esteeming, Protecting, and Preparing the Jews

As British evangelical identity became increasingly tied to the Jews, it morphed as many evangelicals came to understand themselves as people who were to love and esteem the Jews, to serve as their protectors and to prepare the way for them to return to Palestine. This shift is not solely attributable to the historicists, as is evidenced by the work of Thomas Scott (1747–1821), the postmillennialist biblical commentator whose *Commentary on the Bible* was widely read by nineteenth-century British evangelicals and which was written in the early years of the French Revolution. The influence of his commentary can be compared to that of the *Scofield Reference Bible* in the early twentieth century, which was important in promoting dispensational premillennialism. Scott's *Commentary* did much to popularize the notion of a Jewish return to Palestine among its numerous readers throughout the English-speaking world in the nineteenth century, but he was also very important in promoting a positive view of the Jews.

His 1810 sermon "The Jews a Blessing to the Nations, and Christians Bound to Seek Their Conversion to the Saviour" illustrates well how evangelicals were constructing their own identity around their relationship with the Jews, one that emphasized the high esteem Christians should have toward them. Scott argues that those acquainted with the Scriptures should expect that the Jews "would, in every age, be the most distinguished and extraordinary people on earth; and be, in many respects, honoured and made a blessing to the nations above all others of the human race: and likewise that the posterity of Judah would be, by far, the most illustrious of this distinguished people." He goes on to argue that even unbelievers must acknowledge on the basis of objective observation that

> doubtless, the seed of these patriarchs have been, beyond comparison, the most singular people, which ever lived on earth; nay, after making all fair

deductions, they have been honoured by God, and made blessings to mankind above all other nations: and the descendants of Judah have been, and are, incomparably, the most illustrious of that favoured race.[73]

This respect for Jewish achievements was reinforced by Scott's own perception of his duty as a Christian to the Jews:

> I . . . honour the nation to whom God committed his ancient oracles, and by whom they have been communicated to us Gentiles. I honour the race whence prophets, whence apostles, whence Christ himself, arose. I feel myself a debtor, to a vast amount, unto the Jews, from whose Scriptures (for the most, at least, of the New Testament was written by Jews,) I derive all my hope, all my comfort, all my joy in the Lord; and among whom my beloved and divine Saviour received his human nature, and exercised his personal ministry; and it would be a high gratification to me, could I, by any means, repay even a small part of the debt which I owe to that race, of whom it was of old predicted, "that in them should all the nations be blessed."[74]

Scott held to a "quickening of the times," similar to the German Pietists' concept of a "hope for better times," believing that the Jews had a future role to play in divine history. Although a postmillennialist, he looked, as did many evangelicals, to the ultimate conversion of the Jews and their restoration to Palestine and was an early supporter of the LSJ. This interest in biblical prophecy had a much broader religious public than just among the evangelicals; in the nineteenth century churchmen of all stripes and dissenters of all sorts came to be fascinated with the role of the Jews in prophetic understanding as it came more and more to the fore.

Thomas Scott, Charles Simeon, and Edward Bickersteth were three of the most important evangelical writers shaping British evangelical identity in the first half of the nineteenth century, and while the first two were postmillennialists and the last was a historicist premillennialist, all three stand in a tradition I have argued is best characterized as a Christian "teaching of love and esteem" toward the Jews.[75] As Crome observes, "The Judeo-centric basis of restorationist belief . . . led its proponents to look for the coming

---

[73]Thomas Scott, *The Jews a Blessing to the Nations, and Christians Bound to Seek Their Conversion to the Saviour* (London: London Society, 1810), 3.
[74]Scott, *The Jews a Blessing*, 4.
[75]See Lewis, *Origins*, 64-66.

imperial superiority of the Jews, while their belief in England's status as a chosen nation led to anxieties over the nation's responsibilities." Such a belief, as he points out, "militates against a straightforward imperialist reading" of Christian Zionism in the English setting. The leading prophetic writer, Edward Bickersteth, could point "towards Isaiah 50:12, and the warning that the nation that did not serve the Jews would perish: 'How then can we obtain national security? . . . If we do, as a nation, serve Zion, we shall not perish.'"[76] England's meaning and mission were to be found in serving Jewish interests. "The predominance of the British Empire was itself only temporary, fated to wither under the Jewish imperium restorationists found predicted in the Bible; what McNeile described as their 'precedence and royalty of influence and dominion over all people.'"[77] Lord Shaftesbury in writing to his Jewish friend and Christian bishop Michael Solomon Alexander, as he was about to take up his duties as bishop at Jerusalem, could commend his Jewishness in the following way: you are "one of that nation hitherto scattered and faded, before whom we gentiles must eventually fade, to whom everything is promised and to whom everything belongs."[78] Supersessionism this was not.

PROTECTING THE JEWS

> *Support for the Jews, seen as part of a project of spreading toleration and civil rights to persecuted minorities in the Ottoman Empire, was one element of an "imperialism of human rights."*[79]
>
> ANDREW CROME

If British evangelicals came to esteem Jews so highly, one would expect that it would influence their behavior, and clearly it did. The protection of European Jewry and advocacy on their behalf became central to many British evangelicals, especially those associated with the missionary organizations like the LSJ. Evangelicals came increasingly to embrace the idea that the Jews as a people remained a special concern to God; their election as a people

---

[76] Crome, *English National Identity*, 256n226.
[77] Crome, *English National Identity*, 256n230.
[78] Crome, *English National Identity*, 260n242.
[79] Crome, *English National Identity*, 258. See Abagail Green, "The British Empire and the Jews: An Imperialism of Human Rights?," *Past & Present* 199 (May 2008): 175-205.

had not been set aside and they would yet play a role in the unfolding of history. Because of this, evangelicals concerned with the evangelization of the Jews in the nineteenth century (a good number of these evangelists were Jewish converts) were among the chief Gentile opponents of any mistreatment of Jews and were acknowledged by British Jews as such, at the time. These evangelicals were thus markedly different from earlier Christian polemicists and regarded themselves as philo-Semites and firmly rejected the anti-Judaic traditions of both the medieval Catholic Church and of Luther. By the early 1840s British evangelicals were concerned to advance the protection of the Jews throughout Europe and in the Ottoman Empire. The mistreatment of Jews in Palestine was of special concern, and Lord Shaftesbury worked behind the scenes to get the British government to intervene with the sultan of the Ottoman Empire to endorse various schemes that would benefit the Jews and allow them to settle in Palestine.[80]

The Victorian evangelical interest in the Jews was not, therefore, only concerned with efforts to evangelize them, or to enable them to return to Palestine. Individuals like Shaftesbury and those closely associated with him—such as Charlotte Elizabeth Tonna and Edward Bickersteth—and organizations like the LSJ and the Evangelical Alliance were deeply concerned to combat the mistreatment of Jews and to engage in political lobbying on their behalf. It was British evangelicals, more than any other group of English Gentiles, who were most concerned to seek the protection of Jews from those hostile to them.

Paradoxically, Shaftesbury was far more zealous in the cause of a Jewish homeland than were most European Jews; perhaps the greater paradox was that Victorian England's leading Christian Zionist had been encouraged and confirmed in his restorationist views by Jewish converts who were far more zealous in the Zionist cause than most of their fellow Jews. His attempts to influence Lord Palmerston (British foreign secretary and sometime prime minister) would have come to naught unless they had been matched by efforts to create a climate of opinion at a popular level in favor of the cause— through public meetings, newspapers, journals, and books as well as his own speeches, both in and out of Parliament—but especially by a group of highly

---

[80]Material in this paragraph is adapted from the author's earlier work: Lewis, *Origins*, 184-89.

effective female novelists such as Charlotte Elizabeth and Catherine Marsh.[81] Only by moving British public opinion could Shaftesbury and his friends hope to create a climate of opinion in Britain that was sympathetic to Jews and to sustain diplomatic pressure on the Porte (the Ottoman government) to carry through on promises of reform.

Part and parcel of the Christian Zionists' campaign was the attempt to redefine British national identity so as to include Britain's unique responsibility toward "God's chosen people" as Europe's leading Protestant power. The process involved both an acknowledgment of Protestantism's special duty toward the Jews, and the crafting of a new positive image of the Jews as especially worthy of respect: as particularly intelligent, upright, educated, and hard-working. Only in this way could deep anti-Jewish undercurrents be kept in check; Shaftesbury had no doubts about the darker side of the English character as he sought to counter anti-Jewish sentiments in any form.

While these British evangelicals were concerned to read philo-Semitism into the national identity of Protestant England, it was their wider connection with networks of Scottish Calvinists and Continental Pietists that was to expand their influence many times over when it came to dealing with the Near East. And it was in the Near East that these British evangelicals and Continental Pietists were to have an enormous long-term impact.

CHRISTIAN ZIONISTS AND THE TRANSFORMATION OF PALESTINE

> As Britain came to command unchallenged mastery of the seas
> after Trafalgar, and the Ottoman Empire appeared ever more
> unstable, so the possibility of a national restoration of the
> Jews to Palestine became an increasingly realistic proposal.[82]
>
> ANDREW CROME

The impact Christian Zionists had on nineteenth-century Palestine is little understood. The LSJ and the Church Missionary Society were active in Palestine from the 1820s, and their work was followed closely by both English

---

[81]For details on these efforts see Lewis, *Origins*, 189-96.
[82]Crome, *English National Identity*, 210.

evangelicals and German Pietists who cooperated closely on the ground in Jerusalem. They soon became convinced that a British consular presence in Jerusalem was needed, and eventually Lord Shaftesbury was instrumental in the appointment of a British vice consul in 1838 who had impeccable evangelical credentials. This appointment is widely regarded as a turning point in the history of Palestine. Once Britain had diplomatic status in Jerusalem, the other leading powers soon followed suit and the European interest in Palestine grew rapidly throughout the nineteenth century.[83]

The second great object was the establishment of an Anglican church in the city, and the result was the opening of Christ Church in Jerusalem in 1848, after a long and convoluted diplomatic struggle with the Ottoman government. The sultan could not permit the building of a new Christian church; the objection was overcome by designating it as the chapel attached to the British consulate. The third object was the establishment of an Anglican-Lutheran bishopric in Jerusalem, the first incumbent of which was Michael Solomon Alexander, a German Jewish convert. The story of the setting up of the joint bishopric has attracted a considerable amount of historical attention, but again detailed discussion of this has to be sought elsewhere. On examination, it is clear that the English evangelicals' and the German Pietists' interest in the Jews was a major factor in the reshaping of Palestine in the nineteenth century.[84]

Thus it was in the mid-nineteenth century that restorationism began to morph into a movement that was hopeful its political actions could assist the Jewish people to "return to Zion." No longer were restorationists merely hopeful about an eventual return at some point in the vague prophetic future; no longer were they waiting for the mass conversion of the Jews to occur before the restoration. Now they could put their shoulders to the plow and try to make the restoration a reality. Paradoxically, as we will see, there were very few Jews at all interested in the project that was preoccupying more and more Protestants.

---

[83]This paragraph is adapted from the author's previous work: see Lewis, *Origins*, 213-23.

[84]For a detailed accounts of evangelical interest in Palestine, see Ariel, *Unusual Relationship*, chap. 5, and Lewis, *Origins*, chap. 8.

7

PREPARING THE GROUND FOR THE BALFOUR DECLARATION

IN THE LAST CHAPTER I argued that in the mid-nineteenth century Christian restorationism was giving way to an active form of Christian Zionism in light of the shift in prophetic opinion that the Jews would be restored to Zion before, rather than after, their mass conversion to Christianity. This chapter examines how this interest in the Jews and their restoration played out in the late nineteenth century as background to the Balfour Declaration.

The Prayer Meeting Revival of the late 1850s and its lingering impact seems to have contributed to the increasing popularity of dispensationalism. The Plymouth Brethren, among whom it had originated, began to move more into the mainstream of British evangelicalism. The China Inland Mission, which in its origins was profoundly influenced by the Brethren, was formed in 1865 under the leadership of James Hudson Taylor on a distinctly futurist premillennial footing and by 1900 was the largest Protestant missionary society operating in China. Following 1866/1868, the two dates that many historicist premillennialists had set for Christ's return, this form of premillennialism became increasingly discredited, and by the mid-1870s futurist premillennialism was on the ascendant among British evangelicals. The Keswick Convention, which began in 1875, combined its unique version of holiness teaching, premillennialism, and interest in foreign missions to become highly influential in evangelical circles.

The dispensationalists, while believing in the eventual return of the Jews to Palestine, did not have the historicists' enthusiasm about it because its key formulator, John Nelson Darby, believed that the return of the Jews would take place after Christ's return when he would rescue the true Christians from the world in the "rapture." They understood the Jews to be the heirs of

Old Testament Israel, destined to establish a Jewish state in Palestine but only after Christ returned; the Jews would recognize him as their Savior and return to their land.[1] The dispensationalists, while supportive of the evangelization of Jews, did not emphasize the view—as had Philipp Jakob Spener—that Christians had a special responsibility to prioritize the conversion of the Jews and would be held accountable for their failure to attempt their conversion. As Christopher Clark has commented, "The conversionary zeal of the dispensationalists arose not from the fear that failure might subvert the messianic timetable, but from the desire to save individual members of the Jewish people from dying in unbelief."[2] This helps to explain why, in the 1880s, when Shaftesbury's hopes for the return of the Jews and his lifelong desire to aid them in their resettlement were revived, one gets the impression that his fellow evangelicals were supportive of his efforts, but perhaps from the side lines. The Jews would return to Palestine at some distant point and there might be signs that this was going to happen, but relatively few were as enthusiastic as Lord Shaftesbury in working to enable it to happen.

Shaftesbury had been the key political figure promoting Christian Zionism in the 1830s through the 1850s, and while enthusiasm for the cause may have waned after the disappointment of the 1868 failure of Christ to return, Shaftesbury's concern for the Jews did not lessen. He founded the Palestine Exploration Fund in 1865 and spoke at its annual meeting in 1875, urging support of exploration as follows: "Let us not delay . . . to send out the best agents . . . to search the length and breadth of Palestine, to survey the land; and if possible to go over every corner of it, drain it, measure it, and, if you will, prepare it for the return of its ancient possessors, for I must believe that the time cannot be far off before that great event will come to pass."[3] He continued to articulate the "decline thesis" in relation to Palestine, which his mentor Bickersteth had held, arguing that it was "almost without an inhabitant—a country without a people, and look! Scattered over the

---

[1]Christopher M. Clark, "'The Hope for Better Times': Pietism and the Jews," in *Pietism in Germany and North America 1680–1820*, ed. Jonathan Strom, Hartmut Lehmann, and James Van Horn Melton (Farnham, UK: Ashgate, 2009), 36.

[2]Clark, "Pietism and the Jews," 36.

[3]Lord Shaftesbury, speech to the Palestine Exploration Fund Society, *Palestine Exploration Fund Quarterly Report*, 1875, 115-16.

world, a people without a country."[4] He apparently formulated the early slogan "A country without a nation for a nation without a country," which Jewish Zionists later embraced as "A land without a people for a people without a land."[5]

Shaftesbury also continued to believe that there was "a great inclination among the Jews in all parts of the South and the East for their return to the Holy Land."[6] He recalled that before Bishop Alexander had left for Palestine in 1842 to take up his role as the new Anglican-Lutheran bishop in Jerusalem, the bishop had given him a ring that he was still wearing in 1875. On it were inscribed words that he cited as "the grounds of union between us and the poorest Hebrews, though they believe but one half of the Bible: 'Oh, pray for the peace of Jerusalem; they shall prosper that love thee.'"[7] By the 1880s other important voices were joining Shaftesbury in promoting Jewish restoration, and it is clear almost all of them had been associated with or influenced by evangelicalism.[8]

SHAFTESBURY IN THE 1880S

> *England, mighty England, free England, with its world embracing outlook will understand us and our aspirations.*[9]
>
> THEODOR HERZL, FOURTH ZIONIST CONGRESS, 1900

In the early 1880s British evangelicals became preoccupied once again with Jewish matters as the magnitude of Russian Jewry's problem became evident.[10] On becoming czar in 1855, Alexander II initiated a number of reforms,

---

[4]Shaftesbury, speech to the Palestine Exploration Fund Society, 116.

[5]Donald M. Lewis, *The Origins of Christian Zionism: Lord Shaftesbury and Evangelical Support for a Jewish Homeland* (Cambridge: Cambridge University Press, 2009), 145.

[6]Shaftesbury, speech to the Palestine Exploration Fund Society, 116.

[7]Shaftesbury, speech to the Palestine Exploration Fund Society, 117. The sentence is a quotation of Psalm 122:6.

[8]For a discussion of these writers see Lewis, *Origins*, 319-22. See also Shalom Goldman's recent study of Laurence and Alice Oliphant in *Zeal for Zion: Christians, Jews, & the Idea of the Promised Land* (Chapel Hill: University of North Carolina Press, 2009), chap. 1.

[9]World Zionist Organization, *Stenographisches Protokoll der verhandungen des IV. Zionisten Congresses London, 13, 14, 15, 16 August, 1900* (Wien, 1900), 5, quoted in Douglas J. Culver, *Albion and Ariel: British Puritanism and the Birth of Political Zionism* (New York: Lang, 1995), 6.

[10]Much of the following section is adapted from a paper presented in March 2012 to the Lausanne Committee on Jewish Evangelism in San Diego, California. It is reproduced by permission. The paper was entitled "In Light of the Holocaust: Evangelicals, Jews and the Historical Record." www.lcje.net/In%20Light%20of%20the%20Holocaust_Lewis.pdf.

including the relaxation of many of the oppressive measures against the Jews associated with Nicholas I's administration. The rise of Slavophile nationalism in the 1870s was an ominous sign for Russian Jews. Alexander II's assassination in 1881 ended a period of relative peace and prosperity for them, and following his death the situation deteriorated rapidly. Jews were an easy target, especially as one of the seven conspirators involved in Alexander's assassination was a young Jewish woman. A wave of pogroms spread throughout southwestern Russia, some two hundred occurring in 1881 alone. In Warsaw and in the large cities of the Ukraine, as well as in the small towns of Belorussia, mobs attacked Jews, looted their stores and homes, smashed furniture, and generally terrorized the Jewish community, often with the police looking on passively. Hundreds lost their lives, and property damage was extensive, but the psychological impact on Russian Jewry was also significant. By early 1882 "temporary laws" were enacted that legitimized the severe persecution that followed.

A massive migration began of mostly working-class Jews out of Russia, which then had the largest Jewish community in the world, with about five million Jews. About 750,000 left Russia for the West between 1881 and 1905 and another 250,000 left areas of Eastern Europe for the West during the same period. Approximately 80 percent of them went to the United States, while about 100,000 settled in Britain.[11] Jewish nationalism emerged as an important political force and a postliberal pattern in modern Jewish life; rather than follow the assimilationist strategies of Western Jews, some Russian Jews sought new solutions: for some emigration, for some a worldwide socialist revolution, and for others Zionism. The nationalist identity of Jews, which Christian Zionists had so long believed in, was beginning to be realized.

The LSJ was quick to express its sympathy for Russian Jews, and from February 1882 articles in its *Jewish Intelligence* provided the public with details of the events.[12] The vastness of the persecution and the resultant exodus of Jews were seen as a sign from God, presaging "the beginning of a fulfillment of the prophetic Scriptures foretelling the return of the Jews to their own land. . . . The missionaries of the Society rejoice at the protests which

---

[11]Colin Holmes, *Anti-Semitism in British Society, 1876–1939* (London: E. Arnold, 1979), 3.
[12]See "A Few Facts Relating to the Jewish Troubles in Russia," *Jewish Intelligence* (February 1882): 33-37.

Christians everywhere are making against these outbursts, as being not only abhorrent to our common humanity, but also alien to the true spirit of Christianity."[13] Earlier in the century the LSJ committee had been unwilling to take a stand on different prophetic interpretations among its supporters. In 1849 an Anglican clerical supporter had delivered a lecture to its Liverpool branch titled "The National Restoration of the Jews to Palestine Repugnant to the Word of God," which was subsequently published.[14] Now, however, the LSJ was unabashedly restorationist in its public stance. The LSJ did much more than protest; it set up a fund to assist Jews desiring to leave Russia. "The appeal by many Jews to receive protection in mission stations in Europe," Yaron Perry has written, "strengthened the sense of missionary zeal among the London Society members."[15]

The events in Russia deeply disturbed Shaftesbury, reinforcing his view of Russia as intolerant, oppressive, and anti-Semitic. In the twilight of Shaftesbury's life the protection of the Jews again became an ardent concern, as it had been during the Damascus "Blood Libel" Affair of 1840 in which Jews in Damascus were accused of killing a Capuchin monk and his Christian servant and of using the monk's blood to make *matzot*, the unleavened bread for Passover. A number of Jews died in the anti-Jewish riots, arrests, and torture that ensued. British evangelicals, led by Shaftesbury, played a major role in the international outcry that followed.[16] In January of 1882 some British Jews issued a public appeal in *The Times* addressed to Lord Shaftesbury, asking why "no Christian had come forward to assert the principle and practice of true Christianity?"[17] On the 16th of January a letter from Shaftesbury to the editor of *The Times* praised the paper for its reports on the situation in Russia.[18]

---

[13]*Jewish Intelligence* (March 1882): 53.

[14]William Withers Ewbank, *The National Restoration of the Jews to Palestine Repugnant to the Word of God* (Liverpool: Deighton and Laughton, 1849). See Shalom Goldman, *Zeal for Zion*, 16.

[15]Yaron Perry, *British Mission to the Jews in Nineteenth Century Palestine* (London: Frank Cass, 2003), 127.

[16]For a fuller discussion see Lewis, *Origins*, 176-80. In 1858 British evangelicals took the lead in protesting the Edgardo Mortara case, in which an Italian Jewish boy was removed from his parents' home on the pretext of having been secretly baptized as a Christian. The English "Jewish Board of Deputies" publicly thanked the Evangelical Alliance and other Protestant societies for this support in this matter. See Lewis, *Origins*, 198.

[17]Edwin Hodder, *The Life and Work of the Seventh Earl of Shaftesbury, KG* (London, 1886), 3:443.

[18]Letter from the Earl of Shaftesbury to the editor, dated January 14, 1882, *The Times*, January 16, 1882, 8c.

A petition signed by a list of British notables headed by the Archbishop of Canterbury and Lord Shaftesbury calling for a public meeting was published a week later in *The Times*.[19] It took place at the Mansion House in London on February 1, 1882, and the meeting, Shaftesbury reported in his diary, turned out to be "a grand meeting, full, hearty, and enthusiastic."[20] While Shaftesbury doubted that the British government had much leverage with Russia, he was convinced that British public opinion could be influential, as it had been with Nicholas I.[21] His speech to the gathering appealed, in distinctly religious language, to the Russian emperor for the protection of Jews.

Shaftesbury also raised the matter in the House of Lords, urging the government to use its influence with the Russian government. In a letter to a friend he noted, "We had a very short, but very satisfactory, flare up on the Jews in the House of Lords. The Hebrews were in ecstasies."[22] In one of his last public speeches related to the Jews, delivered at the LSJ's annual meeting in 1882, Shaftesbury rehearsed some familiar themes: a strong denunciation of Russian persecution, and an emphasis on the Jews as the "apple of God's eye," quoting his friend Alexander McCaul: "No nation ever injured the Jews without smarting from it." Shaftesbury seemed almost more concerned about the power of anti-Semitism in Germany, which he feared far more than he did Russian anti-Semitism, and warned that "there is, in fact, a great jealousy of that wonderful people [the Jews] who are coming to the front."[23]

On February 24, 1882, another meeting was held at the National Club in London (the headquarters of the Protestant Association). The Dean of Ripon's speech made the point that "this question was pre-eminently a Protestant one. There had been times when the Jews had been harshly treated even by the Christian Church, but happily since the Reformation it had been the aim of the church to bring them to value the truths which were dear to Christians."[24] Specific concern was expressed for a group of about 220 Jewish refugees "who were desirous of emigrating to Palestine as

---

[19] *The Times*, January 23, 1882, 8a.
[20] Hodder, *Life of Shaftesbury*, 3:444.
[21] *The Times*, February 2, 1882, 4c.
[22] Hodder, *Life of Shaftesbury*, 3:444.
[23] *Jewish Intelligence* (June 1882): 150-51.
[24] *The Times*, February 25, 1882, 9e.

agriculturalists."[25] A resolution in support of this group was moved by the Rev. Mr. William Hechler,[26] and when a relief committee was formed, Shaftesbury was the president and Hechler the key activist. Shaftesbury was president of the resultant Syrian Colonisation Fund; a central figure in the movement was Mrs. Elizabeth Finn, the Hebrew-speaking widow of James Finn (longtime British consul in Jerusalem), and the daughter of Shaftesbury's old friend Alexander McCaul, the chief figure in the LSJ.

In Palestine, the LSJ was overwhelmed by the flood of desperate Russian immigrants. It sheltered many at its center in Jaffa, and in Jerusalem.[27] The LSJ missionaries responded so generously that the Jerusalem mission was close to financial collapse and had to be bailed out by the London committee.[28] In England, the LSJ established the Committee on the Persecution of the Jews in Russia and issued a public statement that expressed the hope that "the God of Israel may overrule these trials for the spiritual good of the nation still beloved for the fathers' sake."

William Henry Hechler (1845–1931) worked closely with the relief committee to resettle refugees in Palestine.[29] In 1882 he was dispatched to investigate what was happening in Russia.[30] Hechler was fluent in German, understood Jewish culture, and sympathized with the plight of the Russian Jews. Hechler had been born in Benares, India,[31] the son of a German missionary who had trained both under the Pietist leader Johann Christoph Blumhardt at the Basel Evangelical Mission Institute and then at the Church Missionary Society training college in Islington. Following service in India, Hechler's father had served from 1852 with the LSJ as a missionary to the Jews and had imparted to his son the fervor of his millennialism and especially his passion for Jewish restoration. Hechler was equally at home in British evangelical and German Pietist circles and among the British and Prussian political elite. While he was not a diplomat, he did have personal access to senior German political figures. Trained in theology in both

---

[25] *The Times*, February 25, 1882, 9e.
[26] The report in *The Times* cites him as "the Rev. Mr. Heckler" (!).
[27] *Record*, September 8, 1882.
[28] Perry, *British Mission to the Jews*, 128.
[29] For a nuanced discussion of Hechler, see Yaakov Ariel, *An Unusual Relationship: Evangelical Christians and Jews* (New York: New York University Press, 2013), 91-92.
[30] Paul C. Merkley, *The Politics of Christian Zionism 1891-1948* (London: Frank Cass, 1998), 16.
[31] Merkley, *Politics of Christian Zionism*, 11.

London and Tübingen, he served as a chaplain to Prussian troops during the Franco-Prussian War (1870–1871) and eventually settled in his father's birthplace of Baden, becoming the tutor to Prince Ludwig, the son and heir of Prince Frederick I, the Grand Duke of Baden, and of Princess Louise of Prussia, the only daughter of Kaiser Wilhelm I. Hechler developed a strong rapport with Frederick and Louise, both devout Lutheran Pietists, and imparted his restorationist vision. Prince Ludwig's death in 1876 did not end Hechler's friendship with the family. Hechler returned to England and was commissioned by the LSJ to produce a work on the Jerusalem bishopric. It appeared in 1883. When the Jerusalem bishopric fell vacant, the Prussian government was in line to name the next bishop, and Prince Frederick of Baden suggested to the emperor that Hechler should be the Prussian appointee as the next bishop in Jerusalem.[34]

In Odessa while on his 1882 visit to Russia on behalf of the aid committee, Hechler met Judah Lieb (Leon) Pinsker, a leader of the Hibbat Zion (love of Zion) movement and a pioneer in the emerging Zionist movement. In 1882 Pinsker published an appeal in German to Russian Jews titled *Autoemancipation*, one of the earliest Zionist documents. Hechler vehemently disagreed with Pinsker, who did not think that a Jewish homeland necessarily had to be located in Palestine. While in Russia, Hechler urged on Jews both religious and secular the importance of embracing Zionism.[33] The settlement experiment in Palestine promoted by Hechler eventually failed, and permission was obtained for the group to settle in Cyprus. Shaftesbury was supportive, but in the end the failed project lost him a great deal of money.[34]

Hechler was not dismayed by this failure and in 1882 published his *Die bevorstehende Rückkehr der Juden nach Palästina* (The restoration of the Jews to Palestine according to prophecy). The appointment of Hechler to the Jerusalem bishopric did not materialize because the German government decided to withdraw from the joint bishopric; in 1885 Hechler took up the position as chaplain of the British embassy in Vienna. Eleven years later, Hechler noticed a new publication in a Vienna bookstore titled

---

[34]Alex Carmel, "William Hechler: Herzl's Christian Ally," in *The First Zionist Congress in 1897—Causes, Significance, Topicality*, ed. H. Haumann (Basel: Karger, 1997), 43.
[33]Merkley, *Politics of Christian Zionism*, 16.
[34]Hodder, *Life of Shaftesbury*, 3:509.

Der Judenstaat (The Jewish state), one of the first major statements of the Zionists' case for a self-governing Jewish nation. On March 10, 1896, Hechler introduced himself to the book's author, Theodor Herzl, informing him that "as long ago as 1882, I predicted your coming to the Grand Duke of Baden. Now I am going to help you."[35] Herzl, the founding president of the World Zionist Organization, was Zionism's most effective propagandist; he regarded Hechler as eccentric but useful.

Historians have recognized how Hechler helped Herzl in his propaganda offensive.[36] As Shalom Goldman has observed, "Herzl understood something that many of his less assimilated Jewish associates did not—that the diplomatic success of the Zionist movement was dependent on the help of Christians sympathetic to Zionism."[37] Using his contacts with the Prussian royal family, Hechler introduced Herzl not only to the Grand Duke of Baden but also to the duke's nephew Kaiser Wilhelm II, the last German emperor. In a remarkably short time Herzl moved from being an obscure Jewish writer to the international stage; he was soon being heralded as someone offering a viable solution to the difficulties facing many European Jews: the establishment of a Jewish homeland.[38] Herzl convened the first World Congress of Zionists in Basel, Switzerland, in 1897. His original plan was for the congress to meet in Munich, but German rabbis of "all shades of opinion . . . objected angrily and forced the Zionists" to meet outside of Germany. Public protests followed in Germany, with the rabbis denouncing "Zionism as fanaticism, contrary to the teachings of the Jewish scriptures, and affirmed their undivided loyalty to Germany."[39] Herzl dismissed the rabbis as *Protest-rabbiner* (protesting rabbis) and with his Christian Zionist friend Hechler at his side met with the Kaiser in Istanbul and then again in Jerusalem during Wilhelm II's 1898 tour of Palestine.[40] Through the help of another Christian

[35]Merkley, *Politics of Christian Zionism*, 3. It is significant that the account of this first meeting comes to us from Herzl's diary and not from Hechler himself.

[36]Isaiah Friedman, *Germany, Turkey and Zionism, 1897–1918* (Oxford: Clarendon, 1977), 56-58, 60. See also Shalom Goldman's extended discussion of Hechler and his influence on Herzl in *Zeal for Zion*, 102-17.

[37]Goldman, *Zeal for Zion*, 93.

[38]Material adapted from author's previous work see Lewis, *Origins*, 229.

[39]Thomas Kolsky, *Jews Against Zionism: The American Council for Judaism, 1942–1948* (Philadelphia: Temple University Press, 1990), 17.

[40]Kolsky, *Jews Against Zionism*, 80.

sympathizer, Herzl obtained an audience with Abdul Hamid II, the sultan of the Ottoman Empire.[41]

As the situation in Russia deteriorated, Zionism became a live option among a minority of Western European Jews; yet even in the period from 1897 through to Israeli statehood in 1948, political Zionists were a minority group within world Jewry.[42] It was not until the mid-1890s that Zionism began to establish itself as a viable movement, and not until 1905 that the Zionists settled on Palestine as the only place where that homeland should be established.[43]

By the time of Shaftesbury's death in 1885 there was a strong belief among many pious British Protestants that the Jews were still is some sense "God's chosen people" and were destined to have a national homeland in Palestine. For many this arose out of a belief that such a national home had irrevocably been promised to them in the Bible. For many Britons this was accompanied by a sense that such a homeland was owed to the Jews due to a sense of debt because of centuries of Gentile (especially Catholic) persecution, and that it was Britain's national honor to undertake the lead in righting this historic wrong. For others the idea of a Jewish national homeland was closely linked with their understandings of biblical prophecy and the role that it would play in the unfolding of the "last days" and the return of the Messiah. No one had any idea how such a homeland could be achieved given that Palestine was an integral part of the Ottoman Empire. Small steps, however, such as helping persecuted Jews to settle in Palestine, might in a small way prepare for what was to come.

Some, like Hechler, were convinced that active efforts were needed to accomplish this end, even arguing that attempts to convert Jews to Christianity were no longer appropriate in this "Messianic Age." In 1898 Hechler wrote to a friend in Jerusalem,

> Of course, dear colleague, you look to the conversion of the Jews, but the times are changing rapidly, and it is important for us to look further and

---

[41]Professor Arminius Vanbery of Budapest was the intermediary. Goldman, *Zeal for Zion*, 19.

[42]Stuart A. Cohen, *English Zionists and British Jews: The Communal Politics of Anglo-Jewry, 1895–1920* (Princeton: Princeton University Press, 1982), 3.

[43]The British government's offer of an area of East Africa as a possible site for such a homeland had divided the Zionist movement; for a time some Zionists were willing to consider such a venue.

higher. We are now entering, thanks to the Zionist Movement, into Israel's
Messianic age. Thus, it is not a matter these days of opening all the doors of
your churches to the Jews, but rather of opening the gates to their homeland,
and of sustaining them in their work of clearing the land, and irrigating it, and
bringing water to it. All of this, dear colleague, is messianic work; all of this
the breath of the Holy Spirit announces. But first, the dry bones must come
to life, and draw together.[44]

This was not the first time that "restorationism" became disconnected from
the evangelization of the Jews, and it would certainly not be the last. Hechler,
then, was the sort of "Christian Zionist" whom Herzl and his fellow Zionists
could applaud. Hechler in his hopes for the eventual conversion of the Jews
had given up efforts to procure immediate converts. But Hechler in affirming
the nonnecessity of conversion of Jews to Christianity had, by the definition
of the term I have been using, ceased to be an evangelical. This nonproselytizing Christian Zionism might be welcome in some Jewish circles, but it
involved a critical move away from a core evangelical identity. The title of
Thomas Scott's work *The Jews a Blessing to the Nations, and Christians Bound
to Seek Their Conversion to the Saviour* (1810) is an apt summary of the evangelical view of the importance of seeking the conversion of Jews, and people
like Scott and Shaftesbury would have regarded Hechler's theological shift
unthinkable, even idolatrous, for it gave up on their central concern to see
both the restoration of the Jews to Palestine and their conversion to their
Messiah. Yet the Christian philo-Semitism and the desire for the restoration
of the Jews that nineteenth-century evangelicalism had helped to foster
could take many forms, especially when the pro-Jewish actions of Christians
met with a warm response and acknowledgment from Jews. In such conditions the Romantic influence that had contributed to its rise could eclipse
the proselytizing motive, and talk of a separate, ongoing divine covenant
with the Jews could enable some evangelicals formerly zealous in the cause
to set aside talk of conversion of Jews in the here and now, even if they did
not give up the hope of the same in the more distant future.

For Charles Simeon, Edward Bickersteth, and Lord Shaftesbury, the missiological and the prophetic emphases had come together; for Hechler they

---

[44]Merkley, *Politics of Christian Zionism*, 15-16.

came apart. Even in the 1820s Simeon had expressed concern that an over-preoccupation with prophecy drew its students away from the work of Christ in his death and resurrection (central Pauline emphases characteristic of evangelicals), away "from a doctrine which humbles, elevates, refines the soul . . . to a doctrine which fills only with vain conceits, intoxicates the imagination, alienates the brethren from each other, and by being unduly urged upon the minds of humble Christians, is doing the devil's work by wholesale."[45] Simeon, Bickersteth, and Shaftesbury were so essentially Pauline in their reading and understanding of Scripture, as were most British evangelicals, that millennial theories were always secondary and any millennial speculation that moved away from the missiological imperative of Jewish conversion was to be rejected. As Haddon Willmer has observed, "A prophetically-based philo-Semitism . . . was never basic, never provided the overall framework for most Evangelicalism—it was always derivative, like an implication of what was basic, and it was flexible and dispensable as such implications tend to be and as the change after *circa* 1860 showed."[46]

Christian Zionism appealed most to evangelicals on the margins of British national life, which makes sense of Christian Zionism's attraction to evangelicals situated on Britain's Celtic fringe—especially to Scots and Irish evangelicals who exercised a disproportionate influence in English evangelicalism in the Victorian era. Leaders of the No Popery movement such as Hugh McNeile often had strong Calvinist and Celtic roots (in his case, Irish) and at the same time were strong promoters of philo-Semitism and of Jewish Restoration. In this way these evangelicals sought to remake British identity by emphasizing British responsibilities toward the Jews: a duty both to protect them and to restore them to Palestine, linking their beliefs about Great Britain's identity and mission as Protestant Israel.

The adoption of philo-Semitic views by many British evangelicals in the nineteenth century was part of an ongoing effort at identity construction undertaken by Calvinist evangelicals in the wake of the French Revolution and the tumultuous events of the 1820s that sought to respond both to the resurgence of Roman Catholicism and the emergence of Anglo-Catholicism. This identity picked up on earlier themes that had been current in English

---

[45]Simeon quoted in David Newsome, *The Parting of Friends* (London: Murray, 1966), 11.
[46]Personal communication of Haddon Willmer to the author.

Puritanism, but was deeply influenced as well by the Romantic movement, and by the concern for the Jews prevalent among German Pietists. This emerging identity was also closely related to anti-Catholicism; the Protestant perception of the persecuting nature of the Church of Rome was a deeply ingrained and frequently reinforced perspective shared by many English Protestants. Studies of Europe's anti-Jewish past reinforced the Protestant view that identified this phenomenon with Rome's persecuting nature. The promotion of this philo-Semitic identity and the cause of Jewish restoration to a national homeland were deeply indebted to the work of a group of Jewish converts—Joseph Frey, Joseph Wolff, Philip Hirshfeld, Ridley Haim Herschell, E. S. Calman, G. W. Pieritz, and Bishop Alexander being chief among them. These converts sought to promote a Jewish national identity at a time when most European Jews were not interested in Zionism. However, these prominent converts from Judaism and their fellow evangelicals were deeply interested in the conversion of the Jewish people. Interpretations of prophecy were important in the development of Christian Zionism, but the evangelicals were more missionally minded than they were prophetically motivated —a fact that can easily be lost sight of by concentrating too much on prophetic concerns in a historical analysis of Christian Zionism.

Christian Zionism especially appealed to evangelicals whose own experience "on the margins" created an affinity for the Jews whose experience as a nation was portrayed as being on the margins. Norman Rose in his study of Gentile Zionists in the 1930s notes that often these later Gentile Zionists were characterized by their perception of a "link between the Protestant tradition and the Jewish renaissance," and especially by the parallels between Judaism and Puritanism.[47] In light of these factors, the conception of the Jews as a "people," a "nation," and the concomitant belief that Britain should endeavor to provide them with a "national home" begins to make more sense. The role of Jewish converts in enabling all of this to happen seems a great paradox when considering that the early Zionist movement itself was generally secular and irreligious. Many of the most religious Jews who worked for the creation of a Jewish national home were Jewish Christian ministers, rather than Jewish rabbis.

---

[47]Norman A. Rose, *The Gentile Zionists: A Study in Anglo-Zionist Diplomacy, 1929–1939* (London: Frank Cass, 1973), 75.

Lord Shaftesbury knew that some thought it odd that an English aristocrat should be concerned that his fellow Britons would in his words "behold this nation [the Jews] with the eyes of reverence and affection."[48] He knew that many thought him fanatical to believe so fervently in the restoration of the Jews to Palestine, and yet what he foresaw began to come to pass with the issuing of the Balfour Declaration some thirty-two years after his death. Shaftesbury, having adopted the activist Christian Zionist views of his spiritual mentor, Edward Bickersteth, had employed his skills in persuasion and his political connections to build popular support for the Balfour Declaration.

---

[48]Lord Ashley, "State and Prospects of the Jews," *Quarterly Review* 63, no. 126 (1839): 191.

8

RESTORATIONISM AND CHRISTIAN ZIONISM IN AMERICA FROM THE REVOLUTION TO 1914

[John Nelson] Darby advanced a futurist eschatology in which nothing hindered the imminent rapture of the saints. He was no restorationist, save in a radically futurist sense. Far from being a proud father, Darby would deny any connection to contemporary American Christian Zionism.[1]

ROBERT O. SMITH

CONTEMPORARY DISCUSSIONS OF American Christian Zionism often begin and end with dispensational premillennialism. This chapter problematizes that approach by arguing that Christian Zionism has deeper and older roots than this approach would suggest and that John Nelson Darby, the chief formulator of dispensationalism, was not a Christian Zionist. It explores Darby's views, tracks how they were spread, and examines how his theology was changed and adapted to become friendly to Christian Zionism.

AMERICA AND RESTORATIONISM FROM 1776 TO 1843

America, like England, experienced a surge in prophetic thinking in the 1790s with some Americans interpreting the French Revolution as a signal that America's experience of liberty and republicanism would be exported to the whole world.[2] Perhaps the Jews would soon convert and the Turks

---

[1]Robert O. Smith, *More Desired Than Our Owne Salvation: The Roots of Christian Zionism* (New York: Oxford University Press, 2013), 160.
[2]Smith, *More Desired*, 142.

be overthrown. Napoleon's invasion of the Papal States in 1798 fueled speculation about the papacy's demise and the Jews' return. As Napoleon attacked the Ottomans in Egypt in 1799, he promised to give the Holy Land to Ottoman Jews if they would fight alongside the French, but local Jews "prudently supported the Ottomans, recognizing the quixotic nature of Napoleon's grandiose plans for the Holy Land."[3]

While the postmillennial consensus continued in America, by the late nineteenth century it was being undermined by the rise of theological modernism[4] and after 1868 by the growing popularity of dispensational premillennialism. The historicist premillennialist position also attracted some Americans, most notably through Edward Bickersteth's writings, which were widely influential. Robert K. Whalen has shown that American philo-Semitism and its manifestation in Christian Zionism was in its essence an evangelical project "cut from whole cloth woven in England."[5] The best known home-grown exponent of adventism in America was William Miller (1782–1849), a Baptist farmer from upstate New York who attracted a wide following in early 1840s.[6] Miller predicted Christ would return "about the year 1843," and then when this did not occur, recalculated the date to October 22, 1844. After the "Great Disappointment," Miller was apologetic, but his movement survived and eventually became the Seventh-day Adventist Church. His adventism was retained, but apocalypticism was mixed with a Judaic-influenced Sabbatarianism and observance of Old Testament dietary and sanitary regulations.

Historicist premillennialism did not suddenly fade away in America. Bickersteth's writings continued to be very popular well after Miller's death. American adventists were spread across numerous denominations. Like their British counterparts, they did not necessarily withdraw from society. As Paul Boyer has observed, "Many Millerites saw no contradiction in

---

[3]Clifford A. Kiracofe, *Dark Crusade: Christian Zionism and US Foreign Policy* (London: L.B. Tauris, 2009), 17.

[4]Pietsch argues that postmillennialism was in serious decline well before World War I as theological liberals embraced geologic time and abandoned any apocalyptic intervention in history. B. M. Pietsch, *Dispensational Modernism* (New York: Oxford University Press, 2015), 130-31.

[5]Robert K. Whalen, "'Christians Love the Jews!' The Development of American Philo-Semitism, 1790–1860," *Religion and American Culture* 6, no. 2 (Summer, 1996): 226.

[6]Timothy P. Weber, *Living in the Shadow of the Second Coming: American Premillennialism 1875–1925* (New York: Oxford University Press, 1979), 15.

working for reform while awaiting the end. Angelina Grimke Weld, simultaneously an abolitionist, women's-rights advocate, and avid Millerite," was very much at home with this approach. Many of the key Millerites "were veterans of a variety of reforms, including antislavery, temperance and other causes,"[7] although the Millerites eventually did sever the link between themselves and politics.[8]

Part of the appeal in the American context of radical individualism was Miller's insistence on the democratization of prophetic interpretation. Miller had little formal education and taught that simple believers could investigate for themselves and use their rational powers to verify their conclusions. He saw his work through the eyes of Scottish commonsense realism and considered his approach objective and verifiable, thus affirming both "democratic inclusiveness and the rationalistic aura of the enterprise."[9] On the matter of the Jews, however, Miller stands out as a remarkable exception to the historicist premillennialist consensus. Miller rejected Jewish restoration to Palestine as incompatible with his expectation of the immediate return of Christ: there was simply not enough time for this to occur before the advent.[10] His conclusion was "the Jew has had his day."[11] In this Miller was out of step with the mainstream adventist views in nineteenth-century Britain.

The Rise of Dispensational Premillennialism in America

As suggested in the brief introduction to this chapter, many people assume that Christian Zionism began with dispensational premillennialism (a form of futurist premillennialism) and its idea of a "rapture" of the saints. Dispensationalism was popularized by the prophecy writer and leader of the "Christian Brethren" John Nelson Darby (1800–1882). This assumption is rather remarkable because Darby's own views were far from being politically supportive of Christian Zionism, and his attitudes toward the Jews as a people are complex and hardly likely to be described as advocating a

---

[7]Paul Boyer, *When Time Shall Be No More: Prophecy Belief in Modern American Culture* (Cambridge, MA: Belknap Press of Harvard University Press, 1992), 82.

[8]Smith, *More Desired*, 148-51.

[9]Boyer, *When Time*, 84.

[10]Carl Frederick Ehle Jr., "Prolegomena to Christian Zionism in America: The Views of Increase Mather and William E. Blackstone Concerning the Doctrine of the Restoration of Israel" (PhD diss., New York University, 1977), 334.

[11]Smith, *More Desired*, 150.

"teaching of love and esteem," which we have seen so many British evangelicals embraced in the nineteenth century. Many who would consider themselves to be broadly supportive of dispensationalism and hold to Darby's "secret rapture" belief and are strongly in favor of Christian Zionism have little understanding of what Darby actually said. In fact, dispensationalism has morphed and evolved in the two centuries since Darby began to popularize his views.

Both postmillennialism and historicist premillennialism were strongly restorationist. Dispensational premillennialism—the futurist option that is now far better known—was originally developed by Irish Anglicans associated with Trinity College, Dublin, although its most important systematic popularizer was Darby.[12] His version had its own unique characteristics—particularly related to the idea of "eras" or dispensations, a strong dichotomy between Israel (the Jews) and the church, and an understanding of how to read Scripture "literally." Darby was a prolific writer, but there was little development of his thinking over time. His most ardent apologist acknowledges that "Darby's writings reveal a surprising degree of consistency in his thinking, with very little evidence of any substantial change after 1829."[13] Darby understood the books of Daniel and Revelation to be describing future events rather than the history of the church.

UNDERSTANDING DARBY'S THEOLOGY

Ernest Sandeen, the American historian who pioneered the academic study of dispensationalism with *The Roots of Fundamentalism* in 1970, observed of Darby,

> The will of God seldom blurred before [Darby's] vision. . . . Most unfortunately for his historical reputation, the clarity with which he perceived the will of

---

[12]Darby was from a well-connected and moneyed Anglo-Irish background. Born in London in 1800, he was educated at the elite Westminster School, and studied at Trinity College, Dublin, graduating in 1819; he then trained for the law and was called to the Irish bar in 1822. He soon abandoned the law and was ordained to the Anglican ministry, becoming a dedicated and effective evangelist among the Irish poor. He soon became disillusioned by the close alliance of the state church (the [Anglican] Church of Ireland) with the British government, which he felt was hurting his evangelism. Seeking a more authentic form of Christianity, he left Anglicanism to become a key figure in a small but highly influential group known as the Plymouth Brethren, or simply "the Christian Brethren."

[13]Paul Richard Wilkinson, *For Zion's Sake: Christian Zionism and the Role of John Nelson Darby*, Studies in Evangelical History and Thought (Milton Keynes, UK; Paternoster, 2007), 96.

God was never matched by his ability to write it down. He left a massive set of *Collected Writings* which are almost uniformly unintelligible.[14]

Yet if one is to understand dispensationalism's relationship with Christian Zionism, one has to engage in a detailed study of Darby's theology. Central to this was the Abrahamic covenant of Genesis 12, but his take on the centrality of the Jews is perhaps remarkable but parallels the emphases of Thomas Brightman's historicist postmillennial position discussed in chapter three and reminds one of Andrew Crome's observation about Brightman's approach to Jews and Gentiles: "God had separate earthly plans for each. Even in the millennial period, they would remain radically different. Indeed, the millennium would be a period of Jewish dominion over the earth."[15] Crucial to Darby's approach is the idea that each dispensation is governed by different rules; each dispensation involves "a new test of the natural man" involving commandments and promises.[16]

What is crucially important is that his whole theology revolves around the idea that the Jews are eternally God's earthly people and they will inherit an earthly kingdom, and that Gentile Christians are God's "heavenly people" and can expect a heavenly inheritance.[17] Darby held that this distinction will endure for eternity—with Gentile Christians ruling spiritually in heaven and Jewish believers ruling physically on the earth. Darby frequently cited 2 Timothy 2:15: "Study to shew thyself approved unto God, a workman that needeth not to be ashamed, rightly dividing the word of truth" (KJV). For dispensationalists the phrase "rightly dividing the word of truth" "meant more than keeping one's dispensations straight. At all costs, the dispensationalists insisted, one must maintain the distinction between the two peoples of God."[18] Cyrus I. Scofield published an influential tract in 1888 that

---

[14]Ernest Sandeen, *The Roots of Fundamentalism: British and American Millenarianism 1800–1930* (Chicago: University of Chicago Press, 1970), 31.

[15]Andrew Crome, *Christian Zionism and English National Identity, 1600–1850* (Cham, Switzerland: Palgrave Macmillan, 2018), 53.

[16]Pietsch, *Dispensational Modernism*, 141.

[17]As Paul Wilkinson, a modern defender of Darby, has observed, "This distinction between Israel as the earthly people of God, and the Church as the heavenly people of God, is foundational to Darby's eschatology and was, in his mind, 'the hinge upon which the subject and the understanding of Scripture turns.' It would prove to be 'the mainspring' of his thought." Wilkinson, *For Zion's Sake*, 102.

[18]Weber, *Shadow*, 17-18.

outlined the interpretive method titled *Rightly Dividing the Word of Truth*.[19] Given all the focus in prophetic literature on the millennium, it is surprising that Darby denied that Christians would experience it; he insisted on a sharp dichotomy between this world where the millennium would happen (with Jews at the center of that story) and heaven (where Christians would be).

Darby's approach divided God's dealings with the Jews into six eras, or "dispensations," as he called them, although his "dispensational scheme is not easily extracted from his writings."[20] In each dispensation God had tested his people Israel, and in each test, Israel had failed. Darby's sixth and final dispensation ended with the rejection of Christ by his own people. In response, God put his dealings with the Jews on hold during the church age—he has simply stopped dealing with them—and offered the gospel to the Gentiles, who are promised not the earthly inheritance of a physical kingdom reserved for the Jews but a "heavenly" inheritance that would be spiritually possessed.[21] During the church age, God's dealings with Israel have been paused, or placed on hold; Darby refers to "the church age" as a "parenthesis" in God's dealings with Israel. For Darby the "church age" is a mystery and "mentioned only incidentally, if at all in the prophecies of the Bible."[22] This church age must come to a distinct end before God starts dealing with the Jews again. In his understanding the prophetic passages of Scripture are concerned only with the Jews.

One of the most important prophetic passages that Darby dealt with is Daniel 9:24-27, which speaks of seventy weeks. Dispensationalists following Darby understood the prophet to be talking about seventy weeks, and with each day intended to represent a year (the day-year theory again). This indicated to Darby that the prophet was talking about seventy weeks of seven days, which equaled 490 years. If God had allowed Daniel's prophecy to play out, Christ would have returned some seven years later (after the end of the seventieth week) following his death. To resolve the problem, Darby posited that because of the Jews' rejection of the Messiah, God put his dealings with

---

[19]Pietsch, *Dispensational Modernism*, 184.
[20]Wilkinson, *For Zion's Sake*, 100. Pietsch notes that Scofield arrived at seven dispensations, others writers at three, five, or twelve. Pietsch, *Dispensational Modernism*, 144.
[21]This is not to suggest that Darby eschewed the evangelization of Jews.
[22]Ehle, "Prolegomena," 228.

them on hold and postponed the final week indefinitely.[23] Thus according to Darby, Daniel's seventy weeks are all about the Jews and do not concern the church. As Darby wrote of the church, "We are properly nowhere, save in the extraordinary suspension of prophetic testimony, or period, which comes in between the sixty-ninth and seventieth week of Daniel."[24] The first sixty-nine weeks in which God dealt with the Jews ended with the creation of the church on the Day of Pentecost in the giving of the Holy Spirit, and the seventieth week will resume with "the rapture." The church age is thus bracketed between the sixty-ninth and seventieth week and is not the focus of the prophecies. The distinct end of the Christian era thus occurs at "the rapture," when God will resume focusing on the rescue of his "earthly people" (the Jews) and establishing his earthly kingdom during the seventieth week (or final seven-year period).[25] In a sense, the idea of the rapture is required by the logic of Darby's emphasis on God only dealing with one people at a time. The Gentile believers have to be removed so that God can resume his program and deal with the Jews and set up Christ as King in Zion.

In Ephesians 2:12 Paul insists that Christ broke down the wall of separation between Gentile and Jews. Darby reconstructed it and endowed it with an eternal permanence, for he understood their separate existences as different people as core to his understanding of the Bible, arguing "that as long as the Church believed that she had replaced Israel in the purposes of God, she would remain blind to the 'blessed hope.' Titus 2:13."[26] Darby did not believe that the church and Israel were separate but equal, or that salvation was available apart from the work of Christ. However, he sees Jews as forever separate, with Jews eternally ruling on earth and the Christian saints ruling in heaven. In a way similar to the historicist premillennialists, Darby sees the Jews as the superior and eternally elect people of God and that this

---

[23]Weber, *Shadow*, 17.

[24]Wilkinson, *For Zion's Sake*, 114. Ehle comments, "Whereas earlier Christians had commonly interpreted these weeks as being contiguous as well as successive, the futurists conceived of the seventieth week as separated from the successive sixty-nine weeks, to transpire at an undeterminable time in the future following the rapture of the church from the world." Ehle, "Prolegomena," 282.

[25]The use of the term *rapture* is not original to Darby: Increase Mather used the term in his *Mystery of Israel's Salvation* (1699), where he speaks of "*the rapture of the Saints into the air* to meet Christ." Smith, *More Desired*, 127. It should be noted that Mather's rapturing of the saints is quite different in purpose from that of Darby's. I am indebted to Andrew Crome for this observation.

[26]Wilkinson, *For Zion's Sake*, 104.

will become evident when Christ, having returned, begins to deal with them again, and part of this will involve their restoration to Palestine.

The idea that God dealt differently with people in different "dispensations" gave rise to the term *dispensationalism*. The Old Testament prophecies were for the Jews and were to be read "literally" because they are addressed to God's earthly people; Jews would physically be restored to Palestine and rule there. But New Testament promises to Christians were addressed to a "spiritual" people and were to be read symbolically. Darby was anxious to avoid the common tendency of seeing Old Testament promises to Israel as being fulfilled in the church and used the language of "literal" and "symbolic" to distinguish between the ("earthly" or "literal") promises to the Jews and the ("heavenly" or "spiritual") promises to the church.[27] As Martin Spence has observed: "It was a highly idiosyncratic, and amazingly successful thesis, although not without a number of significant critics, not least from within the Brethren movement itself."[28]

Thus the church's destiny was not "earthly" or "literal," but rather "spiritual" and "heavenly." As Darby himself observed, "The one proper hope of the Church has no more to do with the world than Christ has, who is in heaven."[29] Or again, "Our calling is on high. Events are on earth. Prophecy does not relate to heaven. The Christian's hope is not a prophetic subject at all."[30] The church had no place in God's original plans and only takes center stage because of the Jews' unfaithfulness. As one of dispensationalism's popularizers in the United States, C. H. Macintosh, explained, "It is vain to look into the prophetic page in order to find the church's position, her calling, her hope. They are not there. It is entirely out of place for the church to be occupied with dates and historic events [as the historicists were]. . . . The Christian must never lose sight of the fact he belongs to heaven."[31]

As a dispensational premillennialist, Darby—like Edward Irving and the historicist premillennialists—believed in the imminent personal return of Christ. The postmillennialists, by contrast, could "never expect to be alive

---

[27]Martin Spence, *Heaven on Earth: Reimagining Time and Eternity in Nineteenth-Century British Evangelicalism* (Eugene, OR: Pickwick, 2015), 119.
[28]Spence, *Heaven on Earth*, 120.
[29]Quoted in Spence, *Heaven on Earth*, 119.
[30]Darby quoted in Sandeen, *Roots*, 63.
[31]Weber, *Shadow*, 21.

at the time of Christ's return since it was always at least one thousand years in the future" and were "therefore not greatly concerned with talking about Christ's return in any more than general terms."[32] A key insight came to Darby while recuperating from an injury in 1827: "I saw that the Christian, having his place in heaven, has nothing to wait for save the coming of the Saviour, in order to be set, in fact, in the glory which is already his position 'in Christ.'"[33] Darby insisted that "there is no event, I repeat, between us and heaven."[34]

The historicists had posited that the national conversion of the Jews and their return to their homeland were to be labored for, as events that would occur before his return. Once these were accomplished Christ would return and usher in a new world—heaven would come to earth—and Christians would rule with Christ on earth. Initially, most futurist premillennialists had expected the rapture to occur at the second coming of Christ, at the end of the period of tribulation.[35] Darby agreed with the imminent return of Christ, but conceived of his return in a very different way from the historicists or other futurists. In effect, he argued that there were two "returns" of Christ and that the first one was imminent, but its purpose was not to establish his kingdom on earth in the millennium. Rather it was to snatch away Christians who had been looking for his coming and take them to their eternal spiritual home in heaven. This is another of the innovations that Darby popularized. For Darby, the hope for the church was not a glorious future in the millennium that the historicists looked forward to, but his expectation was that the church would soon be taken away in an "any-moment rapture" to enjoy their heavenly, spiritual inheritance and not an earthly inheritance in the millennium. One day, very soon, the true Christians would simply disappear from the earth. Christ would return to earth later in a public second coming along the lines of Matthew 24. The distinction between these two events is crucial to Darby's doctrine, as he insisted: "The church's joining Christ has nothing to do with Christ's appearing or coming to earth."[36] Or, put more succinctly, "At the rapture, they said,

---

[32]Spence, *Heaven on Earth*, 46-47.
[33]Darby to August Tholuck, quoted in Sandeen, *Roots*, 33.
[34]Smith, *More Desired*, 139.
[35]Weber, *Shadow*, 21.
[36]Sandeen, *Roots*, 63.

Christ will come *for* his saints, and at the second coming, he will come *with* his saints."[37]

Thus, instead of heaven coming to earth with Christ's return (as the historicists maintained), Darby taught that Christ's second coming would be preceded by "the rapture" and "that the unfulfilled biblical prophecies must all wait upon the rapture of the church."[38] Following the rapture, there would be a seven-year period of tribulation (Daniel's "seventieth week"), which would bring dreadful suffering to the earth. During this time the antichrist will be revealed; he will promise peace and security and will dupe the Jews in their newly restored state of Israel, pledging to protect them. He will then show his true colors and demand to be worshiped as divine. To secure his power he will terrorize those who oppose him; during this time (known as "the time of Jacob's trouble") there will be a mass conversion of the Jews to Christianity. At the end of the period of tribulation, nations from the four corners of the earth will attempt to destroy God's people (the Jews) and converge on the valley of Armageddon in northern Israel but will be defeated by Christ, who will return with his previously raptured saints. On his return, Christ will vindicate those who had confessed him and set up his thousand-year kingdom. During these thousand years the prophecies concerning Israel will be literally fulfilled, with a Jewish kingdom ruling the world. Temple worship with daily blood sacrifices will be restored, and Jesus as king will rule from Jerusalem, exercising Jewish control of the world. "Thus all the prophecies originally intended for Christ's first advent (before the Jewish rejection had forced their postponement) will be fulfilled at the second."[39] But at the end of the thousand years there will be a great rebellion, which will be a final showdown between God and the forces of Satan. There will be a final defeat of Satan, then two judgments: the judgment of the world and a judgment of the saints. Thereafter there will be everlasting peace and harmony on earth (ruled by the Jews) and in heaven (ruled by the Christian saints).

Another innovation that caused consternation in Protestant circles was Darby's teaching that the pope was not the antichrist. Many of his contemporaries were suspicious of any futurist scheme of eschatology because

---

[37]Weber, *Shadow*, 21.
[38]Sandeen, *Roots*, 63.
[39]Weber, *Shadow*, 23.

futurism had long been the favored Roman Catholic approach and was popular among Anglican Tractarians.[40] There had been a Protestant consensus since the Reformation that the papacy as an institution (and sometimes also the Turk) was the antichrist (or perhaps Rome was one of the ugly beasts of the book of Revelation). Darby argued that the antichrist was an individual who would arise during the great tribulation to fight against God. The idea of a personal antichrist instead of the papacy as antichrist was regarded by many as strange and objectionable. Many Protestants thought that Darby was soft on Catholicism and was letting the papacy off the prophetic hook. However, given his Irish Protestant background Darby was strongly anti-Catholic.

A third innovation was the rejection of the day-year theory when it came to calculating the 1,260 days of Revelation 11:1-3. Darby used the day-year theory with regard to the 70 weeks of Daniel, but when dealing with the 1,260 days of Revelation 13:3, he argued that they should be interpreted as 24-hour days. The two time periods of Revelation 13:2 and Revelation 13:3 represented for him a total of 7 literal years (3.5 and 3.5), which fit into his understanding of the seventieth week of Daniel. The 3.5 years are described in Revelation 13:2 as 42 months and the second 3.5 years as 1,260 days (a prophetic month being understood as 30 days, thus 42 months × 30 = 1,260 days).

The Reception of Dispensationalism

As observed earlier, dispensationalism became increasingly popular in Britain from the late 1850s as the Brethren movement (which had begun among the social elite) moved down the social scale in the wake of the 1859 Prayer Meeting Revival that began in the United States in about 1857 but hit British shores somewhat later. However, it grew especially rapidly in the 1870s after the huge disappointment experienced by the historicists in the late 1860s, when Christ had failed to appear on schedule.[41] By the 1920s the historicist position had been overshadowed by Darby's futurist views, both in Britain and America.

---

[40]Sandeen, *Roots*, 39n63.

[41]The only major evangelical figure who seems to stand out as a historicist writer in the late nineteenth century was Henry Grattan Guinness, grandson of Arthur Guinness, the wealthy Irish brewer.

Darby journeyed seven times to Canada and the United States between 1862 and 1877, residing in those two countries for about seven years.[42] He also spent considerable time in Switzerland, Italy, France, Germany, Holland, New Zealand, and Australia. Through him and through "Prophetic Bible Conferences" held in the 1870s and beyond, this new eschatology eventually came to characterize much of conservative American Protestantism, reaching denominations like the Presbyterians and other Calvinist-oriented groups, including many American Baptists. Dispensationalism and Christian Zionism—in Britain and America—were both largely restricted to Calvinist and Reformed evangelicals and had little appeal to the Methodists. Evangelical societies aimed at the evangelization of the Jews by 1900 were almost all Calvinist and Reformed in their theological rootage.

The summer Bible conference begun in 1875 and held near Niagara Falls, Ontario, set the pattern for the prophetic Bible conferences.[43] Conservative evangelicals gathered for two weeks each summer at the Niagara conferences to hear doctrine preached and confirmed. Dispensationalists quickly became dominant in the conference leadership. In 1878 the conference produced the "Niagara Creed," a statement of faith that was strongly premillennial and affirmed the essentials that many felt were being questioned by liberal revisionists whom they felt were undermining traditional doctrines. The influence of J. C. Ryle (from 1880 Anglican bishop of Liverpool) can be clearly discerned in these efforts. The published papers of the 1878 conference began with his "Pre-millenarian Creed." Only divine intervention could remedy the contemporary situation, and Ryle warned Christians that they should "expect as little as possible from churches, or governments, under the present dispensation."[44] Although prophetic writers could be bitterly anticapitalist and antisocialist at the same time, many expected little from social reform or attempts to set things right. As Boyer writes, "Jesus and the apostles were not reformers, noted a premillennial leader, so Christians ought 'not attempt in this age the work which Christ has reserved for the next.'"[45]

---

[42]Sandeen, *Roots*, 71.
[43]On the origins of the Bible conference movement see Pietsch, *Dispensational Modernism*, 45-52.
[44]Boyer, *When Time*, 92.
[45]Boyer, *When Time*, 95-96.

Reuben A. Torrey, who worked alongside Dwight L. Moody before becoming a leading figure at Moody Bible Institute and eventually at the Bible Institute of Los Angeles, expressed the dispensational premillennial attitude when "he claimed a premillennial doctrine of the second coming was the ultimate antidote for all infidelity and the impregnable bulwark against liberalism and false cults."[46] Dispensationalism was becoming an identity marker of an important and growing section of "conservative" Protestants— although as Brendan Pietsch and Matthew Avery Sutton have argued the movement in many ways was not conservative but rather "deeply grounded in and reflective of the modernist intellectual currents of their era. While they came to describe their approach as 'conservative' in contrast to modernist methods, there was little that was conservative or traditional about it."[47] Pietsch's book *Dispensational Modernism* argues that "it was not the specific form of premillennial theology that made dispensationalism compelling in America, but its modernist epistemic assumptions."[48]

James H. Brookes (1830–1897), the pastor of a large Presbyterian church in St. Louis, Missouri, has been called "the father of American dispensationalism."[49] Brookes likely met Darby in St. Louis when he preached in Brookes's church, although the significance of Darby's influence on Brookes is debated.[50] Brookes's most popular book was *Maranatha: Or the Lord Cometh* (1874), and his later *I Am Coming* (ca. 1890) rehearsed the same themes. Through his Bible classes, his leadership in the annual Niagara Bible Conference from 1875 until his death, and his many books, as well as his editorship from 1875 until 1897 of *The Truth or Testimony for Christ*, a magazine dedicated to spreading the dispensational gospel, Brookes was a

---

[46]Weber, *Shadow*, 28.

[47]Matthew Avery Sutton, *American Apocalypse: A History of Modern Evangelicalism* (Cambridge, MA: Harvard University Press, 2014), 16.

[48]Pietsch, *Dispensational Modernism*, 9. Pietsch argues that "there were broad, aspirational movements within American Protestantism that placed profound faith in the power of taxonomic and engineering methods to produce confidence in religious knowledge," which helped to give rise to dispensationalism's approach that was fixated on method. Pietsch, *Dispensational Modernism*, 43.

[49]Kiracofe, *Dark Crusade*, 64.

[50]See Pietsch, *Dispensational Modernism*, 215n10. Pietsch notes that Carl Sanders found that Brookes was more influenced by James Robinson Graves, a figure in the American Baptist Landmark movement, and that Brookes displayed little influence attributable to Darby. See Carl E. Sanders II, *The Premillennial Faith of James Brookes: Reexamining the Roots of American Dispensationalism* (Lanham, MD: University Press of America, 2001).

central figure in the late nineteenth-century prophecy movement in America. Pietsch argues that it was Brookes more than anyone else who successfully promoted a new Brethren approach to Scripture that was known as "conversational Bible reading" that worked on the basis of "collecting and organizing Biblical passages according to thematic developments," rather than expositing a single passage of Scripture. His *Bible Reading on the Second Coming of Christ* (1877) brought the approach to a wide audience. Brookes was, "in many respects, the key bridge between Brethren Bible readings and the dispensational hermeneutics that would develop over the next few decades."[51] And it was to Brookes that Cyrus I. Scofield turned after his evangelical conversion in 1879, a man who would become one of the most important purveyors of dispensationalism in the twentieth century.[52]

In 1878 the first of a series of prophetic conferences known as the American Bible and Prophetic Conference was held in New York City. Others followed: in Chicago in 1886; Allegheny, Pennsylvania, in 1895; Boston in 1901; Chicago again in 1914; and Philadelphia and New York in 1918.[53] The dispensationalists had found both their voice and a new urban platform. Even by the turn of the century, however, it is probably the case that premillennialists "were still a small minority within conservative evangelicalism" in America, but their influence was growing steadily.[54] Pietsch argues that the "conference-goers saw themselves not as a fringe, antimodern, belligerent conservative movement, but concerned custodians of mainstream Protestant ideas and clerical authority."[55] The 1878 conference attenders included many with graduate theological degrees; the tone was irenic, the scholarship learned, and there was no concern expressed about liberal theology. "Neither Darby nor his separatistic impulses were in attendance. Darby's works were not cited alongside those of the German scholars so evident in the speeches."[56]

[51]Pietsch, *Dispensational Modernism*, 103.

[52]Timothy P. Weber, *On the Road to Armageddon: How Evangelicals Became Israel's Best Friend* (Grand Rapids, MI: Baker Academic, 2004), 39.

[53]Weber, *Shadow*, 28. Sutton acknowledges the difficulties in estimating the size of the movement and tracks the circulation figures of the leading premillennial journals. Sutton, *American Apocalypse*, 26-27.

[54]Weber, *Shadow*, 29.

[55]Pietsch, *Dispensational Modernism*, 46.

[56]Pietsch, *Dispensational Modernism*, 50.

Much of premillennialism's growth was related to the Bible School movement, which expanded rapidly in the 1880s and was strongly influenced by millenarian teaching.[57] Another important means of its spread were the conferences organized by Dwight L. Moody to promote foreign missions; they did much to motivate missionary volunteers with the "faith missions" and to some extent influenced the Student Volunteer Movement.[58] The emerging fundamentalist movement was a broad and diverse trans-denominational conservative coalition in which dispensational premillennialists eventually made common cause with others, like the Reformed theologians associated with Princeton Seminary, who were amillennial, and with figures like William Jennings Bryan, whose background was Presbyterian and who was vaguely postmillennialist in his orientation.

Dwight L. Moody (1837–1899), the late nineteenth-century revivalist, encountered Darby's teaching in 1872, when he visited Edinburgh and his conversion to dispensationalism brought it prestige and did much to increase its popularity in America.[59] But Moody's embrace of premillennialism did not make him a Christian Zionist—just as it did not make Darby a Christian Zionist. In 1877 Moody commented in a sermon,

> Now I can't find any place in the Bible where it tells me to wait for signs of the coming of the millennium, as the return of the Jews, and such like; but it tells me to look for the coming of the Lord; to watch for it; to be ready at midnight to meet him, like those five wise virgins. The trump of God may be sounded, for anything we know, before I finish this sermon; at any rate we are told that he will come as a thief in the night, and at an hour when many look not for him.[60]

Moody's attitude remains characteristic of many of the Plymouth Brethren down to today; they look for Christ's return and rejoice in the return of the Jews (although they may be surprised that it has happened before the rapture), but stand aloof from the activism of the aggressive, politically engaged Christian Zionists.

While few Protestant seminary professors by 1919 were premillennialists, virtually all of the major American evangelists were, including W. J. Erdman,

---

[57]On the rise of the Bible schools see Yaakov Ariel, *An Unusual Relationship: Evangelical Christians and Jews* (New York: New York University Press, 2013), 75-77.

[58]For a discussion of the prophecy conferences see Ariel, *Unusual Relationship*, 68-73.

[59]On Moody's complicated relationship with the Jews see Ariel, *Unusual Relationship*, 63-67.

[60]W. H. Daniels, *Moody: His Words, Work and Workers* (New York: Nelson & Phillips, 1877), 472.

J. Wilbur Chapman, Reuben A. Torrey, and Billy Sunday. "Belief in the imminent second coming of Jesus Christ gave revivalists a valuable and effective weapon in the war for souls."[61] Time was short; Christ's sudden rapture of his saints might cut off the opportunity for salvation. As Torrey put it, "The common argument today for immediate repentance and acceptance of Jesus Christ is that you may die at any second. That is not the Bible argument. The Bible argument is, 'Be ye ready, for in such an hour as you think not the Son of Man cometh.' Are you ready?"[62]

A huge factor in dispensationalism's growing popularity in America was the *Scofield Reference Bible* (1909, revised 1917), whose explanatory notes "promised the authority of expert interpretations to *any* reader"[63] and spread dispensationalism to a wide audience.[64] Its "particular genius . . . lay not in its prophecy predictions, but in its ability to navigate the tensions between interpretive populism and expertise."[65] Scofield, a convert of Brookes, was ultimately to have more influence in spreading dispensationalism than his mentor. His reference Bible has been judged by Timothy Weber as "the most significant premillennialist publication in the twentieth century"[66] and by James Barr as "perhaps the most important single document in all fundamentalist literature."[67] Counterintuitively, Pietsch makes the argument that "the success of a dispensational product like the *Scofield Reference Bible* came not because it was dispensational but because it was modernist" in its methods and approach and fit the spirit of the age far more than its promoters realized.[68] But he also observes that "an unexpected consequence of the success of the *Scofield Reference Bible*'s interpretive enabling was that 'dispensationalism' slipped out from under the control of the scholarly clerical networks that birthed it."[69] In the late twentieth century, the writings of Hal Lindsey and his *Late Great Planet Earth* and the *Left*

---

[61]Weber, *Shadow*, 52.

[62]Torrey quoted by Weber, *Shadow*, 55.

[63]Pietsch, *Dispensational Modernism*, 174.

[64]For a discussion of Scofield and his Bible see Ariel, *Unusual Relationship*, 73-74, and Pietsch, *Dispensational Modernism*, chap. 7.

[65]Pietsch, *Dispensational Modernism*, 174.

[66]Weber, *Armageddon*, 39.

[67]James Barr, *Fundamentalism* (Philadelphia: Westminster, 1978), 45.

[68]Pietsch, *Dispensational Modernism*, 15.

[69]Pietsch, *Dispensational Modernism*, 177.

Behind series of end-times novels contributed to its ongoing popularity in the United States.

The dispensationalists differed from the historicist premillennialists in their attitudes to the notion of Jewish restoration to Palestine. The historicists believed that Jewish conversion and restoration would happen before Christ's return. But Darby did not expect the Jews would return to the land until after the rapture, during the period of tribulation.[70] He believed that during the period of tribulation the Jews will make a pact with the antichrist, who will arise within a revived Roman Empire. Christ when he returns will defeat the antichrist, secure the land of Israel for the Jews, and enable their return. "While historicist premillennialists agreed with Darby and his followers that the material promises made to the nation of Israel should not be spiritualized, they resisted the notion that there were therefore two peoples of God and two sets of promises."[71] For the historicists there was one hope for both Jews and Christians: a literal, earthly one. For Darby, the Christian hope was heavenly, the Jewish hope was an earthly, "literal" one.

One other sharp contrast between Darby's futurist and the historicist brand of premillennialism was Darby's attitude to the world in general, and to politics in particular. The historicists saw God working progressively in all of history; Darby insisted on quite the opposite—that God distinctly acts suddenly and cataclysmically in judgment. Human effort was of no ultimate consequence; human institutions—including the Christian church—were in apostasy and ruin. True believers should withdraw into small gatherings of individual believers rather than remain in the state churches of Protestantism (which the historicists strongly supported). They should avoid politics altogether and not even vote because to do so would be to signal one's allegiance to the material world and entangle oneself with its evil. Brookes, who promoted Darby's theology in the United States, shared this view of politics. In 1880 he cautioned, "Well would it be if the children of God were to keep aloof from the whole defiling scene. . . . [We] can do more for the country . . . by prayer and godly walk than by being 'unequally yoked together with unbelievers.'" If believers were "alive to Christ," they would be

---

[70]Smith, *More Desired*, 254.
[71]Spence, *Heaven on Earth*, 121.

dead to the world and thus avoid the voting booth because, as Brookes put it, "dead men do not vote."[72]

This view stands in sharp contrast to the social activism and political engagement that characterized the historicist premillennialists, as symbolized by Lord Shaftesbury and by many of the historicist premillennialists associated with Millerism in the United States. It also represents a clear break from pre–Civil War revivalism that was socially engaged, and strongly reformist, inspired in large measure by postmillennial optimism. Ernest Lee Tuveson in his *Redeemer Nation: The Idea of America's Millennial Role* argues that the popularity of America's millennial role reached its apogee around the time of the American Civil War and that "American secular millennialism enjoyed a final efflorescence . . . in the exalted rhetoric with which Woodrow Wilson expressed the nation's war aims in 1917, and in Wilson's doomed campaign to bring the United States into the League of Nations."[73] But while some premillennialists followed Darby (and Scofield) in advocating cultural withdrawal, this picture has been overdrawn. Matthew Avery Sutton has shown that not all premillennialists followed this reasoning. Some of the most popular evangelists—Moody and James Gray, the long-term dean of Moody Bible Institute, A. G. Dixon, J. Wilbur Chapman, and Billy Sunday—remained engaged with social questions and urged Christians to work for the betterment, not the abandonment, of society. Paradoxically they could embrace "the call to exercise influence in politics and culture as aggressively as possible while preparing the world for the oncoming apocalypse."[74]

How, then, does one account for the appeal of dispensational premillennialism to American evangelicals and for its alleged role in the rise of a politically active Christian Zionism in the United States when Darby himself distinctly taught against the expectation that the Jews would return to Palestine in this dispensation? Robert O. Smith's observation is important: "The popularity of dispensational doctrine among American Christians did not depend on Darby alone. His biblical interpretations and theological positions were developed from the same Judeo-centric foundation that had

---

[72]Quoted in Weber, *Shadow*, 93.
[73]Boyer, *When Time*, 229.
[74]Sutton, *American Apocalypse*, 40.

shaped American identity and vocation."[75] Darby drew on elements that had been in the American context since its founding, and the Americans were happy to take aspects of Darby's teaching while discarding others, such as his separatism, his doctrine of the ruin of Christendom, his disdain of politics, his objections to the practices of revivalism, and his lack of enthusiasm for Christian Zionist political efforts. The Plymouth Brethren movement associated with Darby did not flourish in America, but many of Darby's ideas were appropriated, modified, and popularized. As Ernest Sandeen has aptly summarized, "Although not willing to admit their affiliations with his denominational views, Americans raided Darby's treasuries and carried off his teachings as their own."[76]

This transformation was facilitated by the fact that Darby's writings were ponderous, confusing, and therefore difficult to understand. Darby's thought was not original to himself; he adapted from a number of sources.[77] His writings were open to further adaptation, revision, and modification in the hands of his interpreters. As Timothy Weber has argued, "Premillennialists are highly adaptable people" who "can combine their view of the end times with longstanding notions of America's millennial role."[78] Sandeen has argued that Darby's notion of different dispensations, the idea of the church age as a sort of parenthesis in salvation history, and the doctrine of the rapture were kept, while Darby's advocacy of separation from traditional churches was not: "The Americans took what they wanted from his theological bag but refused to forsake their positions with the denominations."[79] But much of his appeal in America came from his apparent devotion to Scripture and the seriousness with which he seemed to treat it, to his ability to make sense of it for people by his literal approach, which "appeared to take the Bible more seriously than the developing modernist approaches."[80] His readers particularly appreciated "his doctrine of grace ('our standing in Christ') and his doctrine of the secret rapture ('the hope of our calling')."[81]

---

[75]Smith, *More Desired*, 153.
[76]Sandeen, *Roots*, 102.
[77]Peter Lee quoted in Smith, *More Desired*, 259.
[78]Weber, *Shadow*, 226, 237, quoted in Smith, *More Desired*, 161.
[79]Sandeen, *Roots*, 101.
[80]Smith, *More Desired*, 266.
[81]Sandeen, *Roots*, 101.

Following Darby, Pietsch argues, the dispensationalists did not simply restate arguments for commonsense induction but rather "became self-trained experts at using internal literary structures of the Bible—numerical constructs, typological themes, and inter-textual references—to reveal the 'scientific' meaning of Scripture."[82] In an age when Americans thought that "the solutions to religious doubts and social problems lay with scientific knowledge," this approach was attractive.[83] The mysteries of Scripture could be unlocked by believers who, under the guidance of the Holy Spirit, "spent years in careful, comparative study of the Bible," employed the proper methods, appreciated the internal coherence of Scripture, and were able to perceive the meaning encoded in "systems of intertextual references, particularly numerical sequences, types and antitypes, literary analogical figures, theological themes, and other intentional ordered systems."[84] It is easy to dismiss the appeal of dispensationalism as the desperate creed of the disinherited, but this was clearly not the case. As Ian Rennie has shown, "Dispensationalism attracted some of the most outstanding evangelicals of the day—and some of the wealthiest."[85]

DISPENSATIONALISM AND JEWISH EVANGELISM

Both historicist premillennialists and postmillennialists had embraced Jewish evangelism. The American dispensationalists also embraced this task enthusiastically, modeling their approaches on German and British efforts—not, however, in the expectation that large numbers of Jews would be converted, but that some Jews would be spared the "time of Jacob's trouble" and lay the groundwork so that there would be a group of as yet unbelieving Jews prepared by the work of Christian evangelists for their role in the end times. At the beginning of the tribulation following the rapture of Christians, some 144,000 Jews (12,000 from every tribe—Revelation 7) would be converted— but the groundwork for their conversion would be the fruit of seeds sown before the rapture. As Yaakov Ariel has written, "It was necessary that there

---

[82]Pietsch, *Dispensational Modernism*, chap. 4.

[83]Pietsch, *Dispensational Modernism*, 96.

[84]Pietsch, *Dispensational Modernism*, 97-98.

[85]Ian S. Rennie, "Nineteenth Century Roots," in *Dreams, Visions and Oracles: The Layman's Guide to Biblical Prophecy*, ed. Carl Edwin Armerding and W. Ward Gasque (Grand Rapids, MI: Baker, 1977), 56.

should be 144,000 Jewish persons who would possess the knowledge of the Gospel (though they have not accepted it), so that they could fulfill their role whenever the rapture might come and the Great Tribulation begin."[86]

Ernst F. Stroeter, who collaborated closely with Arno C. Gaebelein in the Hope of Israel mission in Chicago in the 1890s, argued that the approach to the Jews by the nondispensational missions was responsible for the Jews' un-responsiveness to the Christian message. Ariel summarizes Stroeter's argument made at the prophetic conference in Allegheny, Pennsylvania, in 1895:

> It was only natural that the Jews had refused to convert when all they were offered by the Christian church was the view that they were no longer the chosen people and there was no hope for the reestablishment of the kingdom of Israel. Stroeter complained that Christianity wanted to strip the Jews of the very hopes and beliefs that had kept them alive as a people for so many generations in the midst of hostility and misery. In the field of missions, the Jews had been treated as worse than heathens. Converted heathen were not expected to turn their backs on their people and give up their national aspirations, but converted Jews were forbidden to maintain any ties with their heritage.[87]

The dispensationalists distinguished sharply between different types of Jews. Most of the dispensationalists' efforts in Jewish evangelism were focused on Orthodox Jews, who shared their veneration for Scripture, still anticipated the coming of the Messiah, and prayed for Israel's national restoration. They achieved some modest successes in evangelizing them. "Though many Orthodox Jews instinctively rejected attempts to evangelize them, the dispensationalist messianic terminology that spoke about the appearance of 'the son of David' and the fulfillment of biblical prophecies was not strange to them. There was a common ground for discussion and persuasion."[88] While the Orthodox were believed to be suffering from "judicial blindness," which prevented them from recognizing Jesus as Messiah,

---

[86]Yaakov Ariel, *On Behalf of Israel: American Fundamentalist Attitudes Toward Jews, Judaism, and Zionism, 1865–1945*, Chicago Studies in the History of American Religion 1 (New York: Carlson, 1991), 101.

[87] Ernst F. Stroeter, "The Second Coming of Christ in Relation to Israel," in *Addresses on the Second Coming of the Lord Delivered at the Prophetic Conference, Allegheny, PA., December 3–6, 1895*, ed. Joseph Kyle and William S. Miller (Pittsburgh: W. W. Waters, n.d.), 136-56. Ariel, *On Behalf of Israel*, 107n30.

[88]Ariel, *On Behalf of Israel*, 62.

they would be the group of Jews who would come through the great tribulation and rule in the millennial kingdom. Orthodox Judaism was "the only religious manifestation aside from evangelical Protestantism" that was useful and fitted in with God's purposes.[89] It is understandable, then, that two of the leading American promoters of dispensationalism were for years active in Jewish evangelism: William Blackstone and Arno C. Gaebelein. It is to them that we now turn.

AMERICA'S FIRST QUINTESSENTIAL CHRISTIAN ZIONIST: WILLIAM BLACKSTONE

> *The publication of* Jesus Is Coming *signaled the beginning of a radical new religious movement in the United States and then the world over. By the time of Blackstone's death in 1935, over a million copies of his book had been printed in multiple editions in forty-eight languages, making it one of the most influential religious books of the twentieth century.*[90]
>
> MATTHEW AVERY SUTTON

Matthew Westbrook has argued that "the eschatological program of Darby needed to be *overcome* in an ideologically coherent fashion for activism to justifiably proceed within Christian Zionism."[91] The person who accomplished this feat was William E. Blackstone (1841–1935), who has been called "America's first quintessential Christian Zionist."[92] Blackstone (unlike Darby) was a politically engaged Christian Zionist and laid claim to the leadership of American dispensationalism.[93] Unlike Darby, Blackstone had no formal training and was entirely self-educated, the quintessential self-made man in a highly individualistic culture. Blackstone made his fortune in Chicago real estate but at the age of thirty-seven turned his attention to Jewish evangelism, and to writing. *Jesus Is Coming* (1878) turned out to be a

---

[89]Ariel, *On Behalf of Israel*, 114.

[90]Sutton, *American Apocalypse*, 9.

[91]Matthew C. Westbrook, "The International Christian Embassy, Jerusalem, and Renewalist Zionism: Emerging Jewish-Christian Ethnonationalism" (PhD diss., Drew University, 2014), 68.

[92]Smith, *More Desired*, 163.

[93]On Blackstone see Ariel, *Unusual Relationship*, 78-81 and 85-89. On the social, economic, and political context in which he wrote see Sutton, *American Apocalypse*, 10-12.

runaway bestseller. He became the most popular proponent of dispensational teaching, which he modified and adapted. Although Blackstone professed to follow Darby's teaching, he bent it to his politically engaged
Christian Zionist vision, something Darby never endorsed. Blackstone re-
invented dispensational premillennialism, turning it into an activist
Christian Zionism.

Blackstone acknowledged blending the two competing prophecy
schemes—adopting some futurist aspects but also reintroducing some historicist ones as well. He states this explicitly in one of his writings. Having
outlined the historicist and the futurist positions, he describes his fusion of
the two and concludes, "This we apprehend reconciles into one harmonious
system these two schools of interpretation."[94] Typical of the historicists,
Blackstone was given to date-setting—if not the specific date for Christ's
return, then at least intermediate steps. In 1894 he speculated that "Jerusalem
was captured by the Mohammedans in A.D. 637 and we may expect to see it
delivered in 1897."[95] He also speculated in 1897 that in 1932 "Gentile rule over
Israel must cease forever."[96] In 1923 Blackstone revised that date to 1933.[97]

From the 1880s onward Blackstone had a wide itinerant speaking ministry, often addressing large audiences; he established close friendships with
leading figures in the emerging revivalist tradition. As Sutton observes,
"Fundamentalists like Blackstone . . . spent a half century anticipating the
rapture while simultaneously spreading their message. . . . Their sense of
determination and commitment fueled their relentless passion for expanding their movement. They never forgot that they were under marching
orders."[98] Blackstone regularly taught at three of the key emerging American
Bible schools founded in this era. The founder of Nyack College in 1882 was
A. B. Simpson, a close friend of Blackstone, who credited him with the idea
of founding the school. Blackstone also taught at Dwight L. Moody's Moody
Bible Institute in Chicago, begun in 1886 as the Chicago Evangelical Society
and at California's Bible Institute of Los Angeles founded in 1908 (later
known as Biola College).

---

[94]*The Jewish Era* 2, no. 4 (October 1893): 238-39, quoted in Ehle, "Prolegomena," 259.
[95]*The Jewish Era* 3, no. 4 (Oct. 1894); 4, no. 1 (January 1895): 130, quoted in Ehle, "Prolegomena," 267.
[96]*The Jewish Era* 6, no. 2 (April 1897): 40, quoted in Ehle, "Prolegomena," 270.
[97]Ehle, "Prolegomena," 303.
[98]Sutton, *American Apocalypse*, 209.

In 1887 Blackstone became a founder of the Chicago Hebrew Mission in Behalf of Israel (later simply the Chicago Hebrew Mission and now known as the American Messianic Fellowship). Through its quarterly periodical *The Jewish Era*, he reached a large and expanding audience[99] and churned out new tracts that were printed in the tens of thousands. His writings are deeply aware of the tradition of Christian anti-Semitism, which the German Pietists and English evangelicals had highlighted and continued the emphasis on the belief in the superiority of Jewish achievements even in the face of discrimination—as he wrote in 1892 that when given "a free chance, the Jew outstrips all competitors and rises to leadership in every nation."[100]

In this way Blackstone's impact went far beyond his writing of *Jesus Is Coming*. He was a very wealthy man and able to support himself, dedicating all he had to his one-man crusade to promote his prophetic views and to organize his political lobbying efforts. In 1897 at age fifty-six, he resigned from the Chicago Hebrew Mission, sold his home in Chicago, and determined on a more intense itinerant ministry of preaching, writing, lecturing, and tract distribution.[101] Milton Stewart of Union Oil, who with his brother, Lyman, in 1909 helped to fund *The Fundamentals*, appointed Blackstone the trustee of the Milton Stewart Evangelistic Fund, which in 1916 held $2 million. But Blackstone himself often gave $50,000 of his own money to different charities. (Generously supported by Milton Stewart, Blackstone became a missionary to China for five years, from 1909 to 1914.)

While Darby had said that "there is no event between us and heaven" and disdained politics altogether, Blackstone asserted that Christians should take on a political role and that they should embrace not only the idea that the Jews will convert and return to Palestine but also that American Christians should actively seek to enable this to happen.[102] He did not accept Darby's view that the return would happen after the rapture. Blackstone transferred responsibility from British shoulders to American ones: the

---

[99]Ehle, "Prolegomena," 238.

[100]*The Jewish Era* 1, no. 3 (July 1892): 70, quoted in Ehle, "Prolegomena," 248.

[101]Ehle, "Prolegomena," 268.

[102]Scofield followed Blackstone on this point, but as is argued in chapter six, this was not (contra Samuel Goldman) an innovation. Cotton Mather had argued this position in the eighteenth century, and it was the view that James Bicheno, the leading historicist premillennialist, had argued for in the early nineteenth century. See Samuel Goldman, *God's Country: Christian Zionism in America* (Philadelphia: University of Pennsylvania Press, 2018), 148.

United States was the redeemer nation called to be the modern Cyrus, bringing the Jews back to Zion from exile. "God has chosen America for this role because of its moral superiority to the rest of the world, according to Blackstone, and He will judge it according to how the United States carries out this task."[103] The Puritan "elect nation" was now America and not Britain. As Ariel has commented, Blackstone's theory "amalgamates messianic beliefs and philo-Semitic and pro-Zionist agendas with a strong sense of American patriotism."[104]

In 1888–1889 Blackstone visited Palestine and was impressed by the accomplishments of the recent Jewish immigrants of the "first *Aliyah*"[105] to what he considered to be a desolate land. In that regard he wrote in 1891 of Palestine, "It has a territory of at least ten thousand square miles, with only six hundred thousand population. There is room there for two or three millions more people, and the ancient scriptural limits of the country would largely increase its capacity. . . . Only an independent, enlightened, and progressive government is needed to afford a home for all of Israel who wish to return."[106] The agricultural settlements and new Jewish neighborhoods in Jerusalem were especially important to him, foreshadowing a much greater Jewish presence in a largely Arab land. To him these were "signs of the times" indicating that the Jews would soon be restored to their homeland, and that Christ's return was imminent.[107]

Hearing of the brutal Russian pogroms, he convened an ecumenical conference in Chicago in 1891 called "The Past, Present and Future of Israel," and a number of prominent Christian ministers and Jewish rabbis took part. The result was a unanimous resolution of support for the Russian Jews, although none of the Jewish rabbis present were in favor of the "restoration" of the

---

[103]Stephen Spector, *Evangelicals and Israel: The Story of American Christian Zionism* (New York: Oxford University Press, 2009), 21.

[104]Yaakov Ariel, "'It's All in the Bible': Evangelical Christians, Biblical Literalism, and Philosemitism in Our Times," in *Philosemitism in History*, ed. Joseph Karp and Adam Sutcliffe (Cambridge: Cambridge University Press, 2011), 263.

[105]The First *Aliyah* (literally "ascent") is a term used to describe a wave of Zionist, agriculturally driven immigration to Ottoman Palestine in the years 1882–1903.

[106]*Our Day* 8, no. 46 (October 1891): 241-42, quoted in Ehle, "Prolegomena," 245.

[107]Blackstone also had contact with the "American colony" in Jerusalem, a Christian community built up by Horatio and Anna Spafford, an evangelical but theologically eclectic group with Holiness leanings. See Ariel, *Unusual Relationship*, 104-10.

Jews to Palestine.[108] At the conference, one of America's best-known rabbis made clear his opposition to Zionism. Emil G. Hirsch, the rabbi of the prestigious Chicago Sinai Congregation, and one of the leading figures in Reform Judaism, argued in a plenary address that

> we, the modern Jews, do not wish to be restored to Palestine. We have given up the hope in the coming of a political, personal Messiah. We say, "The country wherein we live is our Palestine, and the city wherein we dwell is our Jerusalem. We will not go back . . . to form again a nationality of our own. . . . Let our religious life be clothed in the symbols of the life we see living round about us. Let our synagogues speak the language of the cities in which we dwell. Let our ceremonial be constituted in harmony with the culture by which we are surrounded."[109]

Other Reform rabbis were more ambivalent about the restoration ideal, being willing to support the emigration and settlement of oppressed Russian Jews in Palestine while not endorsing the Zionist goal of a full-blown Jewish state.[110]

Blackstone's efforts need to be understood in the context of the shifts occurring in the American millenarian movement. He wrote *Jesus Is Coming* in the 1870s, when the futurist option was overtaking the historicist position as the option favored by American millenarians. The fact that he was a layman with no strong denominational ties is characteristic of an anti-denominational and anticlerical trend in late nineteenth-century American conservative Protestantism. In the 1890s the futurist premillennialists split into two camps over the question of whether the personal advent would happen before the seven-year period of tribulation (following Darby) or afterward (the "posttribulation" position). The debates published in prophetic periodicals became personal and nasty, with the same sort of acrimony that had accompanied the early Brethren movement division in the 1840s between the followers of John Nelson Darby and Benjamin Wills Newton. However, by 1910 it was clear that the pretribulationists, following the Darby-Gaebelein-Scofield line, had won the day and this victory was solidified with the publication of Cyrus I. Scofield's reference Bible in 1909.

---

[108]Ehle, "Prolegomena," 240.

[109]George F. Magoun, "The Chicago Jewish Christian Conference," *Our Day* 7 (January–June 1891): 270-71.

[110]Ariel, *On Behalf of Israel*, 77.

The posttribulation premillennial position did not disappear, however. Robert Cameron, Nathaniel West, W. J. Erdman, James M. Stiffler, William G. Moorehead, and Henry W. Frost—all men who had been involved in the Niagara Bible Conferences—were in the minority posttribulation position, believing that the church should expect to experience the tribulation period and not be raptured out of harm's way.[111]

THE BLACKSTONE MEMORIAL OF 1891

Notwithstanding the opposition of assimilationist Jews like Rabbi Hirsch, Blackstone put together the Blackstone Memorial of 1891, which drew on a remarkable spectrum of American leaders to petition President Benjamin Harrison's support for an international conference aimed at restoring the Jews to a home in Palestine—some six years before the first Zionist Conference. Blackstone was careful to avoid antagonizing Russia with direct criticism, aware that this might worsen the situation of Russian Jews, so the memorial began with the question,

> What shall be done for the Russian Jews? . . . The Jews have lived as foreigners in [Russia's] dominions for centuries and she fully believes they are a burden upon her resources and prejudicial to the welfare of her peasant population, and will not allow them to remain. She is determined that they must go. . . . But where shall 2,000,000 of such poor people go?[112]

And then Blackstone's proposed solution:

> Why not give Palestine back to them again? According to God's distribution of nations, it is their home, an inalienable possession from which they were expelled by force. . . . Why shall not the powers which under the treaty of Berlin, in 1878, gave Bulgaria to the Bulgarians and Servia to the Servians now give Palestine back to the Jews? These provinces, as well as Roumania, Montenegro, and Greece, were wrested from the Turks and given to their natural owners. Does not Palestine rightfully belong to the Jews?[113]

As for the Ottomans, the petition argued that "whatever vested rights, by possession, may have accrued to Turkey can easily be compensated, possibly

---

[111]Sandeen, *Roots*, 210-11. There was also a mid-tribulation-rapture option, but it did not gain much traction.

[112]Kiracofe, *Dark Crusade*, 66.

[113]Kiracofe, *Dark Crusade*, 66.

by the Jews assuming an equitable portion of the national debt."[114] No mention was made of its Palestinian Arab inhabitants.

The memorial attracted an enormous amount of attention for the Zionist cause, signed for humanitarian reasons by both Jews and Christians (many of whom were not dispensationalists), and included captains of industry like John D. Rockefeller and J. P. Morgan; leading figures in law (including the sitting chief justice of the US Supreme Court and future Supreme Court justice Louis D. Brandeis, a secular Jew); politicians, including Ohio governor (and future president) William McKinley; and members of Congress. Marnin Feinstein has observed that "no 19th century document dealing with the Jewish question and Palestine, including Herzl's *Jewish State*, evoked as much editorial comment in this country as Blackstone's Memorial."[115] Blackstone thus did much to introduce an activist Christian Zionism into the core of dispensationalism, thereby playing a key role in altering the genetic code of the movement and profoundly influencing the lineage of Christian Zionism.[116]

ARNO C. GAEBELEIN: JEWISH EVANGELIST, PREMILLENNIALIST AUTHOR, AND PROPHECY-CONFERENCE ORGANIZER

That the story of dispensationalism and its relationship with Christian Zionism is not a straightforward one is illustrated by one of Blackstone's contemporaries, Arno C. Gaebelein, who was a key organizer of the surging dispensationalist cause. Gaebelein had worked as a missionary among Yiddish-speaking Jews in New York City. In the 1880s he established The Hope of Israel Mission, approaching Jews through relief and charitable work, as well as by offering popular lectures on Saturdays. Gaebelein was well acquainted with Jewish customs and rites and spoke Yiddish so well that many Jews found it difficult to believe that he was a Gentile. Gaebelein was also for many years the editor of the dispensationalist *Our Hope* magazine and a key figure in Jewish missions.

British and American conservatives watched with great interest the formation of the secular Zionist movement begun in 1897 under Theodor Herzl.

---

[114]*The Missionary Review of the World*, April 1891, IV, NS, 305.

[115]Marnin Feinstein, "The Blackstone Memorial," *Midstream* 10 (June 1964): 76, quoted in J. D. Moorhouse, "'Jesus Is Coming': The Life and Work of William E. Blackstone" (PhD diss., Dallas Seminary, 2008), 4.

[116]On response to the memorial see Ariel, *Unusual Relationship*, 88-90.

As early as 1894 when the first issue of *Our Hope* magazine was published, under the editorship of Ernst F. Stroeter, Gaebelein's close associate, dispensationalist interest was clear. Stroeter "continually declared that the Christian church should be applauding the Jewish colonization of Palestine and should certainly be helping in this endeavor."[117] In 1896 Stroeter traveled to Europe to follow the Zionist developments and returned again to Europe permanently in 1897, and reported to *Our Hope* on the first Zionist congress. With Stroeter out of the picture, *Our Hope* changed its focus as Gaebelein assumed the editorship. Gaebelein was fascinated by the development of Jewish Zionism, but was not as uncritically supportive as Stroeter, Blackstone, or Hechler, and denied that the secular Jewish Zionists were going to be the means of the "restoration." In his *The Conflict of the Ages* he characterized Zionism as follows: "The whole movement is one of unbelief which is displeasing to God, and finally results in new judgments upon Israel's land."[118] It would seem that Gaebelein was closer to Darby's view that the restoration prophesied in Scripture would be accomplished after the rapture. In 1905 he wrote in *Hath God Cast Away His People?*,

> Zionism, we wish to say, is not the divinely promised restoration of Israel. Zionism is not the fulfillment of the large number of predictions found in the Old Testament Scriptures, which relate to Israel's return to the land. Indeed, Zionism has very little use for arguments from the Word of God. It is rather a political and philanthropic undertaking. Instead of coming together before God to search their own Scriptures, humbling themselves before God, calling upon His name, trusting Him, that He is able to perform, what He has so often promised, they speak about their riches, their influence, their Colonial Bank and court the favor of the Sultan. The great movement is one of unbelief and confidence in themselves instead of God's eternal purposes. It is therefore an attempt of the Jewish people to solve themselves the question of their national future and national welfare, without considering the spiritual and the divine side at all. If Zionism succeeds, and no doubt it will, it will be a partial return of the Jews in unbelief to their land. Is such a return anywhere foretold in the Scriptures? We do not know of a single passage which tells us that such should be the case and yet it is evident by all the predicted events which fall into the

---

[117]David A. Rausch, *Zionism Within Early American Fundamentalism, 1878–1918: A Convergence of Two Traditions* (Lewiston, NY: Edwin Mellen, 1979), 229.
[118]Ariel, *On Behalf of Israel*, 115.

closing years of this present age, that in order that these events can be fulfilled, a part of the Jewish nation must be back in the land; while among them is the believing remnant, the great majority will be unbelieving.

Not alone that, but a temple must be built again (and quite often Zionists have mentioned this) and a daily sacrifice be brought (Dan. XI:31). We mention a few Scriptures, which cannot be fulfilled except a part of the Jewish people dwell in Palestine.[119]

Nevertheless, Gaebelein in *Our Hope* was particularly concerned to keep his evangelical readers up to date on the activities of the Jewish Zionists. Many premillennialists thought that Zionism "was probably the beginning of the movement which would bring enough Jews back to the Holy Land 'in unbelief' to start the prophetic countdown to the end of the age."[120] Closely aligned with Scofield, Gaebelein claimed the heritage of the discontinued Niagara conference; by 1902 he was holding prophecy conferences all over the United States, and by 1904 had moved away from direct involvement in the Jewish mission.[121] In effect Gaebelein excommunicated the posttribulationist rapturists within the wider prophecy movement. His organizational initiative was solidified with the publication of Scofield's reference Bible in 1909.

The publication of a series of some ninety essays in twelve books known as *The Fundamentals: A Testimony to the Truth* by the Bible Institute of Los Angeles between 1910 and 1915 sought to affirm conservative Protestant beliefs regarded as foundational to the popular movement that came to bear the name "fundamentalism" as it emerged in the 1920s.[122] Jewish issues are mentioned frequently in the articles, and the second editor of the series was Louis Meyer, a "Hebrew Christian." The article on prophecy was written by Gaebelein, who argued that the inerrancy of the Bible and its supernatural status were reinforced by the biblical prophecies being realized in his day. The emerging fundamentalist movement was broader than just the dispensationalists, but the designation of Gaebelein as the author of this article was an indication of their wider success, which Gaebelein had played a major role in achieving.

---

[119]Arno Clemens Gaebelein, C. I. Scofield, and A. J. Gordon, *Hath God Cast Away His People?* (New York: Our Hope, 1905), 200-201.

[120]Weber, *Shadow*, 137.

[121]Sandeen, *Roots*, 220. Ariel, *On Behalf of Israel*, 109.

[122]On the *Fundamentals* see Ariel, *Unusual Relationship*, 74-75.

Gaebelein differed from Blackstone in significant ways. While Blackstone retained close, personal friendships with leading secular Jews, there is no evidence that Gaebelein had contact with Jews once he left Jewish missions in 1904 to focus on his leadership of the wider dispensationalist cause. He had no connections with the Zionist movement, and his support of Jews returning to Palestine was essentially passive. He never donated to the Zionist cause, which he regarded with suspicion; "he was an observer, condemning its secular character" while paradoxically "rejoicing in its achievements."[123] And yet Zionism's early successes were proof for him that history was unfolding as the premillennialists had predicted; it was a vindication of his prophetic convictions.[124] Within dispensationalism, there remained two streams: an activist Christian Zionist stream following Blackstone; and a passive, yet curious stream, following Darby and Gaebelein. Both groups were convinced that the Jews would eventually return to Palestine but differed as to the timetable and whether they should actively support the Zionist cause.

THE POPE AND THE TURK ECLIPSED BY THE POPE AND THE BEAR

Dwight Wilson in his study of prewar prophetic writings has emphasized how the premillennialists had well-worked-out predispositions: they believed in a Jewish return but also were clearly anti-Russian. The strong anti-Russian sentiments were not solely related to Russian anti-Semitism; both historicist and futurist premillennarians had agreed that Russia was to be identified with "Gog and Magog," in Daniel's prophecy. Up to the late eighteenth century, American prophecy writers had viewed Gog as "the Grand Turk"; the shift from "the Turk-as-Gog" to "Russia-as-Gog" has been traced to the interpretation of a German Hebrew scholar, Wilhelm Gesenius (1786–1842), and his identification was taken on by Darby in articulating dispensationalism.[125] Similarly, a leading British historicist premillennialist, John Cumming, writing in the midst of the Crimean War (1853–1856), which pitted Britain and France against Russia, fighting over the Ottoman Empire, produced *The End* (1855), and developed the Russia-as-Gog theme. By the

---

[123] Ariel, *On Behalf of Israel*, 115.
[124] Ariel, *On Behalf of Israel*, 116.
[125] Boyer, *Shadow*, 154.

late nineteenth century, both British and American writers had embraced this new focus on Russia. As Boyer observes, "At the grassroots level, the vague similarity of 'Rosh' and 'Russia,' 'Meschech' and 'Moscow,' not to mention the undeniable geographic fact that Russia lay north of Palestine, gave the theory a commonsense appeal."[126]

Momentous prophetic events were anticipated, chief of which was to be the restoration of the Jews to Palestine, the rapture, and, of course, the last battle—Armageddon—which would involve Russian aggression against Israel. Beginning in the late nineteenth century, the twin enemies of Protestantism and of the Christian Zionist cause ceased being the pope and the Turk. The Turk as enemy had been displaced by Russia, and all the more so after 1917, when the "Godless Communists" took control of Russia. Russia as the stand-in enemy was to last about seventy years until the rise of radical Muslim terrorism would reassert Islam's place in the prophetic schemes.

[126]Boyer, *Shadow*, 155.

9

THE BALFOUR
DECLARATION OF 1917

His Majesty's Government view with favour the establishment
in Palestine of a national home for the Jewish people, and
will use their best endeavours to facilitate the achievement
of this object.

THE BALFOUR DECLARATION, NOVEMBER 2, 1917

THE BALFOUR "DECLARATION" WAS a simple letter consisting of only three sentences, but it changed the course of world history. It was the single most important political event in the history of Zionism prior to the establishment of the state of Israel. An examination of the influence of Christian Zionism on this declaration moves our discussion into the intricacies of international politics and the general climate of opinion that the Christian Zionists cultivated.

Arthur James Balfour, the British foreign secretary, wrote this letter to Lord Rothschild in early November 1917 to inform this prominent English Zionist of the British government's support of Zionism, and indicated that it would "use its best endeavours to facilitate the achievement of this object." In this brief, typewritten letter, the most powerful and expansive empire known in human history ostensibly committed itself to the Zionist cause in a unique way. A few weeks later British troops under Sir Edmund Allenby captured Jerusalem on December 9. In 1922 the Council of the League of Nations enshrined the commitment made in the Balfour Declaration in its Palestine Mandate, which formally assigned Britain the governing of

Palestine and acknowledged an explicit responsibility to enable the Jews to establish a national home in the country.[1]

BRITISH RESPONSES TO JEWISH PERSECUTION

The declaration needs to be understood in the long history of England's relations with the Jews. As I have argued, Christian support for Jewish restoration had been woven into English identity from the seventeenth century, and English nationalism itself had been forged on the anvil of a peculiar responsibility toward the Jews. Many British Christians had long hoped for England to take concrete actions to facilitate their "restoration" to Zion. Christian "restorationists" had played an important role in arousing the public to support persecuted European Jews for decades, and for Ottoman Jews in the 1840 "Damascus Affair," and again in the 1880s on behalf of Russian Jews. Support for the intent behind the Balfour Declaration has to be sought in the several preceding centuries and not just in the immediate background of its promulgation.

But the immediate background was important. As the situation of Russian Jews grew more dire, Theodor Herzl met in 1903 with Joseph Chamberlain, the British colonial secretary, and with Lord Lansdowne, the foreign secretary, about a possible solution. The Zionists were offered unrestricted Jewish immigration to the British Protectorate of Uganda in East Africa as a place of refuge. Herzl saw this as a temporary sanctuary for Jews who could eventually move to Palestine when conditions permitted. Many Zionists regarded Herzl as a traitor for considering a solution that was not solely Palestine-based. Herzl died in 1904, and although the Uganda scheme was debated at the Zionist conference in 1905, it effectively perished with him.[2] The deteriorating European political situation created the "Second *Aliyah*," a new

---

[1]Tom Segev and Haim Watzman, *One Palestine, Complete: Jews and Arabs Under the Mandate*, 1st American ed. (New York: Metropolitan Books, 2000), 116. The original draft had been drawn up in July 1917 and intended as a short statement of support similar to one that Zionists had elicited from the French government several months earlier. Feedback was solicited from friendly advisers in the Foreign Office, redrafted and shown to Balfour, and more amendments made, and then shown to cabinet, with further revisions. The final wording of the letter was adopted after weeks of to-and-fro discussions within the war cabinet and in dialogue with leading Zionists. For a discussion of the careful and nuanced language of the declaration see Jonathan Schneer, *The Balfour Declaration: The Origins of the Arab-Israeli Conflict* (Toronto: Doubleday Canada, 2010), 335, 373.

[2]Schneer, *Balfour Declaration*, 112.

wave of Jewish immigration to Palestine. From 1904 through to 1914 about thirty-five thousand Eastern European Jews fleeing persecution arrived.[3]

In 1913, when Nahum Sokolow sought to lobby the British Foreign Office, he was ignored. After two months of trying, an official acknowledged that "somebody could see him if he calls, but the less we have to do with the Zionists the better."[4] Turkey, then friendly to Britain, opposed Zionism and thus Sokolow was rebuffed. As Jonathan Schneer comments, Foreign Office officials were insufferable snobs: "When it came to measuring themselves against visitors, no matter how distinguished and no matter where from, they suffered few insecurities."[5] Sir Arthur Nicholson, the permanent undersecretary, would not meet with Sokolow, but his personal private secretary, the Earl of Onslow, did. After Onslow's meeting with Sokolow, his master sniffed, "In any case we had better not intervene to support the Zionist movement. The implantation of the Jews is a question of internal administration [of the Ottoman Empire] on which there is great division of opinion in Turkey. The Arabs and the old Turks detest the movement."[6] Assisting persecuted Jews to settle in Uganda was one thing; trying to help move persecuted Jews to Ottoman Palestine was quite another. Even the experience of teetering on the edge of war did not change the Foreign Office's attitude.

The great majority of British Jews were unsympathetic to Zionism. Some were merely indifferent, but many were openly hostile. At the time, only eight thousand British Jews out of three hundred thousand belonged to a Zionist organization. Most British Jews were desperately poor recent immigrants who had escaped Russian persecution or the pogroms of southern and eastern Europe. Eking out a living in Britain was difficult enough; joining a fantastical movement that advocated moving to a decrepit backwater of the Ottoman Empire had little appeal. The old London Jewish aristocracy were assimilationists, not Zionists. Known as the "Cousinhood," the group was interconnected by marriage among the elite families,[7] and they

---

[3]Caitlin Carenen, *The Fervent Embrace: Liberal Protestants, Evangelicals, and Israel* (New York: New York University Press, 2012), 6.
[4]Schneer, *Balfour Declaration*, 100.
[5]Schneer, *Balfour Declaration*, 108.
[6]Schneer, *Balfour Declaration*, 109.
[7]Schneer, *Balfour Declaration*, 110.

by and large showed only hostility: "They considered themselves to be Jewish Britons, not British Jews, and they abhorred Zionists, who insisted that Jews constituted a separate people or nation."

THE GAME-CHANGER: THE OUTBREAK OF WORLD WAR I AND THE ZIONIST LOBBYING OFFENSIVE

> *The declarations of war in late July and early August 1914 burst upon an unprepared world like a volley of gunshots at a summer garden party.*[8]
>
> JONATHAN SCHNEER

Much changed with the onset of the war. In late October the Ottomans sided with the Central Powers against Britain, and their opposition to Zionism thus no longer concerned the British. Zionists reasoned that if the Ottomans were defeated and their empire carved up by a victorious Britain, then the possibilities for a Jewish homeland would increase dramatically. Between 1914 and 1917 a tug of war ensued between the Zionists and the assimilationists; the anti-Zionist Jews, represented by Lucien Wolf, vied with the Zionists for British government support.

The Zionist lobby was led by Chaim Weizmann, a Russian-born biochemist who had emigrated to England in 1904. He quickly gained access to wealthy British Jews to convince them of the importance and the justice of the Zionist cause. Crucially, he was a top scientist, and his invention of an inexpensive industrial process to make acetone, a key ingredient in explosives, was to make a critical contribution to the British war effort. Historians have long debated to what extent Weizmann's scientific contribution to the war effort affected his success as a lobbyist. (In 1949 Weizmann was elected as the first president of the new state of Israel.) Weizmann was unsurpassed as a lobbyist and remarkably influential in courting key figures in the British political elite and in the Foreign Office who were desperate for any advantage in the war effort that the Zionists could offer.

In the years leading up to the Balfour Declaration, Weizmann and his associates repeatedly argued six points. First point: that the Zionist cause

---

[8]Schneer, *Balfour Declaration*, 112.

represented "International Jewry"—which it did not—it did not even represent British Jewry, but the British government believed them. Second point: that "International Jewry" wanted a homeland in Palestine—another contention that is highly doubtful. As Schneer observes, "The Foreign Office learned from [Weizmann] to believe in Jewish influence upon the world (not hard, many of them believed in it already) and, more to the point, in Zionist influence on the Jews. Weizmann told them that Jews wanted a homeland in Palestine above all else. The Foreign Office believed this too."[9]

Third point: that the Jews (particularly American Jews) were sitting in the wheelhouse of history, with enormous power and virtually unlimited resources, and that they were being courted by the Germans and therefore it was crucial to bring them over to the Allied cause. (Even the French government at the time was concerned that Germany was outbidding the Allies for Jewish support, and many British officials came to believe this as well.)[10] Rumors circulated that powerful American Jews were upset by the anti-Semitism of Russia, a British ally, and thus inclined to the German side; dangling the vague prospect of a Jewish homeland in Palestine might secure American Jewish support.[11] The American Jewish financiers were in fact already overwhelmingly on board with the Allies—but again in all these matters the British believed the Zionists' line. "The government's wartime decision to appeal to the Jews was based on a misconception."[12] In fact, it was based on several misconceptions.

In this period a surprising articulation of this understanding of the overwhelming power of the Jews came from the pen of the British diplomat Mark Sykes in his correspondence with Sharif Hussein's son Prince Faisal in the aftermath of the Balfour Declaration. Hussein was persuaded to lead the Arab Revolt in 1916 against the Ottomans with promises of British assistance. In March 1918, Sykes coached Prince Faisal on his dealings with the Jews, in vaguely providentialist language that is reminiscent of the evangelical philo-Semites like Shaftesbury. Sykes had been born into a prominent Protestant

---

[9] Schneer, *Balfour Declaration*, 367.
[10] Schneer, *Balfour Declaration*, 156.
[11] Schneer, *Balfour Declaration*, 155.
[12] Schneer, *Balfour Declaration*, 153.

family but raised as a Roman Catholic, but his thinking, while fantastical, would have warmed the heart of Christian Zionists:

> I know that the Arabs despise, condemn and hate the Jews, but passion is the ruin of princes and peoples. . . . Those who have persecuted or condemned the Jews could tell you the tale. The Empire of Spain in the old days and the Empire of Russia in our time show the road of ruin that Jewish persecution leads to. You say to yourself what is this race despised, rejected, abhorred, that cannot fight, that has no home and is no nation? O Faisal, I can read your heart and your thought, and there are counselors about you who will whisper similar things in your ear. Believe I speak the truth when I say that this race, despised and weak, is universal, is all powerful and cannot be put down.[13]

The members of the war cabinet that issued the Balfour Declaration undoubtedly had often heard similar arguments. Interestingly this conception was promoted most effectively by three devout Roman Catholics: (1) Mark Sykes; (2) Gerald Henry Fitzmaurice, a British diplomat with long experience in Turkey who was convinced that the Young Turks who had overthrown the Sultan in 1908 "and taken control of the empire were dominated by Jews and *dömnes*, or crypto-Jews";[14] (3) and Hugh James O'Bierne, a much-respected British diplomat. It is unclear what role their common Catholic background had in making them so convinced that "world Jewry" was such a powerful and organized force. Nathan Sokolow, the Zionist lobbyist, once observed of Sykes, "Often he remarked to me that it was his Catholicism that enabled him to understand the tragedy of the Jewish question, since not so long Catholics had to suffer much in England."[15] This belief in the hidden, subterranean power of "Great Jewry" was held by "the bulk of the policy-making elite" of both Britain and France.[16] They could not conceive of questioning that their "notion of Jewish world power was outrageously, egregiously, mistaken; that it was based on romance and myth and age-old prejudice, not upon fact; and that it was at heart profoundly irrational."[17]

---

[13]Schneer, *Balfour Declaration*, 372.
[14]Schneer, *Balfour Declaration*, 153.
[15]Schneer, *Balfour Declaration*, 210.
[16]Schneer, *Balfour Declaration*, 168.
[17]Schneer, *Balfour Declaration*, 168.

Fourth point: that the long-marginalized Russian Jews would be helpful in keeping their country in the war in spite of Russia's long record of anti-Semitism; the reasoning was faulty, and in any event this hope proved a chimera in that five days after the cabinet approved the Balfour Declaration, the Bolsheviks came to power and in December 1917 withdrew Russia from the Great War. Fifth point: that Jews and the British government shared common aspirations—in particular, the defeat of the Ottomans, which was debatable because many Ottoman Jews were fighting *against* the British in Palestine. In 1917 David Ben-Gurion was trying to set up a Jewish battalion in the Turkish army to fight against the British, and Eliezer Ben-Yehuda, the father of the revival of modern Hebrew, also a Zionist, was urging Palestinian Jews to accept the offer of Ottoman citizenship and to enlist in the Ottoman army.[18] Yet, at the same time, a secret Jewish spy ring was working in Palestine against the Ottomans, most of whom eventually paid with their lives for their efforts.[19]

Sixth point: that a Jewish Palestine would benefit British strategic interests in the Middle East, particularly by safeguarding British control of the Suez Canal (even from their wartime allies the French). Convincing counterarguments might have been made to this if the British could have been persuaded that a British-sponsored Jewish homeland would in the long run endanger British strategic interests. The fact that Grand Sharif Hussein had understood that Palestine had secretly already been promised to him by the British did not figure in the debate, nor did the fact that for over a year Arab armies under his command had been contributing "to Britain's successful Middle Eastern military campaign."[20] By March 1916 the British Foreign Office had made up its mind and a prime objective of British diplomacy became the obtaining of Jewish support for the Allied war effort. In their minds "the fate of the British Empire was at stake."[21] For their part, the Zionist lobby under Weizmann's leadership pressed David Lloyd George and Balfour for a British protectorate in Palestine.

---

[18]Segev and Watzman, *One Palestine, Complete*, 16.
[19]Schneer, *Balfour Declaration*, 172.
[20]Schneer, *Balfour Declaration*, 367.
[21]Schneer, *Balfour Declaration*, 162.

Assessing the Influence of Religion
on the Balfour Declaration

Aware of these complex political realities, we can better assess the possible influence of religion on the endorsement of the Balfour Declaration, which is suggested by Tom Segev's quip that "the [Balfour] declaration was the product of neither military nor diplomatic interests but of prejudice, faith, and sleight of hand."[22] The religious and ethnic backgrounds of the British war cabinet perhaps deserve more attention than historians have hitherto given.[23] Much focus has rightly been on the religious backgrounds of David Lloyd George, the British prime minister in 1917, and of Arthur Balfour.

The case of Lloyd George is particularly problematic. In his *War Memoirs*, Lloyd George argued that the declaration was designed to woo American Jewish financial support for the war effort and to induce Russian Jews to use their influence to keep Russia in the war. Barbara Tuchman has discounted such arguments, maintaining that Lloyd George was trying to conceal his religious motives, which he shared with Balfour.[24] Segev, a leading Israeli author who has written extensively on this period, has heaped praise on Jonathan Schneer's *The Balfour Declaration: The Origins of the Arab-Israeli Conflict* (2010) for its probing of recently accessible diplomatic correspondence and its brilliant prose. However, Segev points out that Schneer omits any reference to the fact that the declaration's authors were by and large deeply religious Christian Zionists, thereby lending weight to Tuchman's argument about Lloyd George's hiding of his religious motives.[25]

Such statements, however, need to be compared with what Lloyd George said in 1915, when Asquith's Liberal cabinet considered a memorandum prepared by Sir Herbert Samuel, the Jewish cabinet member, advocating a British protectorate in Palestine. Lord Reading, the (Jewish) lord chief justice, had reported to Samuel that Lloyd George (then the chancellor of the exchequer) was "inclined to the sympathetic side—your proposal appeals to

---

[22]Segev and Watzman, *One Palestine, Complete*, 33.

[23]For a discussion of the religious backgrounds of its members see Donald M. Lewis, *The Origins of Christian Zionism: Lord Shaftesbury and Evangelical Support for a Jewish Homeland* (Cambridge: Cambridge University Press, 2009), 333-34.

[24]Stephen Spector, *Evangelicals and Israel: The Story of American Christian Zionism* (New York: Oxford University Press, 2009), 20.

[25]Tom Segev, "'View with Favor,'" *New York Times*, August 20, 2010, sec. Sunday Book Review.

the poetic and imaginative as well as to the romantic and religious qualities of his mind."[26] But Asquith, the prime minister, had quite a different take on Lloyd George, saying that while Lloyd George supported Samuel's proposal, he "does not care a damn for the Jews or their past or their future, but . . . thinks it would be an outrage to let the Christian Holy Places . . . pass into the possession or under the protectorate of 'Agnostic Atheistic France'!"[27] Schneer appropriately asks whether his concern was more with keeping the French out than allowing Jews in.[28]

It is very difficult to assess how deep Lloyd George's religious sentiments ran. And did they really count for anything in the way he behaved? Apparently not. The quip of one of his cabinet colleagues, Lord Selborne, perhaps put the matter most succinctly: "He would leave anyone in the lurch anywhere if he thought it suited his purpose."[29] We now know from diplomatic correspondence that Lloyd George, even after the issuance of the Balfour Declaration, was prepared to abandon it as he was secretly making promises to the Ottomans that contradicted the intent of the declaration. For a price, the Ottoman Empire might thereby have kept its flag flying in Palestine.[30]

As late as January 1918, British diplomats were working to secure a separate peace with Turkey, which would involve breaking with the Central Powers (Germany, Austro-Hungary, and Bulgaria) and withdrawing from the war. This would allow Britain to redeploy its forces arrayed against Turkey to the German front. Thus it is obvious in hindsight that whatever "Lloyd George gave with one hand he might negotiate away with the other."[31] But to put the negotiations in perspective, the idea of a separate peace with the Ottomans had been around from late 1914, for "Turkey and Britain had no sooner declared war on each other than they opened secret negotiations to try to end it."[32] But the withdrawal of Russia from the war in December 1917 removed what had seemed to be the unsurmountable obstacle to a separate peace with Turkey because up to that point the Russians would

---

[26]Schneer, *Balfour Declaration*, 164.
[27]Schneer, *Balfour Declaration*, 145.
[28]Schneer, *Balfour Declaration*, 145.
[29]Schneer, *Balfour Declaration*, 31.
[30]Schneer, *Balfour Declaration*, 370.
[31]Schneer, *Balfour Declaration*, 370-71.
[32]Schneer, *Balfour Declaration*, 240.

have vetoed any agreement with the Ottomans that did not promise them Constantinople, and the British could not forge an agreement without Russia's approval. Russia's withdrawal made the Ottomans more willing to fight on and to spurn the proffered deal.

It has often been suggested that Palestine at this time was thrice promised to different parties by the British, but in fact "it was promised, or at any rate dangled as bait, four times: before the Zionists and the Arabs, before Picot [the French diplomat] by Sykes in the shape of an as-yet-unformed international consortium, and before the Turks, who would otherwise lose it as a result of war. Of course, during most of our period, for imperial-economic strategic reasons, Britain meant to keep the primary governing role in Palestine for herself."[33]

In retrospect, one can appreciate Lloyd George's dilemma: early in 1917 the situation for the Allies had been growing desperate. Germany was producing U-boats at an alarming rate, and they were seriously endangering British supply lines. British survival was at stake. Although the Americans entered the war in April 1917, American troops did not make it to the European theater until months later and Britain was considering suing for peace with Germany. In the Middle East, the Ottomans had more than held their ground against the British, and Allied troops had paid a devastating toll in lives lost in the Dardanelles. Then Russia underwent its first revolution in March 1917, and if it withdrew from the war because of internal discord, then the Germans would have a great advantage. If Turkey could be removed from the field of combatants, Britain might have a better chance of winning the war.

If Lloyd George's scheming had been successful, not only would the Turks have betrayed the German cause, but the British would have betrayed those Arabs led by Sharif Hussein who (at British urging) had launched the Arab Revolt against the Ottomans in June 1916. If the regime change had happened in Turkey and the new rulers had accepted this proposal, the Balfour Declaration would have been a dead letter because the British had promised them that Turkey would retain Palestine. Whatever his religious background may have been, it would appear that strategic interests were more important to Lloyd George than religious sentiment related to the Jews.

---

[33]Schneer, *Balfour Declaration*, 368.

Arthur Balfour and religious motives? Arthur James Balfour looms large in the history of Zionism and occupies a place of honor alongside Theodor Herzl. The fact that the declaration bore his name is a testimony to this. He played an important role in its preparation and defended it once it became public. As Schneer has observed, "Yet he seems an odd protagonist, scion as he was of the aristocratic Cecil political dynasty, which began in the sixteenth century with Lord Burghley, the adviser to Queen Elizabeth I, and extended down the years to Balfour's uncle, the third marquess of Salisbury, who had served as Conservative prime minister after Disraeli."[34] Lord Salisbury served three times as prime minister (1885–1886, 1886–1892, 1895–1902), being succeeded by his nephew Arthur Balfour in 1902.

Yet this aristocratic background was deeply religious, for Arthur Balfour was raised in a strongly evangelical Scottish Presbyterian home and was nurtured in a Calvinistic evangelicalism similar to that of the Welsh Baptist upbringing of Lloyd George. As Balfour's father died when Arthur was a child, it was his mother, née Lady Blanche Gascoyne-Cecil, who raised him and his seven siblings. (Lady Blanche was thus the older sister of one prime minister [Salisbury] and mother of another.) A wealthy Scottish aristocrat, Lady Blanche was an earnest evangelical who taught her children in daily Bible classes, instilling in her oldest son a remarkable knowledge of the geography of Palestine and familiarizing him with stories of the Old Testament. She was also known for her personal evangelistic efforts, undoubtedly scandalizing those of her own social rank and astounding those of humbler birth by distributing gospel tracts at the railway station in East Linton near the sprawling Balfour family estate in East Lothian in Scotland.[35]

While the adult Balfour shared little of his mother's faith, he does seem to have retained the deep sympathy that she had instilled in him for the Jewish people. When Chaim Weizmann first met him in 1914, he was much surprised to discover an unlikely ally. Balfour listened to the accounts of the woes of the much-despised Jews that Weizmann recounted, and the Zionist leader recalled that Balfour "was deeply moved—'to tears.'"[36] Weizmann

---

[34]Schneer, *Balfour Declaration*, 133.
[35]Material adapted from Lewis, *Origins*, 4. Sydney H. Zebel, *Balfour: A Political Biography* (Cambridge: Cambridge University Press, 1973), 2. Kenneth Young, *Arthur James Balfour* (London: Bell and Sons, 1963), 9.
[36]Schneer, *Balfour Declaration*, 134.

reported to a friend that on leaving "he took me by the hand and said I had illuminated for him the road followed by a great suffering nation."[37] Balfour astounded Weizmann with his parting words: "Mind you come again to see me, I am deeply moved and interested, it is not a dream, it is a great cause and I understand it."[38] The case for religious influence on Balfour is clearly much stronger than it is for his scheming prime ministerial colleague.

The role of "vernacular biblical culture." Eitan Bar-Yosef has observed that "it has become a commonplace to see the Balfour Declaration as the culmination of a rich tradition of Christian Zionism in British culture: a tradition which emerged in the seventeenth century, slumbered in the eighteenth and re-emerged, with a vengeance, in the nineteenth."[39] Accounting for how these ideas spread has proved difficult. Bar-Yosef distinguishes between the highly committed students of biblical prophecy and a more general and diffused "Sunday school" interest in the Jews. Sarah Kochav is right to suggest that the two are linked. The former focused on concepts derived from a literal reading of Scripture; the latter tended to retain images that such readings had created while at the same time often moving from a literal to a metaphorical interpretation of Scripture. As Kochav has written,

> The *image* of the Jew and the Holy Land, moulded by millenarian Evangelicals, was what remained for Lloyd George and his contemporaries, long after the *concepts* of eschatology had vanished. And when we remember this, we see how influential biblical prophecy and the Evangelical movement was in the Restoration of the Jews to Palestine.[40]

Lloyd George and Balfour: shared religious language. Bar-Yosef's emphasis on a "vernacular biblical culture" that framed the Protestant discourse in such a way as to incline (even secular) British Protestants toward Zionism is important. The very language Balfour and Lloyd George repeatedly used concerning the Jews is significant and framed the larger discussion. They speak of "the Jewish nation," "the Jewish people," the "Jewish

---

[37]Schneer, *Balfour Declaration*, 135.

[38]Schneer, *Balfour Declaration*, 135.

[39]Eitan Bar-Yosef, *The Holy Land in English Culture 1799–1917: Palestine and the Question of Orientalism*, Oxford English Monographs (Oxford: Clarendon, 2005), 183.

[40]Sarah Kochav, "Biblical Prophecy, the Evangelical Movement, and the Restoration of the Jews to Palestine, 1790–1860" (paper presented at Britain and the Holy Land 1800–1914 conference, University College London, 1989), 21. This paragraph is adapted from Lewis, *Origins*, 7.

race," and a "Jewish national home." Such language was resisted by assimilationist British Jews but as we have seen had been common parlance among British evangelicals for a very long time. The debate about the influence of religion on the Balfour Declaration needs to take into consideration the language that was at the heart of the internal Jewish debate about Zionism. The contested idea within the Jewish community was whether the Jews constituted a "nation." On this Jews were divided; British Protestants generally were not.

The Great Sanhedrin of 1806 had affirmed that the Jews were no longer a polity and had ceased to have a "national" identity. This view was widely accepted by British Jews, who were largely assimilationists. For them "nationalism came to be regarded as a dangerous heresy which could have perpetuated their alienage."[41] However, the idea of a Jewish national identity, and of world Jewry as constituting a "race" and a "nation," was widespread among British Protestants throughout the nineteenth century.

The popularity of these ideas concerning the Jews among the British political elite was undoubtedly indebted to the rise of racial nationalism in the late nineteenth century.[42] It was because of these identity constructions that British policymakers "so readily and steadfastly believe[d] that Zionism was the key to the Jewish imagination." Such was possible only by positing "the belief that there existed a dominant and unchanging Jewish identity, which was fixed upon the restoration of national life in Palestine. Jewry was therefore perceived to be a very specific type of imagined community, a national community."[43] James Renton and others regard this as a fundamentally mistaken belief promoted by Weizmann and his influential Zionist lobby. "By playing upon policy-makers' perceptions of Jews and ethnic groups, with their portrayal of Jewry as a largely anti-Allied, influential and Zionist Diaspora, they successfully persuaded members of the British Government to pursue a pro-Zionist policy."[44] This perception of the Jews as a "nation" needs to be set, Renton argues, in the context of the emergence of

---

[41]Isaiah Friedman, *The Question of Palestine: British-Jewish-Arab Relations: 1914–1918*, 2nd ed. (New Brunswick, NJ: Transaction, 1992), 32.

[42]This paragraph is adapted from Lewis, *Origins*, 4-6.

[43]James Renton, *The Zionist Masquerade: The Birth of the Anglo-Zionist Alliance 1914–1918* (New York: Palgrave Macmillan, 2007), 3.

[44]Renton, *Zionist Masquerade*, 6.

racial nationalist thought as it developed in European culture in the late nineteenth century. But, while not denying the significance of racial nationalist thought, these characterizations of the Jews as "a people," "a race," and "a nation" were widespread in Protestant evangelical circles by the 1830s, well before the rise of racial nationalism, and as has been seen, these characterizations were most effectively promoted in Victorian England by Jews who had converted to forms of Protestant evangelicalism. The most effective exponents of Christian Zionism were often Jewish converts to evangelical Christianity, who did much to shape the development of popular evangelical thinking in these matters. It was this Protestant religious discourse that marked the family backgrounds of many of the key members of the British political elite responsible for formulating the Balfour Declaration.

Thus Lucien Wolf, the chief opponent of Weizmann's Zionism, could argue that the "national identity" question was the critical one, at the very core of their differences. "Wolf believed that asserting that the Jews constituted a distinct nation would fatally undercut his argument that British Jews really were Jewish Britons" and endanger Jews scattered throughout the world.[45] Anti-Semitism would then have a field day. He argued eloquently that the implementation of the Zionist scheme

> would not only aggravate the difficulties of the unemancipated, and imperil the liberties of emancipated Jews all over the world, but in Palestine itself it would make for a Jewish state based on civil and religious disabilities of the most mediaeval kind, a state, consequently which could not endure and which would bring lasting reproach on Jews and Judaism. Indeed it could not be otherwise with a political nationality based on religious and racial tests, and no other Jewish nationality is possible.[46]

In his mind, and in the minds of other prominent British Jews like Claude Montefiore and Laurie Magnus, Zionism was "an ally of anti-Semitism," and they too warned that "it undermined the security of Jews throughout the world."[47]

---

[45]Schneer, *Balfour Declaration*, 148.
[46]Schneer, *Balfour Declaration*, 150.
[47]Thomas Kolsky, *Jews Against Zionism: The American Council for Judaism, 1942–1948* (Philadelphia: Temple University Press, 1990), 17.

While Balfour appears to have been strongly motivated by his religious upbringing in his attitude toward the Jews, the same cannot be affirmed for Lloyd George. But both of them had been taught to think of the Jews in nationalist terms by their Protestant religious heritage. And thus they naturally leaned toward the Zionist view and away from the assimilationist view, the two views that were struggling for supremacy in the British Jewish community in the lead-up to the Balfour Declaration.

THE COALITION WAR CABINET

The three most influential figures behind the Balfour Declaration were Lloyd George, Balfour himself, and Lord Milner; their support was crucial. The Lloyd George government, formed in December 1916, placed its final decision-making power in the hands of the men belonging to an "inner cabinet" known as the war cabinet. Strange as it may seem, Balfour was never formally a member of the war cabinet, although he served as foreign minister and participated in cabinet debates. The same was true of Edwin Samuel Montagu; while he was a member of the cabinet and fully entered into the debates in his role as secretary of state for India, he was not at the time a voting member of the inner cabinet that endorsed the Balfour Declaration. Among the eight men who served in this inner cabinet between December 1916 and November 1917 were two who had served, or were to serve, as British prime ministers during their lifetimes: Lloyd George (1916–1922) and Andrew Bonar Law (1922–1923). The "Balfour Declaration" came, as it were, ex cathedra from on high and was communicated by the foreign secretary. The coalition cabinet represented all the parties—save the Asquith Liberals—and had a much greater degree of autonomy than any peacetime cabinet. It operated enshrouded in secrecy, gave no reasons for the declaration, outlined no conditions—other than those in the declaration itself—and expected no accountability. The declaration was not debated in either of the houses of Parliament and, like most foreign policy issues, was never approved by a British legislature.[48]

A vigorous historical debate has raged for decades as to the British cabinet's motivation in making this declaration. Early explanations in the

---

[48]This paragraph and the two following are adapted from Lewis, *Origins*, 3-8.

wake of the Great War emphasized the idealism of the British political elite and the religious sympathy among British Protestants for the idea of the restoration of the Jews. This view was most effectively expounded by leading Zionist historians such as Albert Hyamson and Nahum Sokolow, who extolled British benevolence as "driven by a mixture of idealism, religious belief and a desire to redress the past suffering of the Jewish people."[49]

Leonard Stein's 1961 work *The Balfour Declaration* took a very different tack, arguing that the two leading motives behind the declaration were related to the strategic interests discussed above: British propaganda efforts to win support for the war effort among American and Russian Jews, and the advantages such a Jewish homeland would give to British national security, ensuring its strategic military control of the Near East. The availability from the late 1960s of new government documentation led to a downplaying of the propaganda motive, and to an increased focus on Palestine; yet more recently the propaganda motive has come back into vogue with some historians—such as Segev—who focus on what they see as an anti-Semitic impulse.

James Renton has argued in 2007 book, *The Zionist Masquerade: The Birth of the Anglo-Zionist Alliance, 1914–1918*, that a myth of British "proto-Zionism" was created that served the purposes of the Zionist propagandists employed by the British government. In his view the British government's rationale in promoting Zionism in the hopes of influencing world Jewry was based on a series of faulty assumptions carefully reinforced and nurtured by the Zionist lobby. The image promoted was linear, progressive, and vaguely providentialist; history had unfolded in favor of the Jews as a people, Zionist identity had been strengthened, and Britain was to be praised for its role as the protector of God's ancient people. Renton's interpretation stresses "the degree to which the culture of policy-makers, the world-views through which they perceived reality, determined their political choices and strategy."[50]

---

[49]Renton, *Zionist Masquerade*, 85.
[50]Renton, *Zionist Masquerade*, 5.

THE CABINET AND RELIGIOUS MOTIVES?

A close examination of the religious and ethnic backgrounds of the eight men who belonged to the cabinet reveals some notable features.[51] The only member of the cabinet who had been born and raised in England, Lord Curzon, was also the sole English-born Anglican in the war cabinet, and he objected to the Balfour Declaration on practical grounds. He was the only member of the cabinet who had actually been to Palestine and wondered how the Jews would ever get there, and what they might do if they did. He was also concerned about the impact on the Muslim population. Thus Curzon questioned the wisdom of the commitment being proposed and initially opposed Balfour's proposal. (By the early 1920s Curzon was arguing that the British government should abandon the declaration.)[52]

Surprisingly, seven of the eight members had not been born and raised in England. Lloyd George, although born in England, had been raised in Wales and was thought of as Welsh. Scotland had three members (two Labour members, Arthur Henderson and George Barnes, plus the New Brunswick–born Andrew Bonar Law, who from the age of twelve had lived in Scotland). Edward Carson was an Irish Protestant. Five of the members were thus from the Celtic fringe. A seventh member was Jan Christian Smuts, born in the Cape Colony; and the eighth non-English member was the German-born Alfred Milner. Remarkably there was only one English Gentile in the cabinet.

In terms of religious background, seven of the members had been raised in evangelical homes or personally embraced evangelicalism. More specifically, five of these seven had been raised in evangelical Calvinist homes: Lloyd George—Baptist; Lord Curzon—evangelical Anglican; Andrew Bonar Law—(Presbyterian) Free Church of Scotland; Jan Smuts—Dutch Calvinist; Edward Carson—Irish Presbyterian. Three of them were sons of the manse (Curzon, Bonar Law and effectively, Lloyd George). One was a Scottish Methodist—Arthur Henderson. Little is known of the religious backgrounds

---

[51]For an assessment of the religious backgrounds and motivations of the individual members of the cabinet, see David W. Schmidt, *Partners Together in This Great Enterprise: The Rise of Christian Zionism in the Foreign Policies of Britain and America in the Twentieth Century* (Jerusalem: Xulon, 2011), 52-79.

[52]Clifford A. Kiracofe, *Dark Crusade: Christian Zionism and US Foreign Policy* (London: L.B. Tauris, 2009), 80.

of Alfred Milner and George Barnes. But clearly the influence of Calvinist forms of evangelical Protestantism dominated the family backgrounds of the majority of the cabinet members.

Religiously and ethnically, the cabinet was remarkably unrepresentative of Great Britain in either ethnicity or religion. It was dominated by non-English members and by men with Calvinist evangelical upbringings. There were no Roman Catholic members and only one Anglican (Curzon), who was non-practicing. All three of the men who served as prime minister (Lloyd George, Arthur Balfour, and Bonar Law) had been raised in devout evangelical homes. None of the cabinet members were Catholics.

By the 1920s, few of these leading Gentile Zionists self-identified as either evangelicals or as Calvinists, but the influence of the religious culture that had nurtured them disposed them to think of the Jews as a "people," a "race," and "a nation" and thus inclined them toward the idea of a Jewish homeland, and to the idea that Britain had a special role in enabling this to happen. This Calvinist evangelical background did not always dispose these cabinet members toward supporting the Balfour Declaration—Lord Curzon was the son of an evangelical Anglican clergyman but appears both to have rejected his parents' faith and to have lived his life in ways that were diametrically opposite to his clerical father. But the pattern of influence is clear: people representing the fringes of Britain and its empire whose own experience of living on the cultural peripheries gave them a special concern for the Jews, a people living on the edges of European society. And yet these people from the fringes—ethnic, geographic, and religious—constituted the British political elite in 1917 that was responsible for the Balfour Declaration.

Edwin Samuel Montagu, secretary of state for India, was another figure who was close to the war cabinet and participated in its discussions; but he was not a formal member, was firmly anti-Zionist, and was also the only Jewish voice influencing the cabinet debates. Montagu believed a pro-Zionist policy would "prove a rallying ground for anti-Semites in every country in the world,"[53] thus echoing the concerns of Lucien Wolf. An assimilationist, he wanted to be defined first by his English identity, and only secondarily as a Jew. "Ironically, a Jew represented the greatest remaining

---

[53]Schneer, *Balfour Declaration*, 338.

obstacle to cabinet acceptance of the Balfour Declaration."[54] Montagu had firmly opposed his cousin and then fellow cabinet member Sir Herbert Samuel when Samuel had presented the Zionist proposal to cabinet in 1915. He took the matter personally: "He had once remarked that he had been trying all his life to escape the ghetto. Now he understood the Zionists to be trying to push him, and every other assimilated British Jew, back inside."[55] In 1917 he could write, "I deny that Palestine is today associated with the Jews or properly to be regarded as a fit place for them to live. . . . When the Jew has a national home surely it follows that the impetus to deprive [him] of the rights of British citizenship must be enormously increased. Palestine will become the world's Ghetto."[56] Montagu thought Zionism "a mischievous creed,"[57] and his opposition was personal, passionate, and of a vehemence uncharacteristic of dispassionate political discourse. But in any event, Montagu's duties required his presence in India, and he was not at the final meeting of the cabinet that authorized Balfour's declaration to signal his continued opposition.[58]

The Balfour Declaration and Britain's "Free Hand"

As we have seen, even after issuing the Balfour Declaration, Lloyd George was secretly scheming to sacrifice it on the altar of wartime strategy, make a separate peace with Turkey, and allow the Ottoman flag to keep flying over Palestine. The Zionists did not know this, nor did Britain's Arab allies who would also have been stung by so grand a betrayal. Such a scenario would have crushed Zionist hopes and plans. But the Ottomans did not make peace, and the Zionists never learned how close their cause came to being betrayed.

There were two other factors that were crucial for the implementing of the Balfour Declaration. The first was related to America. In April of 1917 the American Congress had declared war on Germany, but crucially, America had not declared war on the Ottoman Empire, even though it was a cobelligerent with Germany. It appears that Woodrow Wilson, a devout

---

[54]Schneer, *Balfour Declaration*, 336.
[55]Schneer, *Balfour Declaration*, 338.
[56]Schneer, *Balfour Declaration*, 337-38.
[57]Kiracofe, *Dark Crusade*, 17.
[58]Schneer, *Balfour Declaration*, 343.

Presbyterian layman, did not want to be at war with the Ottomans because he had been warned by his close friend Cleveland H. Hodge that it would lead to a slaughtering of Protestant missionaries the Middle East.[59] The American failure to declare war on the Ottomans meant that after the war the Americans had no say in what happened with the dismemberment of the Ottoman Empire. Nor, of course, did they join the League of Nations, which in 1922 issued the Palestine Mandate to Britain.

The second factor was related to Russia. In the secret Sykes-Picot Agreement of 1916 the British and French had agreed to partition the empire between them and Russia after the war, granting Russia its long-desired control of Constantinople, the Turkish straits, and Ottoman Armenia, with a French buffer state in the area of Syria, leaving the rest of the empire to the British. "Thus did the Triple Entente divide the prospective Ottoman carcass even before they had skinned it, even before it was dead."[60] However, the situation changed dramatically with the Russian Revolution in February 1917, with Kerensky, the new government leader, insisting that Russia no longer wanted Constantinople or any other territory. The government that emerged after the October Bolshevik Revolution (early in November 1917 according to the Julian calendar, at the very time of the issuing of the Balfour Declaration) followed the same line: the new government disavowed the long-sought-for Russian control of Turkey that Sykes-Picot had envisioned. The Bolsheviks even published the secret agreement in late November 1917, embarrassing the British and French governments, which had made vague promises to Arab leaders to induce them to join the Arab Revolt in June 1916. But Russia's withdrawal from the Great War in December 1917 and its dis-avowal of what had been promised to Russia in the agreement also served to strengthen the British position at the end of the war. The British had borne the heavy lifting in the war with regard to the Ottomans; their French allies had done little fighting and had no troops to occupy the region after the war, leaving the British a relatively free hand in dictating the future of the Ottoman lands. The Arab prince Grand Sharif Hussein had been led to believe that Palestine would be part of his promised Arab federation, but

---

[59]David A. Hollinger, *How Missionaries Tried to Change the World, but Changed America Instead* (Princeton, NJ: Princeton University Press, 2017), 120.
[60]Schneer, *Balfour Declaration*, 165.

exactly what the British had promised and what Hussein understood they had promised turned out to be vague and contradictory, sowing seeds of much future discord and ongoing conflict.

In retrospect there are many what-ifs that affected the events surrounding the Balfour Declaration. What if the anti-Zionist cause had triumphed among British Jews, rather than the Zionist arguments? Weizmann's leadership was critical but fragile, and his victory over his Jewish anti-Zionist foe, Lucien Wolf, seemed unlikely at the start of the war. What if Sharif Hussein had occupied portions of Syria even a few weeks earlier than he did? This would have prevented the British from making the declaration.[61] What if Sharif Hussein had been able to have a powerful diplomat representing his cause in London, who could effectively counter Weizmann's lobbying? Someone, perhaps an Englishman, like Mark Sykes or T. E. Lawrence? But no spokesperson was to be found to oppose the Zionists, and Weizmann was able to carry the day—both against Lucien Wolf and against Hussein and the Arab cause. As Schneer comments, "The Balfour Declaration was the highly contingent product of a tortuous process characterized as much by deceit and chance as by vision and diplomacy."[62]

In the end, with the British having a relatively free hand in determining the fate of the Ottoman territories, rather than simply annex the area for Britain, a mandate system was created whereby French and British influence could be managed through "mandates," a form of government approved of by the League of Nations in 1922. The British Mandate for Palestine thereby ensured that Palestine "would serve as a strategic outpost protecting Egypt and the Suez Canal, the routes to India, and the hydrocarbons of Mesopotamia."[63] But, as has been seen, the British Mandate incorporated in its wording the promise of the Balfour Declaration, committing Britain to support a "homeland for the Jewish people" and pledged to use its "best endeavours" to achieve that goal.

In November 1917 the Balfour Declaration had seemed to many to be a far-fetched dream, one of many promises concocted in the midst of a desperate war to achieve specific strategic aims. Why should Britain be bound

---

[61]Schneer, *Balfour Declaration*, 369.
[62]Schneer, *Balfour Declaration*, 369.
[63]Kiracofe, *Dark Crusade*, 73.

to carry out its promise? After all, Sir Henry McMahon, the chief negotiator with the Grand Sharif Hussein urging on him a revolt against the Ottomans, could write to Lord Hardinge, the British viceroy of India, that "promises made to Arabs need not be binding upon the British government."[64] In the aftermath of the war the British felt little compunction in disavowing many of the promises they made to the Arabs, so why would they not do the same with the declaration? Although by the late 1930s there was a desire by many in Britain that it disavow the declaration, in the 1920s and 1930s the British did in fact honor it and allowed a steady stream of Jewish immigrants to settle in Palestine and entrench themselves in what the Zionists hoped would be not only a Jewish "homeland" but also a distinctly Jewish national state. The ground was being sown with seeds that would germinate into the state of Israel.

But the groundwork was also being laid for the enormous (and fully justified) suspicion of the British on the part of both Zionist and Arab leaders. British double-dealing (or even triple- or quadruple-dealing) had characterized their behavior throughout, focused as they were on gaining whatever advantage might be won by promising whatever to whomever. As Schneer has observed, "Because it was unpredictable and characterized by contradictions, deceptions, misinterpretations, and wishful thinking, the lead-up to the Balfour Declaration sowed dragon's teeth. It produced a murderous harvest, and we go on harvesting it today."[65]

---

[64]Schneer, *Balfour Declaration*, 97.
[65]Schneer, *Balfour Declaration*, 370.

10

AMERICAN CHRISTIAN ZIONISM
FROM 1914 TO 1948

WORLD WAR I AND THE VINDICATION
OF PREMILLENNIALISM

*No event in the fifty years after 1875 did more for the morale of
American premillennialists than World War I. . . . It looked as
though the times had adapted themselves to premillennialism.
Dispensationalists did not change their views to fit the events
of World War I; the war seemed to follow an already existing
and well-formulated premillennial script for the last days.*[1]

TIMOTHY P. WEBER

OUR FOCUS NOW TURNS AGAIN to America to look at Christian
Zionism in the United States up to 1948. By 1917 dispensationalists had a
detailed scenario of "end time" events. Christians would be removed from
the earth when Christ came for his saints in the rapture. But the "times of
the Gentiles" would only end when the power of a revived Roman Empire
would be broken by the personal appearing of Christ at the end of a seven-
year period known as the tribulation. This revived Roman Empire would
consist of a ten-nation confederacy headed by the antichrist. The antichrist
would emerge after the rapture during the tribulation and make a pact with
a newly founded Jewish state, allow the rebuilding of the temple, but after
three years he would turn on the Jews and demand to be worshiped as divine.

---

[1]Timothy P. Weber, *Living in the Shadow of the Second Coming: American Premillennialism 1875–
1925* (New York: Oxford University Press, 1979), 105-6.

In the second half of this seven-year period of tribulation those who refused such blasphemy would be terrorized. Eventually the antichrist's power would be challenged by a confederacy of nations from the north. (Up to 1917 prophecy interpreters were not entirely in agreement whether this referred to the Ottomans or to Russia; after the dismemberment of the Ottoman Empire, the consensus settled on Russia, where it remained until 1989.)[2] The northern confederacy, in league with a confederacy from the south (Egypt), would attack the Jewish state. A group of nations from the east would join in the fray, sending some two hundred million soldiers to engage the conflict in Palestine. The armies of the various confederacies would attempt to try to destroy the people of God (the Jews), but Christ would return with his raptured saints to destroy the evil combatants in the battle of Armageddon, and Jesus would set up his kingdom in Jerusalem to rule for a thousand years.

This whole schema was well in place before the war, and during its course, regular prophecy columns appeared in the most influential of the premillennialist journals: *Our Hope, King's Business, Christian Workers*, and the *Sunday School Times*.[3] The premillennialists were not fearful for themselves because they would be raptured before these events. But they expected to see the European confederacy of ten nations begin to take shape in their day. Thus in the fall of 1914 Arno C. Gaebelein could assure the readers of *Our Hope* that "it is possible that out of the ruins, if this universal war proceeds, there will arise the predicted revival of the great confederacy of Europe. . . . If the Lord tarries still for us, we shall have more to say in our October issue."[4]

The Lord did tarry, allowing premillennialists to map the revived Roman Empire onto the changing map of Europe. With their Bibles in one hand and maps in the other, many premillennialists began to speculate about how this could happen. As most of Germany had not been in the original Roman Empire, it would lose the war and give up some territory that had belonged to Rome; the concession of Alsace-Lorraine to France accomplished this.

---

[2]Paul Boyer, *When Time Shall Be No More: Prophecy Belief in Modern American Culture* (Cambridge, MA: Belknap Press of Harvard University Press, 1992), 102.
[3]Matthew Avery Sutton, *American Apocalypse: A History of Modern Evangelicalism* (Cambridge, MA: Harvard University Press, 2014), 51.
[4]Quoted in Weber, *Shadow*, 108.

The Austro-Hungarian Empire would have to be dismantled, and some of its provinces north of the Danube would come under Russian influence (as eventually happened). Russia would end its association with Europe and develop its influence over nations in northern and eastern Europe (the Russian Revolution of 1917 began this process). The Ottoman Empire would be broken up, and its control of Palestine would end to allow the regathering of the Jews; the Balfour Declaration was seen as initiating these events. Ireland would gain its independence from Britain (which occurred in 1921), as it was not part of the original Roman Empire. All in all "the premillennialists came extremely close to the mark" in most of their predictions. "By any standard of measurement, the premillennialists' record was extraordinary."[5] By the end of the war the premillennialists' predictions seemed to be empirically verified by the way history had unfolded. Timothy Weber observes that overall, "the war earned the premillennialists the best reception they had received since the rise of dispensational premillennialism."[6]

"THE FATHER OF ZIONISM": BLACKSTONE REVISITED

> Mr. [Louis D.] Brandeis [the Supreme Court justice] is perfectly infatuated with the work you have done along the lines of Zionism. It would have done your heart good to have heard him assert what a valuable contribution to the cause your document is. In fact he agrees with me that you are the Father of Zionism, as your work antedates Herzl.[7]

NATHAN STRAUS TO WILLIAM BLACKSTONE, 1916

Three crucial events occurred during World War I: William Blackstone continued to lobby the American government; the Balfour Declaration was promulgated in November 1917; and the British captured Jerusalem a month later. In 1916 Blackstone renewed his political efforts in association with the American Zionist lobby to move Woodrow Wilson to support Zionism, although Wilson was already sympathetic. Blackstone persuaded the

---

[5]Weber, *Shadow*, 112.
[6]Weber, *Shadow*, 115.
[7]Quoted in Shalom Goldman, *Zeal for Zion: Christians, Jews, & the Idea of the Promised Land* (Chapel Hill: University of North Carolina Press, 2009), 26.

Northern Presbyterians and other influential American denominations to endorse a new Memorial to Wilson similar to his 1891 petition to President Harrison.[8] Among the signatories were senior academics and businessmen, but
also the mainline Federal Council of Churches, the Presbyterian and Baptist
ministerial associations, and even the aforementioned Shailer Mathews, the
dean of the University of Chicago Divinity School. Noticeably absent were
Catholic signatories, which is understandable given the Vatican's steadfast opposition to Zionism, a position strongly supported by the American Catholic
bishops up to the establishment of the state of Israel in 1948—and beyond.[9]

Blackstone also collaborated with prominent American Jews in his efforts,
among them Supreme Court Justice Louis D. Brandeis, whose election in
1914 as the chair of the Provisional Executive Committee for General Zionist
Affairs had done much to legitimize Zionism in America. In April 1917
Blackstone sent Justice Brandeis a package, asking him to "kindly place the
enclosed papers in your safe to hold for a few months' time." The subsequent
paragraph of the letter made clear his reasoning: "If, according to my intense
conviction, the Rapture shall occur, and I am caught away, as described in
1 Thess 4:13-18, then will you kindly open the package and read the contents
and do whatever you may seem to you wise and best."[10] Brandeis responded
with a cordial letter assuring him that the envelope had been deposited in
his safety deposit box in Boston.[11] Blackstone also entrusted Brandeis with
executing his will. Blackstone during his lifetime donated to Jewish refugee
causes and left his considerable estate to the Zionist movement.[12] Notwithstanding Brandeis, many in the American Jewish community were not sympathetic to Zionism—whether advocated by Christians or Jews. The British

---

[8]On Blackstone's efforts to influence Wilson see Yaakov Ariel, *An Unusual Relationship: Evangelical Christians and Jews* (New York: New York University Press, 2013), 92-96.

[9]See Adriano E. Ciani, "The Vatican, American Catholics and the Struggle for Palestine, 1917–
1958: A Study of Cold War Roman Catholic Transnationalism" (PhD diss., University of Western
Ontario, 2011). See also Uri Bialer, "Theology and Diplomacy," chap. 4 in *Cross on the Star of
David: The Christian World in Israel's Foreign Policy, 1948–1967* (Bloomington: Indiana University Press, 2005), 72-90.

[10]Carl F. Ehle, "Prolegomena to Christian Zionism in America: The Views of Increase Mather and
William E. Blackstone Concerning the Doctrine of the Restoration of Israel" (PhD diss., New
York University, 1977), 297.

[11]Ehle, "Prolegomena," 298.

[12]Yaakov Ariel, *On Behalf of Israel: American Fundamentalist Attitudes Toward Jews, Judaism, and
Zionism, 1865–1945*, Chicago Studies in the History of American Religion 1 (New York: Carlson,
1991), 88.

ambassador reported to his government in 1920 that "the great mass of [American] Jews appear to be bitterly opposed to the Zionist leaders, and the rich Jews are divided among themselves."[13] In spite of this, by 1920 the American government was committed to supporting Zionism. Significantly, Blackstone's lobbying, while important, was short-lived. As Yaakov Ariel observes, "An examination of Blackstone's tactics reveals that he never tried to establish a lobby or a permanent organization."[14]

American Conservative Responses to the Balfour Declaration and the Fall of Jerusalem

Prophetic speculation was greatly increased by the events of World War I, and hopes were raised that the Ottomans might forfeit their claim to Palestine. The millenarians were enthusiastic over the Balfour Declaration, and many were convinced that General Allenby's entry into Jerusalem in December 1917 was the fulfillment of an event predicted by prophecy—for many it signaled the end of the period when Jerusalem would be "trodden down of the Gentiles" (see Luke 21:24 and Revelation 11:2). Cyrus Scofield put the consensus well when he wrote to a friend, "Now for the first time we have a real prophetic sign."[15] At a prophetic conference held in Philadelphia at the end of May 1918, A. E. Thompson explained its significance:

> The capture of Jerusalem is one of those events to which students of prophecy have been looking forward to for many years. Even before Great Britain took possession of Egypt, there were keen-sighted seers who foresaw the day when God would use the Anglo-Saxon peoples to restore Jerusalem. When the war broke out, there were some of us who were convinced that it would never end until Turkish tyranny was forever a thing of the past in the holy city. When the city was captured, we felt very confident that we could put one hand upon this great event which had stirred the heart of the whole Christian world, and, laying open our Bible at many places in the Prophets, say as confidently as Peter on the day of Pentecost, "This is that which was spoken by the prophets."[16]

---

[13]Quoted in Clifford A. Kiracofe, *Dark Crusade: Christian Zionism and US Foreign Policy* (London: L.B. Tauris, 2009), 84.

[14]Ariel, *Unusual Relationship*, 96.

[15]Boyer, *When Time*, 102n63.

[16]*Light on Prophecy* (New York, 1918), 34, quoted in Ernest Sandeen, *The Roots of Fundamentalism: British and American Millenarianism 1800–1930* (Chicago: University of Chicago Press, 1970), 234.

In November of 1918 Arno Gaebelein developed the same theme at another prophetic conference:

> What rejoicing when it became known that the unspeakably, wicked Turk, with his equally wicked German master had been defeated, that the crescent was downed and the flag of the British Lion wafted over David's City! . . . [The Jewish people] will be regathered from all countries where they are now in dispersion and restored to their God given land. The waste places will be re-built; the land will be once again a land flowing with milk and honey.[17]

Both speakers framed the regaining of Jerusalem with reference to two things. The first is a reference to the ancient enemy "the Turk" (the Prot-estant cipher for Islam), as in the ending of "Turkish tyranny" (Thompson) and "the unspeakably wicked Turk" (Gaebelein). Gaebelein made the point more explicitly when he observed that "the crescent was downed," another reference to Islam. The second is the highlighting of the providential role of English-speaking nations, "when God would use the Anglo-Saxon peoples to restore Jerusalem" (Thompson) and "the flag of the British Lion wafted over David's City!" (Gaebelein). Britain and America as the elect Protestant nations were thus seen as fulfilling the expectation that English and American Puritans had long hoped for in this major step toward the final restoration of the Jews.

THE LIBERAL PUSHBACK: THE FUNDAMENTALIST-MODERNIST CONTROVERSY ERUPTS

The very success of the premillennialists provoked an intensely adverse re-sponse from their opponents. The origins of an organized *fundamentalist movement* have been traced to the emergence of Bible conferences in the 1870s, but this movement consolidated after 1900, particularly with the for-mation of the World's Christian Fundamentals Association in 1919, which was dominated by the more extreme wing of the dispensationalists. The clashes that signaled the emergence of the *fundamentalist controversy*

---

[17] Arno Gaebelein, "The Capture of Jerusalem and the Great Future of that City," in *Christ and Glory: Addresses Delivered at the New York Prophetic Conference Carnegie Hall, November 25–28, 1918*, ed. Arno C. Gaebelein (New York: Publication office of *Our Hope*, 1919), 146-47, quoted in David A. Rausch, *Zionism Within Early American Fundamentalism, 1878–1918: A Convergence of Two Traditions* (Lewiston, NY: Edwin Mellen, 1979), 113.

emerged toward the end of World War I between fundamentalists and the theological liberals whose optimism had been shattered by the war's outbreak.

The conservatives had been divided over the wisdom of the war. Many premillennialists (including most Pentecostals) had promoted isolationism and preached pacifism, making them targets for a liberal attack.[18] Open conflict began in 1917 with the publication of *When Christ Comes Again* by George P. Eckman. This was followed by Shailer Mathews's *Will Christ Come Again?*, which dismissed New Testament apocalypticism as "the mistakes of early Christians."[19] Shailer Matthews and Shirley Jackson Case (both at the University of Chicago) and other social gospel spokesmen launched full frontal attacks on the premillennialists, accusing them of being unpatriotic and suggesting that they were being bankrolled by German money.[20] Case went as far as to accuse premillennialism of being "a serious menace to our democracy" and suggested that premillennialists might prefer a German victory because it "would bring us nearer to the end of the present world."[21]

Such accusations were as unwise as they were spurious, and the contest quickly became one in which both sides tried to prove their patriotism. Conservatives countered by pointing out that much American liberal theology had been learned by its proponents while studying at German universities. Some revivalists like Billy Sunday, William Bell Riley, and R. A. Torrey were strongly pro-military and anti-German. "The conflict," Matthew Avery Sutton observes, "gave premillennialists a perfect opportunity to link their religious beliefs to the Stars and Stripes and to connect liberal theologies with the nation's wartime enemies."[22] After the war the onslaught against the premillennialists from liberal academics and organs like the *Christian Century* was relentless. Once fundamentalist patriotism was strongly asserted, the liberal tactic changed and the accusation became "the more plausible connection with business interests,"[23] a charge that remained fashionable

---

[18]Sutton, *American Apocalypse*, 58.

[19]See Adam Petersen, "'The Premillennial Menace': Shailer Mathews' Theological-Political Battle Against Premillennialism During the First World War," *Journal of Church and State* 60, no. 2 (Spring 2018): 271-98.

[20]Sutton, *American Apocalypse*, 96.

[21]Weber, *Shadow*, 120.

[22]Sutton, *American Apocalypticism*, 62.

[23]George Marsden, *Fundamentalism and American Culture*, 2nd ed. (New York: Oxford University Press, 2006), 206.

among its historians until the 1960s, when scholars generally came to agree the "fundamentalists' deepest interests were more ideological than political."[24] In a sense these liberal attacks were a backhanded compliment and attest to the growing strength of the premillennialists in American Protestantism, demonstrating that premillennialism had arrived.

DISPENSATIONALISTS' ANTI-INTERNATIONALISM: OPPOSITION TO THE LEAGUE OF NATIONS

The mainline Protestant churches campaigned enthusiastically for the United States Senate to ratify the Covenant of the League of Nations in 1920 and "came to invest the League with definite religious meaning and even to associate it with the actual ushering in of the Kingdom of God on Earth."[25] By 1920 all the major Protestant denominations except for the Southern Baptist Convention and a few Lutheran synods had publicly endorsed the League. The Federal Council of Churches did so four times between 1918 and 1920 and urged its member churches to disseminate pro-League literature and to pressure reluctant senators to endorse the League in the ratification debate.[26] The shared optimism of the American left—both secular and religious—had been wounded but had not died on the killing fields of World War I:

> They were sure that they had the numbers and all the requisite historical determinants on their side. World War I had not shattered their optimistic expectations of humanity's progress; on the contrary, liberal internationalists had become more intent on pooling their strength to achieve their varied social goals. They could justify support of the war only if it would indeed bring about the new (social) democracy on which they agreed, and they convinced themselves that this was exactly what was going to happen, both because such was (still) the supposedly inevitable course of ethical evolution and because they themselves would make it happen.[27]

Dispensationalists both in Britain and America decried this as example of human folly and strongly opposed the League. The pushback began in

---

[24]Marsden, *Fundamentalism*, 206.
[25]Markku Ruotsila, *The Origins of Christian Anti-internationalism: Conservative Evangelicals and the League of Nations* (Washington, DC: Georgetown University Press, 2008), 2.
[26]Ruotsila, *Christian Anti-internationalism*, 25.
[27]Ruotsila, *Christian Anti-internationalism*, 26.

Britain, where in 1917 the "Advent Testimony and Preparation Movement" was established under the leadership of F. B. Meyer, a popular premillennialist writer and a well-known figure in the Keswick Holiness movement. Given the imminence of Christ's return, human schemes such as the proposed League of Nations were suspect. At prophecy conferences in America, says Markku Ruotsila, Gaebelein argued that "the inevitable culmination [of the League] would be the eventual reorganization of the whole world into one great 'World Communist Internationale, in which our civilization and religion will be totally destroyed.'"[28]

In 1919–1920, the American dispensationalists campaigned against both the secular and religious supporters of the League, and "a few of them even engaged in political lobbying against the ratification of the League Covenant."[29] The American dispensationalists opposed the League's internationalism on four grounds: it involved cooperation between Christian and non-Christian nations; it was a sinful human initiative that could not secure world peace or social progress, as these could only be achieved by the return of Christ; the United States as a Christian nation should retain its independence, serve as an example to other nations, and only in certain situations enforce right dealing; and finally, the liberal social gospel supporters of secular, pluralist international initiatives were apostate Christians and following their lead would bring God's judgments on America.[30] Further, as Weber has observed, "The majority of the premillennialists agreed that the League was one more step toward the realization of the new Rome and the rise of Antichrist."[31] Not all agreed. Mark Matthews, the Seattle pastor of the largest Presbyterian church in the world, and a dispensationalist but also a strong friend and supporter of Woodrow Wilson, was furious with his fellow premillennialists.[32]

"Christian anti-internationalism" as a stance was not isolationist, as the dispensationalists were interested in global affairs because of their mission work, but their anti-internationalism represented "faith-based opposition to the international organizations that have existed since 1919—political organizations that were secular, invested with worldwide supranational

---

[28]Ruotsila, *Christian Anti-internationalism*, 35.
[29]Ruotsila, *Christian Anti-internationalism*, 2.
[30]Ruotsila, *Christian Anti-internationalism*, 2.
[31]Weber, *Shadow*, 126. See also Sutton, *American Apocalypse*, 75-77.
[32]Sutton, *American Apocalypse*, 77.

authority, and predicated on multilateralism and the equality of all nations and religiocultural traditions."[33] The ongoing hesitations of American conservative Christians regarding the United Nations find their roots in this debate.

The overall political conservatism of the fundamentalists in the 1920s was hardly remarkable, in that it was "little more than a manifestation of commonplace American opinions of the day," although it differed in that it was "tempered by a sense of God's judgment, a sense absent from the patriotism of most Americans."[34] But the cultural alarm that was being sounded in the 1920s was much stronger than it had been before the war, when such expressions were rare and were not linked with an appeal to nationalism. The virtual disappearance of progressive sentiments that had been widespread among the conservatives in the prewar period "is a complex phenomenon related explicitly to fundamentalists' reaction to liberalism's identification with the Social Gospel."[35] The increasingly shrill note of alarm expressed in opposition to the League in 1920 was voiced explicitly in regard to theological modernism, the teaching of evolution, and the rise of communism. The overarching fear was that Christian civilization was under attack and might not survive these challenges, which were increasingly being linked together in the minds of many conservatives.

By 1919 most Americans were aware of the Bolshevik threat. "The premillennialists' earlier predictions concerning the menacing role of Russia in the end times added a degree of plausibility to such fears."[36] The Bolshevik Revolution was understood as another one of the "signs of the times," as referring to the powers from "the north" (Ezekiel 38:6, 15) that would threaten any Jewish entity in the end times. At this point "Zionism-Israel and Communism-Russia became closely intertwined in the minds of American fundamentalists."[37] The fundamentalist movement as it developed in the 1920s in America deliberately wrapped itself in the American flag, viewing itself as the great bastion of Western opposition to the "godless Communists." Such views helped to prepare "the way for the high-profile Christian 'anti-communist crusades' of the early Cold War period."[38]

---

[33]Ruotsila, *Christian Anti-internationalism*, 3.

[34]Marsden, *Fundamentalism*, 207.

[35]Marsden, *Fundamentalism*, 207.

[36]Marsden, *Fundamentalism*, 208.

[37]Kiracofe, *Dark Crusade*, 77.

[38]Kiracofe, *Dark Crusade*, 87.

George Marsden argues that it was in this period that a "great reversal" occurred among the conservative Protestants in the matter of political engagement, for their traditions had "almost always encouraged some political involvement—whether temperance, Sabbath legislation, anti-Masonry, anti-slavery, or any of the other evangelical causes."[39] Following World War I the premillennialist movement was for a time dramatically politicized in the anti-League efforts and then in an anti-evolution crusade. Anomalously the premillennarians looked to one of America's most famous politicians, William Jennings Bryan, to lead that crusade, although Bryan himself, while a fundamentalist, was not a premillennialist (if anything he was a vague postmillennialist) and had a strong record as a progressive politician.

But while conservatives in the 1920s were politicized on the League and evolution issues, their overall political involvement was haphazard, and there was little unity on other political issues. Marsden has argued that aside from their support for Prohibition, and their opposition to Al Smith, the Democratic presidential nominee in 1928 (because of his Catholicism and his opposition to Prohibition), there was no wider political consensus—"except that the church should not be involved in political affairs," reflecting the notion of the "Spiritual Calling of the church."[40] But that involvement did not mean that the dispensationalists should ignore the happenings on the world stage. They were convinced that the Roman Empire would be revived to establish a ten-nation confederacy and looked intently for signs of this happening. With the rise of Benito Mussolini to power in Italy in 1925, a new candidate for antichrist was identified, but his candidacy took several hits in the next decade as he proved himself to be inept, reckless, and not the smooth diplomat expected of the antichrist. He would only do as a "type" or a forerunner of the real thing.[41]

Particularly puzzling for the dispensationalists was the way in which Germany and Russia were behaving. From their interpretation of Ezekiel 38 they were sure that they were to partner together in a northern confederacy in the great tribulation (Gog was by now identified as Russia and Gomer as Germany), but Hitler's deep opposition to communism made this

---

[39]Marsden, *Fundamentalism*, 207.
[40]Marsden, *Fundamentalism*, 208.
[41]On Mussolini, see Sutton, *American Apocalypse*, 213-19.

partnership unlikely.[42] The Nazi-Soviet nonaggression pact of August of
1939 seemed to confirm their prophetic scenario. The dispensationalists
were elated. At a prophecy conference in New York in November 1939, Gaebelein speculated that in light of this clear and remarkable "sign of the times"
that "for all we know, this may be the last prophetic conference which will
be held, for 'our gathering together unto him' [the rapture] cannot be far
away."[43] When in June 1941 Hitler invaded Russia, the prophetic writers
were silent. In general their failures did not thoroughly discourage them;
they reworked their interpretations to accommodate the new realities.[44]

AMERICAN MILLENNIALISM IN THE 1920s

In the 1920s many conservative Christians continued in their traditional
denominations—particularly the Northern and Southern Presbyterians,
the Baptists, and the Congregationalists—and did not withdraw from their
traditions under the strain of the fundamentalist controversy. But the
leaders of the millenarian movement by the 1920s differed from the pre-
1900 leaders in that "few of these leaders possessed any firm denominational ties and that most of them were affiliated with Bible institutes."[45]
Such schools had emerged beginning in the 1880s, initially designed to
equip laypeople in domestic evangelism and as Christian workers, and
then began to train people to serve as foreign missionaries. By the 1920s,
many of the millenarian leaders were sitting loose to denominational affiliation. Ernest Sandeen observes that "denominational loyalties seemed
much less important to twentieth-century millenarians than to their nineteenth-century predecessors."[46] In the late 1800s "denominational affiliation, though deprecated and deemphasized, was ordinarily considered
necessary."[47] In fact, many of the older generation of leaders had thought
it unwise to operate without denominational affiliation. By the 1920s that
was changing.

---

[42]Boyer, *When Time*, 166. On attitudes to Russia see Sutton, *American Apocalypse*, 221-22.

[43]Timothy P. Weber, *On the Road to Armageddon: How Evangelicals Became Israel's Best Friend*
(Grand Rapids, MI: Baker Academic, 2004), 92.

[44]On premillennialists' attitudes to Hitler see Sutton, *American Apocalypse*, 219-21, and on the 1941
German attack on Russia, see 280-83.

[45]Sandeen, *Roots*, 239.

[46]Sandeen, *Roots*, 240.

[47]Sandeen, *Roots*, 240.

Distrust of the mainline denominations' susceptibility to liberalism was a factor for some. Sandeen contends that by the 1920s for many dispensationalists traditional denominations were effectively replaced by nondenominational institutional structures, chief of which were the Bible institutes, which often began behaving like denominations.[48] These schools took on roles far more wide-ranging than an educational mandate might suggest. Moody Bible Institute developed its own financial-support base and a student-recruitment network among a host of sympathetic churches. In the 1930s it ventured into radio broadcasting and published its own periodical, *Moody Monthly*. Links with specific foreign missionary societies, particularly faith missions like the China Inland Mission, were also forged, with the school both training the missionaries and linking them to a wider conservative constituency that supported the workers on the mission field. The close alliance of dispensationalism with the faith-mission approach pioneered by James Hudson Taylor of the China Inland Mission and reinforced in the Bible school movement was to be critical in the internationalizing of dispensational teaching and in turn of Christian Zionism in the twentieth century. Some schools like Moody held their own conferences for their alumni and further consolidated connections through summer conferences. Weber has commented, "Such activities produced tremendous loyalties among its constituents and friends, many of whom had deeper ties to the Institute than they did to their own denomination. As a parody of a popular gospel song put it, 'My hope is built on nothing less / Than Scofield's notes and Moody Press.'"[49]

Many of these evangelicals' identities were bonded less by denomination than by the Bible school network of friends and acquaintances, which constituted their primary community of allegiance. In these ways, the nature of American fundamentalism was morphing in the early twentieth century and the millenarian movement was shaping the fundamentalist movement that emerged in the 1920s. Given these factors, conservatives could not agree on an interdenominational structure to rival the National Council of Churches of the mainline denominations until the founding of the National Association of Evangelicals in 1942.[50]

---

[48]For details on the development of the Bible schools see Sutton, *American Apocalypse*, 150-60.
[49]Weber, *Shadow*, 174.
[50]On its founding see Sutton, *American Apocalypse*, 284-90.

THE ROLE OF CHRISTIAN ZIONISM IN
AMERICAN FUNDAMENTALISM

Understanding this background is important in explaining the role that the Christian Zionist cause played in American fundamentalism in the 1920s, for it was something that could bring together disparate groupings of evangelicals, regardless of their millenarian views, or their denominational affiliations or lack of one. Whether they were historicist or futurist premillenarians, they could all agree on the prophetic significance of signs indicating the return of the Jews to Palestine. In early nineteenth-century Britain, many key postmillennialists, as well the resurgent historicist premillennialists, could agree on the return of the Jews to Palestine as a prophesied event to be expected by Christians. And the American millenarian movement throughout the nineteenth century—except for the Millerites—had been able to agree on one point, and that was their confident prediction that the Jews would return to Palestine.

The Christian Zionist vision offered dispensationalists hope, comfort, and something on which they could experience a degree of unity even with those who were outside of the dispensational tent. Hope was important, especially because the dispensational view of the future was so bleak: their Bible teachers told them that institutional churches were becoming apostate and Christianity's public influence was waning. Earthquakes would increase, floods would occur, wars would break out. But it also offered comfort, for while those who hoped in human progress would be bitterly disappointed, the true believers would be removed to heaven in the rapture. While others might experience the chaos they read about in their daily newspaper, the premillennialists had in their prophetic schemas a superstructure in which such events could be comprehended.

> By having a pre-existing script, premillennialists were able to explain the events of their time and, as dispensationalists understood so well, once a historical event was placed somewhere within God's eternal plan, it lost its ability to terrorize. That is why premillennialists could be so calm and so hopeful in the face of a dismal and catastrophic future.[51]

---

[51]Weber, *Shadow*, 127.

The flip side of this hope was the confidence that premillennialism engendered. As Sutton observes, "In a darkening age, they alone understood the significance of cascading world events. While the rest of humanity naively marched toward the coming tribulation, fundamentalists looked forward to the rapture and then millennial bliss."[52]

Christian Zionism served to unify many conservative evangelicals across denominational and prophetic differences. The very divisiveness of the fundamentalists of the 1920s appears to be one reason for the increasing appeal of prophecies concerning the Jews: Christian Zionism was a banner under which a wide coalition of conservative evangelicals could work. The signs of the times were clear: God was up to something in his dealings with the Jews, as millenarians had been saying for decades—indeed, for four centuries— and corroborating evidence for this view was found on the front pages of the newspapers they read. Surely here was confirmation of their long-held and deeply cherished hope for the restoration of the Jews being accomplished before their eyes. An accompanying sense of being on the right side of history, of their long-ridiculed beliefs being vindicated, filled many millenarian hearts. While they may have been divided on the details, there was a unity in celebration of prophecy being fulfilled—especially in both the Balfour Declaration and the fall of Jerusalem.

CHRISTIAN ZIONISM AND EVANGELIZING THE CHOSEN PEOPLE

As discussed above in chapter six, a distinctive characteristic of evangelicalism is its concern with personal conversion, and dispensationalists were concerned with trying to convert Jews to Christianity, however much this might be resented. Premillennialists (unlike William Hechler) would not abandon the attempt and "were able to stress the evangelization of the Jews while at the same time they supported Jewish nationalist aspirations."[53] Premillennialists were convinced that they had an edge in such work. As James Brookes claimed, "No man is fit to preach to the Jews unless he believes in the personal coming of the Messiah." It was important to show observant Jews that their hope of restoration to Palestine "is founded on the

---

[52]Sutton, *American Apocalypse*, 211.
[53]Weber, *Shadow*, 141.

coming of Messiah."[54] Premillennialists founded new evangelistic societies targeting American Jews, and employed many of the approaches developed in the eighteenth century by the German Pietists, and refined in the nineteenth by the London Jews' Society.[55] By the middle of the twentieth century American Christian missions to the Jews came to be dominated almost entirely by premillennialists. Disagreements had emerged about the degree of contextualization that would be allowed for Jewish converts, but in the end the view that converts should assimilate into conservative evangelical churches prevailed.[56]

Weber contends that in the half century between 1875 and 1925 premillennialists, while concerned with Jewish evangelism, "were fierce opponents of anti-Semitism in any form, and they frequently called themselves the friends of Israel."[57] Sutton, however, argues that in the 1920s "many fundamentalists, like Americans more generally, harbored strong anti-Jewish prejudices" and that some were anti-Semitic.[58] Much may come down to how one defines *anti-Semitism*, which I take to mean racially based hatred of Jews.[59] The fundamentalists would generally have been horrified to have been called anti-Semitic, but clearly some of them employed negative stereotypes of individual Jews while they professed to love Jews as a people and some made "repeated references to ugly stereotypes."[60]

Paul Boyer has raised the troubling question as to whether premillennialism might actually have served (perhaps unwittingly) to encourage anti-Semitism. David Rausch in his *Zionism Within Early American Fundamentalism* has argued vigorously that the premillennialists were philo-Semitic and strongly opposed anti-Semitism. Rausch apparently does not consider Jewish stereotyping by some of the prophetic writers to constitute anti-Semitism. Rausch, claims Boyer, does not acknowledge "the way premillennial belief encouraged a passive view of anti-Semitic outbreaks as foreordained 'chastisements' or 'corrections.'"[61] Boyer also points out the philo-Semitism

---

[54]Weber, *Shadow*, 142.
[55]For a description of such work in the early twentieth century see Weber, *Shadow*, 143-57.
[56]For a discussion of this matter see Weber, *Armageddon*, 123-28.
[57]Weber, *Shadow*, 154.
[58]Sutton, *American Apocalypse*, 125.
[59]This is not to say that the Jews are a separate race, but anti-Semites characterized them as such.
[60]Sutton, *American Apocalypse*, 125.
[61]Boyer, *When Time*, 218.

Rausch emphasized was of a special variety. "Prized for their role in biblical times and their high place in Christ's millennial kingdom, Jews in their present 'unbelieving' state were viewed far more ambivalently. They had a glorious past and future; only the present posed problems."[62]

David Wilson has documented a strain of what he terms anti-Semitism in pre-1945 prophecy writings but makes the subtle point that "those who believe that the Jews face endless chastening and persecution for their collective guilt in rejecting and crucifying Jesus, even if they are not openly anti-Semitic, are more inclined to 'expect the phenomenon of anti-Semitism and tolerate it matter-of-factly.'"[63] In Wilson's view, premillennialists were conditioned by their interpretation of Scripture to expect anti-Semitism as a fact of life, and while pro-Zionist they did little to decry inhumanity toward the Jews. However, as Boyer points out, prophecy writers after World War II often denounced anti-Semitism, especially "prophecy writers involved in Jewish missionary work," and as time passed "prophecy popularizers routinely denounced anti-Semitism."[64] As Boyer acknowledges, anti-Semitism seems to have largely vanished from postwar premillennialism.

Keeping the larger picture in view is helpful. In the nineteenth century premillennialists of the historicist variety were at the forefront of the protests against Russian anti-Semitism, and in the past quarter century at least, both in America and abroad premillennialists have emerged as vigorous opponents of anti-Jewish and anti-Israeli expressions. Yet Boyer is correct in pointing out that "at the heart of dispensationalism lies the assumption that Jews are essentially and eternally *different*. The view of 'the Jew' is not necessarily hostile, but he is always *separate*, a figure whose special traits and destiny arouse endless speculation."[65] As Frederick J. Miles put it in a book on prophecy in 1943, "Unique in origin, the Jew is equally unique in racial purity. . . . We cannot assimilate and absorb the Jew. *He remains a Jew*."[66] And as we have seen, Darby made such a radical separation between Jew and Gentile and taught that the separateness would endure throughout eternity, with Christians ruling from heaven,

---

[62]Boyer, *When Time*, 219.
[63]Boyer, *When Time*, 219.
[64]Boyer, *When Time*, 220.
[65]Boyer, *When Time*, 220.
[66]Boyer, *When Time*, 220.

Jews from earth. This underlines Boyer's view that "the Jew's cosmic *otherness* in the premillennial system encouraged subtle stereotyping that, if not consciously 'anti-Semitic,' nevertheless shaped perceptions of what one popularizer called 'that Strange People, the Jews.'"[67]

Joel Carpenter in his study of the reorganization of American fundamentalism in the 1920s and 1930s has commented that "the most astonishing sign of the times for fundamentalists, and the one which they were most ready to explain in prophetic terms, was the rise of anti-Semitism and the widespread persecution of the Jews."[68] Both before and after their resettlement in Palestine they believed that the Jews were to undergo "the time of Jacob's trouble" (citing Jeremiah 30:7). These troubles would be horrendous, but in the end Christ would return to bring deliverance to the Jewish people.

The dispensationalists' attitudes to the Jews were thus both complex and ambivalent.[69] They were eager to evangelize Jews, and often experienced deep hostility from the Jewish community for doing so. In some cases, warm and friendly relationships between Christians and Jews were established, often because of the common concern for the Zionist cause. American premillennialist journals like their British counterparts—particularly the publications of the London Jews' Society—were ever on the watch for anti-Semitism, and while they decried the mistreatment of Jews they expected that such actions might move Jews to consider the Zionist option and return to Palestine.[70]

But at times, some fundamentalists promulgated stereotypes of Jews that mixed suspicion with affection. This was not the case with Jewish-Christian evangelists in general, or with William Blackstone. As Ariel has observed, there are "almost no remarks in his writings that portray the Jews as greedy or malicious, or that attribute any other unpleasant characteristics to them."[71] In a speech to Zionists in 1918, Blackstone outlined what he considered to be the three options for contemporary Jews: First, they could become "true Christians" by embracing Christ as Lord and Savior, but he expected few would follow this

---

[67]Boyer, *When Time*, 221.
[68]Joel A. Carpenter, *Revive Us Again: The Reawakening of American Fundamentalism* (New York: Oxford University Press, 1997), 97.
[69]For a fuller discussion of this matter see Weber, *Armageddon*, 129-53.
[70]Weber, *Armageddon*, 136.
[71]Ariel, *On Behalf of Israel*, 63.

option. Second, they could become "true Zionists," but he understood these "true Zionists" as religiously motivated Jews who hold fast to messianic hopes for the restoration of the Jews to Palestine (which was pretty rare of those Jews who were active Zionists). The third option was the assimilationist path and to resist the Zionist appeal. Blackstone's dispensationalist views left no room for "genuine, non-Zionist Jewishness," which left the dispensationalists open to the charge of anti-Semitism, which they strongly denied.

An ambivalence toward the Jews, however, can be seen in the ministry of Blackstone's contemporary Dwight L. Moody, who often referred to the Jews in his sermons, in which he expressed "many common prejudices against Jews."[72] Yet while prejudiced, Moody was not an anti-Semite. Ariel has commented, "His attitude toward the Jewish people included elements of appreciation and hope," and while given to stereotyping, "it was far from demonic or diabolic."[73] At one point Moody was quoted as saying that French Jews in a meeting in Paris had boasted having "killed the Christian God"; an angry protest ensued in the American Jewish press, and Moody apologized, claiming he had been misquoted and saying that he respected the Jews.[74] In 1893 Moody welcomed to Chicago the Lutheran minister and politician Adolf Stoecker to work alongside him in evangelism given his success with the German working classes. Stoecker, however, was a leading and virulent anti-Semite, but Moody trusted him and "did not bother to check the accusations against him."[75] Occasionally some dispensationalists expressed hostility toward the Jews—particularly irreligious, "unbelieving" Jews—and at times appeared indifferent to their suffering. Some pointed to reasons why Jews might have brought trouble on themselves, while others attributed anti-Semitism to demonic activity.

Some premillennialists were worse. Isaac M. Haldeman, a leading New York City Baptist minister, penned a book, *Signs of the Times*, in 1911 in which he recapped the long sad history of anti-Semitism and then, as if to offer it as a way of explanation of the shortcomings of Jewry, wrote,

---

[72] Ariel, *On Behalf of Israel*, 21.

[73] Ariel, *On Behalf of Israel*, 32.

[74] Ariel, *On Behalf of Israel*, 33. For a discussion of American Jewry's hostile attitude to Moody see David A. Rausch, *Communities in Conflict: Evangelicals and Jews* (Philadelphia: Trinity Press International, 1991), 57-61.

[75] Ariel, *On Behalf of Israel*, 33.

Because they had no recourse; because all men were their enemies, and every hand against them, their character responded to the times and its usage. Unable to defend themselves with arms, they seemed to fawn, to yield, took advantage of their foes, cheated when they could, and lied themselves out of threatened danger. These were their only weapons of defense, and when caught in the attempt to so defend themselves against the assaults of other Gentile aggressors, were smitten and persecuted a thousandfold—each characteristic of apparent duplicity justifying the Gentile his murderous attack.[76]

And yet Haldeman immediately goes on to reaffirm in his own way his belief in divine care for the Jews:

God used the Gentile nations as his rods wherewith to correct his disobedient people; at the same time he warned these nations that while he would not make a full end of the Jews, he would make a full end of them.

He has kept, and is keeping, his twofold promise.

He has laid his hand on the nations that persecuted them. No nation has touched them and not paid the penalty in sorrow, in suffering, or national shame.[77]

Similar ambivalent sentiments had been expressed by James H. Brookes in his 1893 tract *How to Reach the Jews*.[78]

There were other egregious expressions by premillennialist spokesmen that reinforced Jewish stereotypes and rationalized social discrimination. Presbyterian minister Charles C. Cook, writing in 1921 in *The King's Business*, published by the Bible Institute of Los Angeles, is an example:

The Jewish race is morally fully capable of doing all that is charged against it. It is at present rejected of God, and in a state of disobedience and rebellion. . . . As a race Jews are gifted beyond all other peoples, and even in their ruin, with the curse of God on them, are in the front rank of achievement; but accompanying traits are pride, overbearing arrogance, inordinate love for material things, trickery, rudeness and an egotism that taxes the superlatives of any language. Oppressed are they? Indeed, and subject to injustice more than any other race, and yet never learning the lesson of true humility. . . .

These cheap adulations [of editors, ministers, and politicians] are usually based on no better foundation than self-interest, for the unregenerate Jew

---

[76]I. M. Haldeman, *The Signs of the Times* (New York: Charles C. Cook, 1911), 437-38.

[77]Haldeman, *Signs of the Times*, 438.

[78]Ariel, *On Behalf of Israel*, 28.

usually has a very unattractive personality. There is a reason for his being *persona non grata* at resorts and in the best society; who can deny it?[79]

Such views are clearly bigoted and reinforced popular stereotypes; but to call them racially based hatred of Jews (my definition of anti-Semitism) is problematic.

PREMILLENNIALISTS AND *THE PROTOCOLS*

Some of the more surprising examples of this ambivalence come from the pens of several fundamentalist leaders, including Christian Zionists who thought of themselves as philo-Semites, like Arno Gaebelein and James M. Gray, president of Moody Bible Institute. Both were impressed by *The Protocols of the Elders of Zion*, a document that claimed to be a Jewish plan for world domination popularized in America by Henry Ford in his newspaper, *The Dearborn Independent*. While the *Times* of London exposed it as a flagrant forgery as early as 1921, its appeal only grew. In the early 1920s Gaebelein mentioned *The Protocols* several times in his journal, *Our Hope*, and expressed his belief that the document came "from the pen of apostate Jews"—the people he believed were behind Bolshevism and other international revolutionary movements. Weber writes,

> Gaebelein was especially struck by how many Jews were involved in the illegal liquor business and how many criminals had Jewish last names, facts that fit well with the conspiracy's plan to undercut society's morals and stability. Gaebelein believed there was something especially loathsome about the chosen people doing such things. Since God expected more from them, their sins were worse than other people's. "There is nothing so vile on earth as an apostate Jew who denies God and His Word."[80]

In his *The Conflict of the Ages* (1933) Gaebelein cataloged at length a list of conspiracies that he believed had plagued America. While he questioned the authenticity of *The Protocols*, he still regarded much of it as believable. Thus Gaebelein and others, "like the anti-Semites they condemned, blamed

---

[79]Charles C. Cook, "The International Jew," *King's Business* 12 (November 1921): 1087, and Dwight Wilson, *Armageddon Now! The Premillenarian Response to Russia and Israel Since 1917* (Tyler, TX: Institute for Christian Economics, 1991), 76. As quoted in Weber, *Armageddon*, 132.
[80]Weber, *Armageddon*, 132.

Jews for the mess the world was in."[81] James M. Gray, while emphasizing his opposition to anti-Semitism, also acknowledged that to him the *Protocols* sounded "authentic." Eventually, under heavy criticism in 1935, Gray began to backtrack and insisted that Moody Bible Institute had never officially promoted *The Protocols*. While he never retracted his claim that the work was "a clinching argument for premillennialism," he decided it would be better to confine his comments to Scripture alone.[82] Blackstone, however, rejected *The Protocols* as anti-Semitic propaganda and wrote to the editor of Ford's *Dearborn Independent* to insist,

> I do not believe for a moment that the Jews have any organization for securing control of the government of the world, neither do I believe that they were at all instrumental in the production or propagation of the so-called protocols, and it is amazing to me that such anti-Semitic propaganda could be established in this country as well as in England.[83]

The extreme wing of the fundamentalists represented by the Baptist preachers William Bell Riley, the sometime editor of *The Christian Fundamentalist*, and Gerald Winrod were more extreme in their views, regarding Franklin Roosevelt's administration as communist in disguise.[84] Riley, even under heavy criticism from his old friend and associate J. Frank Norris, would not back down, and in 1939 Riley published a new work *Wanted—a World Leader!* in which he went even further in his vitriol toward the Jewish conspiracy he saw threatening the world.[85] Winrod was thoroughly unrepentant in his determined defense of Hitler; in 1942 he was arrested for sedition by the American government, although the case ended in a mistrial when the judge hearing the case died in its early stages.[86]

But there was also significant pushback from other premillennialists, especially those active in Jewish evangelism, who strongly rebuked fellow fundamentalists for such statements and for the embrace of *The Protocols*. In

---

[81]Weber, *Armageddon*, 130.

[82]Weber, *Armageddon*, 139.

[83]Ariel, *On Behalf of Israel*, 64.

[84]The premillennialists were generally united in their opposition to Roosevelt. See Sutton, *American Apocalypse*, chap. 6.

[85]Weber, *Armageddon*, 141.

[86]Weber, *Armageddon*, 140. See also Ariel, *Unusual Relationship*, chap. 8, "Evangelical Christians and Anti-Jewish Conspiracy Theories," for a fuller discussion of attitudes to the *Protocols*.

1933 the *Hebrew Christian Quarterly Alliance* castigated evangelical periodicals such as the *Moody Monthly*, the *Sunday School Times*, and *Revelation* for endorsing *The Protocols*. Joseph Cohn of the American Board of Missions to the Jews severely criticized Gaebelein for his *Conflict of the Ages*.[87] Harry A. Ironside, pastor of the flagship Moody Church in Chicago, added his public rebuke to dispensationalist leaders, grieved as he was "to find that the Protocols are being used not only by godless Gentiles, but even by some fundamentalist Christians to stir up suspicion and hatred against the Jewish people as a whole."[88] "By the late 1930s, other dispensationalists were ready to condemn the *Protocols* as an outright forgery that should never have been taken seriously, no matter how much it seemed to confirm prophetic expectations."[89]

Dispensationalists' Response to Hitler

While the dispensationalists sincerely believed that they were the best friends of the Jews and often condemned anti-Semitism, Weber comments that "they often accepted anti-Semites' analysis of why Jews were despised in the world. This perspective made dispensationalists remarkably susceptible to anti-Semitic conspiracy theories and Nazi propaganda during the 1930s."[90] Weber's assessment should be qualified with the word *some*—their perspective made some of the premillennialists susceptible. Certainly Blackstone was not, and even before Hitler rose to power, Gaebelein had adopted an anti-Nazi position, rejecting their racial theories and decrying their attempt to eliminate Judaic features of Christianity. He made a connection between Nazi anti-Semitism and what he considered to be its hostility to orthodox Christianity. As Ariel acknowledges, "His premillennialist views served, in this case, as a wall against Nazi propaganda."[91] And yet he came away from a visit to Germany in 1937 appreciative that Hitler was preventing the growth of what he considered to be Jewish-inspired Bolshevism. He commented, "There is no question in my mind that Hitler was an instrument of God to save Germany and Europe from the Red Beast."[92]

---

[87] Weber, *Armageddon*, 138.
[88] Weber, *Armageddon*, 138n38.
[89] Weber, *Armageddon*, 139-40.
[90] Weber, *Armageddon*, 130.
[91] Ariel, *On Behalf of Israel*, 116.
[92] Weber, *Armageddon*, 143.

As the Nazis took power in Germany, some premillennialist leaders—notably James Gray of Moody Bible Institute—hesitated to be critical of Hitler because of cautions from German pastors who played down the anti-Semitism of the Nazis, while many others protested vociferously, especially Jewish Christian evangelists.[93] In the early 1930s it seemed that many dispensationalists—as indeed, many Americans more generally—were genuinely confused as they struggled to understand Hitler and what was taking place in Germany. Firsthand observation of the situation in Germany by various dispensationalist leaders in the mid-1930s produced sharply differing assessments.[94] A study of Protestant journalism in the 1930s found that "fundamentalists were the best informed of any American Protestants on the Jews' situation in Europe,"[95] but at the same time they produced little positive action beyond expressions of sympathy and outrage, and some refugee relief efforts. Interest in prophecy seems to have reached a fever pitch by the late 1930s, but there were a few who wondered whether all this focus on prophecy was entirely helpful to the health of American evangelicalism. Some feared that an "obsession with scouring the news for hints of the antichrist took time and energy away from the work of helping to save humankind from the coming tribulation. "But is it not a fact," W. W. Shannon asked, "that many of the saints will cross the city and go many miles to hear about the Antichrist, but they would not cross the street to try to win a soul for Christ?"[96] Scofield had warned that prophetic study was not meant to encourage such speculation, but rather was intended to develop "present character, not future prediction." Its proper outcomes were friendship and intimacy with God, hope and optimism.[97]

CHRISTIAN ZIONISM AS AN EVANGELICAL IDENTITY MARKER

Christian Zionism may not have been the cause they understood as their "community of primary allegiance," but it was emerging for many evangelicals as a key identity marker of their form of Christianity. But while an identity marker, for many it was not yet a political cause. The dispensationalists

---

[93]See Weber, *Armageddon*, 142-46, for a discussion of this matter.
[94]Weber, *Armageddon*, 143.
[95]Carpenter, *Revive Us Again*, 99.
[96]Sutton, *American Apocalypse*, 229.
[97]B. M. Pietsch, *Dispensational Modernism* (New York: Oxford University Press, 2015), 164.

largely saw themselves as outside of the mainstream of American political life, and most felt that their hope was in heaven, and not to be placed in political action. Thus as Stephen Spector has observed, "American premillennialists were mainly passive in their support for Israel prior to 1948, though with the conspicuous exception of William E. Blackstone."[98]

In their publications, such as *Our Hope* magazine (edited by Frank Gaebelein, Arno's son), Moody Bible Institute's *Moody Monthly*, the Pentecostals' *Evangel*, and the Bible Institute of Los Angeles's *The King's Business*, the Christian Zionists kept their constituencies abreast of developments in the Jewish world, the Zionist movement, and in particular, what was happening in the growing Jewish community in Palestine. They were heartened in the 1920s and 1930s with the British government's allowing a steady influx of Jewish immigrants and approved of the British administration of the Palestine mandate. The opening of the Hebrew University (1925) and of the port of Haifa (1932) were seen as signs of Jewish progress toward the goal of a homeland in Palestine. They opposed British government restrictions on Jewish immigration and became alarmed by Arab hostility and violence toward the *Yishuv* (the Jewish community in Israel). In 1931 James Gray, the president of Moody Bible Institute, cautioned in *Moody Monthly* that those who attempted to block God's plans for the Jews would not succeed.[99] While there was some divergence among premillennialists in their view of Arabs, the general consensus was that they were Ishmael's descendants, the son of Abraham by his wife's handmaiden, Hagar. But the land had been promised to Isaac, the son of promise, the father of the Jews. In the 1930s anti-Arab sentiments were frequently repeated in dispensationalist discourse.

While the millenarian Christian Zionists had a cause, it was not yet a political cause, and millenarian-motivated Christian Zionism did not yet have a discernible political impact in America, as it arguably had had in Britain. Blackstone's efforts with his 1891 petition of President Harrison and his new petition effort in 1916 to influence President Wilson were the most important political campaigns that American Christian Zionists had mounted. The 1916 petition was endorsed by the general assembly of the

[98]Stephen Spector, *Evangelicals and Israel: The Story of American Christian Zionism* (Oxford: Oxford University Press, 2009), 20.
[99]Ariel, *On Behalf of Israel*, 266.

Presbyterian Church, USA, and it was that denomination that presented it to President Wilson, indicating how many within mainline Protestantism had come to support Blackstone's agenda.[100] But mainline Protestantism was not uniform on this matter. The *Christian Century* from 1917 remained opposed to Zionism, and repeatedly argued that "the great majority of Jews in the world were either uninterested in a Jewish state, or 'are more or less opposed to it.'"[101] Even in 1948 when opinion polls indicated that 80 percent of Americans supported the establishment of a Jewish state, the *Christian Century* maintained its opposition.[102]

From 1945 to 1948 much of the American religious support for Israel came from the mainline Protestant denominations—the *Christian Century* notwithstanding—rather than from the heirs of the fundamentalists of the 1920s, who were generally passively supportive but not very politically active. As Caitlin Carenen has argued, "American [mainline] Protestants had undergone a dramatic shift in attitudes—from ambivalence about Jewish suffering in the early 1930s to effective mobilization on behalf of the Zionist cause by 1945."[103]

In the United States the leading mainline theologian Reinhold Niebuhr supported Zionism on theological (although not prophetic) grounds.[104] Niebuhr "was convinced that the hegemonic powers owed Jews a nation-state not only as security against persecution in the future but also as 'a partial expiation' for the vexed history of Jewish-Christian relations."[105] In Europe, Karl Barth, the founder of the theological movement known as "neo-orthodoxy," which was so influential in both Europe and America, also endorsed Zionism.[106]

---

[100]Ariel, *On Behalf of Israel*, 85.

[101]Hertzel Fishman, *American Protestantism and a Jewish State* (Detroit: Wayne State University Press, 1973), 29.

[102]Goldman, *Zeal for Zion*, 21.

[103]Caitlin Carenen, *The Fervent Embrace: Liberal Protestants, Evangelicals, and Israel* (New York: New York University Press, 2012), 17.

[104]On Niebuhr see Fishman, *American Protestantism*, 68-70, and Samuel Goldman, *God's Country: Christian Zionism in America* (Philadelphia: University of Pennsylvania Press, 2018), 107-16. See also Robert Benne, "Theology and Politics: Reinhold Niebuhr's Christian Zionism," in *The New Christian Zionism: Fresh Perspectives on Israel and the Land*, ed. Gerald McDermott (Downers Grove, IL: IVP Academic, 2017), 221-48.

[105]Goldman, *God's Country*, 117.

[106]For an extended discussion of Barth's view, see Mark R. Lindsay, "Karl Barth and the State of Israel: Between Theology and Politics," chap. 4 of *Barth, Israel, and Jesus: Karl Barth's Theology of Israel* (Aldershot: Ashgate, 207), 59-85.

The leadership of mainline Protestant Christian Zionism in the second half of the twentieth century was profoundly influenced by James Parkes (1896–1981), a British Anglican minister who in the 1920s had begun to campaign against anti-Semitism; he helped to rescue Jewish refugees in the 1930s and worked tirelessly to promote respect for the Jews. He also ardently opposed the evangelization of the Jews. His *The Conflict of the Church and Synagogue: A Study in the Origins of Anti-Semitism* (1934) looks at the first eight centuries of Christian history to understand the origins of antagonism between the two and lays the blame squarely on supersessionist doctrine.[107]

His pro-Jewish advocacy was taken up by two American Methodist scholars. Roy A. Eckardt (1918–1997) was to become a friend of Parkes. He published his first book on the subject in 1948, *Christianity and the Children of Israel*, and two decades later *Elder and Younger Brothers: The Encounter of Jews and Christians* (1967). In his view God's covenant with the Jews is eternal and not superseded by the church, which has been brought into the Jewish family and therefore Christians should be committed to the welfare of the Jews and of the state of Israel. Over the next several decades he published many books advocating such views.[108]

The other leading figure carrying the torch for Christian Zionism in the mainline churches was Eckardt's friend Franklin H. Littell (1917–1998), a leading figure in the establishment of Holocaust studies. Littell had spent about ten years in postwar Germany as a religious adviser to the American High Command and had become a student of the Holocaust. He became a forceful public spokesman rejecting supersessionism, which he termed "theological anti-Semitism."[109] His *The Crucifixion of the Jews* (1975) takes specific aim at the *Christian Century*, which for him represented "an endemic cultural Antisemitism."[110]

Jewish Anti-Zionism and the Great Reversal

Paradoxically, the strongest American opposition to Zionism came from a

---

[107]James Parkes, *The Conflict of the Church and the Synagogue: A Study of the Origins of Anti-Semitism* (London: Soncino, 1934).

[108]On Eckardt, see Franklin H. Littell, "In Memoriam: Roy Eckardt," *Journal of Genocide Research* 1, no. 1 (1999): 11-12.

[109]Franklin H. Littell, *The Crucifixion of the Jews* (New York: Harper & Row, 1975), 25.

[110]Littell, *Crucifixion*, 73.

group of Reform Jews, who represented the traditional antipathy of the American Jewish community. Reform Judaism was the main religious expression of German Jewish immigrants from central Europe prior to 1880. Enlightened, rational, and progressive, it prided itself on being a purely spiritual community which rejected the notion that Jews constituted a nation. Many Reform rabbis castigated Zionism. But the demographics of American Jewry were changing quickly: in the period between 1880 and 1920 the American Jewish community grew rapidly with the influx of Eastern European Jews, who soon constituted the overwhelming majority. These newcomers were far more likely to identify themselves in national or ethnic terms, and thus were more easily drawn into the Zionist cause. Jewish Zionism in America grew after World War I under the leadership of Louis D. Brandeis. Although it declined in the 1920s, it began to grow again in the 1930s and by the 1940s was becoming very influential. In 1940 the World Zionist Organization launched a campaign to woo American Jews, and anti-Zionist Jews responded by forming the American Council for Judaism in 1943. But as Thomas Kolsky has concluded, "Once the story of the Holocaust became fully known in 1945, any serious chances for the success of anti-Zionism were doomed."[111] Even after independence in 1948 the American Council for Judaism maintained its opposition to the state of Israel, but its influence waned.

In the postwar period the anti-Zionists had significant friends in the American State Department, chief among them being Secretary of State George Marshall.[112] These anti-Zionists were dismayed when Truman surprised them with his immediate and unilateral recognition of the state of Israel within hours of its declaration of independence, making the United States the first nation to recognize the new state. The lobbying efforts of a group of powerful liberal Protestants was important behind the scenes, reasoning that Christian anti-Semitism had been responsible for the Holocaust and that therefore Christian America should make amends and support the establishment of the Jewish state, an act of atonement on behalf of Christendom.[113]

---

[111]Thomas Kolsky, *Jews Against Zionism: The American Council for Judaism, 1942–1948* (Philadelphia: Temple University Press, 1990), 5.
[112]Goldman, *Zeal for Zion*, 27.
[113]See Carenen, *Fervent Embrace*, chap. 2.

Truman's motives in recognizing Israel have been debated endlessly by historians.[114] He was facing an upcoming election (which many thought he would lose), and he was dependent on American Jewish finances, needing to win the electoral votes of New York State with its large Jewish population. In private Truman frequently complained about being pushed around by "the Jews" but ended up doing their bidding, then whined to friends about being told what to do. In a 1945 diary entry he expressed his personal skepticism about the idea that the Jews were God's elect people: "The Jews claim God Almighty picked 'em out for special privilege. Well, I'm sure he had better judgment. Fact is, I never thought God picked out any favorites."[115] Later he put his own spin on events and sought to take credit for his pro-Israel policies, claiming he was "the Cyrus" of modern times.[116] Truman's denominational heritage was liberal Baptist, but his background reflected no particular sympathy for a religiously motivated Christian Zionism.

Assessing Christian Zionism's Impact in This Era

Carl F. Ehle's study of Blackstone argues that there were three ways in which Christian Zionism abetted political Zionism. First, he maintains that individual Christians like Blackstone in America and William Hechler in Germany helped the Jewish Zionists to achieve certain political objectives through their lobbying and through their connections with senior government leaders in Germany and the United States. It is widely acknowledged that Hechler acted as an important liaison between Herzl and European royalty, and the German Kaiser through his close friendship with the Kaiser's uncle, the Duke of Baden.[117] Second, he argues that the Christian Zionists in this period helped to facilitate Jewish acceptance of the Zionist cause. He points to sociological theorist Samuel Halperin, who has reasoned that "large sections of every minority group are oriented in their values and daily lives toward the dominant majority culture rather than to their own

---

[114]For a recent discussion of Truman's role, see Walter L. Hixson, *Israel's Armor: The Israel Lobby and the First Generation of the Palestine Conflict* (New York: Cambridge University Press, 2019), chap. 2.

[115]Quoted in Goldman, *God's Country*, 120.

[116]For a discussion of this see Goldman, *Zeal for Zion*, 27-28.

[117]Ehle, "Prolegomenon," 343.

groups."[118] Halperin further argues that, "in fact, prominent non-Jewish supporters of a Jewish state may be said to have mattered considerably more
than similarly situated Jews"[119] and that "the existence of this coalition of
Jewish and Christian Zionist or Christian pro-Palestine interests decisively
facilitated the acceptance of Zionist claims by American Jews."[120] Ehle's third
conclusion is perhaps less controversial: that the Christian Zionists in this
period promoted "a receptive environment for Zionist propaganda" among
some non-Jews. Clearly Blackstone was the most important American
Gentile in this regard, and his activities parallel those of Hechler in Germany,
although there is no indication that either of them was aware of the other.

---

[118]Samuel Halperin, "Zionism and Christian America: The Political Use of Reference Groups," *The Southwestern Social Science Quarterly* 40, no. 3 (1959): 225-26, quoted in Ehle, "Prolegomena," 244.
[119]Halperin, "Zionism and Christian America," 225-26, quoted in Ehle, "Prolegomena," 244.
[120]Halperin, "Zionism and Christian America," 236, quoted in Ehle, "Prolegomena," 245.

11

CHRISTIAN ZIONISM
AND DEVELOPMENTS
IN PALESTINE

FROM THE BALFOUR DECLARATION
TO ISRAELI INDEPENDENCE

BRITAIN AND THE PALESTINE DEBACLE

Any aid too that we can nationally render to their peaceful
return (without sanctioning their impenitence or any injustice
to others), will be graciously accepted by the God of Abraham,
of Isaac and of Jacob, and will bring down blessings on the
country rendering such aid. (Ps cxxii.6 Gen xii:3)[1]

EDWARD BICKERSTETH, 1836

With Great Britain's pledge in the Balfour Declaration to establish a Jewish "homeland," the situation in Palestine changed dramatically. The Zionists were eager that the British allow Jewish immigration, but this policy was met with fierce resistance from Palestinian Arabs. With the rise of Arab nationalism and large numbers of persecuted Jews desiring to immigrate, the British were faced with the thankless task of policing an Arab population that resisted Jewish immigration and Zionists who demanded more.

The dream of balancing human rights. A line in the Balfour Declaration asserted that the aspirations of the Jews would be squared with protecting

---

[1]Edward Bickersteth, *The Restoration of the Jews to Their Own Land: In Connection with Their Future Conversion and the Final Blessedness of Our Earth*, rev. ed. (London: Seeley and Burnside, 1841), xci.

the rights of non-Jews, "it being clearly understood that nothing shall be done which may prejudice the civil and religious rights of existing non-Jewish communities in Palestine." In a letter solicited by the war cabinet to sound out Jewish attitudes to the proposed declaration, Joseph Herman Hertz, the chief rabbi of the United Kingdom, lauded this wording:

> The draft declaration is in spirit and in substance everything that could be desired. I welcome the reference to the civil and religious rights of the existing non-Jewish communities in Palestine. It is but a translation of the basic principles of the Mosaic legislation: "And if a stranger sojourn with thee in your land, ye shall not vex him. But the stranger that dwelleth with you shall be unto you as one born among you, and thou shalt love him as thyself" (Lev 19:33, 34).[2]

Rabbi Hertz's reassurance on this point set a high moral bar for the Zionists.

The Zionists were more realistic than Hertz and were fully aware that success would eventually require the displacement of Arabs if there was to be a viable Jewish-majority state. The first step was the purchase of land (largely from absentee owners living in other parts of the Middle East) and then the piecemeal eviction of tenant farmers. The concept of a population "transfer" of Arabs out of the anticipated Jewish state had been discussed in Zionist circles from the start of the movement; in the 1930s it was hoped by some that the British would carry this out. From the late 1930s there were hopes that millions of Polish Jews might be resettled in Palestine with inducements suggested for the Arabs to move en masse to Syria or another Arab area to make way for them. "All understood that there was no way of carving up Palestine which would not leave in the Jewish-designated area a large Arab minority (or an Arab majority)—and that no partition settlement with such a demographic basis could work."[3] During World War II, even some Arab officials conceded the need for partition of Palestine and the transfer of both Arabs and Jews to their respective areas.[4]

Growth of Arab hostility: riots of 1920–1921. Palestinian Jews early on adopted a policy of only employing Jews on their farms and small-scale industries, not wanting to be politically and economically dependent on

---

[2]Christopher Sykes, *Two Studies in Virtue* (London: Collins, 1951), 222.
[3]Benny Morris, *The Birth of the Palestinian Refugee Problem Revisited* (Cambridge: Cambridge University Press, 2004), 59.
[4]Morris, *Revisited*, 58-60.

Arabs. A policy of separate development kept most Jews apart from their Gentile neighbors. But hostility toward the Jewish settlements was strong enough for the emergence of Jewish military groups as early as 1907 to guard such settlements. The idea of Jewish self-defense had been around for some time given the experience of the Russian pogroms of the 1880s and in particular the Kishinev pogrom of 1903 in Russia.[5] As Shalom Goldman has commented, "A rallying cry of the early Zionists was that a Jewish territory in Palestine would enable Jews to defend themselves against their enemies."[6] The need for such self-defense in Palestine became increasingly evident.

In April 1920 rioting occurred in Jerusalem, leaving some five Jews and four Arabs dead. It was becoming obvious that British plans for continued Jewish immigration would be met by strong resistance from Arab nationalists. In response to these events the Haganah (literally "The defense") was formed in June 1920, a military force that would eventually evolve to become the core of the Israel Defense Forces. Throughout the 1920s, Arab nationalist unrest "demonstrated the growing hatred of the Palestinian masses—egged on by a mixture of real and imagined religious and nationalist grievances, and Muslim preaching—for the burgeoning Zionist presence."[7]

The British attitude to Palestine was in flux. Lord Curzon, who had been critical of the declaration in the war cabinet in 1917, was by the early 1920s actively seeking to make it a dead letter and wanted it ignored. But the British government did take actions that helped to forward the Zionist cause, actions strongly supported by Winston Churchill. In 1920 David Lloyd George's government appointed Sir Herbert Samuel, a nonpracticing Jew and a moderate Zionist, as the first high commissioner for Palestine. His appointment was greeted with strong hostility from Palestinian Arabs, both Christian and Muslim.

Continued Jewish immigration and Jewish purchases of Arab land were highly contentious issues, and British military officials warned the government of dire consequences from an enraged Arab population. Similar warnings had been issued in the wake of the conquest of Jerusalem in 1917.

---

[5] Shalom Goldman, *Zeal for Zion: Christians, Jews, & the Idea of the Promised Land* (Chapel Hill: University of North Carolina Press, 2009), 29.

[6] Herzl tended to play down this need in his writings and in his 1902 novel, *Old-New Land*, envisioned Arabs living as satisfied and successful partners with Jews, grateful for the prosperity they had brought to Palestine. Goldman, *Zeal for Zion*, 28-29.

[7] Morris, *Revisited*, 10.

The British government had downplayed any talk of General Allenby's entry into Jerusalem being cast in terms of a new Christian "crusade," aware that this would inflame Muslim feelings not only among the Arabs in the Middle East but also among Muslims in British India. The Jerusalem riots of 1920 were only a foretaste of what was to come.

1929 Arab riots. In August 1929 rioting occurred when a long-simmering dispute over access to the Wailing Wall in Jerusalem turned violent. The riots spread throughout Palestine; some 133 Jews and about 110 Arabs were killed. There was a good deal of destruction of Jewish property and some seventeen Jewish communities were evacuated. Palestine was again at the top of the British political agenda, where it would remain until World War II. The presenting issue was the growth of the Jewish community, which between 1917 and 1939 expanded from 83,000 (about 7 percent of the population), to over 400,000 (about 28 percent).[8]

The government response produced the Passfield White Paper of 1930, which took a largely pro-Arab line and greatly angered the Zionists. The British were confused, angry, and uncertain about what to do; British policy toward Palestine veered one way, then the other, in part because the Foreign Office favored the Arabs while the Colonial Office favored the Zionists. There was no consistency regarding the British attitude to the flow of immigrants or to the question of partition. Arthur Koestler's observation is apt: "In fact, the main characteristic of British policy in Palestine up to 1939 was the absence of any consistent design."[9] The British were concerned on several fronts: the British fleet was stationed at Haifa, and it was also an important hub for its oil pipeline and rail system. In 1935 Italy conquered Abyssinia, underlining Palestine's strategic importance for protecting British interests in the region and its access to the Suez Canal and its Indian possessions.

The ongoing influence of "Sunday school Zionism." Throughout this period there are traces of what might be termed a "Sunday school Zionism" in the backgrounds of important political players—of Winston Churchill, T. E. Lawrence (of Arabia), Arthur Balfour, and David Lloyd George, who all

---

[8]Timothy P. Weber, *On the Road to Armageddon: How Evangelicals Became Israel's Best Friend* (Grand Rapids, MI: Baker Academic, 2004), 164.
[9]Clifford A. Kiracofe, *Dark Crusade: Christian Zionism and US Foreign Policy* (London: L.B. Tauris, 2009), 96.

had a cultural memory influenced by the philo-Semitic and pro-Zionist atmospheres of their upbringings. There were also two important military figures who were influenced by this sort of Sunday school Zionism. The first is Lieutenant-Colonel John Henry Patterson (1867–1947), an Anglo-Irish Protestant officer who during World War I commanded the Zion Mule Corps and later a group of soldiers known as the Jewish Legion. Benjamin Netanyahu regards Patterson as "the commander of the first Jewish fighting force in nearly two millennia. And as such, he can be called the godfather of the Israeli army."[10] Patterson was also the godfather of Netanyahu's brother, Johnathan, who was named after him. An Irish Protestant, Patterson wrote in favor of Zionism and befriended many leading Zionists, including Professor Benzion Netanyahu, Benjamin's father.

The second was Orde Wingate, the grandson of a Protestant missionary to the Jews and the son of Plymouth Brethren missionaries to India (where he was born). His mother instilled in him his mission to the Jews: "She taught me that I must live by the Bible, and that I must help the prophecies of the Bible to come true. It was she who told me to befriend the Jews, and help them to fulfill the biblical prophecy and return to Palestine."[11] Wingate was a high-ranking British intelligence officer stationed in Palestine in 1936 who believed fanatically that he had a religious duty to facilitate the creation of a Jewish state. In the early 1940s he acknowledged that he had never met a Jew before arriving in Palestine, but "long before I reached Palestine I knew what the Jews were seeking, understood what they needed, sympathized with their aims, and knew they were right."[12] Wingate established a special unit made up of British soldiers and Jewish volunteers from the Haganah called the Night Squad, which was tasked with countering Arab terrorism.[13] Among the soldiers he trained were Generals Yigal Allon and Moshe Dayan, who later confessed that Wingate had taught them all they knew about warfare.[14]

---

[10]Ron Ross, "The Christian Godfather of the Israeli Army," *Christian Today*, August 13, 2019, https://christiantoday.com.au/news/the-christian-godfather-of-the-israeli-army1.html.

[11]Goldman, *Zeal for Zion*, 30.

[12]Goldman, *Zeal for Zion*, 30.

[13]This eventually developed into the Palmach, an elite fighting force that eventually formed the backbone of the high command of the Israel Defense Forces.

[14]For further details see Goldman, *Zeal for Zion*, 29-30.

DISPENSATIONAL RESPONSES TO THE PALESTINE DEBACLE

There was no consensus among dispensationalists as to whether the influx of Jewish immigrants was the final restoration of the Jews, or whether that would only occur with the second coming. A few even speculated that Zionism was "doomed to failure, because, as they claim, it is a man-made movement, which leaves God out of all considerations."[15] Such discordant views died away as the years went by and by 1948 had virtually disappeared. From the 1920s onward, American dispensationalists were generally enthusiastic supporters of the British in Palestine and its favoring of the *Yishuv* and Zionism. One author in a pamphlet, *Israel in Covenant and History*, made the case that the Jews had six titles to the land; no mention was made of the rights of the Arabs.[16] As the American premillennial press observed the events of the 1920s, they were interpreted through the lens that "Arabs were descendants of Ishmael, who, not being the promised heir of the land given by God to Abraham, had been cast out."[17]

Throughout the dispensationalist discussions there was an antipathy to the Arabs, which "was not derived from any hatred of the Arabs themselves or of their actions, but simply was inherent in the premillenarians' view of Biblical restorationism."[18] In the 1920s some dispensationalists "continued to hold the naïve view that desertion by the Turks had left Palestine a great vacuum that was sucking the Jews back by some inevitable law of nature. Many never even considered the question of the justice or injustice of the Jews replacing or overpowering the native—Arab existence was completely ignored."[19] Continuing into the 1930s the premillennial view was almost entirely anti-Arab. God had given the Holy Land to the Jews, and the Arabs had best adapt to that reality. The dispensationalists throughout the 1920s and 1930s opposed any attempt by the British to abandon its Balfour commitments; they also strongly opposed calls for restrictions on Jewish immigration.[20]

---

[15]Dwight Wilson, *Armageddon Now! The Premillenarian Response to Russia and Israel Since 1917* (Tyler, TX: Institute for Christian Economics, 1991), 69.

[16]Wilson, *Armageddon Now*, 66.

[17]Ruth Mouly and Roland Robertson, "Zionism in American Premillennial Fundamentalism," *American Journal of Theology and Philosophy* 4, no. 3 (1983): 106.

[18]Wilson, *Armageddon Now*, 71.

[19]Wilson, *Armageddon Now*, 72.

[20]Wilson, *Armageddon Now*, 93.

The 1929 riots were widely reported in the premillenarian press in America and England. There was no doubt in their minds that the end of "the times of the Gentiles" would soon be realized and that Palestine would come under Jewish control. As the Bible Institute of Los Angeles's journal put it, "Regardless of whether the question is settled by arbitration or by the sword, the Jew is, according to the Scriptures, the rightful owner of Palestine."[21] The *Pentecostal Evangel* argued, "During the whole of the work of Jewish colonization not a single Arab has been dispossessed; every acre of land acquired by the Jews has been bought at a price fixed by the buyer and the seller."[22] A writer in *The King's Business*, while willing to acknowledge some Jewish share of blame for the events of 1929, managed to slight both Jews and Arabs in his assessment of the events:

> As in most unfortunate incidents, there has been fault on both sides. It is quite evident that the Jew has not come to Palestine to live with the Arab, but quite apart from him. The Jew in Palestine is frequently bigoted, and often carries "a chip on his shoulder." It is well known that the Jews themselves were partly to blame for the riots of 1929. But this does not justify the Arab for his falsehoods which helped to incite the trouble, nor for the murder of men, and even women and children, of which he is guilty. It was an Arab massacre, in which Jews sought to defend themselves.[23]

Defenses of Arab rights were rare; there were a few cogent appeals for justice for the Arab population, but they mattered little to most premillennialists.[24]

Arab Revolt: 1936–1939

In 1936 a yet-more-serious Arab revolt began as Palestinian nationalists attacked the British and the Zionists; some two thousand Arabs were killed in combat (Arab estimates put the figure over five thousand), and much lower deaths among Jews (between ninety-one and several hundred). The British supported Jewish militias like the Haganah and courted a rival Palestinian clan, the Nashashibis, who collaborated with the British and the Zionists to crush the revolt. The British army resorted to the systematic destruction of

---

[21]Wilson, *Armageddon Now*, 73.
[22]Wilson, *Armageddon Now*, 73.
[23]Wilson, *Armageddon Now*, 89.
[24]Wilson, *Armageddon Now*, 104.

Arab homes, the execution or exile of many of the Palestinian leaders, especially members of the dominant Husseini clan, driving some of them into the arms of the Nazis. The putting down of the revolt greatly weakened Palestinian society, both politically and militarily, which in turn set it up for defeat by the Zionists in 1948.

On the diplomatic front, the British responded with the "Peel Commission" in 1937, which recommended ending the Palestine Mandate and the imposition of a partition. All of the strategic places (especially Haifa) would remain in British hands; Jews would be granted their area (20 percent of the land) and Arabs theirs (more than 70 percent), but British interests would not be abandoned. The Zionist leadership saw this proposal positively and called for further negotiations of the details; the Arab Higher Committee rejected partition, and demanded the immediate ending of the Palestine Mandate, the prohibition of further Jewish immigration, and the establishment of an Arab state in all of Palestine with vague promises to Jews already there. The Woodhead Commission was set up, but its recommendations were rejected by all parties early in 1939. Finally in May of 1939 a government white paper was issued that proposed a Palestinian state that would accommodate both Jews and Arabs; Jewish immigration would be capped at seventy-five thousand over a five-year period, and no further Jewish immigration after 1944 would be allowed without Arab consent. Sale of Arab land to Jews was also severely curtailed. The Arabs were promised independence within a decade, and assured that they would remain the majority. With the prospect of another war, Britain in May 1939 established a pact with Turkey; wartime strategy required the British to put any talk of a pro-Zionist policy on hold.

These British actions were decried in the dispensationalist press. One explanation proffered for Britain's betrayal was that she was trying to placate Muslims in British India, but the journal *Our Hope* expressed its confidence that whatever the British motives were, it was convinced that "they *shall* go back to their land. . . . How and when the White Paper will be repudiated we do not know, but that in the end it *shall* be non-effective is a certainty."[25] The white paper's policies remained the official British position until it formally

---

[25]*Our Hope*, quoted in Wilson, *Armageddon Now*, 106.

handed over responsibility for Palestine to the United Nations in 1947, although it did not withdraw its troops until May 1948. The restrictions on Jewish immigration made the British odious to the Zionists. British soldiers and colonial officials became the targets of the Jewish terrorist organizations —especially after the war—for these policy decisions had left millions of European Jews stranded with no place to turn.

The Zionist Focus Shifts to America

In the early 1930s the international Zionist movement realized it had to focus on building support in America, and the United States soon became its main focus. As has been seen, American Reform Judaism was strong among the long-standing German Jewish community in America and was traditionally anti-Zionist. Assimilationist American Jews rejected the notion that Jews constituted a nation.[26] The new Zionist political initiative in America provoked "the final and most bitter Jewish attack on Zionism before the creation of a Jewish state."[27] The Zionists knew they also needed Christian allies in their cause. As early as 1932 the American Palestine Council took the lead in courting conservative American Christians.[28] Its public language was coded in such a way as to attract the support of dispensationalists: "The fulfillment of the millennial hope for the reunion of the Jewish people with the land of its ancient inheritance, a hope that accords with the spirit of biblical prophecy has always commanded the sympathy of the liberal Christian world."[29]

In the 1930s and early 1940s new organizations emerged that sought to harness the Zionist sympathies of mainline Protestants who were motivated by humanitarian concerns, rather than by prophecy: the Pro-Palestine Federation of America (1932), the Christian Council on Palestine (CCP), and the American Christian Palestine Committee. The CCP was the most important of these organizations, attracting the support of Reinhold Niebuhr, the leading American theologian whose "Christian realism" supported a Jewish homeland on ethical (but not prophetic) grounds.

---

[26]The Pittsburgh Platform of 1885 reflected the ideology of American Reform Judaism, which was embraced by the majority of American Jews, many of whom were of German descent. The fifth paragraph of the platform states, "We consider ourselves no longer a nation, but a religious community." Thomas Kolsky, *Jews Against Zionism: The American Council for Judaism, 1942–1948* (Philadelphia: Temple University Press, 1990), 22.

[27]Kolsky, *Jews Against Zionism*, 18.

[28]Kiracofe, *Dark Crusade*, 101.

[29]Kiracofe, *Dark Crusade*, 102.

In 1940 international Zionists moved their headquarters to the United States. Efforts were focused on Congress, and in particular on the Democratic Party. The rise of Hitler had alarmed American Jews in the 1930s, and the British white paper of 1939 restricting Jewish immigration to Palestine—and then in 1944, halting Jewish immigration entirely—shocked American Jews and did much to sway anti-Zionist Jews to the Zionist cause. Walter Hixson has recently published a study of the early years of the pro-Israel lobby in the United States titled *Israel's Armor: The Israel Lobby and the First Generation of the Palestine Conflict.*[30] Hixson sees the large conference of American Jews that gathered at the Biltmore Hotel in New York in May 1942 as the birthplace of the lobby. It issued the Biltmore Program, which called for unrestricted Jewish immigration, and immediate, full Jewish statehood. As he observes, "The extensive lobbying efforts of American Zionists predate the creation of Israel and flourished throughout the first generation [1942–1967] of the special relationship."[31] The Jewish pro-Israel lobby was masterful in producing results: "On multiple occasions, American diplomats, advisers, and all four presidents [Truman, Eisenhower, Kennedy, Johnson] became frustrated and angry at the pressures placed upon them by Israel and its domestic supporters. Yet whenever US leaders or diplomats appeared to challenge Israeli actions and policies, the lobby counterattacked and typically proved highly effective in achieving its aims."[32]

The British Dilemma: the Militant Zionists

> *[Britain] had in 1917 somewhat rashly let themselves in for a romantic adventure and did not know how to get out of it.*[33]

ARTHUR KOESTLER

Emboldened by American Zionist support and by the turning of the tide in the war in both Europe and the Far East, by 1944 the Jewish Agency in Palestine

---

[30]Walter L. Hixson, *Israel's Armor: The Israel Lobby and the First Generation of the Palestine Conflict* (New York: Cambridge University Press, 2019).

[31]Hixson, *Israel's Armor*, 1.

[32]Hixson, *Israel's Armor*, 2.

[33]Arthur Koestler, *Promise and Fulfilment: Palestine 1917–1949* (New York: Macmillan, 1949), 16.

began to act as if it was already an independent government, much to the chagrin of the British colonial officials.[34] As the story of what had happened to European Jewry at the hands of the Nazis became known, public opinion in the West began to swing toward the opening of Jewish immigration to Palestine, and eventually to Jewish statehood. The British tried to prevent Zionist ships from making their way to Palestine, both before and after the war in an attempt to honor the promises made to the Arabs in 1939, but this policy was unpopular and difficult to implement. British soldiers in Palestine found themselves arresting illegal Jewish refugees, some of whom they had liberated from the concentration camps, and having to inter them in camps in Palestine before sending them back to Europe.

Anti-British violence flared again in Palestine, but now much of it came from Jewish nationalists, and British diplomats and soldiers were the target. In 1940 Avraham Stern broke with the Irgun (the Revisionist Irgun Zvai Leumi—IZL) to found Lehi (Lohamei Herut Yisrael, or LHI, or Freedom Fighters of Israel, or Stern Gang) as a new and more radical terrorist organization bent on expelling the British from Palestine. Stern had decided that Zionists could not support the Allies any more than the Fascists, and was determined to use whatever means necessary to evict the British from Palestine, including making a pact with Germany if it would agree to a Jewish homeland. Stern was killed in 1942, and Yitzhak Shamir took over the leadership of the organization. (Shamir in the 1980s and early 1990s served two terms as Israeli prime minister.) Lehi orchestrated a guerilla war in which Jewish terrorists killed British police, hung British soldiers in retaliation for the execution of Lehi operatives, and placed bombs in public buildings. It tried several times unsuccessfully to assassinate Sir Harold MacMichael, the British high commissioner. In November 1944 Shamir organized the assassination of the British diplomat Lord Moyne (Walter Guinness of the Irish brewing family), in Cairo. This action infuriated the moderate Zionist leaders, and "they began cooperating with the British to eradicate the organization."[35] Yet from 1945 to 1948 Lehi and the Irgun carried out

---

[34]Kiracofe, *Dark Crusade*, 109.
[35]Weber, *Armageddon Now*, 166.

numerous attacks on British soldiers, the Palestine rail system, and British boats, provoking anti-Jewish riots in Liverpool, Manchester, and Glasgow.

The Palestinian leadership that had been crushed by the British in the Arab revolt of 1936–1939 had sided with the Axis powers, receiving support from them even during the revolt. Mohammed Amin Al-Husseini (ca. 1897–1974) and his followers had supported an anti-British revolt in Iraq in 1941 and then moved to Germany, where they worked for the Nazi government, with Al-Husseini broadcasting German propaganda, seeking to enlist Muslims in the Balkans for the Nazi war effort.[36] David Brog argues that Al-Husseini was present at the conference of the German military leadership in January 1942 that decided to pursue the "Final Solution of the Jewish Question," and encouraged the Nazis to pursue this path. Brog would seem to suggest that the Arab reaction to Zionism contributed to some degree to the Holocaust. There were efforts to try Al-Husseini as a war criminal once the war was over, but he escaped and took up residence in exile in Egypt, where he directed Palestinian terrorism aimed at Israel. Palestine's Jews had of course generally opposed the Nazis, and some twenty-eight thousand Palestinian Jewish volunteers fought for the British, gaining military experience that would serve them well in the coming conflict with the Palestinian Arabs. The *Yishuv's* economy was dramatically strengthened during the war, as it became a military workshop for the British army, and the skills and infrastructure so gained were of great value in preparing for what was to come.

AFTER WORLD WAR II

In July 1945 Churchill, a strong Zionist, was defeated by Clement Attlee, whose Labour government was strongly pro-Arab. The staggering cost of maintaining an occupation force in Palestine and the ongoing Jewish resistance to British rule made the government eager to withdraw from Palestine. But the British were beholden to the United States, both for its support during the war and for much-needed American postwar loans to rebuild its shattered economy. Churchill was no longer in power, and Franklin Roosevelt was gone, having died in April 1945. Roosevelt had been very cautious

---

[36]See David Brog, *Reclaiming Israel's History Roots, Rights, and the Struggle for Peace* (Washington, DC: Regnery, 2017), 116-19.

in his dealings with Palestine and had "favored a trusteeship arrangement for Palestine in which Muslim, Jewish, and Christian interests would be protected,"[37] the very sort of arrangement that the Zionists and many Palestinians rejected.

Harry S. Truman was much more supportive of the American Zionists, so while the United Kingdom lost a strongly pro-Zionist leader, the United States gained one. The immediate problem was the huge number of Jewish refugees eager to emigrate to Palestine, but who were prevented from doing so by the British cap on immigration. In August 1945 Truman sent a letter calling on the British government to allow the immigration of one hundred thousand Jews to Palestine. The British responded by suggesting the establishment of an Anglo-American Committee on Palestine, which recommended that Palestine become a trusteeship under the auspices of the United Nations. American Zionists were too powerful in the American Congress for its recommendations to be acted on. The Zionists didn't want a trusteeship; the Biltmore Program insisted on a Jewish state.

The Palestine Mandate expired in April 1946 with the death of the League of Nations, and the British were eager to hand responsibility for Palestine to the new United Nations in 1947. But by then Palestine was experiencing a civil war, and Zionist paramilitary groups like the Irgun, the Haganah, and the Stern Gang (Lehi) were making the British role in Palestine unsustainable. Attacks on British troops by Zionist extremists became commonplace, and the British public was angry with what they regarded as rank ingratitude toward them by many Palestinian Jews. The British army, having helped to liberate the death camps, was now trying to restrain the Zionists, who were now determined to rid Palestine of the British. By 1946 even many of the moderate Zionists were turning against the British and were coming to favor an armed uprising. Early in that year the British tried to crack down on the resistance by means of mass arrests, but to no avail. In July 1946 the Irgun, under the direction of Menachem Begin, bombed the British administrative headquarters at the King David Hotel in Jerusalem, killing ninety-one people, among them British officials, Jews, Arabs, and innocent civilians. The British army in Palestine was facing a determined

---

[37]Kiracofe, *Dark Crusade*, 111.

foe, supposedly the people they were protecting while waiting for the end of the Palestine Mandate.

Dispensationalists followed these events closely, and some were troubled by them. From time to time discordant voices were raised, as in the case of T. A. Lambie's article in *The Sunday School Times* in May 1946. While he followed the standard dispensationalist line of argument regarding the Jews taking possession of Palestine—"God has decreed it. It must be so"—he evidenced a measure of cognitive dissonance in regard to justice for the Arabs so displaced:

> Of course [the Jews'] right to the land cannot be maintained apart from God.
> . . . The Arab people in the land do have rights from almost every human
> viewpoint. These rights can never be ruthlessly trampled under foot, and it is
> difficult to imagine their having a change of heart and becoming willing to
> admit the Jews. An irresistible force seems to be meeting an immovable body
> and how God's purpose for Israel will work out in its inflexible course we can
> only wonder. It will be worked out, and all that most of us can do about it is
> to watch, to pray, and to believe.[38]

THE UNITED NATIONS' PARTITION PLAN

The British planned to hand responsibility for Palestine over to the United Nations on May 15, 1948. In May 1947 the new United Nations Special Committee on Palestine (UNSCOP) was established and in August recommended the partition of Palestine.[39] In November 1947 the United Nations General Assembly endorsed partition. The measure, Resolution 181, made it through the Security Council following the surprising about-face of the Soviet Union, which many had been expected to veto the plan. The Soviets apparently believed that Israel, being a socialist project, might align with them once it achieved independence. The vote in the General Assembly on November 29, 1947, was 33 to 13 with 10 abstentions and reflected the influence of American government lobbying to achieve the result. In the end,

---

[38] Wilson, *Armageddon Now*, 171.

[39] This proposal was more generous to the Zionists than the Peel Commission's recommendations in 1937: 56 percent (instead of 20 percent) of the area would go to the Jews—although much of this area was desert; about 42 percent would go to the Arabs (Peel had proposed 70 percent). Jerusalem and Bethlehem were to be under international control.

Resolution 181 was never implemented; contrary to popular understanding, the United Nations did not vote to establish a Jewish state, it merely recommended partition to the parties involved and a way forward that was not taken. The United Nations did not have the authority legally to partition Palestine, nor did it confer "upon the Zionist leadership any legal authority to unilaterally declare the existence of the Jewish state of Israel."[40]

The Zionists were jubilant; the Arabs, furious. The head of the Arab Higher Committee, Al-Husseini—the Nazi collaborator, from exile in Egypt—rejected the plan; a three-day general strike was called; and a series of attacks on Jews in the cities and on the roads began. The first attack occurred the day after the UN resolution was passed. Two buses were ambushed, and seven Jewish passengers killed. On the 2nd of December an Arab mob began attacking Jews in Jerusalem, burning and looting their shops. Within twelve days of the resolution's passing, some eighty Jews had been killed and many more wounded. By the end of December 1947 some 140 more Jews were killed.[41]

THE ARAB STATES RESPOND

The surrounding Arab states quickly rejected the partition plan and mobilized volunteers, finances, and arms to aid the Palestinians. Between January and March 1948 several thousand volunteers organized under the Arab Liberation Army reinforced the Arab Palestinian cause. Soon a full-blown civil war was in progress. The British plan for an orderly transfer of power to the United Nations was in ruins, and they tried to remain neutral, wanting as smooth and peaceful a withdrawal as possible. On May 14, 1948, David Ben-Gurion proclaimed Israeli independence, just as the Palestine Mandate was to expire at midnight on that day.

ASSESSING WHAT HAPPENED IN 1947 AND 1948

We turn to examine the events in the months leading up to the establishment of the Israeli state. Brog, a Jewish apologist for Zionism, is the cousin of former Israeli prime minister Ehud Barak and was executive director of

---

[40]Jeremy R. Hammond, "The Myth of the U.N. Creation of Israel," *Foreign Policy Journal*, October 26, 2010, https://foreignpolicyjournal.com/2010/10/26/the-myth-of-the-u-n-creation-of-israel/.
[41]Brog, *Reclaiming*, 129.

Christians United for Israel. In his recent *Reclaiming Israel's History: Roots, Rights, and the Struggle for Peace* he acknowledges,

> Israel has committed sins both small and large. Israeli soldiers have killed innocent Arab civilians—and not always by mistake. Israeli commanders have expelled Arabs from their villages and destroyed their homes—and not always in cases of clear military necessity.
>
> We now know about these Israeli transgressions in detail. We know about them because Israeli scholars have documented them. And we know about them because the Israeli media has publicized them. Such is life in a free society.[42]

Brog is referring to the school of liberal Zionist writers known as the New Historians led by Benny Morris, who have examined what happened before and after the declaration of independence. These historians have challenged the narrative presented in Israeli school textbooks that the Arabs in the Jewish-designated area of Palestine left their homes and properties when called on by Arab authorities and that they were responsible for opposing the United Nations partition scheme and duly suffered as a result. And that these Arabs were responsible for their own fate and paid the price of exile in refugee camps in Syria and Lebanon.

The larger picture I have already sketched: Arab-Jewish rivalry had surfaced in the 1920s and 1930s, and the crushing of the Arab revolt in the late 1930s had driven Al-Husseini into the arms of the Nazis, whom he had encouraged to pursue the destruction of world Jewry in the Holocaust. From his place of exile in Cairo, Al-Husseini sought to direct the anti-Zionist forces and obliterate the Jewish presence in Palestine. The Zionists, among whom were many Holocaust survivors, were determined to secure the homeland promised to them by the British, in the form of a sovereign state with a Jewish majority. The fact that some of their Arab opponents had collaborated with the Nazis raised the stakes for the Zionists, who feared obliteration in the land where they sought to settle.

THE ESCALATION OF THE CONFLICT: DECEMBER 1947–MARCH 1948

Early in December 1947 the Irgun and Lehi started acting independently of the Zionist mainstream and renewed the tactic that they had employed

---

[42]Brog, *Reclaiming*, ix.

between 1937 and 1939 of "placing bombs in crowded markets and bus stops."[43] In February and March of 1948, Arabs retaliated using the same tactic. The mainstream Haganah during this period also employed terror but normally sought to be more discriminate and to limit its "violence in scope and geographically to areas already marked by Arab-initiated violence."[44] Between December 1947 and March 1948 the Arabs generally took the initiative in attacking Jewish vehicles and protected convoys. Jewish defense forces adopted a defensive stance, but this soon proved untenable. Arab villages often were located atop hills overlooking key roads, which gave them a strategic advantage. In February and March of 1948 Arab ambushes on Haganah convoys increased, and Zionist forces experienced major defeats, particularly on the road linking Tel Aviv with the Jewish area of West Jerusalem. A siege of Jerusalem was effectively strangling the one-hundred-thousand-strong Jewish community in the city, and isolated Jewish communities were blockaded. By the end of March 1948 over nine hundred Jews had been killed and a figure more than double that had been wounded. The "war of the roads" was one that the Jews were clearly losing.

The Palestinian leadership under Al-Husseini fanned the deep hatred of the Jews in Arab Palestine. This loathing contributed to the fear of what would happen to Arabs in Jewish-controlled areas, and by late March 1948 the exodus of Palestinian Arabs from the areas set aside in the partition plan was well underway. The violence to that point had occasioned the flight of many of the middle and upper classes from the large towns, notably Haifa, Jaffa, and Jerusalem and surrounding communities. The Arab rural population in the heartland of the Jewish region fled.[45] They feared Jewish military power and doubted their own, hoping perhaps to be rescued by the surrounding Arab states. They expected they would soon return to their homes when the Zionists were defeated. To this point there was no grand strategy of removal in effect. "Neither the *Yishuv* nor the Palestine Arab leadership nor the Arab states during these months had a policy of removing or moving the Arabs out of Palestine."[46] Many children and elderly people

---

[43]Morris, *Revisited*, 66.
[44]Morris, *Revisited*, 66.
[45]Morris, *Revisited*, 148.
[46]Morris, *Revisited*, 139.

moved to areas in Palestine where Arabs might have safety in numbers, because of the advice or orders of Arab military commanders. The Arab Higher Committee generally opposed flight, but they were unable to halt it.[47]

The deteriorating situation at the end of March 1948 caused the Jewish military groups to reexamine their response and decided that the only viable defense was an offense. At the same time, in the second half of March, the United States "had proposed that a United Nations trusteeship be imposed on Palestine, signaling a (possible) retreat from support for partition."[48] A new form of trusteeship beyond the May 14 would involve more foreign rule and was totally unacceptable. There was a growing fear that continued Zionist military defeats might undermine what had been promised, and the deteriorating military situation and the prospect of an invasion by neighboring Arab states contributed to the change of tactics. The Zionists felt their backs were against a wall, and that they were running out of time. Unless they consolidated their internal control and neutralized Palestinian opposition within the Jewish zone, they would not be able to deal with prospective and increasingly bellicose invaders. The arrival of shipments of arms from Czechoslovakia strengthened the Zionist cause at a pivotal time and contributed to the resolve to respond aggressively to the Arab attacks.

THE ZIONIST OFFENSIVE: APRIL TO MAY 14, 1948

By the end of March 1948, the Arabs had gained the upper hand in the countryside and often blocked roads between areas where the Jews were concentrated, and outlying communities, notably West Jerusalem with its large Jewish population, an area south of Bethlehem, kibbutzim west of the Sea of Galilee, and the northern approaches to the Negev desert.[49] The British army, planning its withdrawal and experiencing lethal Stern Gang/Lehi attacks on its troops, was both unable and reluctant to protect Jewish traffic. Ben-Gurion feared the loss of Jerusalem to the Arabs and a slaughter of Jerusalem's Jewish population. The main military group, the Haganah, sought to limit its response to Arab hostility, fearing that aggressive action would drive the Arab masses into the arms of the radicals. Given the open

---

[47]Morris, *Revisited*, 139.
[48]Morris, *Revisited*, 13-14.
[49]Morris, *Revisited*, 66.

civil war by the end of March 1948 some one hundred thousand of the wealthier Arabs of Jaffa, Haifa, Jerusalem, and Jewish-dominated areas had fled east or out of the country altogether. From the end of March 1948 to May 14, Jewish militias went on the offensive operationalizing a military plan (Plan D—for Hebrew *dalet* as it was called). Morris argues,

> Plan D was not a political blueprint for the expulsion of Palestine's Arabs: It was governed by military considerations and geared to achieving military ends. But, given the nature of the war and the admixture of populations, securing the interior of the Jewish State and its borders in practice meant the depopulation and destruction of the villages that hosted the hostile militias and irregulars.[50]

What appears to be the case is that an unofficial and never formally endorsed campaign to put pressure on the Arab population was instituted as a military necessity. It sought to relocate Arabs outside of the area designated for Israel in the partition plan, and then to extend Israeli control over area not assigned to the new Jewish state. Aiding the Zionists was the Palestinians' eagerness to leave; the Zionists had not expected the Palestinians to leave en masse so quickly and were surprised by the size and scope of the exodus.[51]

The Palestinian militias, assisted by Arab Liberation Army sympathizers, were disorganized and poorly coordinated, hampered by Arab disunity and internal weaknesses. The result was that "Palestinian military power was crushed and Palestinian society was shattered."[52] For their part, the Zionists were better trained, much more highly motivated, had superior arms and administrative skills, and had a better-educated and more-experienced military. The unity and single-mindedness of the Jews was crucial, as Morris observes: "Their motivation was strongly reinforced in the 1930s and 1940s by the onset in eastern and central Europe of anti-Semitic oppression and, then, the Holocaust, which rendered supremely urgent the establishment of a safe haven, in the form of an independent Jewish polity, for the world's unwanted, assailed and endangered Jews."[53] The kibbutzim, the experiment in communal living that had arisen in Jewish Palestine, had

---

[50]Morris, *Revisited*, 164.
[51]Morris, *Revisited*, 166.
[52]Morris, *Revisited*, 14.
[53]Morris, *Revisited*, 14.

from the beginning been designed with self-defense in mind and they were prepared for conflict: "Like most *kibbutzim*, the *Yishuv* in macro saw itself as a community without a choice—it was statehood or bust, and bust, given the depth of Arab enmity for Zionism, meant a possible repetition, on a smaller scale, of the Holocaust."[54]

With this context in mind, it is perhaps easier to understand some of Israel's "sins both small and large" that Brog refers to above, among the most famous of which is the Deir Yassin massacre. On April 9, 1948, the Irgun and Lehi attacked the Palestinian Arab village of Deir Yassin near Jerusalem with over one hundred victims dead (some accounts put the number at 250), including women and children. Initially the Zionists denounced the attack, and later Menachem Begin insisted there had been no "massacre." Morris has studied in depth the event and the historiography that followed and has concluded that both combatants and noncombatants were killed in the course of the house-to-house fighting, and after the fighting, groups of prisoners and noncombatants were killed in separate, sporadic acts of frenzy and revenge.[55] Brog acknowledges that: "Yet there is credible evidence that some of Deir Yassin's residents—both combatants and civilians—were killed after the fighting had ended. Such murders are war crimes, pure and simple."[56] The remaining villagers were then expelled. Morris offers the caveat: "But this was no Srebrenica."[57] Retaliation from the Arab side was swift: a Jewish medical convoy was attacked on Mount Scopus, resulting in the deaths of seventy-seven doctors, medical personnel, students, and patients.[58]

The prospect of similar treatment was a great incentive for Arabs to flee for their lives—especially those living in areas with a substantial Jewish population, leaving behind their homes and property. If further incentives

---

[54]Morris, *Revisited*, 16.

[55]For details see Benny Morris, *1948: A History of the First Arab-Israeli War* (New Haven, CT: Yale University Press, 2008), 124-25.

[56]Brog, *Reclaiming*, 139. It is important to note that a respected Israeli historian has recently challenged this widely accepted version of what happened at Deir Yassin. See Elizer Tauber, *Deir Yassin: Sof Hamitos* [*Deir Yassin: The end of the myth*] (Hebrew text) (Modi'in, Israel: Kinneret Zmora-Bitan Dvir, 2017).

[57]Benny Morris, "The Historiography of Deir Yassin," *Journal of Israeli History* 24, no. 1 (2005): 100-101.

[58]Wilson, *Armageddon Now*, 172.

were needed, they were given. Morris argues that ethnic cleansing was the tacit, unstated military policy, although

> no expulsion policy was ever enunciated and Ben-Gurion always refrained from issuing clear or written expulsion orders; he preferred that his generals "understand" what he wanted. He probably wished to avoid going down in history as the "great expeller" and he did not want his government to be blamed for a morally questionable practice.[59]

The Arab media trumpeted the reports of the massacre hoping to rouse Arabs to fight, but it had the opposite effect. It triggered fear and created panic, which accelerated the flight of Arabs from Palestine's villages and towns. The result surprised even the Zionists.[60] As Morris observes, "The exaggerated descriptions broadcast on Arab radio stations for weeks undermined morale throughout Palestine, especially in the countryside."[61] In responding to an Arab Liberation Army offensive at Mishmar Ha'emek between April 4 and 15 (simultaneous with Deir Yassin), "for the first time, Ben-Gurion explicitly sanctioned the expulsion of Arabs from a whole area of Palestine."[62] Some three hundred thousand Palestinians fled the Jewish terrorist groups before the 1948 war even began.

After Independence

The day after the declaration of independence, the British withdrew and the armies of Jordan, Syria, Egypt, and Iraq invaded Palestine. While allegedly wanting to defend the Palestinians and prevent a Jewish state, there was no firm desire to establish a Palestinian one on the part of the Arab states. The Jordanians clearly wanted to occupy as much of Arab Palestine as they could.

---

[59]Morris, *Revisited*, 597. Morris has written several books to chronicle exactly what happened. His 1987 work *The Birth of the Palestinian Refugee Problem* debunked the myth that Palestinians fled because ordered to by Arab leaders. He pointed the finger at Israeli involvement in ethnic cleansing, rape, murder, and terrorism all designed to remove as many Arabs as possible (population "transfer" as it was called). His work was revised as *The Birth of the Palestinian Refugee Problem Revisited* using more recently available archives, and in it he demonstrates that the Haganah had orders to uproot the Arab villagers, "transfer" them out of Israeli territory, and destroy their villages. Ari Shavit, another Israeli writer and Zionist, has long written for *Haaretz*, a leading Israeli newspaper. Shavit has covered similar ground to Morris in his work *My Promised Land: The Triumph and Tragedy of Israel* (New York: Spiegel and Grau, 2013).

[60]Morris, *Revisited*, 239-40.

[61]Morris, *Revisited*, 264.

[62]Morris, *Revisited*, 240.

Up to independence, the Zionists lost about two thousand dead; after that date they lost about another four thousand in defeating the invading Arab armies.

In the weeks following it became clear that the invading armies were no match for little Israel:

> The swift collapse of almost all the Palestinian and foreign irregular forma-tions and of civilian morale, and the spontaneous panic and flight of most communities meant that Jewish commanders almost invariably did not have to face the dilemma of expelling: Most villages were completely or almost completely empty by the time they were conquered.[63]

By July 1948 the tide of the battle had turned against the Arab armies, and by the end of December 1948 they had in effect been defeated. The Israelis now controlled four-fifths of Palestine, considerably more than had been promised in the partition plan. But the casualties of the war were numerous and the refugee situation desperate.[64] Final United Nations estimates of the total number of Palestinian Arab refugees were between 800,000 and 900,000. Morris more recently has put the figure at about 700,000.[65] Many of them ended up in refugee camps in Syria, Jordan, and Lebanon, where many of their descendants still live today. The new Israeli government was not supportive of suggestions that once hostilities had ended these displaced people be granted the "right of return."[66] The Arab countries that had at-tacked Israel were not much interested in these refugees either; rather they took the initiative in expelling the Jews living in Arab lands, many of whom became refugees whom Israel welcomed.

In 1948 the new Israeli government was unwilling to agree to a right of return of displaced Palestinians. By mid-1949 it was no longer even con-ceivable; much of the abandoned Arab land and buildings had been shared

---

[63]Morris, *Revisited*, 265.

[64]An account of events from a Palestinian Christian perspective has been written by Alex Awad, the pastor of the East Jerusalem Baptist Church, whose father, an unarmed civilian, was killed on May 24, 1948, in Jerusalem. Alex Awad, *Palestinian Memories: The Story of a Palestinian Mother and Her People* (Jerusalem: Bethlehem Bible College, 2008), 39.

[65]Morris, *Revisited*, 602-4.

[66]Both the United States and the United Nations pressed Israel to allow the return of Palestinian refugees to no avail. See Hixson, *Israel's Armor*, 67-71. The UN diplomat, the Swedish Count Bernadotte, who championed a peace plan was assassinated in September 1948 by Lehi, the terrorist organization then headed by Yitzhak Shamir, a future Israeli prime minister. Hixson, *Israel's Armor*, 58.

out to Jewish settlements, new settlements had occupied abandoned land, and a flood of Jewish immigrants (many of those expelled from Arab countries) had taken up occupation of Arab agricultural land and of much empty Arab housing, both in the cities and towns of Israel.[67] The new state—with generous financial backing from the Truman administration—welcomed Jewish immigrants with open arms. Between May 1948 and December 1951 some seven hundred thousand Jewish immigrants arrived and occupied the abandoned buildings and land.[68] "Allowing back Arab refugees, Israel argued, would commensurately reduce Israel's ability to absorb Jewish refugees from Europe and the Middle East."[69] The refugeedom of the Palestinian exiles was becoming permanent.

Assessing blame in these matters is a complex and difficult business and is not the focus of this book. There were egregious actions by both Arabs and Jews. Ben-Gurion in a speech to Mapai (the Workers' Party) in 1938 attributed Arab hostility to the following: "We are the aggressors, and they defend themselves." The Palestinian Arabs think Palestine "is theirs, because they inhabit it, whereas we want to come here and settle down, and in their view we want to take away from them their country."[70] As Morris concedes, "The displacement of Arabs from Palestine or from the areas of Palestine that would become the Jewish State was inherent in Zionist ideology and, in microcosm in Zionist praxis from the start of the enterprise."[71]

However, as Morris argues, the United Nations in November 1947 had recommended the partition of Palestine, and the rejection of this proposal by the Palestinians was at the heart of the civil war between November 1947 and May 14, 1948:

> There were also powerful vengeful urges at play—revenge for the Palestinian onslaught on the *Yishuv* during December 1947–March 1948, the pan-Arab invasion of May-June, and the massive Jewish losses. In short, the Palestinians were being punished for having forced upon the *Yishuv* the protracted, bitter war that had resulted in the death of one, and the maiming of two, in every

---

[67]Morris, *Revisited*, 588.
[68]Morris, *Revisited*, 382.
[69]Morris, *Revisited*, 599.
[70]David Ben-Gurion in 1938, quoted in John Quigley, *Palestine and Israel: A Challenge to Justice* (Durham, NC: Duke University Press, 1990), 25.
[71]Morris, *Revisited*, 588.

100 in the Jewish population. The Arabs had rejected partition and unleashed the dogs of war. In consequence, quite understandably, the *Yishuv's* leadership—left, center and right—came to believe that leaving in place a hostile Arab minority (or an Arab majority) inside the state would be suicidal.[72]

CHRISTIAN ZIONIST RESPONSES TO THE
HOLOCAUST AND TO ISRAELI INDEPENDENCE

By the late 1930s American dispensationalists had by and large become critical of Hitler and were warning of his determination to persecute the Jews. But dispensationalists had for decades been warning that the Jews were going to face terrible suffering, and when events in the 1930s began to unfold as they had predicted, they fit it into their prophetic schema. In 1937 Charles G. Turnbull, the editor of the widely circulated *Sunday School Times* (the flagship publication of American fundamentalism), argued that German Jews were experiencing divine punishment for their "deliberate, persistent, and continued apostasy," just as they had been judged by God in the past.[73] Others replayed a similar line: God loved the Jews but was chastising them through their persecutors; the persecutors, however, were not exempt from God's judgment on their terrible actions, and God would punish them in turn. "In this way, dispensationalists could see the Nazis playing a role in the prophetic plan at the same time they viewed Hitler and his men as monsters who deserved to be damned by God."[74] Lewis Sperry Chafer, the leading theologian at Dallas Theological Seminary, made such an argument after the war: "Jehovah may chasten His people and even use the nations to that end, but invariably judgment falls on those who afflict Israel."[75] The dispensationalists believed that, however evil and fierce Hitler was, he would not succeed in his attempt to eliminate the Jews. While God might allow terrible suffering, he would not allow their extinction; they had to be returned to a Jewish state in Palestine and play their role in the end times, although they believed that the suffering in the "time of Jacob's trouble" would be worse

---

[72]Morris, *Revisited*, 596.
[73]Weber, *Armageddon*, 147.
[74]Weber, *Armageddon*, 147.
[75]Weber, *Armageddon*, 147.

than the Holocaust.[76] While they grieved the mistreatment of European Jewry, they felt there was little they could do to stop it, although they did initiate efforts as early as 1939 to provide relief for Jewish refugees. They hoped, as well, that this suffering might result in a new openness to the Christian gospel.

Quite understandably, the Christian Zionists responded enthusiastically to the establishment of the Israeli state. They had been predicting this event for decades and interpreted it all within their religious framework. The evangelical religious press in America was ecstatic, and every development of the fledgling state was followed with great interest. They were particularly delighted with the flood of Jewish immigrants who flocked to the new country. John F. Walvoord, president of Dallas Theological Seminary, expressed concerns with the plight of the hundreds of thousands of Palestinian refugees.[77] While critical of Arab hostility to Israel, the evangelical press "expressed a belief that the land of Israel could maintain an Arab population alongside its Jewish inhabitants and that Israel had an obligation to respect human rights and treat the Arabs with fairness."[78] A number of evangelical groups had long-standing mission work in Arab countries and were genuinely concerned with the plight of the dispossessed. There were other conservative voices raised at the time criticizing the Israeli response to the refugee situation. The *Pentecostal Evangel* cited John L. Meredith's evaluation of the situation: "If they continue to treat Arab refugees as Europe treated the Jewish refugees, Israel will be laying the groundwork for hatreds that may well produce the 'time of Jacob's trouble,' foretold in Jeremiah 30:7."[79] Donald Grey Barnhouse, one of the most prominent American evangelical pastors, who had a long tenure as the pastor of the prestigious Tenth Presbyterian Church in Philadelphia, was editor of the prophecy journal *Revelation*. In 1949 he warned, "Israel must remember that there are promises to Ishmael as well as to Isaac, and they will drink a bitter cup if they continue in their

---

[76]See Gershon Greenberg, "The Rise of Hitler, Zion, and the Tribulation: Between Christian Zionism and Orthodox Judaism," in *Comprehending Christian Zionism: Perspectives in Comparison*, ed. Goran Gunner and Robert O. Smith (Minneapolis: Fortress, 2014), 247-70.

[77]John F. Walvoord, *Israel in Prophecy* (Grand Rapids, MI: Zondervan, 1962), 19.

[78]Yaakov Ariel, "'It's All in the Bible': Evangelical Christians, Biblical Literalism, and Philosemitism in Our Times," in *Philosemitism in History*, ed. Jonathan Karp and Adam Sutcliffe (Cambridge: Cambridge University Press, 2011), 268.

[79]*Evangel*, December 11, 1948, quoted in Wilson, *Armageddon Now*, 140n84.

cruel and heartless way. The land has been sworn to Jacob, yes, but Jacob is to rule it one day in righteousness and not in cruelty."[80]

At the time these early cautions were rarely heeded by Christian Zionists, and since then they have generally not engaged with the issues raised by the New Historians and acknowledged the facts associated with the events surrounding the attaining of Israeli independence. Surely if at the time an Israeli cabinet minister was concerned with the reports in late 1948 that officers in the Israel Defense Forces had, in his words, "committed Nazi acts," that should give pause.[81] As will be seen in succeeding chapters, the concern that Walvoord and others had for the impact of these "prophetic events" on Palestinians continued to resurface after Israeli independence.

Before 1948 key leaders like Arno Gaebelein had been critical of the irreligious Jews, and as has been seen, he and others did not believe that a secular Zionist movement could be the way the final restoration of the Jews would be accomplished. But with Israeli independence and the fledgling state's seemingly miraculous survival when it was immediately attacked by the surrounding Arab nations, it seemed clear that the Jews were being returned "in unbelief," contrary to Darby's understanding of the prophetic plan. In the 1930s Christian Zionists had often been critical of unbelieving Jews, some even engaging in caricatures that reinforced ethnic stereotyping, and had been harshly critical of their ethics in various fields. Now however, the actions of the emerging Jewish state being set up "in unbelief" were less easily questioned because it was believed that prophecy was being fulfilled—even if not quite in the way that had been anticipated. For some, their particular prophecy understandings seemed to trump everything else, including Jewish and Christian ethics that mandated concern for the widow, the orphan, the stranger, the dispossessed, and the many prophetic warnings of the Hebrew Scriptures about the moving of property boundaries.

Brog argues persuasively that Israel's contemporary critics hold it to a much higher standard than they do other nations that have engaged in ethnic cleansing, population transfers, and the like, accusing it of the

---

[80]*Evangel*, July 16, 1949, 7, quoted in Wilson, *Armageddon Now*, 140n85.

[81]After reading Israeli military reports of the Israel Defense Forces' involvement in a massacre in November 1948, one Israeli cabinet member, Aahron Cisling, declared in cabinet on the 19th of November, "I couldn't sleep all night. . . . This is something that determines the character of the nation. . . . Jews too have committed Nazi acts." Morris, *Revisited*, 488.

occupation of Palestine, and the resulting statelessness and refugeedom of many Palestinians.[82] But as observed above, Chief Rabbi Joseph Hertz in commending the Balfour Declaration to the British war cabinet in 1917 had set a high moral standard, citing "the basic principles of the Mosaic legislation": "And if a stranger sojourn with thee in your land, ye shall not vex him. But the stranger that dwelleth with you shall be unto you as one born among you, and thou shalt love him as thyself." (Lev 19:33, 34)."[83] Rabbi Hertz had endorsed a standard to which Israel's critics can appeal.

---

[82]Brog, *Reclaiming*, ix-xxv.
[83]Sykes, *Two Studies in Virtue*, 222.

12

AMERICAN CHRISTIAN ZIONISM SINCE 1948

Christian interest in the Jewish resettlement of Palestine in the nineteenth and twentieth centuries and Christian support of the Jewish Zionist cause have derived first and foremost from Christian messianic hope, and a specific mode of interpretation of biblical passages. Pro-Israel sentiments and concern for the physical well-being of Jews derive from the function of the Jews in the advancement of history toward the arrival of the Lord. While such Christians have often shown dedication and warmth toward Jews and Israel, they see themselves as supporting and working toward a great cause, in fact the greatest of all, the unfolding of the messianic age and the establishment of the kingdom of God on earth.[1]

YAAKOV ARIEL

THE ISRAELI DECLARATION OF INDEPENDENCE on March 14, 1948, ushered in a new era for Christian Zionism. In Jerry Falwell's view it was "the most important date since Jesus' ascension to heaven."[2] Christian Zionists believe strongly that the state of Israel is ordained by God, a fulfillment of biblical prophecy and solid evidence of God's direct intervention

---

[1]Yaakov Ariel, "'It's All in the Bible': Evangelical Christians, Biblical Literalism, and Philosemitism in Our Times," in *Philosemitism in History*, ed. Jonathan Karp and Adam Sutcliffe (Cambridge: Cambridge University Press, 2011), 284-85.

[2]Stephen Spector, *Evangelicals and Israel: The Story of American Christian Zionism* (Oxford: Oxford University Press, 2009), 27.

in history. For them Israel sits on the land promised by God to Abraham and his descendants. As John Hagee put it, "[This was] the Royal Land Grant that was given to Abraham and his seed through Isaac and Jacob with an everlasting and unconditional covenant."[3] Helping dispersed Jews return to Israel has become a religious duty for many Christian Zionists.

Israeli independence is commonly regarded as a miracle: Israel is a unique nation created by divine fiat. With Israeli independence, a sense of urgency entered into the veins of Christian Zionists. Many speak of Israel as "God's prophetic clock," and that clock is counting down the time till Christ returns. As Stephen Spector observes, "In the dispensationalist view, the clock had stopped but began to tick again with the birth of the State of Israel."[4] Sean Durbin argues that for Christian Zionists "modern Israel's establishment and expansion served a decisive blow to the liberal Protestants and Higher Critics who had abandoned the inerrancy of the Bible and inadvertently contributed to the production of the fundamentalist movement in the first place."[5]

DISPENSATIONALISM'S DILEMMA

While Spector's and Durbin's observations are accurate in describing how many dispensationalists think about Israeli independence, this spin on the event represents a major shift in traditional dispensational thinking. John Nelson Darby disavowed any event between him and heaven. For him God's prophetic clock would be activated by the rapture, not the establishment of a Jewish state. According to classical dispensationalism articulated by Darby, "God's heavenly/spiritual people (the church) are removed so that God's earthly people (the Jews) can receive their as-of-yet unfulfilled promises, including restoration to Palestine—a view which was derived from a 'literal' reading of the scriptures but losing a significant measure of plausibility after the establishment of Israel in 1948."[6] Crawford Gribben has observed that

---

[3]Faydra Shapiro, *Christian Zionism: Navigating the Jewish-Christian Border* (Eugene, OR: Cascade, 2015), 55.
[4]Spector, *Evangelicals and Israel*, 28.
[5]Sean Durbin, *Righteous Gentiles: Religion, Identity, and Myth in John Hagee's Christians United for Israel*, Studies in Critical Research on Religion 9 (Leiden: Brill, 2019), 37.
[6]Crawford Gribben, *Writing the Rapture: Prophecy Fiction in Evangelical America* (New York: Oxford University Press, 2009), 9.

"the claim that 1948 was a fulfillment of prophecy profoundly undermined the coherence of dispensational ideas."[7] Dispensationalist theology was being revised to comply with the unfolding of history. But as I have argued, this shift had already been initiated by William Blackstone in the late nineteenth century, who sought to reconcile futurist and historicist forms of premillennialism; Blackstone did not believe that one had to wait for the rapture before the return of the Jews could be accomplished, hence his strong advocacy of an activist Christian Zionism. Just as the nineteenth-century historicist premillennialists had run into credibility problems with their date-setting, the dispensationalists eventually experienced the same with their sequencing of events related to the rapture. A formal reworking of the system was required, but in the euphoria surrounding the establishment of Israel, these details were ignored and classical dispensational prophecy interpretation was adjusted to fit the new reality. In 1967 a new edition of the *Scofield Reference Bible* appeared "with revised annotations to reflect the new reality that Israel had been (re)established prior to—rather than after, as initially speculated—the rapture," and this revised approach was incorporated into Hal Lindsey's *The Late Great Planet Earth* in 1970.[8] Sutton's critique is apt: dispensationalism's "theology is flexible enough and malleable enough that its proponents can and do constantly adjust/update it to match the changing geo-political situation. This is their *modus operendi*, not an exceptional event."[9]

PERIODIZATION

In tracking American Christian Zionism since 1948 the historian is faced with the dilemma of breaking the seventy-plus years into smaller periods. We will consider the movement chronologically, dividing the history into four periods: (1) from 1948 to the eve of the Six-Day War in 1967; (2) from the Six-Day War through to 1979; (3) from the rise of the Moral Majority in 1979 through to the election of George H. W. Bush in 1989; and then (4) from 1989 to today—the era of Robertson and Hagee. In each period we will look at the political contexts, the key players, the cultural and theological shifts

---

[7]Westbrook, "Christian Embassy," 51n28.
[8]Durbin, *Righteous Gentiles*, 37.
[9]Matthew Avery Sutton, personal communication to the author, December 19, 2019.

during the period, and consider the ways in which Christian Zionism has
morphed and changed over time.

Period One: The Shift in American Christian Support for Israel from 1948 to 1967

Protestant mainline support for the establishment of Israel in 1948 was important, but after independence the leadership of Christian Zionism began
to shift away from the Protestant mainline to an influential political lobby
spearheaded largely by dispensationalists that came increasingly to affect
American foreign policy. The Israeli state since the 1950s has been increasingly aware of this American Christian Zionism and has courted its leaders
as people of influence in the corridors of power in Washington. A lack of
American Roman Catholic interest in Christian Zionism reflected the Vatican's traditional opposition to Zionism. The suppression of millennialism
more generally (discussed in chapter one) meant that Catholics had little of
the sense of urgency that Protestants felt in their desire to prepare themselves for the second coming. Catholics were also not as enthusiastic about
the belief that America was an "elect nation"; thus the Protestant linking of
America with Israel had little appeal. Furthermore they did not naturally
think in terms of "covenant," which was important to the Protestant understandings of both America and Israel.[10]

Shift in Catholic attitudes to Israel. It is important to set alongside these
developments a shift in Catholic attitudes to Israel and Zionism in the post–
World War II period. Jacques Maritain (1882–1973), a leading Catholic philosopher of the twentieth century, was perhaps the most important single
person advocating the reappraisal of Catholic attitudes toward the Jews and
Judaism. Born into a French Protestant family, as a young man he became a
skeptic. He and his friend Raissa Oumansoff, the daughter of Russian Jewish
immigrants, vowed to commit suicide within a year if they were unable to
find meaning in life. In 1904 they married and soon thereafter were baptized
into the Catholic Church. However, neither of them ever considered that
Raissa had ceased to be a Jew. From the 1930s Maritain campaigned against
anti-Semitism. He spent the war exiled in New York City but was invited by
Charles de Gaulle in 1945 to serve a three-year term as French ambassador

---

[10]See Samuel Goldman, *God's Country: Christian Zionism in America* (Philadelphia: University
of Pennsylvania Press, 2018), 135.

to the Vatican. A major proponent of democracy and human rights, his ambassadorial position enabled him in 1946 (with the support of his friend Giovanni Battista Montini—later Pope Paul VI) to press Pope Pius XI to issue a papal encyclical denouncing anti-Semitism. The pope refused, insisting that he had already made his opposition to anti-Semitism clear to a large group of Holocaust survivors several months earlier.[11] Significantly, Maritain disagreed with those who made a direct connection between theological anti-Judaism and anti-Semitism[12] and in particular rejected James Parkes's argument that anti-Semitism was "a creation of the Christian Church."[13]

Maritain was a major figure in Vatican II and influenced the writing of *Nostra Aetate*, which dealt with Roman Catholicism's relations with other religions, particularly Judaism. It repudiated the charge of deicide made against the Jews and the traditional "teaching of contempt" toward the Jews. But Maritain was deeply wounded by the final wording of the document, which deleted the word *condemn* in relation to manifestations of anti-Semitism.[14] From the 1920s Maritain had advocated a Jewish return to Palestine "both as a temporal answer to antisemitism and as a prelude to fulfilling biblical prophecy,"[15] and he maintained his strong Christian Zionist position in spite of the church's reluctance to endorse Zionism or recognize the Israeli state (which only happened in 1993).

Two other Catholics were influential Christian Zionists in this period. John M. Oesterreicher (1904–1983) was born into a Jewish family in Moravia, converted to Catholicism as a young man, and was ordained a priest in 1927. Engaged throughout the 1930s in fighting anti-Semitism, he fled to France and then the United States. In the 1960s he was active in petitioning the Vatican to repudiate anti-Semitism and was involved in a major way in drafting *Nostra Aetate*.[16] The other important Catholic was Rose Thering (1920–2006), a sister in the Dominican order who in 1968 became a colleague of Oesterreicher at Seton Hall University in New Jersey. Thering's

---

[11]Richard Francis Crane, "'Heart-Rending Ambivalence': Jacques Maritain and the Complexity of Postwar Catholic Philosemitism," *Studies in Christian-Jewish Relations* 6 (2011): 8.

[12]Crane, "Heart-Rending," 11.

[13]Crane, "Heart-Rending," 12.

[14]Crane, "Heart-Rending," 13.

[15]Crane, "Heart-Rending," 14.

[16]His Christian Zionism is clearly outlined in John M. Oesterreicher, "The Theologian and the Land of Israel," *The Yearbook of Judaeo-Christian Studies* 5, no. 17 (1970): 231-43.

doctoral work examined the portrayal of Jews in Catholic school textbooks and is thought to have influenced the drafting of *Nostra Aetate*. Like Oesterreicher, Thering was an outspoken supporter of Israel. All three of these figures—Maritain, Thering, and Oesterreicher—had come to embrace a "teaching of love and esteem" toward the Jews, which this book has argued is a major theme running throughout Christian Zionist history.

The resurgence of evangelicalism. Dispensationalism and Christian Zionism have also morphed since 1948. Evangelical and fundamentalist Christians had largely stood on the sidelines during the debate about America's recognition of Israel because of their general lack of political clout. Many of them had rejoiced at its founding, believing that it was a clear fulfillment of biblical prophecy. Since then, however—and especially since the 1967 Six-Day War—many of them have emerged as Israel's most zealous defenders and its most active political supporters.

The 1950s saw a boom in church building and church attendance, and the concomitant growth of American denominations as veterans returned home from the war hoping to build a good life for themselves and their families in a more stable environment. For many, church attendance and denominational affiliation were evidence of that desire. During this period American evangelicalism experienced a resurgence, with new leadership being offered in the person of Billy Graham, who had come to prominence through his 1949 Los Angeles crusade. By the mid-1950s he was a figure of national importance and the acknowledged leader of the "neo-evangelicals"—more moderate leaders anxious to distance themselves from the separatist tendencies of the fundamentalist leaders of the 1920s. In the words of Matthew Avery Sutton, they sought to transform "fundamentalism from a dispersed, decentralized movement into one carefully directed by a powerful and culturally influential white male elite."[17] Fuller Seminary, begun in 1947, offered intellectual leadership to the new conservative coalition. In 1956 *Christianity Today* commenced publishing, offering serious reflection on contemporary issues. With the financial backing of the Graham circle, it sought under the editorship of Carl F. Henry to provide a theological alternative to the *Christian Century*.[18]

---

[17]Matthew Avery Sutton, *American Apocalypse: A History of Modern Evangelicalism* (Cambridge, MA: Harvard University Press, 2014), 295.

[18]For background on Henry's internationalism, see Lauren Frances Turek, *To Bring the Good News*

Developments in Israel in the period from 1948 to 1967. American evangelicals were profoundly interested in events in the Middle East. Two key military events occurred between 1948 and 1967. The first is largely forgotten today. The new Eisenhower administration came into power in 1953 and was less inclined to support Israel than Truman's had been. The Israelis were building waterworks within a demilitarized zone, channeling Jordan River water into Israeli territory, in defiance of the United Nations. The American government punished Israel by secretly withholding aid. In October 1953 an Israeli woman and her two children were killed by an explosive device set by a Palestinian terrorist in a border area. In response, two days later a special army unit of the Israel Defense Forces under the direction of Ariel Sharon launched a premediated night attack on the village of Qibya (also spelled Kibya), a mile inside Jordan. *Time* magazine reported that sixty-six men, women, and children had been massacred:

> The Israelis moved into Kibya with rifle and Sten guns. They shot every man, woman and child they could find, then turned their fire on the cattle. After that, they dynamited 42 houses, a school and a mosque. . . . The villagers huddled in the grass could see Israeli soldiers slouching in the doorways of their homes, smoking and joking, their young faces illuminated by the flames. By 3 A.M., the Israelis' work was done, and they leisurely withdrew.[19]

Up to this point Israel had been favorably portrayed in the American media in spite of the fact that the Qibya operation was only one of a series of "reprisal operations" undertaken by the Israeli government in the 1950s and 1960s in response to attacks by Arab militants on Israelis.[20] This massacre seriously damaged Israel's reputation. Its enormously disproportionate response and the deliberate killing of innocent civilians shocked many. Abba Eban, the Israeli ambassador to the United States, wrote that the Qibya massacre "brought our international standing to the edge of the abyss. . . . This

---

to *All Nations: Evangelical Influence on Human Rights and US Foreign Relations* (Ithaca, NY: Cornell University Press, 2020), 1-4.

[19]"Israel: Massacre at Kibya," *Time*, October 26, 1953, 34, quoted in Doug Rossinow, "'The Edge of the Abyss': The Origins of the Israel Lobby, 1949–1954," *Modern American History*1, no. 1 (2018): 34. For a discussion of the Qibya massacre, see Walter L. Hixson, *Israel's Armor: The Israel Lobby and the First Generation of the Palestine Conflict* (New York: Cambridge University Press, 2019), 91-94.

[20]See Benny Morris, *Israel's Border Wars, 1949–1956: Arab Infiltration, Israeli Retaliation, and the Countdown to the Suez War* (Oxford: Clarendon, 1993).

operation was the first since the establishment of our state that world Jewry refused to identify with. . . . Even Deir Yassin did not evoke such nausea."[21] Matters were not helped when Ben-Gurion put out a story that the incident was a case of irate Israeli settlers taking matters into their own hands when it was clear that this had been a direct, premeditated operation of the Israel Defense Forces.[22] The United States supported a strong rebuke of Israel in the UN Security Council for both the Qibya massacre and the Jordan River diversion and made public its previously secret decision to withhold economic aid to Israel. The incident, however, served to galvanize American Jews' support of the pro-Israel lobby.[23] Its importance is underlined by Hixson's argument that in the period from 1945 to 1967 the pro-Israel lobby was remarkably effective in overcoming what it perceived as "the 'pro-Arab bias' of American professional diplomats."[24]

In July 1956 the Egyptian president Gamal Abdel Nasser nationalized the Suez Canal and closed the Straits of Tiran to Israeli shipping, which Israel regarded as an act of war. In October 1956 Israel, together with France and Britain, seized the Suez Canal, precipitating the Suez Crisis. Britain and France landed paratroopers along the canal with the twofold aim of regaining control of it and ousting Nasser. The United States and Russia strongly opposed these actions, and Israel, France, and Britain were forced to back down. Israel angered Eisenhower by demanding guarantees of its security before it withdrew from territory it had occupied, which it finally did only in March 1957.[25] Although the war was largely a disaster for Israel, it won two concessions: it held on to part of the Sinai, which was its first territorial acquisition since 1949,[26] and received an American guarantee of Israeli shipping through the Straits of Tiran.[27]

American Christian Zionists were generally fully supportive of Israel's attack on Egypt and incensed by Eisenhower's stance. America was putting

---

[21]Eban quoted in Rossinow, "Edge of the Abyss," 34.

[22]Rossinow, "Edge of the Abyss," 37. For a fuller discussion see Ronen Bergman, *Rise and Kill First: The Secret History of Israel's Targeted Assassinations*, trans. Ronnie Hope (New York: Random House, 2018), digital ed., 56-57.

[23]Rossinow, "Edge of the Abyss," 36.

[24]Hixson, *Israel's Armor*, 3.

[25]For details see Hixson, *Israel's Armor*, 109-10.

[26]Goldman, *God's Country*, 133.

[27]Caitlin Carenen, *The Fervent Embrace: Liberal Protestants, Evangelicals, and Israel* (New York: New York University Press, 2012), 105-6.

its oil interests ahead of its duty to "bless Israel" and would suffer divine judgment. Believing that Israel's expansion was prophetically foreordained, many dispensationalists "expected wars to continue as Israel extended its borders at Arab expense."[28] However, the crisis did prompt some self-questioning among American evangelicals. In 1956 *Christianity Today* discussed events in the Holy Land. One participant was Oswald T. Allis from Westminster Theological Seminary. Allis was not a dispensationalist and argued that the restoration of the Jews had been "unjust." His views were countered by Wilbur T. Smith, "America's best known prophecy expounder of the postwar era," and author of the bestselling *This Atomic Age and the Word of God* (1948).[29] Smith had taught at Moody Bible Institute before becoming a founding professor of Fuller Seminary. Smith advocated a standard dispensationalist view, arguing that the establishment of Israel was a fulfillment of biblical prophecy and Christians were bound to support Israel.[30]

The courting of American evangelicals before 1967. The courting of American evangelicals by the Israeli state began in the 1950s.[31] Billy Graham's pastor, W. A. Criswell, the pastor of First Baptist Church, Dallas, and a leading figure in the conservative Southern Baptist Convention, visited Israel in the early 1950s and met with David Ben-Gurion. He vigorously promoted Christian Zionism among Southern Baptists and reinforced his commitment by leading tours to Israel on a regular basis. In 1959 Ben-Gurion met with Oral Roberts, a well-known American faith healer, television evangelist, and Pentecostal leader. In 1960 Billy Graham, who often expressed his support for the state of Israel throughout his long ministry, returned from a much-publicized trip to Israel singing its praises.[32]

In 1961 Ben-Gurion's office helped to organize the World Conference of Pentecostal Churches in Jerusalem and even minted a state medal for the

---

[28]Dwight Wilson, *Armageddon Now! The Premillenarian Response to Russia and Israel Since 1917* (Tyler, TX: Institute for Christian Economics, 1991), 177.

[29]Boyer, *When Time*, 118.

[30]Wilson, *Armageddon Now*, 178.

[31]Ironically, in 1950 the Israeli government had feared the influx of large numbers of Roman Catholic pilgrims and had done everything it could to discourage them. See Uri Bialer, *Cross on the Star of David: The Christian World in Israel's Foreign Policy* (Bloomington: Indiana University Press, 2005), 189.

[32]Goldman, *God's Country*, 153. See also Daniel G. Hummel, *Covenant Brothers: Evangelicals, Jews, and U.S.-Israeli Relations* (Philadelphia: University of Pennsylvania Press, 2019), 1.

2,589 delegates.[33] He personally greeted the conference, tailoring his words to the Christian audience: "Today we are privileged to see the fulfillment of the prophecy and promise of the Bible."[34] Following the Six-Day War the Israeli government worked closely with American evangelicals to promote evangelical tourism as a major way of building American evangelical support for Israel. The Israeli Ministry of Religious Affairs printed a special issue of its journal *Christian News From Israel*, to keep Western Christians up to date with Israeli events.

Judeo-Christianity. Important changes were happening in America that would affect Jewish-evangelical relations. During the Second World War an appeal to the "Judeo-Christian tradition" was employed as a way to distinguish liberal democracy from Nazi tyranny, but after the war it came to be deployed against the Soviet threat. In the wake of World War II, American Jews were moving more into the mainstream of American life and the language of American civil religion increasingly adopted the concept of "Judeo-Christian" values, which were set over against atheistic communism. This concept was advanced by president-elect Eisenhower in a speech in December 1952 in which he reasoned that "our form of Government has no sense unless it is founded in a deeply felt religious faith, and I don't care what it is. With us of course it is the Judo-Christian [*sic*] concept but it must be a religion that all men are created equal."[35] As Samuel Goldman has commented, "The 'Judeo-Christian concept' was a way of including all Americans—Protestants, Catholics and Jews—in a common front against Soviet tyranny."[36] This notion emphasized the common heritage of Protestantism, Catholicism, and Judaism, which accounted for American exceptionalism and more broadly for Western culture. In the early 1950s "Judeo-Christianity became for many Americans a core identity read into the Bible and projected into the world."[37] These values were increasingly set over against atheistic communism as the Iron Curtain descended across Europe.

Daniel Hummel has argued that "the turn to Israel undertaken by both American evangelicals and Jews in the postwar period emerged as much out

---

[33]Spector, *Evangelicals and Israel*, 144.
[34]Spector, *Evangelicals and Israel*, 144.
[35]Goldman, *God's Country*, 132.
[36]Goldman, *God's Country*, 132.
[37]Hummel, *Covenant Brothers*, 40.

of communal debates over identity and theology as by other forces,"[38] such as evangelical prophecy concerns. A new coalition of American Jews and evangelicals was forming that would help to create a "bipartisan consensus over American diplomatic, political, and financial support for the state of Israel,"[39] although on virtually every other political issue socially liberal American Jews and socially conservative American evangelicals disagreed. Francis Schaeffer, a leading evangelical intellectual and apologist associated with the L'Abri community in Switzerland, advocated the concept of "cobelligerency" whereby evangelicals were encouraged to work alongside others on specific issues of mutual concern but with whom they disagreed on important theological issues. This approach was crucial to the success of the Christian Zionists.

Another development making for closer Christian-Jewish ties was the rise of the academic study of biblical archaeology pioneered by William Foxwell Albright, perhaps the greatest archaeologist of the twentieth century. Albright helped to shape a specifically evangelical understanding of "Judeo-Christianity," which emphasized Christian indebtedness to Jewish history, helping them "to denounce anti-Semitism as un-Christian and un-American."[40] America was to be aligned not just with the history of the Jews revealed in biblical archaeology but with God's providential care of the Jewish state of Israel, the responsibility for which rested mainly on America, the primary custodian of the shared Judeo-Christian tradition.[41] This evangelical take on "Judeo-Christianity" brought the biblical story line of archaeology "into the Cold War. And through this biblical lens, Judeo-Christianity stood alone, opposed by atheistic communism, secularist betrayers of the tradition, and unremitting hatred directed toward the most potent symbol of the historical reality of Judeo-Christianity: the state of Israel."[42]

By the late 1950s shared interest began to allow for increased interaction and mutual exchange between American Jews and evangelicals. In 1963 the National Association of Evangelicals for the first time invited a Jewish rabbi,

---

[38]Daniel G. Hummel, "*His Land* and the Origins of the Jewish-Evangelical Israel Lobby," *Church History* 87, no. 4 (December 2018): 1126.

[39]Hummel, "*His Land*," 1120.

[40]Hummel, *Covenant Brothers*, 42.

[41]Hummel, *Covenant Brothers*, 42.

[42]Hummel, *Covenant Brothers*, 54.

Marc Tannenbaum from the American Jewish Committee, to address the organization.[43] In some circles Tannenbaum came to be referred to as the "apostle to the Gentiles" (Romans 11:13). Such moves that sought to blur Jewish and Christian identities were contested. To some there seemed to be a drift toward a "dual covenant" theology popular in liberal Protestant circles that there is one means of salvation for Gentiles through Christ but a different path to God for Jews. Thus the argument was made that Jews should not be evangelized by Christians. Concerns were expressed about Billy Graham's comments to reporters before his 1957 New York crusade when he explained that those who "made decisions for Christ" would be referred to ministers in their own faith tradition: "We'll send them to their own churches—Roman Catholic, Protestant or Jewish. . . . The rest will be up to God."[44] What the local rabbi was expected to say to a congregant who had made a decision for Christ was unclear. In practice the Graham organization sent inquirers to evangelical churches.

The most penetrating theological critique of this shift came from the Lithuanian Jewish-Christian theologian Jakob Jocz, who protested what he saw as the secularizing and pluralistic tendencies within the theological shift to an emphasis on the commonalities rather than the differences between Christianity and Judaism. He first expressed these views in *The Jewish People and Jesus Christ* (1949) and most thoroughly in *The Jewish People and Jesus Christ After Auschwitz* (1981). (Jocz's father and family members had died at the hands of the Gestapo.) His arguments are reminiscent of the nineteenth-century evangelical authority on Judaism Alexander McCaul, discussed above in chapter six, who had contrasted the theological differences between rabbinic Judaism and Christianity. As Hummel has observed, "Jocz severed the essential linkage of Judeo-Christianity and offered the rudimentary arguments for a critical evangelical approach to Christian Zionism."[45] But Judeo-Christianity promoted interest in Israel and thus laid "the groundwork for a realignment of Christian Zionism around Judeo-Christian identity."[46] This new self-understanding catalyzed Christian Zionism in the 1950s and

---

[43]Hummel, *Covenant Brothers*, 48.
[44]Hummel, *Covenant Brothers*, 49.
[45]Hummel, *Covenant Brothers*, 57.
[46]Hummel, *Covenant Brothers*, 57.

1960s, under the leadership of evangelical power brokers like G. Douglas Young, the dynamic founder of what became known as the American Institute of Holy Land Studies in Jerusalem.[47] Part of this involved an unshakeable commitment to Christian Zionism and the Israeli state.

Another consequence of the adoption of the language of "Judeo-Christian" civilization and the emerging American evangelical-Jewish alliance—especially after 1967—was the eventual hardening of differences with Muslims later in the century.[48] While anti-Semitic and anti-Zionist attitudes were growing in the Arab world in the 1950s and 1960s, they were not yet a feature of radical Islamic politics. As Hummel has observed, "Into the 1970s the specter of Islamic fundamentalism and terrorism remained on the margins of Jewish-evangelical reconciliation."[49]

Christian Zionism in the Kennedy-Johnson era. It was John F. Kennedy who first spoke of America's "special relationship" with Israel.[50] His administration was much more friendly to Israel than Eisenhower's, providing it with considerable financial, military, and economic aid. In 1962 the United States ended its embargo on American weapon sales to Israel with the sale of Hawk surface-to-air missiles in what it said was a move to counter sales of Russian military arms to Arab nations.[51] Lyndon Johnson's administration was even more friendly. Johnson had a long pro-Jewish record going back to the 1930s, having done everything in his power to rescue European Jews from the Holocaust. Although raised in an evangelical home,[52] he qualified as a Jew under religious law given his ancestry, and his aunt was an active Zionist. In a manner reminiscent of David Lloyd George, he would later tell a meeting of B'nai B'rith: "The Bible stories are woven into my childhood memories as the gallant struggle of modern Jews to be free of persecution is woven into our souls."[53]

---

[47]For a study of Young and his involvements see Hummel, *Covenant Brothers*, chap. 3.

[48]Hummel, *Covenant Brothers*, 98.

[49]Hummel, *Covenant Brothers*, 101.

[50]Durbin, *Righteous Gentiles*, 25.

[51]Hummel, *Covenant Brothers*, 53.

[52]Yaakov Ariel, *An Unusual Relationship: Evangelical Christians and Jews* (New York: New York University Press, 2013), 180.

[53]Lawrence Davidson, "Christian Zionism and American Foreign Policy: Paving the Road to Hell in Palestine," *Logos* 4, no. 1 (Winter 2005): http://www.logosjournal.com/issue_4.1/davidson_printable.htm.

American Jewish Zionists were also helpful in this shift. American Jews had established the American Zionist Committee on Public Affairs in 1954 in the wake of the Qibya massacre, and in 1963 it was renamed the American Israel Public Affairs Committee.[54] The change of name involved dropping the word *Zionist* to accommodate many wealthy Jews (especially those associated with the American Jewish Committee) who were neither Zionist nor anti-Zionist. These "non-Zionist" Jews had not supported Israel's founding but were sympathetic to the Jewish community in Palestine. Once Israel was established, they wanted to be supportive but did not self-identify as Zionists. By the 1960s the American Israel Public Affairs Committee's power had increased substantially when it was able to help "secure U.S. weapons sales and generous U.S. government assistance to Israel, and later it would continue to strengthen the political and strategic ties between the two polities."[55]

Before 1967 the key figure in the dialogue between American Jews and mainline Protestants was Rabbi Marc Tannenbaum, but the top priority in these talks was not Israel or Zionism. Joint areas of concern were the civil rights movement, opposition to the Vietnam War, and poverty. The White House was more interested in courting the mainline churches than evangelical figures like Billy Graham. In ecumenical circles Judaism was widely regarded as one more religious denomination alongside the various Protestant groupings and Roman Catholicism—all under the umbrella of Judeo-Christianity. The tendency was to view Jews as belonging to an "ethnicity" rather than a race or nation. In these conversations, Jason Olson has argued that "Jews portrayed Judaism as an equal denomination lest American Christians be persuaded that Jews were not equal Americans."[56] All of this would change dramatically after the 1967 Six-Day War. American Jewish Zionists would begin to build bridges to the American evangelical Christian Zionists. As Samuel Goldman has observed, "The emergence of American Christian Zionism on the right did not occur automatically. It required the shock of Israel's victory in the Six-Day War to galvanize a combination of dispensational eschatology, American patriotism, and pop-culture fixation into a movement."[57]

---

[54]It has become the largest and by far the most well-funded Jewish-Zionist lobby group (with revenue of $77.7 million in 2014).

[55]Rossinow, "Edge of the Abyss," 25.

[56]Jason M. Olson, *America's Road to Jerusalem: The Impact of the Six-Day War on Protestant Politics* (Lanham, MD: Lexington, 2018), 2.

[57]Goldman, *God's Country*, 155.

Period Two: The Billy Graham Era from the Six-Day War to 1979

The turning point: the Six-Day War.

> *Since the French Revolution in the last years of the eighteenth century and the Napoleonic Wars at the beginning of the nineteenth, no political-military event has provided as much fuel to the engines of Christian prophetic belief as did the short war between Israel and its neighbours in June 1967.*[58]

YAAKOV ARIEL

> *Israel's overwhelming victory drastically reordered the Middle East and transformed the Arab-Israeli conflict into a global struggle that allowed Americans—both Christians and Jews— to see themselves as partisans in it.*[59]

DANIEL HUMMEL

In November 1966 a Palestinian Liberation Organization mine attack, launched from the West Bank, killed three Israeli police officers. The Israelis retaliated by attacking a Jordanian police station. Anti-Israeli riots in the West Bank followed, seriously undermining the Jordanian king. On May 14, 1967, President Nasser mobilized troops in Sinai; four days later the United Nations secretary general agreed to Nasser's request to remove the UN Emergency Force from Sinai and Sharm El Sheikh. Nasser then announced that in spite of American guarantees made by President Eisenhower in 1957 about the Straits of Tiran, he was closing them to Israeli shipping. Promising "destruction of Israel," Nasser formed a pact with Jordan; Syria mobilized its troops; and Iraqi forces began gathering in Jordan in the hopes of "driving Israel into the sea."[60] Tensions were extremely high with the Soviets backing their Arab allies and the United States under President Johnson staunchly supporting Israel, even in view of Soviet threats of a war with the United

---

[58]Ariel, "It's All in the Bible," 268.
[59]Hummel, "*His Land*," 1127.
[60]Olson, *America's Road*, 45.

States. On the 2nd of June the commander of the Jordanian army boasted, "I cannot imagine that even a single Israeli is going to be left alive once the battle begins."[61] As Jason Olson comments, "The evidence demonstrates that Israelis sincerely feared a widespread and Holocaustic destruction of the Jewish State."[62]

Nasser's actions were regarded by the Israelis as acts of war. The Israeli intelligence organization, Shin Bet, recruited a double agent who persuaded the Egyptians that Israel was going to enter the war with a ground offensive. On the 5th of June the Israeli Air Force caught the Egyptians off-guard by launching preemptive airstrikes against their airfields, thereby securing Israeli air supremacy. On the ground the Israelis invaded the Gaza Strip and the Sinai. Syria and Jordan entered the conflict almost immediately on mistaken reports from the Egyptians that they had defeated the Israeli air strike. The Israelis then launched counterattacks against the invading Jordanian Army. The Israel Defense Forces seized East Jerusalem and the West Bank from Jordan, and the Golan Heights from Syria. Some three hundred thousand Palestinians fled the West Bank, and about one hundred thousand Syrians left the Golan Heights to become refugees. In the wake of the war Jewish communities were expelled from countries across the Arab world, with many of them going as refugees to Europe, America, or Israel.

American Protestant responses to the Six-Day War. As American evangelicals were turning to Israel, mainline Protestants were turning away. From about 1953 liberal Protestantism had become increasingly critical of Israel, and this intensified following the Suez Crisis in 1956.[63] This shift accelerated dramatically following the Six-Day War, as they became increasingly critical of the Israeli state as an occupying force in Arab lands. Many "mainliners" were broadly Christian pacifists. The pro-Israel Christian realists associated with Reinhold Niebuhr, the American Christian Palestine Committee, and the journal *Christianity and Crisis* took a very different view from the pacifist mainliners. After 1967 American Jews were appalled that years of interreligious dialogue with mainline Protestants and Roman

---

[61]Quoted in Olson, *America's Road*, 46.
[62]Olson, *America's Road*, 46.
[63]See Carenen, *Fervent Embrace*, chaps. 4 and 5.

Catholics had achieved so little. In general, however, Americans did not follow the lead of the liberal Protestants. Most Americans were "swept up in the euphoria of Israel's rapid and sweeping victory," and generally very supportive of Israel as the "perceived underdog" in the conflict.[64] A very different response came from the evangelicals whose ascendency in American Protestantism was becoming evident. Jerry Falwell's observation in 1984 that evangelicals "converted to support for Israel at a very rapid pace" over a "twenty year" period is telling.[65]

The implications of the Six-Day War for American-Israeli relations and American foreign policy were profound: "The reality of Israeli victory, overwhelmingly celebrated by evangelicals and fundamentalists, heralded a new era for Protestant interest in the Holy Land and Judaism."[66] The victory had brought a number of biblical sites under Israeli control; of supreme importance was Jerusalem. For Christian Zionists its capture was a fulfillment (or a further fulfillment) of Luke 21:24, marking the end of the "times of the Gentiles"—many had understood the fall of Jerusalem in 1917 in light of this verse: "They will fall by the sword and will be taken as prisoners to all the nations. Jerusalem will be trampled on by the Gentiles until the times of the Gentiles are fulfilled." The return of Christ must therefore be very close. Dispensationalist thinking now regarded the establishment of the state of Israel in 1948 as pivotal in the unfolding of the prophetic timetable; the capture of Jerusalem by Israel was yet one more crucial step. (All of this, as I have pointed out, was not part of the prophetic timetable of John Nelson Darby, who had expected these events to follow the rapture.) John F. Walvoord, president of Dallas Theological Seminary, reasoned that Israel's taking of the old city of Jerusalem was "one of the most remarkable fulfillments of biblical prophecy since the destruction of Jerusalem in A.D. 70."[67] Many Christian Zionists were convinced that God had fought for Israel. As Caitlin Carenen has observed, "The evangelical response to Israeli military prowess and land acquisition between 1967 and 1979 permanently altered [American] evangelical Protestant political behavior and set the foundation

---

[64]Carenen, *Fervent Embrace*, 136.
[65]Merrill Simon, *Jerry Falwell and the Jews* (Middle Village, NY: Jonathan David Publishers, 1984), 88, quoted in Hummel, "*His Land*," 1123.
[66]Carenen, *Fervent Embrace*, 141.
[67]Quoted in Spector, *Evangelicals and Israel*, 28.

for the dynamic political engagement that would characterize evangelical Protestants in the 1980s."[68] The American evangelical response, while overwhelmingly positive, was not universal, and most dissenters were people who were involved in evangelical missions in Arab countries.[69]

Changes in Jewish-Christian relations. The 1967 war had an enormous impact on American Jews. In mid-May of 1967 according to Rabbi Arthur Hertzberg, "the mood of American Jewry underwent an abrupt, radical, and possibly permanent change."[70] In just over two weeks, American Jews gave over $100 million to the United Jewish Appeal for its Israel Emergency Fund. A much-heightened concern for Israel among American Jews linked a new Jewish self-understanding between Jewish peoplehood and "the land." Some rabbis now emphasized the religious aspect with Rabbi Hertzberg, arguing that Judaism "beyond any doubt, created the indissoluble emotional and historic connection. The State of Israel . . . is necessary for the continuity of Judaism and Jews."[71] This was quite a momentous shift in Jewish religious attitudes toward Israel, a country founded in large part by secularists who understood that Israel was to be the home of Jews, and never intended it to be the homeland of Judaism. Yaakov Ariel has noted that in the early twentieth century "both Orthodox and Reform Jewish leaders noticed that Zionism secularized Jewish yearnings for redemption in Palestine at the expense of traditional religious values."[72] The early Zionists were "mostly young anti-traditionalist Jews, [who] often understood that move as an act of rebellion against their parents' world and mentality, at times relating to their choice as a conversion into a new faith."[73] Now their embrace of secular Zionism was being reinterpreted as consistent with traditional spiritual longings, whereas half a century earlier the rabbinic consensus was that it was a repudiation of rabbinic Judaism. Rabbi Marc Tanenbaum, whose

---

[68]Carenen, *Fervent Embrace*, 134.

[69]See David Rausch's account of the protests of James L. Kelso in *Christianity Today* in 1967. Kelso was an evangelical who had been the moderator of the United Presbyterian Church and a long-time missionary in Arab countries. David A. Rausch, *Communities in Conflict: Evangelicals and Jews* (Philadelphia: Trinity Press International, 1991), 147-48.

[70]Hummel, "*His Land*," 1129.

[71]Hummel, "*His Land*," 1130.

[72]Yaakov Ariel, "Zionism in America," in *Oxford Research Encyclopedia of Religion* (Oxford: Oxford University Press, 2017), 10, https://doi.org/10.1093/acrefore/9780199340378.013.434.

[73]Ariel, "Zionism in America," 11.

friendship had a major impact on Billy Graham, made clear to Christian Zionists the implications of the new orthodoxy: "There will be no future Jewish-Christian dialogue unless Jews insist that Christians face and accept the profound historical, religious, cultural, and liturgical meaning of the land of Israel and of Jerusalem to the Jewish people."[74]

In the wake of the war, American Jews came to accept the enthusiastic support offered by American Christian Zionists. Hummel, in trying to make sense of this surprising alignment of groups that were opposed on so many social issues, has reasoned that after the Six-Day War, American Jews adopted a renewed emphasis on the Zionist concept of a Jewish "peoplehood" (which had been a commonplace in Christian Zionist thinking for several centuries), but now it was resonating with both religious and nonreligious Jews:

> Israel became a more prominent marker of group identity for both commu-
> nities: for evangelicals as a historical and prophetic symbol of biblical au-
> thority and for Jews as a core component of peoplehood. Counterintuitively
> to the prevailing scholarly understanding, affirming religious identity did not
> limit political cooperation; it provided a new opportunity for cooperation.[75]

The three issues central to this cooperation are covenant, land, and mission. The concept of covenant was from the earliest colonial times core to Protestant concepts of America's calling, and the idea of a shared covenant with the Jews had long informed Christian Zionist thinking. This obser-vation recalls Andrew Crome's comments mentioned in the introduction: in Christian Zionist thinking national identity formation fueled by prophecy and oriented toward the fulfillment of a national mission involves the pos-itive "othering" of the Jews, but it is a positive othering in which Gentile nations, even the United States, can only experience a form of secondary election. Israel is *the* chosen nation; while in the words of Abraham Lincoln, America is God's "*almost* chosen people."[76] Chosen Christian nations never replace Israel as *the elect nation*, thus complicating the way one thinks about prophecy and national identity. As Samuel Goldman has argued, "Rather

[74]Marc Tanenbaum quoted in Judith Herschkopf Banki, *Christian Reactions to the Middle East Crisis: New Agenda for Interreligious Dialogue* (New York: American Jewish Committee, 1967), 15-16, cited in Hummel, "*His Land*," 1130.

[75]Hummel, "*His Land*," 1123.

[76]Speech of Abraham Lincoln to the New Jersey Senate, February 21, 1861, Abraham Lincoln Online, http://www.abrahamlincolnonline.org/lincoln/speeches/trenton1.htm.

than Daniel's seventieth week or Isaiah's foretelling of the restoration of Jerusalem, the core idea of Christian Zionism is that God's relationship with the Jewish people [the covenant] was not severed with the advent of Christ. What many Christian Zionists hope to do is to return that idea to the centrality that they believe it deserves."[77]

The second issue is the land. Christian Zionists interpreted the Old Testament land promises to still be in effect. "The land" as an eternal gift was understood literally to be true and ongoing. After the Six-Day War both Israeli and American Jewish leaders pivoted in their use of the language of Jewish peoplehood. Formerly Jewish nationhood was associated with Judaism as a faith; latterly Jewish nationhood became associated with the Jewish faith, but now with "the land" as an integral component. Yona Malachy made the argument that "Judaism as [it] understands itself" is "the tripartite union of religion-people-land."[78] Or as the Israeli scholar R. J. Zwi Werblowsky put it, "Israel's life is bound up with its land, the 'land of Zion and Jerusalem.'"[79] These sentiments were common among Christian Zionists. What is surprising is that religious Jews had traditionally insisted on just the opposite: that the land was central to Jewish identity but would only be restored to the Jews by the Messiah, and to insist on the fulfillment of the religion-people-land linkage before his coming was regarded by most religious leaders in the history of Judaism as heterodox. This new appropriation of the Jewish religious tradition by Zionists like Tannenbaum became the new orthodoxy: the Zionist project, which had long been opposed by the mainstream of the rabbinic tradition, was now regarded as its fulfillment, not as its abandonment. Not waiting for the Messiah to accomplish the return was now asserted to be consistent with Judaism, not a rejection of the same.

The third component is the stumbling block of Christian mission that had to be worked around or set aside. By the 1950s the mainline Protestant denominations had shut down their mission outreaches to the Jews,[80] but the

---

[77]Goldman, *God's Country*, 175.

[78]Quoted in Hummel, *Covenant Brothers*, 83.

[79]Quoted in Hummel, *Covenant Brothers*, 83.

[80]See Ariel, *Unusual Relationship*, 123-24. Ariel's whole chapter, "Instructing Christians and Jews: Evangelical Missions to the Jews," in *Unusual Relationship* is particularly helpful in its description and assessment of evangelical missions to the Jews.

evangelical effort to reach the Jews, first pioneered by the German Pietists and embraced by nineteenth-century British evangelicals, and then taken up with a passion by the dispensationalists, was deeply felt by Jews around the world. Ariel has tracked these efforts in his *Evangelizing the Chosen People* and has highlighted the ubiquity of these efforts, something that is well-known in the Jewish world but that few Gentiles are aware of:

> Like their British counterparts, American groups ventured out to evangelize a global Jewish community that, at its peak on the eve of World War II, comprised no more than sixteen million people (and would be much diminished after the war), making the Jews one of the most evangelized people on earth. From Warsaw to Cape Town, and from Buenos Aires to Montreal, evangelical missions interacted with Jews via educational, medical, welfare, and literary projects. The missions served as a link between two sets of cultures: that of evangelical Protestants and that of the Jews. The missions' large and varied literature was intended to educate both communities, Protestant and Jewish, and bring them to adopt a Christian premillennial vision.[81]

These efforts in America were focused on poor Jewish immigrants who often appreciated the benefits that they received without responding to the missionaries' message, but were resented by acculturated middle-class Jews, "who were often at the forefront of Jewish anti-missionary activity and rhetoric."[82] Now it was being made clear that the price of Jewish cooperation with evangelicals was for them to tone down any talk of converting the Jews and at least to distance themselves from any mission work that consciously targeted them. From the early 1950s, as Hummel has shown, evangelical missionaries in Israel shifted away from an evangelical theology that emphasized the proclamation of the gospel to the Jews in the hope of individual conversions. Given the severe restrictions on religious liberty imposed by the Israeli government, which reflected the inherited religious policy of the Ottomans and the British, efforts to convert Jews were seen as threatening to Israel's society and state. (Many American evangelicals protested these restrictions, and their calls for increased religious freedom were an important sticking point between many American evangelicals and Israel.)

---

[81] Ariel, *Unusual Relationship*, 114.
[82] Ariel, *Unusual Relationship*, 117.

But some missionaries began to speak of a theology of "witness" that emphasized Christian brotherhood with Jews and abandoned any talk of conversion. Christian witness in Israel involved showing solidarity with Israel's Jewish population, especially in its unstinting support of Zionism.[83] The new "witness" theology was pioneered by Southern Baptist missionaries in Israel but is most clearly illustrated in the person of G. Douglas Young, who had strong connections to American evangelicalism as a key figure in the Evangelical Free Church of America and as the dean of Old Testament at Trinity Theological Seminary (later Trinity Evangelical Divinity School) in Deerfield, Illinois. His American Institute of Holy Land Studies in Jerusalem had a wide base of American evangelical support. Young, as shown in his unpublished notes, clearly believed that the conversion of the Jews would only happen after the rapture, and thus he could "dismiss Jewish missions as unnecessary and counterproductive to the real mandate imposed on Christians in the present age to reconcile with Jews as the two chosen peoples of God."[84] This accorded well with the new "witness theology" approach. Like William Hechler in the 1890s, who had made a similar theological move, it was music to the ears of the Jewish Zionists with whom they sought to work.

The new witness theology reached a much wider audience when presented at the first World Congress on Evangelism, held in Berlin in 1966, organized and funded by the Billy Graham Evangelistic Association. The shift was seen in the only document on Jewish-Christian relations that emerged from the Berlin Congress, and in Graham's keynote speech to the Congress.[85] Hummel comments, "Christian witness, as it traveled from Jerusalem to Berlin into the highest echelons of postwar evangelicalism, prefigured the orientation of the later Christian Zionist movement."[86] This shift was seen more openly in 1973, when Graham publicly distanced himself from missions solely directed at Jews, and similar moves were made by those who succeeded him as Christian Zionist leaders in the 1970s and 1980s, specifically Young and John Hagee.[87] In 2006 Rabbi Scheinberg, who was

---

[83]See Hummel, *Covenant Brothers*, chap. 1.
[84]Hummel, *Covenant Brothers*, 33.
[85]Hummel, *Covenant Brothers*, 33.
[86]Hummel, *Covenant Brothers*, 33.
[87]On Hagee see John Hagee, *Should Christians Support Israel?* (San Antonio: Dominion, 1987), 124-25, 127.

known as Hagee's unofficial rabbi, asserted in a *Jerusalem Post* article that Hagee believed in a dual-covenant theology and that he had done so for twenty-five years, and that Falwell accepted it as well. Falwell responded immediately, strongly denying the assertion. Hagee acknowledged that he did not seek to proselytize at his events but denied embracing a "dual covenant."[88] However, the water was further muddied by Hagee in his *In Defense of Israel* (2007), which confusingly seemed to embrace dual-covenant theology, claiming that "the Jews did not reject Jesus as Messiah; it was Jesus who rejected the Jewish desire for him to be their Messiah."[89] The gospel was not intended for Jews, only for Gentiles. As Hagee put it, "The message of the gospel was from Israel, not to Israel!"[90] Jewish missions were pointless in this age. After an outcry from many evangelicals, Hagee walked back some of his statements in his 2009 revised edition.[91]

The trend in Christian Zionist circles was pinpointed by Wayne Hilsden, the Pentecostal pastor of King of Kings Assembly in Jerusalem, in a speech to the Feast of Tabernacles put on by the International Christian Embassy Jerusalem in October of 2006:

> How did Rabbi Aryeh Scheinberg come to the conclusion that John Hagee along with Jerry Falwell and other Christians have come to accept this two covenant theology? I don't believe he ever heard John Hagee or Jerry Falwell ever say that gentiles go to heaven through Jesus and Jews get to heaven through Moses. I don't believe they ever said that. But this rabbi has gone to so many pro-Israel rallies and so many Jewish-Christian dialogue events but he's never heard a gospel presentation by any of these people. So it appears to him they must have forsaken the exclusivity of the gospel message and that the gospel really isn't that vital, for Jewish people at least.[92]

Hilsden's comments echo the words of W. W. Shannon from the early 1940s (quoted in chapter eleven) about those evangelicals preoccupied with

---

[88]Faydra L. Shapiro, "The Messiah and Rabbi Jesus: Policing the Jewish-Christian Border in Christian Zionism," *Culture and Religion* 12, no. 4 (2011): 468, DOI: 10.1080/14755610.2011.633537.

[89]John Hagee, *In Defense of Israel* (Lake Mary, FL: Frontline, 2007), 145. The whole argument is developed on 132-45.

[90]Hagee, *In Defense*, 134.

[91]See Robert O. Smith, *More Desired Than Our Owne Salvation: The Roots of Christian Zionism* (New York: Oxford University Press, 2013), 19-21, and Shapiro, "Rabbi Jesus," 470.

[92]Shapiro, "Rabbi Jesus," 469.

prophecy interpretation who follow the crowds to learn about the antichrist but would not walk across the street to share their faith.

The historian is hard-pressed not to see that the impact of Christian Zionism on evangelical theology has sometimes led some of its proponents away from classic evangelical theology about the centrality of Christ and the universal claims of the Christian gospel. Evidence of the secularizing effects of Christian Zionism is hard to ignore—notably Hechler and Hagee. It parallels the secularizing effect that Zionism had had on Judaism, which Orthodox and Reform rabbis had lamented early in the twentieth century. In the case of Christian Zionism, it may be that this shift was facilitated by their long-standing focus on the Jews as a "people" or "nation," rather than the Jews as individuals. German Pietism had focused on the latter and promoted evangelism of the Jews, something nineteenth-century evangelicals had warmly embraced. Much of contemporary Christian Zionism so focuses on the Jews as a collectivity that it can lead to a downplaying or a sidelining of the focus on the conversion of individual Jews.

Israeli courting of American evangelicals after the Six-Day War. Following the war the Israeli government began to take much more seriously the matter of American Christian Zionist support. The Department of Christian Affairs dispatched Yona Malacy, a Polish-born scholar with a doctorate from the Sorbonne, to study American Christian Zionism. He established contacts with leading evangelicals and visited several seminaries, including Biola College (formerly the Bible Institute of Los Angeles, where William Blackstone had often lectured), which responded by issuing its "Proclamation Concerning Israel and the Nations," expressing strong support for Israel and warning that "the true people of God should not be found in league with those who oppose the will and work of God for Israel."[93] Malacy returned to Israel to edit the Department of Christian Affairs' publication *Christian News From Israel*. Posthumously his findings were published as *American Fundamentalism and Israel: The Relation of Fundamentalist Churches to Zionism, and the State of Israel* (1978).

Israel had been on the search for Christians whose theologies would legitimate the Jewish state and talk about it in a way that used the new

---

[93]Quoted by Spector, *Evangelicals and Israel*, 145.

language about Jewish peoplehood being bound to the concept of the land. Such shared language would build on the mutually shared religious tradition and foster active Christian involvement in promoting Zionism. Eager Christian Zionists were only too willing to serve in this way, thereby assuring themselves that they were "blessing Israel" and working for its divinely ordained flourishing.[94]

The unique role of Billy Graham.

> Institutionally, the Christian Zionist movement [in America] has direct lineage in postwar white evangelicalism, especially the social and religious networks stemming from Billy Graham's ministries.[95]
>
> DANIEL HUMMEL

This courting of American evangelicals was most successful in its wooing of Billy Graham. Graham had inherited dispensationalism from his upbringing, but like Dwight L. Moody, on whom he modeled his ministry, he tended to downplay its details.[96] His preaching often focused on the second coming of Christ, and throughout his ministry he exuded a warm regard for Israel. In 1967 the American Jewish Committee arranged a face-to-face meeting with Graham. Several meetings occurred, including a two-hour conversation with Golda Meir, who sought to leverage Graham's close relationship with Richard Nixon, who was generally cool toward Israel, still smarting from the fact that he only garnered 17 percent of the Jewish vote in the 1968 elections.[97] In March of 1970 Meir asked Graham to intervene with his friend in the Oval Office to ensure that America would sell military jets to Israel.[98]

Graham could be helpful in other ways. In 1970 the Billy Graham Evangelistic Association produced a movie titled *His Land*, which featured British evangelical pop singer Cliff Richard. It warmed the hearts of

---

[94]For a discussion of what "blessing Israel" means, and how it functions in Christian Zionism, see Durbin, *Righteous Gentiles*, chap. 7.

[95]Hummel, *Covenant Brothers*, 245n6.

[96]Grant Wacker, *Heaven Below: Early Pentecostals and American Culture* (Cambridge, MA: Harvard University Press, 2001), 45.

[97]Hummel, *Covenant Brothers*, 90.

[98]Hummel, *Covenant Brothers*, 90.

American dispensationalists as well as American and Israeli Jews. There were, in fact, two cuts of the movie—the original was sixty-seven minutes and included an evangelistic pitch in the last twelve minutes asking viewers "to invite Jesus into your heart."[99] But the Graham organization also produced a fifty-five-minute version for Jewish audiences that did not have the evangelistic ending.[100]

It was essentially a travelogue in which Richard, accompanied by Graham's song leader and choral director, Cliff Barrows, visited the sites of Christ's life in Israel, portraying the land filled with happy, hard-working Jews, eager (it would seem) to play the roles designated for them by dispensationalists. The lyrics of Richard's songs were strongly pro-Zionist, and the central message: all of this is God's land; God has given it to the Jews as an eternal possession; they are in their land; here they will remain. It was hailed by Tannenbaum as "perhaps the most beautiful, sympathetic portrayal that has been made by any Christian since the creation of the Jewish state."[101] Ariel has judged that it presented Israel in "favorable and glorious terms."[102] It was undoubtedly a major boon to American evangelical tourism in the Holy Land. At a ceremony where Graham was given the American Jewish Committee's national interreligious award, Rabbi Tannenbaum commented, "Israel's political leaders—from Golda Meir to Menachem Begin—could quote 'chapter and verse' of times when Graham provided assistance." Graham responded, speaking of "the debt I owe to Israel, to Judaism and to the Jewish people."[103] Yet Graham, like Arno Gaebelein before him, held negative views of Jews, which he privately expressed to Richard Nixon in 1972 and later would haunt him.[104]

A crucial publication. A new surge of interest in prophecy after the war was capitalized on by Hal Lindsey, whose *The Late Great Planet Earth*

---

[99]Hummel, "*His Land*," 1140.

[100]Hummel, "*His Land*," 1141.

[101]*Christianity Today*, November 18, 1977, quoted in Ruth Mouly and Roland Robertson, "Zionism in American Premillenarian fundamentalism," *American Journal of Theology and Philosophy* 4, no. 3 (1983): 104. Some evangelicals protested the one-sided portrayal, notably Bert De Vries, a professor of history at Calvin College. See Rausch, *Communities in Conflict*, 150.

[102]Yaakov Ariel, *Evangelizing the Chosen People: Missions to the Jews in America, 1880–2000* (Chapel Hill: University of North Carolina Press, 2000), 198.

[103]Ariel, *Evangelizing the Chosen People*, 108.

[104]Graham privately blamed Jews for their stranglehold on media and the general moral decline of America. Shapiro, *Navigating*, 72-73.

appeared in 1970. It has been described as "among the greatest successes in modern publishing."[105] A graduate of Dallas Theological Seminary, Lindsey popularized his version of dispensational premillennialism for a new generation and reached out in a readable, catchy, and dramatic fashion to an audience well beyond those who were interested in academic and arcane discussions of prophecy.[106] His work made its way into bookstores, newsstands, and supermarkets; it has sold over thirty-five million copies, been translated into thirty-five languages, and a film version was produced, narrated by Orson Welles. Lindsey has been spinning out sequels ever since, reworking and reframing his end-times scenarios to take into account political changes as he goes. Building on the fascination of prophecy novelists of the 1950s and 1960s with the implications of a world with atomic weapons, "Lindsey . . . relentlessly turned the Bible into a manual of atomic-age combat."[107] But as B. M. Pietsch points out, "Lindsey represented a departure from early dispensational traditions. He emphasized premillennialism and beliefs about the Rapture, and he hid his epistemic methods and interpretative strategies, differing dramatically from dispensational modernists who took pains to make their methods—and the need for methods—explicit."[108] In the wake of Lindsey, a fascination with prophecy prediction rather than modernist methodology spawned a new wave of prophecy writers claiming the dispensationalist label.

Christian Zionist lobbying for Israel.

> *For the first time, [in the 1970s] dispensationalists believed that it was necessary to leave the bleachers and get onto the playing field to make sure the game ended according to the divine script.*[109]

TIMOTHY WEBER

---

[105]Goldman, *God's Country*, 158.

[106]For a consideration of some of the reasons for its success, see Goldman, *God's Country*, 158-62.

[107]Boyer, *When Time*, 127.

[108]B. M. Pietsch, *Dispensational Modernism* (New York: Oxford University Press, 2015), 210.

[109]Timothy P. Weber, *On the Road to Armageddon: How Evangelicals Became Israel's Best Friend* (Grand Rapids, MI: Baker Academic, 2004), 14. This should be qualified, for as Hummel has argued, from "the 1920s, evangelical and fundamentalist leaders were politically active in conservative politics, preaching the virtues of limited government, free market economics, and social conservatism." Hummel, "*His Land*," 1126.

In the decades following the 1967 war, American Christian Zionists emerged as a powerful pro-Israel lobby in the United States, seeking "massive American support for Israel in terms of money, arms, and diplomatic backing."[110] This was particularly seen during the Yom Kippur War in October 1973, which began with a coordinated surprise attack on Israel by Egypt and Syria on the Jewish Day of Atonement. Initially the Israelis fared badly. In Israel, Christian Zionists actively supported the Israel Defense Forces,[111] and in the United States Graham implored President Nixon to intervene, assuring him that the "majority of Evangelicals were strongly supportive of Israel."[112] Graham's lobbying of Nixon on behalf of Israel was rumored and later confirmed.[113] Following Graham's conversation, a huge American airlift of supplies occurred, which proved decisive, and a cease-fire was achieved. It is hard to know how important Graham's actions were, but certainly Graham's friend Rabbi Tannenbaum considered them significant. Hummel speculates that in light of these events "postwar evangelical Christian Zionists reached the height of their influence in the years 1973–1976."[114] In the aftermath of the Yom Kippur War the American Jewish Committee, in league with Douglas Young, sought to expand evangelical support in America and shifted the focus from Graham to evangelical leaders in theological education and in churches, hoping to "promote theological change as a step towards political mobilization."[115] Central to this strategy was a series of conferences held in New York City beginning in 1975 that involved key evangelical and Jewish leaders.[116]

The lobbying accorded well with the American self-understanding of its special relationship with the Jews that had been part of American identity since the eighteenth century, but in the 1970s and 1980s, this partnership fit comfortably with the realities of the Cold War: Israel was a valuable partner in the struggle against communism, and many of the Arab countries had

---

[110]Ariel, "It's All in the Bible," 269.

[111]Hummel, *Covenant Brothers*, 141.

[112]Hummel, *Covenant Brothers*, 142.

[113]Hummel, *Covenant Brothers*, 129n6. Nixon was much less favorable to Israel than Kennedy had been in spite of his religious upbringing. Ariel asserts that he was raised in an evangelical Quaker home. Ariel, *Unusual Relationship*, 180.

[114]Hummel, *Covenant Brothers*, 130.

[115]Hummel, *Covenant Brothers*, 147.

[116]See Hummel, *Covenant Brothers*, 149-51.

leaned toward the Soviet Union. But with the rise of international terrorism and the killing of Israeli athletes at the Munich Olympics in 1972,
violence escalated in the Middle East and Americans came to understand
the Arab-Israeli conflict in ways "that associated Palestinian nationalism
with terrorism and cast Israel on the front lines of a jihadist threat."[117] Increasingly both Jews and American Christian Zionists began to see any
international criticism of Israel as evidence "of a 'new anti-Semitism' mas-
querading at anti-Zionism."[118]

All of this came at a time of rising evangelical influence in American
politics, symbolized for many by the election of Jimmy Carter—a self-identified evangelical—in 1976. While Carter proved to be a disappointment to
conservative evangelicals on several fronts, his evenhandedness in dealing
with Egypt and Israel was particularly objectionable to many dispensationalists. In 1977 the Egyptian president, Anwar Sadat, shifted Egyptian foreign
policy and sought a rapprochement with Israel. Unhappy with its relationship with the Soviet Union, reeling from the costs of war with Israel, and
struggling with a stagnant economy, Sadat sought peace with Israel and
warmer relations with the United States. The result was negotiations at Camp
David, Maryland, that began a process that resulted in a peace accord between Egypt and Israel. Israel returned the Sinai Peninsula to Egypt (captured in 1967), and Egypt promised to allow Israeli ships use of the Suez
Canal. It was hoped that this would lead to similar agreements with other
Arab countries, but most were hostile to the whole plan. Egypt was subsequently expelled from the Arab League. These efforts involving "land for
peace" were denounced by many American dispensationalists because they
contradicted their belief that Israel was prophesied to expand its borders to
include all of the land that they believed God had promised to ancient Israel.

PERIOD THREE: THE JERRY FALWELL ERA; THE RISE OF THE MORAL MAJORITY IN 1979 UNTIL ITS DEMISE IN 1989

In spite of the Israeli and American Jewish embrace of evangelicals post-
1967, there were "no evangelical political action committees, grassroots organizations, or lobby groups dedicated to pro-Israel political support in

---

[117]Hummel, *Covenant Brothers*, 152.
[118]Hummel, *Covenant Brothers*, 153.

1970."[119] In the 1970s some conservative American Christians became disturbed by evidence of a significant moral decline in America and began making common cause with conservative Catholics and Mormons who shared their social views. Jerry Falwell early in his ministry had disavowed any interest in politics, insisting that preachers are called to be soul winners, not politicians.[120] It has been suggested that the shift away from these views resulted in the ending of the "fundamentalist exile" that is alleged to have begun in 1925 after the disastrous Scopes Monkey Trial.[121] However, the supposed "exile" in the 1930s and 1940s had been related as much to the dispensationalists' choosing to inhabit the political wilderness given their deep and sustained opposition to Roosevelt and his New Deal and their dissatisfaction with Truman rather than from a disinclination to be involved in politics.[122] As Sutton has shown, it was in the 1940s that American evangelicals reversed their First World War tendencies toward pacifism and "baptized Christian fundamentalism in the waters of patriotic Americanism. For the rest of the century they positioned themselves as the legitimate guardians of the nation."[123] The establishment of the National Association of Evangelicals in 1942 was central to their reengagement in national religious and political life. In 1948 it opened an office in Washington to lobby for evangelical concerns.[124]

The rise of the Christian Right in America. The significant shift came in the late 1970s, when for the first time American evangelical political involvement became decidedly partisan, building on the party realignment that had been going on since about 1960. The emergence of the new Christian Right involving groups like the Moral Majority, which Jerry Falwell founded in 1979, the Religious Roundtable, and eventually, Pat Robertson's Christian Coalition evidenced a new configuring of dispensationalists' engagement in politics, something that conservative Republican strategists were eager to

---

[119]Hummel, *Covenant Brothers*, 118.
[120]Durbin, *Righteous Gentiles*, 39. For details on Falwell's early years see Susan Friend Harding, *The Book of Jerry Falwell: Fundamentalist Rhetoric and Politics* (Princeton, NJ: Princeton University Press, 2000), 12-18.
[121]The term is Susan Harding's. See Harding, *Falwell*, 61.
[122]See Sutton, *American Apocalypse*, chap. 8, "Christ's Deal Versus the New Deal."
[123]See Sutton, *American Apocalypse*, 263-92.
[124]Sutton, *American Apocalypse*, 324.

harness.[125] Many of the rank-and-file supporters were dispensationalists who had become convinced that they had a moral and patriotic duty to stand up for their views and to be counted politically, specifically in their pro-Israel views. The politicized tourism that the Israeli government had been encouraging was beginning to "generate grassroots political mobilization."[126]

Menachem Begin, the former head of the terrorist organization Irgun, served as Israeli prime minister from 1977 to 1983 and was particularly drawn to the Christian Zionists, developing a friendship with Jerry Falwell, honoring him in 1981 with the prestigious Jabotinsky Award over the protests of the rabbinical head of Reform Judaism.[127] With this friendship, Falwell began a tradition of establishing connections with all the Israeli prime ministers to follow. Falwell promoted Christian tourism to Israel, bringing thousands of freshmen from his Liberty University for study tours; he was also a vocal political supporter of the Likud Party's controversial settlements in the West Bank, the Israeli preemptive strike in 1981 on an Iraqi nuclear reactor,[128] and the Israeli 1982 invasion of Lebanon.[129] In an interview with *Christianity Today* in 1981 Falwell articulated his understanding of America's role as an "elect" nation, echoing themes articulated a century earlier by William Blackstone: "God has raised up America in these last days for the cause of world evangelization and for the protection of his people the Jews. I don't think America has any other right or reason for existence than those two purposes."[130] In so reasoning, Falwell was echoing a theme that runs throughout the post–World War II prophecy literature: that America has risen to power "for such a time as this" (quoting the book of Esther).

Hummel argues that between 1976 and 1984 American Christian Zionists in a close partnership with American Jews were an integral part of

---

[125]Sutton points out that up to the late 1970s conservative evangelicals had not been wedded to the Republican Party. Sutton, *American Apocalypse*, 353-54.

[126]Hummel, *Covenant Brothers*, 118.

[127]Spector, *Evangelicals and Israel*, 148.

[128]Famously, Prime Minister Begin phoned Falwell to ask him to rally support for Israel in the wake of the international reaction to the attack on Iraq's nuclear facility. For details, see Durbin, *Righteous Gentiles*, 58-62.

[129]Weber, *Armageddon*, 219.

[130]"Interview with the Lone Ranger of American Fundamentalism," *Christianity Today*, September 4, 1981, 25, quoted in Mouly and Robertson, "Zionism," 97.

a well-organized and effective pro-Israel lobby in Washington. "In less than a decade, Christian Zionism transformed into a cause of the Christian right and into a far more politically organized movement."[131] Although the evangelicals and most American Jews were at loggerheads on social issues, the coalition "remained animated by the goal of reconciliation and committed to the security of Israel."[132] The Christian Right and the Israeli Right had found common cause. They "aided each other and provided crucial support in times of distress, encouraging both an alarm for encroaching right-wing politics and harder-edged support for Israel among American Jewish leaders and lobbyists."[133] In this period Graham stepped back from pro-Israel politics, moderated his political statements (perhaps out of a concern for their impact on evangelicals in Arab countries), and dissented from the Moral Majority coalition that Falwell was building. Falwell soon replaced Graham as the most important American Christian Zionist leader.[134]

Premillennialism and the Reagan presidency.

> Ezekiel tells us that Gog, the nation that will lead all of the other powers of darkness against Israel, will come out of the north. Biblical scholars have been saying for generations that Gog must be Russia. What other powerful nation is to the north of Israel? But it didn't seem to make sense before the Russian revolution, when Russia was a Christian country. Now it does, now that Russia has been communistic and atheistic, now that Russia has set itself against God. Now it fits the description of Gog perfectly.[135]

RONALD REAGAN, 1971

By 1981 the American Christian Zionist movement in its alliance with the Christian Right had succeeded in moving "from an elite effort to a popular and

---

[131]Hummel, *Covenant Brothers*, 161.

[132]Hummel, *Covenant Brothers*, 161.

[133]Hummel, *Covenant Brothers*, 161.

[134]Hummel, *Covenant Brothers*, 164. Olson points out that Graham was aware of the negative impact his views might have on Christians in the Arab world, and his friend Rabbi Marc Tannenbaum attributed this to Graham's reticence to speak publicly about his private lobbying efforts. Olson, *America's Road*, 171.

[135]Boyer, *When Time*, 162.

grassroots movement."[136] Falwell was its spokesman, having advanced a popular political Christian Zionism far more deliberately and effectively than Graham. Christian Zionist influence was clear in its impact on Ronald Reagan, when he became president in 1981, and the "premillennialists found themselves with unprecedented access to power, and it did not take long for the news media to detect premillennialists in the new administration."[137] Reagan had a deep, personal, and abiding interest in biblical prophecy and was fascinated by his reading of Hal Lindsey's *Late Great Planet Earth*.[138] In 1983 Reagan delivered a speech to the National Association of Evangelicals in which he famously referred to Soviet Russia as the "evil empire,"[139] an assessment that would have been consistent with Lindsey's view. During his incumbency America continued to offer Israel political support and generous financial and military aid.

PERIOD FOUR: THE ERA OF ROBERTSON AND HAGEE FROM 1989 TO TODAY

> *[Falwell's] reign [as the leader of American Christian Zionism]*
> *was short lived. Even at its political apex the Christian right,*
> *and Christian right Zionism, was headed toward disarray.*[140]
>
> DANIEL HUMMEL

By 1986 Falwell's Moral Majority was in decline, and he stepped down from leadership of the financially strapped movement. In the late 1980s the public moral failings of leading figures such as Jimmy Swaggart and Jim and Tammy Faye Bakker seriously damaged the public credibility of the Christian Right. With the end of the Cold War in 1989, the Soviet threat was gone and the Christian Right seemed to fade quickly. In the same year Falwell announced that the Moral Majority was disbanding given that it had achieved its political goal of establishing the Christian Right as an integral part of American political life. Over the course of the next thirty years the leadership and dynamic of American Christian Zionism would shift once again—this time to charismatic and Pentecostal Christians.

---

[136]Hummel, *Covenant Brothers*, 184.
[137]Weber, *Armageddon*, 200.
[138]Boyer, *When Time*, 142.
[139]Crawford Gribben, "Rapture Fictions and the Changing Evangelical Condition," *Literature and Theology* 18, no. 1 (March 2004): 79.
[140]Hummel, *Covenant Brothers*, 184.

The charismatic (or renewalist) Zionists moved in and dismantled "the Falwell-led Christian right's grip on the movement and then reconstituted American Christian support for Israel under their own leadership."[141] The way for this was paved by Pat Robertson, a televangelist who emerged as a leading American Christian Zionist in the 1980s and 1990s and blazed the trail for the rise of John Hagee, on whom the mantle of Christian Zionist leadership fell by the mid-2000s. Their leadership signaled "the shift of Christian Zionism in American politics toward an open embrace of conservative and right-wing allies in both the United States and Israel."[142] In spite of the many currents at play in American Christian Zionism in the post-Falwell era, it was Robertson who more than anyone else solidified "the ascendancy of Spirit-centered Christians on the Christian right and the Christian Zionist movement" in America.[143]

Robertson was a Virginian like Jerry Falwell, being the son of a US Democratic senator. A graduate of Washington and Lee University, he studied law at Yale before converting to Christianity in his mid-twenties and deciding to become a Baptist minister. In 1960 at the age of thirty he founded the Christian Broadcasting Network based in Portsmouth, Virginia, and started his television talk show, *The 700 Club*, in 1966, which proved to be very profitable. In 1977 he founded Christian Broadcasting Network University (renamed Regent University in 1990). By the late 1970s he became increasingly strident in his criticisms of American culture and vied with Falwell for leadership in the world of televangelists, but his charismatic theology was still suspect in some conservative circles, which limited his influence. Unlike Falwell he did not have personal contacts with Israeli politicians.

Robertson, however, was not a typical dispensationalist in that he believes in a posttribulation rapture,[144] and at one point he sounded like an historicist premillennialist in date-setting Christ's return by the end of 1982.[145] Then again, by 1982 in his book *Secret Kingdom*, "deep fissures had emerged in Robertson's eschatology, as he both embraced the standard premillennial position, and espoused a breathtakingly optimistic postmillennialism.

---

[141] Hummel, *Covenant Brothers*, 186.
[142] Hummel, *Covenant Brothers*, 187.
[143] Hummel, *Covenant Brothers*, 194.
[144] Weber, *Armageddon*, 206.
[145] Weber, *Armageddon*, 205.

Through Christ, he proclaimed, we can enjoy the millennium here and now. 'There *can* be peace; there *can* be plenty; there *can* be freedom.'"[146] Influenced for a time by "dominion theology" associated with C. Peter Wagner, he urged that conservative Christians actively engage in politics and claim dominion over secular matters. Hummel credits his move from the second tier of Christian Zionist leaders to his 1986 announcement that he would run for president; he eventually came in second to vice president George H. W. Bush in the Iowa caucuses.[147] Although his candidacy failed, it convinced him of the importance of grassroots political organization. In 1989 he established his Christian Coalition, which sought to fill the vacuum left by the Moral Majority's demise, and by the early 1990s his focus was on how Christians could mobilize for political action. Its effectiveness was seen in its acknowledged influence in the Republican National Convention, and its breakthrough came in 1994, when the Republicans achieved their first majority in the House of Representatives since 1952.

The very name Christian Coalition sounded more ominous to American Jews than the failed Moral Majority in which they had been subsumed. As Timothy Weber has commented, "As Robertson's book *The New World Order* [1991] made clear, Robertson was much more interested in stopping the forces of one-worldism than in explaining or proving the elaborate dispensationalist system."[148] The particular difficulty was that critics felt Robertson had singled out Jews as key players in his conspiracy theory expounded in *The New World Order* and went on the attack, notably the Anti-Defamation League, which produced a report that was scathing in its criticisms.[149] This was countered by a *New York Times* ad signed by a number of prominent Jewish conservatives who defended Robertson from accusations of anti-Semitism. Another defender was Rabbi Yichel Eckstein, who had worked closely with Robertson and whose International Fellowship of Christians and Jews was dependent on evangelical support. As Hummel summarizes, "With the help of Eckstein, Robertson had managed to salvage a record of incoherent and controversial positions into a learning experience that reinforced

---

[146]Boyer, *When Time*, 138.
[147]Hummel, *Covenant Brothers*, 196.
[148]Weber, *Armageddon*, 207.
[149]Hummel, *Covenant Brothers*, 197.

the Christian right's centrality to Christian Zionism."[150] But Robertson failed to build an institutional center for Christian Zionism, and in the 1990s, while there were "outbursts of support for Zionism," little was accomplished. In 1997 the Christian Coalition's key organizer, Ralph Reed, resigned, and in 2001 Robertson withdrew. The Coalition continued for a few years in the political wilderness. Christian Zionism was down but not out.

The Left Behind series. The great publishing success story in this period was the Left Behind series written by Tim LaHaye and Jerry B. Jenkins. It included sixteen apocalyptic novels written between 1995 and 2007. Total sales for the series have been estimated at sixty-five million copies. Unlike the earlier *Late Great Planet Earth*, the series is prophecy in narrative form and focuses on the postrapture world in which a small group of Christian converts constitute the "Tribulation Force," which struggles against the "Global Community" and its leader, the antichrist, who turns out to be an unknown Romanian politician who becomes secretary of the United Nations and promises to bring about peace and order. The antichrist, Nicolae Jetty Carpathia, succeeds in moving the two mosques from the Temple Mount in Jerusalem to "New Babylon."[151] The enormity of the novels' popularity was only matched by the storm of protests from Jews and Catholics (and presumably Romanians) who were offended by the story line.[152]

Russia, the collapse of communism, and prophetic rethinking. The end of the Cold War following the dismantling of the Berlin Wall meant that the well-established enemy of the West was no longer Soviet Russia, and this had profound implications for American Christian Zionism. For seventy years dispensationalists had identified the Soviet Union as the Gog and Magog spoken of in Ezekiel 38–39 as the leader of the coming northern confederacy. Paul Boyer in his exhaustive study of prophecy popularizers in America between 1945 and the early 1990s has argued that this core dispensational belief became "firmly embedded in the belief system of millions of Americans"[153] and in turn "helped shape U.S. Cold War attitudes—supplying

[150]Hummel, *Covenant Brothers*, 198.

[151]Ariel, "It's All in the Bible," 282.

[152]For discussions of the Left Behind series see Ariel, *An Uncommon Relationship*, 46-57, and Sherryll Mleynek, "The Rhetoric of the 'Jewish Problem' in the *Left Behind* Novels," *Literature and Theology* 19, no. 4 (November 2005): 367-83, and Gribben, "Rapture Fictions," 77-94.

[153]Boyer, *When Time*, 174.

theological reinforcement of the rigidly hostile view of the Soviet Union that pervaded American culture for several postwar decades."[154] He observes,

> We must keep the larger picture in view: from the end of World War II to the closing years of the twentieth century, scores of prophecy writers, in books selling millions of copies, as well as TV and radio preachers reaching more millions of individuals, taught that Russia's destruction is explicitly foretold in a sacred text which most Americans revere as divinely inspired. We cannot fully understand Cold War politics and culture without close attention to this religious component.[155]

The collapse of the Soviet bloc in the early 1990s presented a problem in that "the mainstays of post–World War II prophecy teaching were suddenly gone."[156] Some argued that the situation was only temporary; most ignored the problem and sought to change the subject. Instead of an obsession with Russia, the new focus was the emergence of a new world order that had long been a theme in dispensational thinking, harkening back to their fears of the League of Nations in the 1920s.

The other threat that came to displace the focus on Russia was the reviving of a focus on Islam as the longer-term enemy of the West, and for Robertson and others this merged with the talk of "one-worldism." From the early 1970s with the oil crisis of 1973, dispensational writers had become increasingly interested in the rise of Islamic fundamentalism. Such concerns increased after the 1979 Iranian Revolution, and by the early 1980s the Islamic threat had increasingly come to the fore. The Iraqi invasion of Kuwait in 1990 turned out to be a huge boon for dispensationalist writers, with sales of *The Late Great Planet Earth* once again taking off and a whole new spate of prophecy books being published. And with the new conflict in the Middle East, Bible teachers advanced a new line of interpretation—namely, that "Iraq was really the Book of Revelation's Babylon,"[157] not Russia. Russia as the great enemy of the West was being replaced by Islamic fundamentalism, which was now seen as the common enemy of Christians and Israel. As a leading figure in the National Association of Evangelicals put it in 2003,

---

[154]Boyer, *When Time*, 174-75.
[155]Boyer, *When Time*, 175.
[156]Weber, *Armageddon*, 204.
[157]Weber, *Armageddon*, 208.

"Evangelicals have substituted Islam for the Soviet Union. The Muslims have become the modern-day equivalent of the Evil Empire."[158]

The Oval Office and Israel: From George H. W. Bush to the Trump era. Reagan's successor, George H. W. Bush (president from 1989 to 1993), was reliant on Christian Zionist support and followed a policy that was clearly pro-Israel. Bill Clinton (president from 1993 to 2001) was a nominal evangelical. He had been raised in an evangelical home[159] and was a member of a Southern Baptist church, but received little support from conservative evangelicals. In a 1994 speech to the Israeli Knesset, he recalled the words of his former Baptist pastor W. O. Vaught: "If you abandon Israel, God will never forgive you. . . . [He] said that it is God's will that Israel, the biblical home of the Jewish people, continue forever and ever. . . . Your journey is our journey, and America will stand with you now and always."[160] While historians have found little other evidence of Christian Zionist influence on Clinton, Ariel has commented, "Yet it is important to be aware of the fact that the roots and cultural background of the American president, who opened his administration to Jews more than any president before him and showed deep concern for Israel, were in the American Bible Belt with its scriptural vision of Israel."[161]

Clinton's successor, George W. Bush (president from 2001 to 2009), regarded himself as a committed conservative evangelical, and he was very sensitive to premillennialist Christian Zionists.[162] The events surrounding 9/11 led to a comment by Bush a few days later in which he called for a "war on terrorism." This was followed by what was perhaps the greatest gaffe of his presidency when he said, "This crusade, this war on terrorism, is going to take a while."[163] The use of the word *crusade* was met with dismay in the Arab and Muslim world, conjuring up the disastrous religious and military

---

[158]Spector, *Evangelicals and Israel*, 57.

[159]Ariel, *Unusual Relationship*, 182.

[160]Daniel G. Hummel, "Foreign Policy and Religion: U.S. Foreign Policy Toward Israel," in *Oxford Research Encyclopedia of Politics*, ed. Paul A. Djupe, Mark J. Rozell, and Ted G. Jelen (Oxford: Oxford University Press, 2019), 1-2, https://doi.org/10.1093/acrefore/9780190228637.013.988.

[161]Ariel, "It's All in the Bible," 270.

[162]For details on George W. Bush's relationship to Israel see Ariel, *Unusual Relationship*, 183.

[163]George W. Bush, "Remarks by the President upon Arrival," Office of the Press Secretary, 16 September 2001. https://georgewbush-whitehouse.archives.gov/news/releases/2001/09/20010916 -2.html.

crusades of the High Middle Ages. The "war on terror" was understood by many in the Muslim world to be, in fact, a war on Islam as a key aim of American foreign policy. One study of public opinion in four leading Muslim nations at the time showed that large majorities of those populations embraced the view of American intentions that it was really warring against Islam, and thus they strongly endorsed the view that American troops should be withdrawn from all Muslim countries.[164] Durbin has observed that "it is hard to underestimate the role that events such as 9/11 had on American views of Muslims, and their corresponding view of Israelis"[165] as "the creation and identification of a united enemy that is against both Christianity and Judaism helps to define who belongs and who does not."[166] These events have been frequently used by Christian Zionist speakers to develop "a shared sense of affinity—if not identity—among Americans and Israelis" and underline "the role that fears of Islamic terrorism have had and continue to have in further entrenching American affinity for Israel."[167] Sean Durbin comments,

> Just as American Christians brought Jews and Israel into the fold of Judeo-Christian civilization as part of a strategy of broadening their fight against communism, so too has this new threat of terrorism enabled them to define themselves as purveyors of a ("true") God-fearing civilization that is at the core of Western civilization, versus what they construe as a backward and barbarous enemy in the thrall of a false, satanically-inspired ideology.[168]

Barak *Hussein* Obama was the president whom the dispensationalists were least pleased with.[169] His middle name reminded them of the former president of Iraq whom the United States had overthrown, and fueled suspicion that Obama was a closet Muslim and that he favored Islamic nations over American interests. Well before he was elected, Christian Zionists were concerned about remarks by Jeremiah Wright, Obama's pastor, which they considered anti-Semitic.[170] Obama's unwillingness to veto a censure of

---

[164]Clifford A. Kiracofe, *Dark Crusade: Christian Zionism and US Foreign Policy* (London: L.B. Tauris, 2009), 44.

[165]Durbin, *Righteous Gentiles*, 47.

[166]Durbin, *Righteous Gentiles*, 121.

[167]Durbin, *Righteous Gentiles*, 47.

[168]Durbin, *Righteous Gentiles*, 47.

[169]See Durbin, *Righteous Gentiles*, 176-90.

[170]For a fuller discussion of attitudes to Obama see Durbin, *Righteous Gentiles*, 19-51.

Israel by the United Nations Security Council in 2016 that condemned the West Bank settlements—a first for any American president—especially upset them. Obama's relationship with Benjamin Netanyahu was probably the worst of any American president with an Israeli prime minister since Israel's founding.

The Trump administration's attitude to Israel was far more friendly than Obama's. In 2017 President Trump recognized Jerusalem as Israel's capital and announced that it would move its embassy there from Tel Aviv. On May 14, 2018, the American embassy was opened in Jerusalem, on the seventieth anniversary of Israel's declaration of independence. Vice President Mike Pence was present to represent the United States; he had been the head of the Christian Zionist lobby in Congress when he served as a congressman from Indiana in the early 2000s. In November 2019 the American Secretary of State Mike Pompeo announced that the United States no longer regarded Israeli settlements in the occupied territories as contravening international law.[171] The Trump administration's actions were widely seen as a reward by Trump to his Christian Zionist supporters.

The John Hagee era of American Christian Zionism, 2006 forward.

> *Of all the leaders [directing] . . . the efforts of American Christians into the world of practical politics on behalf of Israel, Hagee and CUFI are among the most renowned and effective. . . . In the years following the founding of CUFI in February 2006, it has rhetorically framed its growth and relative success not merely as just another political lobbying group, but as God's instrument for fulfilling his purposes in the world on behalf of Israel.[172]*
>
> SEAN DURBIN

Christians United for Israel (CUFI) asserts that it is the largest American pro-Israel group.[173] It was formed in 2006 by John Hagee, the pastor of

---

[171]Lara Jakes and David M. Halbfinger, "In Reversal, U.S. Sides with Israel on Settlements," *New York Times*, November 19, 2019, A1 N.

[172]Durbin, *Righteous Gentiles*, 54.

[173]For details on Christians United for Israel see Durbin, *Righteous Gentiles*.

Cornerstone Church in San Antonio, Texas, after Benjamin Netanyahu asked him if he could do something to unite American Christians in support of Israel.[174] CUFI claimed over ten million members in 2021.[175] Netanyahu offers his personal endorsement on its website: "I consider CUFI to be a vital part of Israel's national security."[176] The key person in the organization from 2006 to 2015 was David Brog, a conservative (nonmessianic) Jew and the cousin of former Israeli prime minister Ehud Barak. Brog enlisted the help of other Jews, including Ari Morgenstern as communications director, who "ensures CUFI's messaging is consistent with what Brog wants—which is to convey that evangelical Christians support Israel, yet (to his Jewish supporters) are also 'safe' because CUFI will never proselytize."[177] Unlike other organizations, it seems virtually impossible to ascertain CUFI's annual income,[178] but if their seven million registered members are giving on average only $20 a year to the organization, then its income could well be over $140 million, putting it ahead of the income of the International Fellowship of Christians and Jews, which had an income of $121 million in 2017.

Hagee was able to succeed where Falwell and Robertson had failed in that he created a national grassroots organization focused on Christian Zionist objectives. Hagee's health-and-wealth prosperity gospel in Pentecostal clothing was anathema to Falwell but quite similar to Robertson's. Yet it was "Hagee, more than any Christian Zionist before him, [who] bound prosperity theology and Genesis 12:3 [the injunction to bless Israel] together and placed them at the center of his thinking about Israel."[179] Hagee had been active in Christian Zionist circles since visiting Israel in 1978, but it was his beginning a "night to Honor Israel" in his Texas church in June 1981 that propelled him into Christian Zionist leadership. The celebration blended American and Israeli nationalism with great fanfare. So successful was this

---

[174]This story is frequently recounted by CUFI speakers, including Hagee in Netanyahu's presence. Durbin, *Righteous Gentiles*, 56-57.

[175]CUFI.org, accessed January 21, 2021.

[176]Benjamin Netanyahu, "How You Can Bless Israel," http://cufi.convio.net/blessingisrael/Blessing Israel_Booklet_2015.pdf, accessed January 21, 2021.

[177]Troy Anderson "Where Your Israel Donation Really Goes," *CharismaNews*, October 22, 2013, https://www.charismanews.com/opinion/standing-with-israel/47005-where-your-israel-dona tion-really-goes.

[178]The author contacted the organization, but they do not disclose financial information to the public.

[179]Hummel, *Covenant Brothers*, 202.

occasion that it became an annual event and attracted attention from grateful Israeli politicians. His embrace of prosperity-gospel themes in the early 2000s was evident in a number of his books, and he established close links with other popular figures on the Christian right.[180] Together they emphasized covenantal commands of Scripture that would unlock divine blessings on America and American Christians. In the minds of the prosperity gospel Zionists "it was up to Christians to prompt God's blessings, and the Bible explained the process clearly."[181] Durbin summarizes the role that "blessing Israel" plays in this context: "The act of 'blessing' Israel helps Christian Zionists further define and enact their identity, and, in the process, locate themselves in sacred history as agents of God helping to facilitate the implementation of his plans in the world."[182]

Hagee espouses elements of dispensational theology, such as the eternal separation of Jews and Gentiles. Darby had said that the Jews will reign with Christ on earth because they are his earthly people; Gentile believers are God's heavenly people and they will reign with Christ in heaven. Hagee echoes this in his exegesis of Genesis 22:17: "I will multiply your descendants as the stars of heaven and as the sand which is on the seashore" (RSV). Hagee unpacks this in a Darbyite fashion, arguing that the stars represent the church (the Gentiles) who are God's spiritual seed, but "the sand of the seashore" "is earthly and represents an earthly kingdom with a literal Jerusalem as its capital city. Both stars and sand exist at the same time, and neither ever replaces the other. Just so, the nation of Israel and the church exist at the same time and do not replace each other."[183] But as Durbin and Spector have argued, it would seem that the Christian Zionists in Hagee's camp are not motivated by eschatology alone. Social and political factors, even contemporary events, are important influences as well.

Durbin's recent (rather polemical) study of Hagee and his organization examines the mentality that he believes suffuses this expression of Christian Zionism. He asserts that Christian Zionists associated with CUFI operate out of a worldview that they claim can be read off the pages

---

[180]Hummel, *Covenant Brothers*, 204.
[181]Hummel, *Covenant Brothers*, 206.
[182]Durbin, *Righteous Gentiles*, 240.
[183]Hagee quoted in Durbin, *Righteous Gentiles*, 128.

of Scripture in a straightforward manner and think of themselves as people who understand the ultimate truth about the direction of history that this reading of Scripture has revealed to them. Central to this worldview is their understanding that whenever Scripture talks about "Israel" it is talking about Jews and, by extrapolation, modern-day Israel. Put simply: in the minds of the Christian Zionists, the ancient Israelites "are synonymous with modern Israelis."[184]

They believe that those who do not share this worldview are clearly on the wrong path, however well-meaning they may be, including those Christians (both liberals and conservatives) who fail to agree with their views. Often the Christian Zionist discourse offered by people like Hagee demonizes those who disagree with them and attributes their opposition or lack of support to Satan. Their reading of Christian Zionist history is called on to prove to themselves that far-sighted Christians like Lord Shaftesbury and William Hechler were on God's side, just as they are. Those who doubted them were aligned with anti-Semitic forces just as their opponents are. The other great enemy besides wrong-headed Christians are Arabs, whose opposition can be traced back to the biblical rivalry between Isaac and Ismael.[185] Christian Zionists and the Jews are on God's side; Americans and Israelis are united as defenders of "Judeo-Christianity." Both stand opposed to the Arabs and Islam (which are often equated). America and Israel are sharers of "Judeo-Christianity," covenant brothers in God's eyes. And Christians are repeatedly called on to "bless" the Jews, which entails financial sacrifice and political support, all subsumed under religious duty.

With this mentality and message Hagee has managed to create a popular movement that has garnered the support of both Jews and Christian Zionists. Under his leadership "Hagee and CUFI became the preferred pro-Israel lobby group in the Trump administration and prominent source of evangelical identification with the White House."[186] Even some Orthodox Jews in Israel have been drawn to cooperate with Hagee, encouraged by his willingness to downgrade Jewish evangelism in order to assist and defend the Christian Zionist cause.

---

[184]Durbin, *Righteous Gentiles*, 103.
[185]Durbin, *Righteous Gentiles*, 122-31.
[186]Hummel, *Covenant Brothers*, 209.

Just as the onset of the Cold War had provided Christian Zionists with a threat to Israel that could serve to unite Jews and Christians under the umbrella of "Judeo-Christianity," so also radical Islam presented them with an opponent that replaced the Soviet Union as the existential threat. The election of Mahmoud Ahmadinejad as president of Iran in 2005 soon became the new focus. His repeated threats to wipe Israel off the map and his pursuit of nuclear weapons made the Iranian threat a top priority. The Christian Zionist framing of the Iranian threat often appealed to the book of Esther, which recounts the attempt by Haman, a Persian official, to destroy the Jewish people, and drew parallels between him and the Iranian leader.[187] Within the interpretive framework of the Christian Zionists, "just as Satan used Haman to attempt to prevent Jesus's *first* coming by destroying all of the Jews in the world, Ahmadinejad's threats to destroy Israel are connected with Satan's desire to prevent Jesus's *Second* Coming, which for Christian Zionists is intimately connected to a Jewish Jerusalem."[188] Esther is an example of someone who allowed herself to be used by God—like "righteous Gentiles" throughout history who have stood by the Jews—and Christian Zionists are to emulate her in their support for Israel. She becomes a paradigm as an individual "whom God chose to use to save his chosen people from destruction, and further reveal himself in history. And she is also an example that Christian Zionists today invoke in order to attach their own work to what they construe as a similarly urgent call."[189] In Durbin's view, these enthusiasts do not regard the book of Esther as an artifact of history; its concerns are human instrumentality, engagement in spiritual warfare, and the assertion that anyone can become a pivotal actor in God's plans. The account of Esther is employed to "reconstitute political activities as acts of religious devotion,"[190] ironically so because the book of Esther is not a prophetic book and never mentions the name of God.

Christian Zionists frequently write themselves into Scripture, and are often urged to be "watchmen" on the wall for Israel. This picks up the language of Isaiah 62:6: "I have posted watchmen on your walls, Jerusalem."

---

[187]See Durbin, *Righteous Gentiles*, chap. 3.
[188]Durbin, *Righteous Gentiles*, 98.
[189]Durbin, *Righteous Gentiles*, 99.
[190]Durbin, *Righteous Gentiles*, 116.

Christian watchmen are "to have a heart for Israel" and the Jewish people. A shared Christian Zionist identity is nurtured and enacted through prayer, financial gifts, and/or political lobbying. "Such acts, when prefaced with various scriptural references, act to re-define individuals as 'watchmen on the wall,' inserting them into the biblical text as divinely inspired subjects whom God has chosen to help further his will at a particular juncture in history."[191]

Assessing the Christian Zionists' Political Impact

Just how important all this lobbying has been since 1967 is a matter of dispute. Some writers make it sound like the Christian Zionist lobby determined American foreign policy. Samuel Goldman has questioned whether this is an exaggeration, pointing out that

> no investigation, however, demonstrated that these strategies diverted U.S. foreign policy far from its recent course. According to many analysts, the Bush White House pursued the same goals in its relations with Israel— security cooperation, promotion of economic ties, and a negotiated two-state settlement—as had the Clinton administration. . . . A majority of Americans regarded Israel as a friend and had for years. U.S. foreign policy reflected that fact, no matter who sat in the Oval Office.[192]

This observation would appear correct, at least until the presidency of Donald Trump, whose administration exhibited exuberant support for Israel and included Christian Zionists, most notably his vice president, Mike Pence.

Weber has argued of an earlier era that the dispensationalists' influence "was more indirect and subterranean: It created a certain passivity about the inevitability of military buildups, failed peace talks, deepening crises, and nuclear war. If such things were going to happen no matter what, then there was no use trying to do anything about them."[193] While this may have been the case with many Christian Zionists up to about 1970, it is doubtful whether this analysis is applicable to the period since then. Durbin has challenged this perspective in his study of CUFI: since the 1970s the newly active

---

[191]Durbin, *Righteous Gentiles*, 103.
[192]Goldman, *God's Country*, 174.
[193]Weber, *Armageddon*, 203.

Christian Zionists have both nurtured their apocalyptic outlook (although they often downplay the apocalyptic emphasis when relating to outsiders) and promoted political involvement. He observes that they are not seeking to "hasten Armageddon" but rather seeking to be God's instruments to block activities that might imperil God's intentions. Clearing the way for God's work to be accomplished in the world is their goal, and "it is through this work that ostensibly ordinary political action becomes reconstituted as a form of religious practice." Rather than "forcing God's hand" they are simply "walking in the mantle of Esther."[194]

---

[194]Durbin, *Righteous Gentiles*, 116.

13

AMERICAN CHRISTIAN ZIONIST ACTIVITIES AND ORGANIZATIONS

AMERICAN CHRISTIAN ZIONISTS have been busy on at least three fronts. First, in the United States they educate church groups about Israel, distribute pro-Zionist materials (books, CDs, etc.), mobilize prayer support for Israel, organize pro-Zionist tours to the Holy Land, and lobby the American government on policies and budget decisions related to Israel.[1] Politically this generally means strong support for the Republican Party as political polling shows that Republicans are—by a wide margin—much more pro-Israel than Democrats. Second, in Israel they generously support Israeli charities, helping to fund Jewish immigration to Israel, and work to provide social services such as food banks, aid to the elderly, and support to Israeli soldiers. Third, in both the United States and in Israel many of them support evangelistic work among the Jewish people. Many of these activities are channeled through local churches across America. Others are sponsored by a multitude of different agencies; some dedicated to spreading the Christian Zionist message; others, to evangelism; while others focus on a particular philanthropic cause usually subsumed under the theme of "blessing Israel."[2]

TWO KEY ORGANIZATIONS THAT CHRISTIAN ZIONISTS SUPPORT

International Fellowship of Christians and Jews. Aside from CUFI (discussed in chapter twelve), there are two organizations that find strong

---

[1]Jeremy M. Sharp, "U.S. Foreign Aid to Israel," Congressional Research Service, April 10, 2018, https://fas.org/sgp/crs/mideast/RL33222.pdf.

[2]Christian Zionists are generous givers. Their donations to Zionist and Jewish causes amounted to roughly $130 million in 2017, but this amount does not include the income of the largest of the groups, Christians United For Israel, whose income could well have surpassed this total.

support among Christian Zionists.[3] The lion's share of American Christian Zionist charitable giving has gone to (the late) Rabbi Yechiel Eckstein's International Fellowship of Christians and Jews, which was founded in 1983 and raises a huge amount annually[4] from 1.6 million Christian donors, "making it the largest Christian-supported humanitarian agency helping Israel and the Jewish people around the world,"[5] although it is not a Christian organization. It claims to have raised over $1.4 billion to help Jews in Israel and throughout the diaspora. It enlists Christians as advocates for Israel, and to fight anti-Israel bias wherever it is manifested. The Fellowship has a program (Guardians of Israel) that distributes food and medical care to the poor; another called Isaiah 58 focuses on care for Russian Jews; On Wings of Eagles helps needy Jews from around the world to emigrate to Israel; and Stand for Israel is particularly focused on prayer and political support for the fight against anti-Semitism, especially in the media.[6]

Many Christian Zionists apparently operated under the impression that Rabbi Eckstein was a messianic believer (that is, a Jewish Christian), but he was in fact an orthodox rabbi. (Eckstein died suddenly in early 2019.) In a 2014 article titled "Where your Israel Donation Really Goes," *Charisma* magazine reported that "some organizations [supported by evangelicals] not only fail to support Messianic believers, but often use donations to support initiatives that actually hinder those brothers and sisters in Christ. One such example is International Fellowship of Christians and Jews."[7] Eckstein's access to evangelicals was aided by his friendships with Pat Robertson and Jerry

---

[3]In addition to CUFI and the two described in some detail below, there also others, whose websites often indicate that they have national offices spread throughout the world: the Unity Coalition for Israel based in Kansas and claiming to be "the largest network of Pro-Israel groups in the world," representing "more than 40 million Americans"; Bridges for Peace; Christian Friends of Israeli Communities; the Jerusalem Prayer Team, which claims sixty-seven million members (and has endorsements on its website from two former Israeli prime ministers); Christian Friends of Israel; National Christian Leadership Conference for Israel (formerly Christians Concerned for Israel); and Eagles' Wings based in Clarence, New York, but very active in Israel.

[4]It had a 2017 income of $121,344,000. ProPublica Nonprofit Explorer, "International Fellowship of Christians & Jews," https://projects.propublica.org/nonprofits/organizations/363256096.

[5]International Fellowship of Christians and Jews, "Rabbi Yechiel Eckstein, 1951–2019," https://www.ifcj.org/who-we-are/leadership/rabbi-yechiel-eckstein/.

[6]Ifcj.org website, accessed September 28, 2017.

[7]Troy Anderson "Where Your Israel Donation Really Goes," *CharismaNews*, October 22, 2013, https://www.charismanews.com/opinion/standing-with-israel/47005-where-your-israel-donation-really-goes.

Falwell and support from evangelical leaders such as Jerry Rose, the late Jamie Buckingham, and the late Robert Walker, a prominent evangelical publisher.

International Christian Embassy Jerusalem. The second organization with very high visibility in the Christian Zionist world, and "the most visible and best known Christian Zionist organization in Israel,"[8] is the International Christian Embassy Jerusalem (ICEJ). Its roots go back to the early 1970s, when expatriate Christian Zionists in Israel began gathering weekly for prayer and discussed ways in which they could counter the growing anti-Israeli sentiments in Western Christian churches. Influential in this was the Hebrew Roots movement, which wanted to explore the points of contact between the Jewish and Christian faiths, to build bridges with Jewish Israelis, and to appropriate the Hebrew language and Jewish symbols in Christian worship. Furthermore, they wanted Christians to be physically present in Israel because they believed the land to belong eternally to the Jews, and thus Christians had a responsibility to obey Isaiah 40:1 to comfort God's people.[9] The conviction—indeed the "revelation"—of the importance of Christian celebration of all three Jewish feasts became central to their faith and practice. Christians from all the nations of the world should fulfill the injunction of Zechariah 14:16 (frequently cited by the ICEJ): "And it shall come to pass that everyone who is left of all the nations which came against Jerusalem shall go up from year to year to worship the King, the Lord of hosts, and to keep the Feast of Tabernacles."[10] A key leader was Jan Willem van der Hoeven,[11] a Dutch minister who suggested that they begin gathering Christian Zionists from around the world annually in Jerusalem to celebrate the Feast of Tabernacles (Sukkot), which commemorates the exodus from Egypt. The first such celebration took place in October 1979 and ended with a march of the Christian Zionists

---

[8]Yaakov Ariel, "'It's All in the Bible': Evangelical Christians, Biblical Literalism, and Philosemitism in Our Times," in *Philosemitism in History*, ed. Joseph Karp and Adam Sutcliffe (Cambridge: Cambridge University Press, 2011), 271.

[9]Matthew C. Westbrook, "The International Christian Embassy, Jerusalem, and Renewalist Zionism: Emerging Jewish-Christian Ethnonationalism" (PhD diss., Drew University, 2014), 18.

[10]NKJV quoted by Westbrook, "Christian Embassy," 18.

[11]Van der Hoeven was for a time the guardian of the "Garden Tomb" in Jerusalem and is now the director of the International Christian Zionist Center in Jerusalem. See International Christian Zionist Center, "ICZC International Director; Jan Willem Van Der Hoeven," https://iczcusa.org /about-us/international-director-board.

dressed in native costume through the streets of Jerusalem, waving their own nations' flags along with the Israeli flag.

In 1980, when Israel announced that Jerusalem would become the Israeli capital, the United Nations Security Council condemned the move and called on members states to withdraw their diplomatic missions from Jerusalem; about a dozen governments complied. To affirm Israel's control of Jerusalem, the Christian Zionists started the International Christian Embassy Jerusalem. Matthew C. Westbrook comments, "For Christian Zionists, historical memory and unfolding eschatology find their apex in a united, Jewish-controlled Jerusalem. It was in this context of unfulfilled desire that U.N. Resolution 478 was felt by these Christians to be in opposition to the divine purpose for history and for Israel."[12] Teddy Kollek, the mayor of Jerusalem, immediately welcomed the organization, and the Israeli political establishment has generally been enthusiastic about ICEJ ever since. Although ICEJ financial support from the United States is modest (just over $3 million in 2016) compared to the other players, the ICEJ has a remarkably high profile in Israel. It has sponsored a number of creative initiatives and generally downplays proselytism.

Its Feast of Tabernacles regularly attracts about five thousand attendees from around the world. Its leadership is largely European rather than American, and it appears to have a much more international following, especially in Africa, South America, and Asia. It claims satellite branches in eighty-five countries, including eight new branches in countries with a Muslim majority, and one in Cuba. It has an impressive media production department that operates in seven languages, producing booklets, DVDs, audiotapes, and a web and television focus.[13] It is also very active in philanthropic work in Israel—particularly focused on care for the elderly and immigrants—distributing money to various Jewish and Israeli causes, often to Israeli public agencies. While the ICEJ claims that its work is religious and not political, that is quite evidently not the case. It works hard to get Christian Zionists throughout the world to lobby their governments to take a pro-Israeli line; it repeatedly lobbied the American government to move its embassy to Jerusalem, opposed any "land for peace" agreement, and regularly

---

[12]Westbrook, "Christian Embassy," 22.
[13]For a fuller account of the ICEJ see Ariel, "It's All in the Bible," 271-75.

boasts that it has used its influence to move Majority World leaders, especially in Africa, in a pro-Israel direction.[14] Israeli prime ministers have frequently addressed the Feast of Tabernacles, and the World Jewish Congress has often expressed its appreciation of the ICEJ.

Traditionally Israelis have been reluctant about such Christian-based charity, but those hesitations are being overcome as organizations like ICEJ and Christian Friends of Israel have categorically rejected proselytizing in Israel. Now even Israeli-based institutions and agencies are actively soliciting donations from evangelicals: Leket, the Israeli food bank; the Israel Disabled Veterans organization; and even the Israeli emergency medical service organization, Magen David Adom, all have their "Christian Friends of. . . ." fundraising arms. The decline of American Jewish funding of Israel and Israeli causes has contributed to this trend of seeking Christian charitable giving.[15] Thus Yaakov Ariel has observed,

> The phenomenon of Christians supporting Jewish and Zionist causes is full of paradoxes. Being committed, indeed fervent, evangelicals or pietists, Christian supporters of Israel insist on the exclusivity of their faith as the only true fulfillment of God's commands and as the only means to assure people's salvation. The Christian philo-Semite relations to the Jews have therefore been characterized by two conflicting sentiments, one supportive and appreciative, and the other critical and patronizing.[16]

How the supportive and appreciative sentiment is worked out on the ground has been described by Faydra Shapiro, who has personally observed the hard and unnoticed work of hundreds of Christians, and has expressed her utter surprise at the willingness of poor ultra-Orthodox Jews to accept practical help and food from these Christians over the opposition of their rabbis. Shapiro observed such work as a participant-observer and comments, "The day-in, day-out support of Jews in Israel requires a great deal of organization, hard work, and patience. There are no tambourines or banners here, no flag waving, dramatic political activism, or impassioned

---

[14]Timothy P. Weber, *On the Road to Armageddon: How Evangelicals Became Israel's Best Friend* (Grand Rapids, MI: Baker Academic, 2004), 217.

[15]Judy Maltz, "Once Taboo in Israel. Now It's on the Rise. Why?," *Haaretz*, August 16, 2016, https://www.haaretz.com/israel-news/.premium.MAGAZINE-once-taboo-in-israel-evangelical-aid-is-on-the-rise-why-1.5424590.

[16]Ariel, "It's All in the Bible," 283-84.

speeches, just a group of hardworking folks who believe themselves to be doing God's work by ensuring that poor Jewish kids in Israel get breakfast."[17]

Christian Zionists and *Aliyah* (Jewish Immigration to Israel)

Helping dispersed Jews move to Israel has become a religious duty for many Christian Zionists. The immigration of Jews is something that they believe God has promised, and their support for *aliyah* is a means of their participation in the fulfillment of biblical prophecy. Thus the "return of the Jews" is hugely significant, and many want to help through their giving, prayer, and direct involvement to accomplish this end, enabling people to immigrate and helping them settle into Israeli society. Many millions of dollars are given to this end each year, and hundreds of thousands of Jews have been aided in their move to Israel. Private groups like Nefesh b'Nefesh[18] (Jewish souls united) receive funding from evangelical Christian Zionists through the International Fellowship of Christians and Jews and John Hagee Ministries,[19] but there are numerous evangelical organizations facilitating *aliyah*, often focusing on different areas of the world: the Cyrus Foundation;[20] Helping His Chosen Return (from North and South America); Operation Exodus of the Ebenezer Fund;[21] and Operation Jabotinsky of Livids Ord—a Swedish charismatic megachurch (both primarily focused on the former Soviet Union), and others that are concerned with Ethiopia and India.

While American Christian Zionists tend to be conservative on immigration into the United States, they are enthusiastic about Jewish immigration to Israel because for many of them it is "not a matter of public policy, but rather an issue of divine prophecy."[22] And many believe that this movement is a precursor to the spiritual revival that is to come on the Jews. "For Christian Zionists, Jewish immigration to Israel is part of a theological vision of restoration and reconciliation, in which the mundane details of

---

[17]Faydra Shapiro, *Christian Zionism: Navigating the Jewish-Christian Border* (Eugene, OR: Cascade, 2015), 43.

[18]Nefesh b'Nefesh, https://nbn.org.il.

[19]Shapiro, *Navigating*, 57.

[20]Cyrus Foundation, http://cyrusfoundation.org.

[21]Operation Exodus, http://operation-exodus.org.

[22]Shapiro, *Navigating*, 58.

migrant experience are overlooked in favor of the perceived cosmic significance of the immigration itself."[23]

A central figure in this story is Israel's first prime minister, David Ben-Gurion, the resolutely secular Jew who has become a Christian saint of sorts in Christian Zionist circles. They celebrate him not as the founder of a secular and secularizing state but as a divinely ordained leader who was perhaps secretly sympathetic to Protestant religious influences. He is believed to have kept a copy of Hal Lindsey's *The Late Great Planet Earth* on his bedside table, and his warm friendships with Christian Zionists are celebrated. In the narrative popular among Pentecostal and charismatic Zionists, Ben-Gurion's emigration to Palestine in 1906 is linked with the Azusa Street revival, which is cited as the birth of Pentecostalism. Another Pentecostal revival known as the Latter Rain Revival of 1948 (discussed in chapter fourteen) is tied symbolically with the gaining of Israeli independence in the same year, and the beginning of the Jesus People movement is dated in 1967, when the Six-Day War occurred. As one pastor explained to Shapiro, "Everything that happens in Israel is directly related to what's happening in the church. . . . We need to realize that Israel's restoration directly affects something great for the Gentiles."[24]

CHRISTIAN ZIONIST AMBIVALENCE ABOUT ISRAEL

Christian Zionists are not uncritical of Israeli policy and sometimes criticize the Israeli government on public-policy issues—such as abortion—that are close to their hearts. And yet, for Christian Zionists, Israel "is the only nation-state in the world that matters, supernaturally speaking. The land itself is felt to be cosmically aligned with forces of good."[25] While Israel has not yet realized its full potential, which it will one day when the people, the land, and the God of Israel are in perfect alignment, it will do so in the end. This vision allows Israel to be in the minds of the Christian Zionists the "global 'true north' for the nations of the world, exporting an all-powerful orientation that locates other nations on the cosmic stage. Israel constitutes

---

[23]Shapiro, *Navigating*, 60.

[24]Shapiro, *Navigating*, 60.

[25]Faydra L. Shapiro, "Living in the Hour of Restoration: Christian Zionism, Immigration, and Aliyah," in *Comprehending Christian Zionism: Perspectives in Comparison*, ed. Goran Gunner and Robert O. Smith (Minneapolis: Fortress, 2014), 169.

the center, an *axis mundi* around which transnational actors can flow."[26] The Gentile nations can be redeemed by blessing Israel, their locality sanctified, their callings esteemed. By standing with Israel the Gentiles become Christian nations. Shapiro comments, "The Jews in place, sovereign in the land of Israel, and a state whose policies are more (or less) in line with God's plan, has the power to unlock a wealth of spiritual blessing to the supranational Gentile church."[27]

CHRISTIAN ZIONISM AND HOLY LAND TOURS

Christian Zionists are eager to visit Israel, and the Israeli government has, since the 1950s, been even more eager to have them. The courting of American evangelical pastors went into overdrive in the 1970s and the 1980s, with the Israeli Ministry of Tourism aggressively recruiting American evangelical pastors for all-expense-paid "familiarization tours" in an effort to induce them to bring their flocks to Israel—using the Israeli airline El Al and employing Israeli Ministry of Tourism guides and Israeli ground transportation companies.[28] Daniel Hummel has a chapter in his recent book *Covenant Brothers* titled "Sightseeing Is Believing," which chronicles the way this remarkable level of cooperation unfolded.[29] The Israeli state learned that encouraging Christian pastors to visit Israel was a great way to induce American evangelical tourists (almost three-quarters of whom are women, the bulk of whom are also retirees)[30] to travel to Israel and spend their foreign currency, thereby helping to make tourism a pillar of the Israeli economy. Fostering the Israel-evangelical connection is not just good politics; it is also good business.

What these sightseers see is often carefully choreographed. Shapiro notes that "the 'local culture' enjoyed by Christian Zionists is—with few exceptions—Jewish. Arab/Palestinian hotels, shops, restaurants, products, cities, and sites are explicitly avoided, with an appeal to participants that they are in

---

[26]Shapiro, *Navigating*, 69.
[27]Shapiro, *Navigating*, 69.
[28]Weber, *Armageddon*, 215.
[29]Daniel G. Hummel, *Covenant Brothers: Evangelicals, Jews, and U.S.-Israeli Relations* (Philadelphia: University of Pennsylvania Press, 2019), chap. 5.
[30]Hillary Kaell, *Walking Where Jesus Walked: American Christians and Holy Land Pilgrimage* (New York: New York University Press, 2014), 4, 12.

Israel to support and 'bless' the Jewish people in their homeland."[31] A host of evangelical-oriented tour groups have sprung up in recent years, and key dispensationalist missions to the Jews have incorporated tours into their work.

Tours have become an important practice shaping and reinforcing Christian Zionist beliefs, a new and somewhat unique form of religious pilgrimage. The standard Christian Zionist tour combines a mix of distinctly religious sites related to the ministry of Jesus, commonly the "Garden Tomb," which they generally prefer over the Church of the Holy Sepulchre as the site of Christ's burial, a baptismal site (the Yardenit) on the Jordan River, and for the prophecy set, a visit to Megiddo, where they expect the battle of Armageddon to occur. But as Shapiro has observed, "the sites of Jesus' life and ministry or significant events in the early church are given surprisingly little weight."[32] Many of the traditional religious sites are either Orthodox or Catholic, but "these sites serve evangelicals as almost 'anti-sites,' representing a Christianity gone wrong, ones connected with paganism and anti-Semitism."[33]

On the other hand, political sites associated with the Israeli state are important—the Knesset (Parliament), Independence Hall, and a military cemetery (Har Herzl). "In the Christian Zionist world view, the state and its political history are explicit manifestations of the divine plan for the world, justifying—if not actually requiring—visits to sites like the Parliament or Mount Herzl military cemetery, that scholars tend to associate with 'civil religion.'"[34] Ironically, Christian Zionists show little interest in key sites linked to Christian Zionist history: notably Christ Church in Jerusalem, the Protestant cemetery in Jerusalem, or Tabor House, Conrad Schick's home built in 1882.[35]

These tours are well-planned and influenced by the Israeli Ministry of Tourism, with Zionist tour operators who are eager to show Israel in the best possible light. Encounters with modern Israelis are entirely focused on meeting Jews, not Arabs, and certainly not Arab Christians. They hear from recent Jewish immigrants waxing eloquent about their "restoration," and

---

[31]Shapiro, *Navigating*, 50.
[32]Shapiro, *Navigating*, 51.
[33]Shapiro, *Navigating*, 50.
[34]Shapiro, *Navigating*, 52.
[35]On Shick see Donald M. Lewis, *The Origins of Christian Zionism: Lord Shaftesbury and Evangelical Support for a Jewish Homeland* (Cambridge: Cambridge University Press, 2009), 306-7.

meet victims of war and persecution, visit the Holocaust museum, and hear a consistent message that reinforces the Christian Zionist story. The tours are designed to ensure that the participants meet local Jews, eat in Jewish restaurants, buy Jewish wine, and exist in a Jewish bubble. All of this is framed in the narrative of "blessing Israel": one evangelical pastor told Shapiro that he encouraged his flock to voluntarily pay "more than the asking price for all products and services, in direct contrast with the common practice in Israel of haggling for cheaper prices" as a way of "blessing Israel."[36] For Christian Zionists these tours constitute a pilgrimage—"a significant, meaningful, religious act . . . a performance, a display of solidarity with what they perceive to be an embattled, wrongly isolated nation."[37]

Christian Zionism and Jewish Mission

> "Brotherhood"—a term with a largely theological resonance for
> Christian Zionists—has become the dominant cultural and
> political paradigm within the movement. Christian Zionist
> advocates of brotherhood seek to address, and suppress, the
> historical evangelical yearning to convert Jews or watch the
> world descend into fiery judgment.[38]
>
> Daniel Hummel

The "critical and patronizing" aspects of evangelical theology are seen by Ariel as related to the issue of Christian evangelization of Jews, and there is tension within Christian Zionism over this issue. From its beginning evangelicalism has been focused on sharing the Christian gospel. As has been seen, it was the German Pietists and the English evangelicals who pioneered Christian missions specifically toward the Jews in the eighteenth and nineteenth centuries. As Ariel writes, "Missions to the Jews have occupied an important place on the philo-Semitic agenda and have come to characterize the messianic-oriented Christian interaction with the Jews even more than

---

[36]Shapiro, *Navigating*, 53.
[37]Shapiro, *Navigating*, 52-53.
[38]Hummel, *Covenant Brothers*, 3.

pro-Zionist activity."[39] The mission to the Jews, particularly for many premillennialists, is closely intertwined with their prophetic hopes. While some Christian Zionists are willing to forgo evangelism of Jews in Israel, many are not. Groups like the American Messianic Fellowship and Friends of Israel combine a pro-Zionist stance with a concern to evangelize, as does Jews for Jesus. The conversion of significant numbers of American Jews to Christianity in the 1970s and 1980s—with many joining the charismatic movement—led to the emergence of "messianic Judaism." Jewish converts began to exercise leadership in American evangelicalism, forming their own "messianic congregations" in the United States; similar messianic congregations have been formed in many parts of the world, including Israel.[40]

The relationship between evangelicals and the Israeli government has been fraught with tension over the issue of proselytizing. In 1978 the Begin administration responded to the demand of Orthodox members of the Knesset and proposed a law that would ban the offering of financial incentives by Christians to Jews to convert. It was based on an unfounded fear that converts were being so "bought," and little came of the legislation because the government was reluctant to enforce it. In the mid-1990s initiatives were proposed that would prohibit Christian missionary activity, and an initial measure passed in the Knesset. But there was a storm of protest worldwide from evangelicals who insisted that this was a violation of Israel's commitment to democracy, and the government was flooded with protest mail. Benjamin Netanyahu, then prime minister, had originally been supportive of the proposed law, but soon did an about-face and opposed it. Ariel comments,

> The aborted attempts at curtailing missionary activity in Israel highlighted the paradoxical nature of the relation of philo-Semitic Christians toward Jews: the evangelization of a people they see as chosen and whose country they strongly support. It also points to the nature of Israeli *realpolitik*: accepting help from Christians, some of whose values and agendas contradict their own.[41]

---

[39] Ariel, "It's All in the Bible," 276.
[40] For an overview see Yaakov Ariel, "A Different Kind of Dialogue: Messianic Judaism and Jewish-Christian Relations," *Crosscurrents* 62, no. 3 (2012): 318-27, and Ariel, *An Unusual Relationship: Evangelical Christians and Jews* (New York: New York University Press, 2013), chap. 12.
[41] Ariel, "It's All in the Bible," 279.

A Surprising New Alliance: Religious Jewish Zionists and Christian Zionists

Since 1967 a surprising new partnership has emerged between religious Jewish Zionists and some of the more radical Christian Zionists. Historically devout Jews have regarded Christian Zionists as people with hostile intent in their desire to bring about their conversion. This new alliance is therefore both surprising to all and concerning to many, especially because the alliance is united in achieving two controversial goals: supporting and expanding Jewish settlement in the territories occupied by Israeli troops during the Six-Day War, and the rebuilding of the third temple.

The Zionist movement was from its inception secular, and largely Marxist, with few rabbis supporting the cause. Most in fact opposed it. There were no Orthodox rabbis who attended the First Zionist Congress in 1897 from Eastern Europe and only three from the rest of Europe.[42] Among the Orthodox, both the ultra-orthodox Hasidim and their opponents (the Mitnagdim —literally "opponents") objected to the "Lovers of Zion movement" (Hovevei Zion), which embraced mainstream secular Zionism.

The rabbinic tradition not only resisted secular Zionism but was concerned too about religiously motivated Zionists, anxious about their mysticism and messianic tendencies. Rabbinism had long been threatened by messianic movements—Christianity being the most successful—but the Bar Kokhba revolt of AD 135 was another. Both were felt to have done lasting damage to Jews. Such fears were reinforced in the 1660s, when a charismatic rabbi, Sabbatai Sevi, claiming to be the Messiah, gathered a large following of fellow Ottoman Jews and induced them to sell their goods and follow him to Palestine. The whole movement ended as an unmitigated disaster when Sabbatai apostatized and converted to Islam in 1666. Rabbis had thus long been suspicious of the messianic impulse.

The Six-Day War was the catalyst for change. Gershom Gorenberg has argued that "the Six-Day War did more than create a new political and military map in the Middle East. It also changed the mythic map, in a piece of the world where myths have always bent reality."[43] It was only in the wake

---

[42]Shalom Goldman, *Zeal for Zion: Christians, Jews, & the Idea of the Promised Land* (Chapel Hill: University of North Carolina Press, 2009), 273.
[43]Goldman, *Zeal for Zion*, 271.

of the war that the religiously motivated Zionists began to gather a significant following—even some secularists joined them, attracted by their zeal and their reimagining of Zionism. By the mid-1970s the religious Zionists had emerged as a power to be reckoned with.

In 1974 Gush Emunim (The bloc of the faithful) was founded as an activist movement seeking to promote Jewish settlement in the suddenly acquired "occupied territories" from the 1967 war. Ironically, under the leadership of Rabbi Zvi Yehuda Kook (1891–1982), son of Rabbi Abraham Isaac Kook, Gush Emunim soon changed direction, turning its back on its nonmessianic heritage, as well as its socialism and pragmatism. As Joshua Hovsha has observed, "Here the secular Zionist movement and the government of the state it produced are validated as agents of the divine, perhaps best defined as unwitting messianic emissaries."[44] Gush Emunim became an important religious and political movement, and came to dominate the settler movement. These religious Zionists were convinced that the Israeli victory was "an act of God moving in history to bring about the full redemption of Israel."[45] Without the secular Zionists being aware of the religious significance of what they had done, they were being cast into a religious role in a reimagined messianic Zionist history.

The early settler movement had been secular, weak, and ineffective; now armed with a religious, even messianic vision, it was transformed to become powerful and highly effective. Its determination to solidify the Israeli state's territorial expansion by moving hundreds of thousands of Jews into the occupied territories (or "liberated" territories) received support from many in the Likud Party and even members of the Labour Party. These messianic Zionists even managed to persuade some secular Israelis to either join or support the settler movement. The settler movement in both Gaza and the West Bank thus grew rapidly in the 1970s; the 1977 election saw the pro-settler government of Menachem Begin gain power. In the 1980s considerable support came from Ariel Sharon, the famous general and later Likud prime minister (2001–2006).

---

[44]Joshua Hovsha, "Clashing Worlds: Religion and State Dualism in Jewish Political Thought" (master's thesis, the University of the Witwatersrand, Johannesburg, South Africa, 2015), 51.
[45]Goldman, *Zeal for Zion*, 283.

The movement led to a change in settler attitudes toward the Arabs, as Arab resistance was now characterized as a manifestation of their "Amalekite" heritage, playing the biblical role of implacable enemies of Israel. The Arabs were standing in the way of the divine imperative to occupy the land. Negotiation or compromise was not to be contemplated. The land of biblical Israel had to become the land of the state of Israel. The original vision of the Zionist pioneers had been based on principles of human rights and democracy, with all people entitled to political freedom. The new messianic ideology was particularist, nationalist, and exclusive; hostility toward outsiders was endemic to its vision. In the words of Rabbi Shlomo Aviner, "Settlement of the land outweighs any moral considerations one might have for the national rights claims of the *goyim* in our land."[46] These religious/messianic Zionists see both the original secular Zionists and the settler movement as a means of hastening messianic redemption, even if the secular Zionists had not been aware of their role in the divine plan of redemption.

The settler movement was shaken in 1981 by the Israeli government's implementation of the 1979 peace agreement with Egypt in which it returned territory to Egyptian control. The settlers resisted the turnover, and the Israeli army had to remove Jewish settlers by force. A similar situation occurred in 2005, when Israel returned the Gaza Strip to Palestinian control. With the rapid growth of the Jewish population in the occupied territories, the religious/messianic fervor lessened, but their influence remains powerful. In all of this strong support has been given to the settler movement by many American Christian Zionists,[47] especially by John Hagee and his CUFI. Sean Durbin has argued that "active support for Israel's expansionist policies . . . became part of the domestic social contest between Fundamentalists and liberal Protestants in the United States."[48] We now turn to the other issue on which the religious/messianic Zionists made common cause with some Christian Zionists: the matter of the third temple.

---

[46]Goldman, *Zeal for Zion*, 287.

[47]For a case study see Elizabeth Phillips, "Saying 'Peace' When There Is No Peace: An American Christian Zionist Congregation on Peace, Militarism, and Settlements," in Gunner and Smith, *Comprehending Christian Zionism*, 15-31.

[48]Sean Durbin, *Righteous Gentiles: Religion, Identity, and Myth in John Hagee's Christians United for Israel*, Studies in Critical Research on Religion 9 (Leiden: Brill, 2019), 40.

Rebuilding the Temple

The disciples' question to the risen Jesus in Acts 1:6, "Lord, are you at this time going to restore the kingdom to Israel?" reflects traditional Jewish expectations of the Messiah: When will you restore the kingdom? In the question there is a shared assumption common to the disciples, many contemporary Christian Zionists and a growing number of Jewish religious Zionists, that a Jewish kingdom is soon to be restored. The key questions are of agency and timing. The disciples were clearly hoping for a restoration of Jewish hegemony and the establishment of an earthly kingdom. Jesus' response is enigmatic: "It is not for you to know the times or dates the Father has set by his own authority" (Acts 1:7). Was he indicating that the question was out of place and the expectation would never be realized in the way they anticipated, or were their assumptions correct, but their timing was off?[49]

Today similar expectations are being put forward by Jews who long for the establishment of a theocratic Jewish state, the rebuilding of the temple on Mount Moriah where the Al Aksa Mosque is currently situated, and the reinstitution of blood sacrifices in the temple, and even for some the reconstitution of a Jewish kingship. Prior to the Six-Day War the Temple Mount /Haram al-Sharif had been under the authority of the Muslim Religious Council in Jerusalem, and it was the decision of the Israeli defense minister, Moshe Dayan, to continue that arrangement. The messianic Zionists and the Christian Zionists were incensed. In 1967 Shlomo Goren, the chief rabbi of the Israeli army, rebuked Dayan for failing to blow up the Mosque of Omar in order to make way for the building of the third temple.[50] Since the early 1970s some Christian Zionists have been cooperating with Jewish Temple Mount enthusiasts to hasten its rebuilding.[51] Ariel summarizes their influence in this way: "The Jewish movements that have striven to build the temple would not have acted as they did if it were not for evangelical Christians providing encouragement and assistance."[52]

---

[49]The Christian Zionist interpretation is made by Mark S. Kinzer in "Zionism in Luke–Acts: Do the People of Israel and the Land of Israel Persist as Abiding Concerns in Luke's Two Volumes?," in *The New Christian Zionism: Fresh Perspectives on Israel and the Land*, ed. Gerald R. McDermott (Downers Grove, IL: IVP Academic, 2016), 141-65.

[50]Goldman, *Zeal for Zion*, 281.

[51]For a full treatment of this see Ariel, *Unusual Relationship*, chap. 11.

[52]Ariel, *Unusual Relationship*, 203.

Both the *Late Great Planet Earth* and the Left Behind series highlight the importance of the rebuilding of the temple. While John Nelson Darby thought that the Jewish temple would eventually be rebuilt after the rapture, it was not something he expected his followers to be planning for or helping to make happen. It was Blackstone who in the 1870s had added new "signs of the times" that had to be fulfilled, chief of which was the return of the Jews to Palestine. But since 1948 another expectation came to characterize dispensational premillennialism for many: the rebuilding of Herod's temple.

The idea of rebuilding the temple has not historically been common in Judaism, although it is significant that Avraham Stern, the founder of the terrorist group Lehi (a.k.a. the Stern Gang), had articulated in 1940 some "18 Principles of Rebirth," the last of which was, "18. THE TEMPLE: The building of the Third Temple as a symbol of the new era of total redemption." The secular socialist Zionists were uninterested in it, but "guerrilla Zionist groups" like the Stern Gang and some right-wing Zionist groups thought of it as "the embodiment of Jewish sovereignty over the Holy Land" even before Israeli independence.[53] But as Tomer Persico points out, many of these enthusiasts for the temple (whom he calls "mythical Zionists") were not particularly religious Jews and "aspired not for a religious revival but for a national one, and used Jewish mythical sources to fuel their passion for political independence. For them, the temple was an axis and focal point around which 'the people' must unite."[54]

Until the 1970s, however, the prospect of building the temple found little traction among Israeli Jews, whether religious or secular. The Mishnah, the compilation of Jewish law by the rabbis, regarded the Temple Mount as sacred and that purification rituals were needed for a Jew before entering it. These rites require the ashes of a red heifer, a now-extinct animal, and thus "most observant Jews at the time accepted the rabbinical ban and saw entrance to the Temple Mount as taboo."[55] But since 2010 rabbinic prohibitions have been relaxed somewhat and the number of Jewish visitors has increased dramatically. Recently Third Temple activists have become convinced that

---

[53]Tomer Perisco, "The End Point of Zionism: Ethnocentrism and the Temple Mount," *Israel Studies Review* 32, no. 1 (Summer 2017): 1.

[54]Perisco, "End Point," 4.

[55]Ariel, "It's All in the Bible," 280.

the building of the Third Temple will usher in the messianic times and thus have been "preparing sacred temple objects and architectural plans and leading weekly pilgrimages to the Mount."[56]

In August 1969 a mentally unbalanced Australian, Dennis Michael Rohan, who had been influenced by reading material from Herbert W. Armstrong's "Worldwide Church of God" (which was regarded as a cult by most evangelicals) decided to take matters into his own hands in hastening the return of Christ. He set fire to the pulpit of the El-Aqsa Mosque on the Temple Mount, hoping to clear the ground for the rebuilding of the temple. Rioting in Jerusalem followed, and the Islamic world was inflamed. Premillennialists have sought to use persuasion to advance their cause regarding the rebuilding of the temple, hoping to promote the idea among Orthodox Jews. The late Chuck Smith (d. 2013), pastor of Calvary Chapel in Costa Mesa, California, was very supportive and even hosted Stanley Goldfoot, the founder of the Jewish "Temple Mount Foundation" to lecture in his church. Goldfoot was a secular right-wing activist and a former member of the Stern Gang. Goldfoot became "the Israeli contact person for evangelical Christians advocating the rebuilding of the temple."[57] An American archaeologist associated with Smith worked with Goldfoot to use high-tech devices to establish the original location of the temple but was prevented from doing so by Israeli police. Some theorized that the temple was located between the two mosques on the Temple Mount, the El-Asqa and the Dome of the Rock, and therefore could be rebuilt without interfering with either of these structures that are holy to Muslims.[58]

The prospect of a rebuilt temple has garnered a lot of interest among many premillennialists and has led to a search for ways to breed red heifers, in order to allow Jews to be ritually pure so as to access the Temple Mount. Others have been fascinated with details of the temple's interior design, its sacrificial rites, and the garments and utensils needed to re-create ancient Jewish worship. There has been a significant response among some observant Israeli Jews, most prominently from a group known as the Temple Mount Faithful (or more fully the Temple Mount and Land of Israel Faithful

[56]Rachel Z. Feldman, "Putting Messianic Femininity into Zionist Political Action: The Race-Class and Ideological Normativity of Women for the Temple in Jerusalem," *Journal of Middle East Women's Studies* 13, no. 3 (November 2017): 395.
[57]For details on Goldfoot, see Ariel, *Unusual Relationship*, 205.
[58]Ariel, "It's All in the Bible," 281.

Movement), whose stated aim is "Not Only to Remember the Destruction but to Build the Third Holy Temple in the Lifetime of Our Generation."[59] The leader of the group, Gershon Salomon, has been supported by Pat Robertson. Periodically the group attempts to hold prayer vigils on the Temple Mount and would like to install a cornerstone for the prospective temple.

Rachel Z. Feldman has argued that the Temple Mount activists through their "pilgrimages" to the site are hoping to "strategically help extend Israeli sovereignty over the mount through the format of a cathartic spiritual and touristic journey."[60] They frame their activity "in the language of the liberal state, claiming that Jewish access to the Temple Mount is a matter of 'human rights' and 'religious freedom.'"[61] She further asserts that the Israeli state is helping to fund these activities. The Temple Institute, the leading Third Temple organization, currently receives national service volunteers (noncombat army duty) and substantial annual funding from the Ministry of Culture, Science, and Sports; the Ministry of Education; and the Ministry of Defense to support its projects. There is substantial political support in the Knesset for the Temple Mount enterprise with a "Temple Lobby" seeking to advance their cause: "United by a desire to reclaim the Temple Mount, an unlikely alliance is forming in the *Knesset* between secular nationalists and the religious nationalists who desire to see Israel transformed into a biblical theocracy."[62]

Critics warn that this is an extraordinarily dangerous issue. The Temple Mount is one of the most holy sites to Muslims, and any attempt to undermine it could provoke a holy war. Timothy Weber cautions, "In their commitment to keep Israel strong and moving in directions prophesied in the Bible, dispensationalists are currently supporting some of the most dangerous elements in Israeli society. . . . By lending their support—both financial and spiritual—to such groups, dispensationalists are helping the future they envision come to pass."[63]

---

[59]Temple Mount and Land of Israel Faithful Movement, "Tisha B'Av March 2017 Report," https://templemountfaithful.org/events/details-of-the-2017-tisha-b-av-march-of-the-temple-mount-faithful.php.

[60]Rachel Z. Feldman, "Temple Mount Pilgrimage in the Name of Human Rights: The Use of Piety Practice and Liberal Discourse to Carry Out Proxy-State Conquest," *Settler Colonial Studies* 8, no. 4 (2018): 2, DOI:10.1080/2201473X.2017.1397943.

[61]Feldman, "Temple Mount Pilgrimage," 3.

[62]Feldman, "Temple Mount Pilgrimage," 6.

[63]Weber, *Armageddon*, 249-50.

AMERICAN CHRISTIAN ZIONISM: THEMES AND OBSERVATIONS

One of the most interesting studies of recent American Christian Zionism is Stephen Spector's *Evangelicals and Israel: the Story of American Christian Zionism*. Spector conducted extensive interviews with American evangelical leaders, pastors and laity, the representatives of many Christian Zionist and Jewish organizations, as well as with American and Israeli officials and diplomats. He immersed himself in the Christian Zionist world, attending many worship services, meetings, and prayer events and conferences. He also studied their publications, mailings, websites, and books, and the scholarly literature on the subject.

This immersion in Christian Zionism led him to unexpected conclusions. He was surprised to hear repeated declarations of love and support by evangelical Christians for Jews. The providentialist reading of history related to God's blessing and judging of nations in relation to the treatment of the Jews was a common refrain. He concludes that "Christian Zionist beliefs comprise a complex system of scriptural mandate, historical justification, political conviction, and empathic connection. Much of it is founded on God's mystery, and on love."[64] Spector's conclusion is supported by Shapiro's observation that "focusing overly much on the political does a disservice to the complex and powerful motivations and implications of this world view."[65]

Spector also observed that many articulated a negative view of Palestinians, and insisted that the land was given to Abraham and not to his firstborn son, Ishmael, "whom they take to be the ancestor of the modern Arabs."[66] He sees this as key to the standard Christian Zionist take on the Arab-Israeli conflict.[67] Spector's observation is reinforced by Paul Boyer, who points out that this is a theme running through American popular prophecy books, sermons, TV and radio broadcasts, and religious magazines in the post–World War II period: "In summary, among the many demonic forces foreordained to shape history's course in the last days, communistic Russia and its allies, the Arabs and the darker-skinned peoples of

---

[64]Stephen Spector, *Evangelicals and Israel: The Story of American Christian Zionism* (New York: Oxford University Press, 2009), 26.
[65]Shapiro, *Navigating*, 44-45.
[66]Spector, *Evangelicals and Israel*, 26.
[67]Spector, *Evangelicals and Israel*, 27.

Africa and Asia, loomed large."[68] Boyer contends that a specific anti-Arab bias is discernible throughout much of post-1948 prophecy writing: "In addressing Mideast issues specifically, most prophecy writers either ignored the Arabs or treated them as an obstacle to be removed. While portraying Jewish nationalism as a 'divine call back to the Holy Land,' writes Dwight Wilson, they presented Arab nationalism as 'a sinister demonic force.'"[69] Their dispensational interpretation necessitated the removal of Arabs, not only from the Temple Mount area, but also "from most of the Middle East. The scriptural basis of this view was both inferential—they stood in the way of God's promises to the Jews—and explicit. Wilbur T. Smith in 1967 cited God's curse on 'mount Seir' (which he took as a reference to modern-day Arabs) recorded in Ezekiel."[70] Boyer's judgment is that "however unwittingly, premillennialist popularizers over the decades contributed to the anti-Arab biases and stereotypes that pervaded U.S. mass culture."[71] It is possible that the premillennarians' anti-Arab stance has been as helpful to the Israeli state as the pro-Zionist stance of the Christian Zionists. The dispensationalists' tendency to lionize Jews and demonize Arabs plays well in Israeli political circles and helps to keep America onside with Israel.

Spector notes that Christians are to love and support the Jews but observes that Christian Zionists are divided on whether Christians should proselytize Jews, or just stand with them in loving support and solidarity. Christian Zionists regularly call on their followers to obey the injunction of Psalm 122:6 to "pray for the peace of Jerusalem" and to comfort the Jews following the injunction of Isaiah 40:1-2, a passage traditionally emphasized in Christian celebration of the incarnation at Christmas and read in conjunction with its fulfillment in the birth of Christ:

> Comfort, comfort my people,
>   says your God.
> Speak tenderly to Jerusalem,
>   and proclaim to her

---

[68]Paul Boyer, *When Time Shall Be No More: Prophecy Belief in Modern American Culture* (Cambridge, MA: Belknap Press of Harvard University Press, 1992), 169.

[69]Boyer, *When Time*, 200-201.

[70]Boyer, *When Time*, 200.

[71]Boyer, *When Time*, 203.

that her hard service has been completed,
    that her sin has been paid for,
that she has received from the LORD's hand
    double for all her sins.

However, Spector points out that American Jews are generally not getting the evangelicals' message regarding their love of the Jews, and are almost as distrustful of evangelicals as they are of Muslims.[72] They often fear that the professed "love" is a cloak for conversionist designs and obscures the Christian Zionist belief in a dark future for the Jews in the tribulation. As one Christian Zionist confessed to Spector, although he had made it his life mission to serve Jews, he and others felt "that our Jewish friends are tolerant of every one but us." He then elaborated: "Christians despise you because you're not proselytizing. Jews despise you because [they think] you are. It's so hard, so lonely. There's so much discouragement. If you didn't have this from God, there's no way you could stand up to this."[73]

Related to this is the evangelicals' talk of the Jews as "the apple of God's eye" (citing Zechariah 2:8, "for whoever touches you touches the apple of his eye")—an emphasis I have noted that was common among German Pietists of the eighteenth century. Christian Zionists argue that Christians should be grateful for the role that the Jews have played in maintaining ethical monotheism throughout the centuries, and of course, for the greatest gift (from a Christian standpoint), of a Jewish messiah, Jesus Christ. Hagee makes the connection: "In return for these many gifts, . . . Christians should give practical support to the modern state of Israel, as Paul says in Romans 15."[74] As Spector comments, "This verse has become central to Christian Zionists, an important basis for the enormously generous amount of charity that they give to Israel every year."[75] But the verse most often used to inspire Christian Zionist philanthropy toward contemporary Jews is Romans 15:27, which reads, "They were pleased to do it, and indeed they owe it to them. For if the Gentiles have shared in the Jews' spiritual blessings, they owe it to the Jews to share with them their material blessings." The incongruity of using this

---

[72]Spector, *Evangelicals and Israel*, viii.
[73]Spector, *Evangelicals and Israel*, 31.
[74]Spector, *Evangelicals and Israel*, 32.
[75]Spector, *Evangelicals and Israel*, 32.

verse is that Paul is asking Gentile Christians to support Jewish converts to Christianity, rather than urging support for a secular Jewish state that opposes Christian proselytizing of Jews.

Spector was also surprised by these Christian Zionists' eagerness to adopt Jewish religious symbols as their own. This is consistent with the theme that I have stressed about the role of Christian Zionism in evangelical identity formation—the symbolism has long been there, but it seems that this emphasis on Jewish symbols, while not new, has become more important for many Christian Zionists. Jewish symbols have become a badge of Christian identity for many people associated with this movement: shofars, the star of David, and a host of Jewish symbols and practices are promoted and embraced in this milieu. Spector observed the common emphasis on the ingathering of the Jewish people to "Zion" as something that the Christian Zionists believe is central to their eschatology, citing the influence of dispensational premillennialism. One expression of this fascination with Judaism has led to what is called the Hebrew Roots (or sometimes Hebraic Roots) movement, but many evangelicals are cautious about it.[76]

Spector also encountered a strong refrain of Christian repentance over the historic mistreatment of Jews in Christian Europe and its full manifestation in the Holocaust. Again, as I have noted, this theme was there in the early Luther, in the Puritans, in the German Pietists, and again reemerged very strongly in British evangelicalism in the 1830s and 1840s. But in the twenty-first century the Christian Zionists have taken this theme to new levels. Interestingly, the burden of the blame for this is not placed on the shoulders of the medieval church, nor used as a stick with which to beat Roman Catholicism, as it had been in earlier expressions of Christian Zionism. Protestantism is not excused, although often Christian Zionists see Satan behind historical hatred of the Jews. But this emphasis has led to some Christian Zionist organizations such as Eagles' Wings to seek to mobilize Christians to actively oppose expressions of anti-Semitism and to serve as goodwill ambassadors for Israel.[77] The same is true of other leading Christian Zionist organizations, CUFI and ICEJ.

---

[76]For a discussion of this movement see Shapiro, *Navigating*, 27.

[77]Spector, *Evangelicals and Israel*, 33.

And finally, Spector notes the phenomenon of the Christian Zionists wedding their support for Israel to their opposition to Islamic terrorism, as many now see Islam itself as the chief enemy of both Israel and the West. Many espouse a conspiracy theory that Islam is bent on world domination and that there is a war being waged against the West by militant Islam. In this they find support from scholars such as Bernard Lewis, the British Jewish historian and the leading expert on the history of the Middle East, and the Israeli historian Benny Morris. Lewis argues that Muslim law from an early stage of Islamic history urged its "followers to wage war on unbelievers until all mankind either embraces Islam or submits to the authority of the Muslim state,"[78] while "Morris notes that it is a basic tenet of Islam that any land conquered by Muslims remains perpetually sacred Islamic land (*Dar Al Islam*)."[79] The result is that extremist Muslims and many Christian Zionists see the world in dichotomous terms as a battle between good and evil, each being convinced that they are on the right side. In the view of American Christian Zionists, Israel is "America's crucial ally in a war against Islamic extremists."[80] This anti-Muslim message, of course, is not entirely new given the fact that the Reformers saw Islam as one of the two great threats to Protestantism. What is surprising is that the other traditional foe of Protestantism, the Roman Catholic Church, seems to have disappeared in these scenarios.

Another fact stands out when it comes to some of the key leaders of Christian Zionism, and that is the disavowal of any desire to convert Jews. The Israeli government's policy is that it is willing to work with Christian Zionists if they agree not to proselytize. Again, this is reminiscent of the direction that William Hechler went in the late 1890s, although for Hechler the nonproselytizing decision seems to have involved a dual-covenant theology—one for the Jews and one for Christians. The difficulty for any observer is that there is such a wide spectrum of views within Christian Zionism, with some believing strongly in the Reformation doctrine of *solus Christus*—that salvation for both Jews and Gentiles is ultimately only through Jesus Christ—while others take the view that they will leave those

---

[78]Spector, *Evangelicals and Israel*, 62.
[79]Spector, *Evangelicals and Israel*, 62.
[80]Spector, *Evangelicals and Israel*, 7.

matters up to God to sort out in the end—sometimes advocating an uncon-scious pluralism, or a form of dual-covenant theology.

As I have noted, in spite of all these protestations of love for the Jews and Israel, American Jews remain largely unconvinced, and there remains a "widespread distrust of Christian Zionists' motives" in the US Jewish community.[81] In 1991 David Rausch wrote perceptively about the under-lying reasons for this distrust. As he pointed out, while many American evangelicals understand themselves as philo-Semitic and pro-Israel, studies of the major evangelical publishers of Sunday school curricula done in the 1980s provided evidence that substantiated and reinforced Jewish fears that such teachings were anti-Judaic and anti-Semitic.[82] Thus, as Rausch wrote at the time, "For the average [American] Jewish person, anti-Semitism and evangelicalism go hand in hand."[83] In attempting to understand this, Rausch suggests that the term *cognitive otherness* de-scribes the state of American Jewry and American evangelicalism. Evan-gelical beliefs are so radically different from those of Jews—they tend to look for divine intervention in their lives, they regard Scripture as au-thoritative, if not inerrant. In short the evangelical view "trades on a set of assumptions about human life and the universe that are unimaginable for most modern [American] Jews." He elaborates: "This 'cognitive otherness' makes the evangelical appear at times incomprehensible, at times men-acing to the Jew. To hold the beliefs that evangelicals apparently do re-quires, many Jews tend to think, a sacrifice of intellect, indeed a sacrifice of cognitive citizenship in the modern world."[84] All of this feeds fears that "the ancient poisons of anti-Judaism" are "more alive in those whose Chris-tianity is more raw, unrefined, unreconstructed. To the extent that evan-gelicals represent that 'old time religion,' they represent a Christianity relatively undiluted by the 'civilizing' elements of modern culture. This thesis (which is quite false, as it turns out) allows Jews to relate today's evangelicalism to yesterday's persecutorial Christianity."[85]

---

[81]Spector, *Evangelicals and Israel*, 10.
[82]David A. Rausch, *Communities in Conflict: Evangelicals and Jews* (Philadelphia: Trinity Press International, 1991), 67-83.
[83]Rausch, *Communities in Conflict*, 84.
[84]Rausch, *Communities in Conflict*, 85.
[85]Rausch, *Communities in Conflict*, 86.

Spector, however, did not find that these Jewish perceptions of evangelicals —as described by Rausch—were borne out in the American Christian Zionists whom he encountered. He was most surprised by the flexibility and lack of rigidity on the part of the Christian Zionists. Where he expected intransigence, he discovered pliability:

> In examining evangelical beliefs, I expected to find a theological rigidity, especially about the end-times, that issued in political obduracy. . . . I found instead an unexpected pragmatism, flexibility, and nuance in evangelicals. This was true even of many of the most ardent Christian Zionists. I also found a lot of disagreement and uncertainty about the end of days. Even born-again leaders who are sure in their convictions and invoke God's wrath for anyone who divides His Land, nevertheless showed a wholly unanticipated humility about knowing God's plan.[86]

The stereotypical view of evangelicals that Spector expected to be borne out was not confirmed because contemporary American Christian Zionism does not fit the characterizations of "old time religion." It is new in many of its developments because it exists in a post-Holocaust world and after Israeli independence. It has, in a sense, taken over the "teaching of love and esteem" with a vengeance and is eager to distance itself from the sort of errors associated with earlier formulations of Christian Zionism that could indulge in negative stereotyping of Jews.[87] The "teaching of love and esteem" has been expanded to become the "teaching of love, esteem, and blessing," for the emphasis on "blessing Israel" has become paramount.

Spector attributes this adaptability in large measure to the radical individualism of American evangelicals. American evangelicalism is a descriptor of a broad movement, which is generally unsystematic, remarkably pragmatic, and highly fragmented. And for all the focus on prophecy, Spector observes, "many born-again Christians have only a very vague notion of Israel's role in the final days, and even among evangelical elites there is remarkable diversity and nuance in their beliefs."[88] Some 51 percent of American evangelical leaders "are in favor of a Palestinian state on land that

---

[86]Spector, *Evangelicals and Israel*, viii-ix.
[87]I am indebted to Daniel Hummel for his reflections on this matter.
[88]Spector, *Evangelicals and Israel*, 161.

God promised to Abraham, as long as it doesn't threaten Israel!"[89] Caitlin Carenen reached a similar conclusion in her study of the political and religious landscape shifts in America between 1980 and 2008: "Evangelical Protestants undertook their own theological innovations through a de-emphasis on end-of-times eschatology to focus more on the command to bless Israel to garner blessings for the United States."[90] Instead the focus has shifted to the twin goals of opposing anti-Semitism and expressing support for "Israel and its land acquisitions as part of a biblical mandate," which now dominate the American Christian Zionist agenda.[91] More recently Daniel Hummel has argued along similar lines:

> In its most activist circles today, Christian Zionism is less about apocalyptic theology or evangelism than it is a range of political, historical, and theological arguments in favor of the state of Israel based on mutual and covenantal solidarity. In recent years, a type of nation-based prosperity theology, promising material blessings to those who bless Israel, has played a prominent role.[92]

As Shapiro has observed, for American Christian Zionists "the exceptionalism of America is only superseded by the exceptionalism of Israel."[93]

Spector's conclusions fit well with the overall argument of this book regarding Christian Zionism. Christian Zionists' beliefs about Israel and the Jews are closely tied to their self-understanding as participants in a divine drama that many will admit they don't understand very well. Christian Zionism is an identity marker for them; it gives them a sense of purpose, of belonging to an international community that transcends race and national identity. It gives many a sense that Jerusalem is their spiritual home, the geographic center of God's purposes for humanity—not Rome, or Geneva, or Wittenberg. As Gila Gamliel, an Israeli cabinet minister (Likud), put it in 2011 when addressing Christian Zionists gathered for the Day to Pray for the Peace of Jerusalem: "Jerusalem is not holy because of *Camp David*,

---

[89]Spector, *Evangelicals and Israel*, 161.
[90]Caitlin Carenen, *The Fervent Embrace: Liberal Protestants, Evangelicals, and Israel* (New York: New York University Press, 2012), 210-11.
[91]Carenen, *Fervent Embrace*, 211.
[92]Hummel, *Covenant Brothers*, 3.
[93]Shapiro, "Hour of Restoration," 148.

Jerusalem is holy because of *King David*."[94] Shapiro comments, "Contemporary Israel becomes a kind of litmus test, both for manifesting the truth of the Word of God, and for manifesting the individual's or the nation's commitment to realizing God's will in the world."[95] Thus in their minds, the biblical nation of Israel is equated with the modern state of Israel, which makes the latter "uniquely and cosmically powerful in its reconnection of the people of Israel in the land of Israel, according to the word of the God of Israel. Now that the Jews are 'in their place' this association between the contemporary nation-state and its cosmic role, the political world and the symbolic, is extremely strong."[96] Even some translations of the Bible used by Christian Zionists have changed the Old Testament language that speaks of "the Israelites" when speaking of the Jewish people to "the Israelis" to make the connection clear.

Many American Christian Zionists still embrace dispensational premillennialism, but as we have seen, earlier forms of Christian Zionism before the mid-nineteenth century were not dispensationalist, and in fact, as will be seen in the next chapter, dispensationalism may well be losing some of its appeal among Christian Zionists outside of America. While many are vague on how and when the end times will unfold, for them it is enough to know that they stand with others to bless Israel and to take their part in the unfolding of God's mysterious purposes for his chosen people.

---

[94]Gila Gamliel, October 2, 2011 quoted in Shapiro, *Navigating*, 54.
[95]Shapiro, *Navigating*, 54.
[96]Shapiro, *Navigating*, 56-57.

14

CHRISTIAN ZIONISM IN RENEWALIST AND GLOBAL MOVEMENTS

THE PAST THREE DECADES have witnessed the emergence of "renewalist Zionism"—an umbrella term used to describe the transnational and trans-denominational forms of Pentecostal/charismatic Christian Zionism. Much of its leadership comes from outside the United States. Christianity's growth in the Global South has significant implications for the future of Christian Zionism. An examination of the history of Pentecostalism and the stages or "waves" of Pentecostal/charismatic history is called for that tracks attitudes to Zionism and Israel along the way. I will conclude with a discussion of the nature of the new face of Christian Zionism beyond the United States.

THE CHANGING FACE OF CHRISTIAN ZIONISM

In the past half century Christianity has been in retreat in some of the areas formerly considered as its heartland—Europe and the English-speaking world—but it has been expanding rapidly in other locations. The form of that expansion has often been new expressions of evangelicalism in Pentecostal and charismatic movements.[1] The difficulty of tracking the global expansion of Christian Zionism becomes apparent when one realizes that while there are indications that Christian Zionism is alive and well—indeed thriving in the Global South—very little academic study has focused on this phenomenon outside of the North Atlantic world. Paul Freston, a leading

---

[1]For accounts of this expansion see Donald M. Lewis, ed., *Christianity Reborn: The Global Expansion of Evangelicalism in the Twentieth Century* (Grand Rapids, MI: Eerdmans, 2004), and Lewis and Richard V. Pierard, eds., *Global Evangelicalism: Theology, History and Culture in Regional Perspective* (Downers Grove, IL: IVP Academic, 2014).

expert on evangelical involvement in politics in the Global South, argued in 2009 that the spread of evangelicalism had—up to that point—only a very limited impact on support for Christian Zionism.[2] He suggested three possible reasons for this: the prophetic concerns of Christian Zionists were not as pressing; Majority World evangelicals experienced little post-Holocaust guilt; and they felt less endangered by Islamic terrorism. More recently Freston has argued that this is changing.[3] This may be due in part to American and European Christian Zionists seeking to compensate for loss of support for Christian Zionism at home by recruiting new followers in the Majority World and the Israeli government's attempts to strengthen its support abroad.

The change is evident in Daniel Hummel's 2017 comment on those attending the International Christian Embassy Jerusalem's celebration of the Feast of Tabernacles: "The usual list of Christian Zionist leaders over the last forty years has been overwhelmingly American, white, and deeply influenced by apocalyptic theology. The new face of Christian Zionism, however, is mostly *not* American, white, English-speaking, or overly concerned about the end of history."[4] Israel's new allies in the Global South are Pentecostal and charismatic Christians who far outnumber their American cousins and "are driven less by apocalypticism and more by a type of nation-based prosperity theology."[5] If Christians in Nigeria, Brazil, and China are increasingly found in the ranks of Christian Zionists, the long-term geopolitical implications could be significant.

Glocalization at Work

A sociological concept is helpful in understanding what is happening with Christian Zionism beyond the West. Sociologists have observed two trends

---

[2]Paul Freston, "Christianity: Protestantism," in *Routledge Handbook of Religion and Politics*, ed. Jeffrey Haynes (London: Routledge, 2009), 42.

[3]Paul Freston, "Christian Zionism Finding New Sources of Growth in Global South?," *Religion-Watch* 34, no. 10 (October 2019): www.religionwatch.com/christian-zionism-finding-new -sources-of-growth-in-global-south/. See also Paul Freston, "Bolsonaro, o populismo, os evangélicos e América Latina," in *Novo ativismo político no Brasil: os evangélicos do século XXI?*, ed. José Luis Pérez-Guadalupe and Brenda Carranza (Rio de Janeiro: Konrad Adenauer Stiftung, forthcoming).

[4]Daniel Hummel, "The New Christian Zionism," *First Things*, June 2017, www.firstthings .com/article/2017/06/the-new-christian-zionism.

[5]Hummel, "New Christian Zionism."

in regard to globalization: on the one hand, the homogenizing effects of global business, media, and other factors are moving the world toward a global village, and yet on the other hand, there are powerful nationalist forces that are resisting and pushing back against these trends. One way that international corporations have sought to cope with the pushback is to allow local adaptations of global brands: thus in a McDonald's restaurant in Tokyo you can order Shakachiki red pepper chicken; in New Delhi, a McPaneer Royale; in Costa Rica, a McPinto Deluxe; or in Cairo, a McArabia. Sociologists call this phenomenon "glocalization"—a new word that brings together the global thrust with local adaptations.

In the morphing of Christian Zionism in the twenty-first century, we have a religious example of glocalization at work. In seventeenth-century England, Protestants conceived of English national identity in terms of its being an "elect" nation with its special relationship with the Jews, "*the* elect nation." In Puritan America this tradition was adapted so that America took on this special role and even in the founding of the new republic in the 1770s, this understanding of America's special relationship with the Jews was an important aspect of the emerging American national identity. Today this phenomenon is being replicated many times over as Christian Zionists throughout the world conceive of their own nation in relationship to Israel. This continues this same tradition—in effect, it globalizes the same national identity fixation on a particular nation's relationship with Israel. Any nation can become a "Christian nation" by "blessing Israel."

Christian Zionism thus becomes closely linked with two nation-states, or two people groups. Christian Zionists thus function with a dual identity—not simply as Christian Zionists for Israel, but particularly as Brazilian Christian Zionists for Israel, or Zambian Christian Zionists for Israel, or even Cherokee Nation Christian Zionists for Israel. As Faydra Shapiro has observed, it is "thanks to a transnational attachment to Israel that the local nation-state is redeemed";[6] or even, an indigenous tribal identity is validated through a unique association with the "tribes of Israel." These nations become in some sense "Christian nations"—that is, individually they become "elect/chosen" nations through their support and blessing of Israel,

---

[6]Faydra Shapiro, *Christian Zionism: Navigating the Jewish-Christian Border* (Eugene, OR: Cascade, 2015), 61-62.

the uniquely elect nation. Recently the Israeli government has been working hard to establish relations with indigenous people, presenting "Israelis as the prototypical first nation."[7]

Thus contemporary Christian Zionism, while it is a global phenomenon, reinforces local identities and succeeds as it revalidates national identities, both the individual nations from which its adherents come and the state of Israel. Andrew Crome has argued this involves a positive form of "othering." As Freston has written, "It creates a unique form of dual nationalism through promoting another nation. It can even offer an alternative way of conceiving of 'national identity' and 'national mission' in nations of uncertain constitution."[8] This leads to new providentialist readings of contemporary politics. The injunction to "bless" the Jews becomes—once again as so often in the Christian Zionist past—the ground for interpreting the rise and fall of nations. The blessing also applies to churches that embrace Christian Zionism: it is seen as a means of securing church growth and becomes easily (and often) tied into prosperity-gospel readings of Scripture.

CHRISTIAN ZIONISM AND POLITICS

There is a long history of Christian Zionism influencing British and American foreign policy. The same pattern can now be seen in parts of the Global South. A few examples will suffice. In 1991, when the one-party state of Kenneth Kaunda came to an end in Zambia, Kaunda was replaced by Frederick Chiluba, a Pentecostal Christian Zionist, who reversed his predecessor's pro-Arab stance and within seven weeks of coming to office recognized Israel and broke off relations with Iran and Iraq.[9] In December 2017 Jimmy Morales, the evangelical president of Guatemala (the most strongly Pentecostal country in Latin America), announced that his country would follow the lead of the United States and move its embassy to Jerusalem. (President Morales was courted by the Israeli government, and an honorary doctorate was bestowed on him by the Hebrew University of Jerusalem in 2016.) The election of Jair Bolsonaro as president of Brazil in 2018 was achieved with strong support from evangelical Christian Zionists, and Brazil indicated it

---

[7]Freston, "Global South."
[8]Paul Freston, personal communication to author, 2018.
[9]Paul Freston, *Protestant Political Parties: A Global Survey* (Aldershot, UK: Ashgate, 2004), 84.

would join the United States and Guatemala in moving its embassy to Jerusalem, although Bolsonaro later was forced to walk back his promise.

Given the rapid growth of charismatics/Pentecostals and the emergence of democratic structures in many of their countries, the expectation is that their governments' foreign policies may become "more accountable to these growing populations of Pentecostals."[10] It is certainly the hope of Israeli policymakers that this will be the case. Timothy H. Shah, the lead investigator of the Pew Forum's 2006 study of renewalist Christianity, notes that "there is an emerging, active attempt to organize Pentecostals and other evangelicals in a pan-global effort to support Israel, to offer sympathy and support."[11] Israeli initiatives to encourage this can be traced back to the early 1950s.

ESTIMATING THE SIZE OF THE CONSTITUENCY

The word *renewalist* is an umbrella term to refer to Pentecostal-like movements that emerged in the twentieth century. The term embraces classical Pentecostals, the charismatic Christians that emerged in the 1960s within mainline Protestantism and Roman Catholicism, and neo-charismatics who are often associated with new independent charismatic churches and denominations, and more recently the independent network charismatics. In 2010 the number of renewalists was put at 614 million by Vinson Synan, and more conservatively in 2011 by the Pew researchers at 584 million.[12] It may well be the case that renewalists now represent the majority of Christians actively practicing their faith.

The affinity of these renewalists with pro-Israel attitudes was evident in the findings of the Pew examination of evangelicals and renewalists; the American pattern that showed distinctly pro-Israel attitudes among Pentecostals and renewalists (even among American Black Pentecostals, many of whom were angered with Israeli support of the apartheid South Africa government in the 1980s) was repeated across the ten countries surveyed, with Pentecostals and renewalists being more supportive of Israel than both their fellow citizens and

---

[10]Timothy H. Shah, "Pentecostal Zionism? The Role of Israel in Global Politics," Center for Religion and Civic Culture, January 19, 2011, https://crcc.usc.edu/pentecostalism-and-politics/.
[11]Shah, "Pentecostal Zionism."
[12]Matthew C. Westbrook, "The International Christian Embassy, Jerusalem, and Renewalist Zionism: Emerging Jewish-Christian Ethnonationalism" (PhD diss., Drew University, 2014), 13-14.

other Christians.[13] Such pro-Israel views were higher in the Philippines, India, and Nigeria, which were dealing with Muslim insurgencies or terrorism. Significantly, Catholic renewalists were decidedly less supportive than the Protestant renewalists. As Timothy Shah has observed, "There is an undeniable theological element to that [finding] which does cross regional and international boundaries."[14] Their strong support for Christian Zionism caused Shah to summarize their findings succinctly: "Does the international Israeli lobby speak in tongues? The answer is yes."[15] We now turn to look at the historical relationship between Pentecostalism and Christian Zionism.

RENEWALIST ZIONISM: PENTECOSTALS AND THE CHARISMATICS

As has been argued, there is no such single thing as "Christian Zionism"; there are in fact many different "Christian Zionisms." The standard explanation of Christian Zionism by a number of contemporary scholars is that it is essentially (1) American in origin, (2) Darbyite in inspiration, and (3) consistently inspired by dispensational premillennialist history.[16] This is seriously flawed on all three points. Christian Zionist thinking can be traced to the second generation of the Protestant Reformation and not just to the nineteenth century. Darby's views may have constituted the construct known as "dispensational premillennialism," but his views were not original to him and the essence of his system (his single-minded futurism) was abandoned by his leading American disciple, William Blackstone, who self-consciously sought to merge historicist premillennialism with futurism. Matthew C. Westbrook, the leading scholar of renewalist Zionism, has argued that there is no "single thing called 'dispensationalism.'"[17] Its most recent reformulators acknowledge that the movement is still evolving and being reworked. A one-size-fits-all dispensational premillennialism is a straw man that serves the critics of Christian Zionism well as a whipping boy but makes little sense historically.[18] As Westbrook comments, "The error

---

[13]The countries surveyed were the United States, Guatemala, Brazil, Chile, Nigeria, Kenya, South Africa, India, the Philippines, and South Korea.

[14]Shah, "Pentecostal Zionism."

[15]Shah, "Pentecostal Zionism."

[16]Westbrook, "Christian Embassy," 63-80.

[17]Westbrook, "Christian Embassy," 82.

[18]Westbrook argues that this standard account is misleading and explores why it has been perpetuated, and the impact this has had on the study of Christian Zionism. Westbrook, "Christian Embassy," 64-82.

suggesting that dispensationalism and Christian Zionism are coterminous movements . . . is an error that allows for easy caricature."[19]

Christian Zionism and Premillennialism in Late Nineteenth- and Early Twentieth-Century Missions

The period stretching from the late nineteenth to the early twentieth century was one in which evangelical missions expanded rapidly, much of it undertaken by "faith missions," which built on the example of James Hudson Taylor and his China Inland Mission founded in 1865. However, little work has been done on the extent to which Christian Zionist ideas were exported by late nineteenth-century British and American missionaries. Pietsch has noted that many missionaries were influenced by the rise of Bible schools and prophecy conferences, but argues that "even more importantly, the *Scofield Reference Bible* had perhaps its greatest impact in the twentieth-century Protestant missionary movement."[20] The China Inland Mission was enormously influential in China by 1900, and it is widely recognized that dispensational premillennial theology was an important theological impetus. The Keswick Holiness movement did much to motivate many conservative evangelicals to serve overseas and undoubtedly did much to promote dispensational views and indigenize Christian Zionism in the far-flung missionary outreach of the movement.[21] As John Wolffe and Mark Hutchinson have observed, "faith missions entrenched Keswick spirituality in the global village."[22]

In America, Lyman Stewart, who with his brother Milton Stewart had funded the widespread distribution of *The Fundamentals*, also played a key role in the founding of the Bible Institute of Los Angeles (later Biola) in 1908 on a strict dispensational-premillennial basis. A strong Christian Zionist, he also funded missionary work in Korea and China (where Blackstone served for a time with Milton Stewart's funding) and underwrote the Scofield Bible Correspondence series, the editorial committee of the *Scofield Reference Bible*, and a Korean Bible school and the Hunan Bible Institute in China. He also covered the cost of translating the *Scofield Reference Bible* into Korean

---

[19]Westbrook, "Christian Embassy," 79.

[20]B. M. Pietsch, *Dispensational Modernism* (New York: Oxford University Press, 2015), 205.

[21]For a discussion of Keswick see John Wolffe and Mark Hutchinson, *A Short History of Global Evangelicalism* (Cambridge: Cambridge University Press, 2012), 124-30.

[22]Wolffe and Hutchinson, *Global Evangelicalism*, 130.

and Chinese. In all of this Stewart sought to sow the seeds of Christian Zionism in the Korean and Chinese churches.[23] Much more detailed local studies need to be done for us to appreciate how central the Christian Zionist message was in these mission contexts.[24]

THE PENTECOSTALIZATION OF CHRISTIAN ZIONISM

While the story of dispensational-premillennial missions in relation to Christian Zionism needs much more exploration, that is only part of the story, for over the course of the twentieth century the theological foundations of Christian Zionism were Pentecostalized, particularly in regions beyond America. The Pentecostals (and for the most part, their charismatic stepchildren) generally rejected the Calvinist framework that had undergirded earlier forms of Christian Zionism, and replaced it with a providentialism of their own: the early Pentecostals were a long way from traditional Calvinism, but they did believe strongly in an all-powerful God who intervened in history, and they were convinced that God was sovereignly raising up the Pentecostal movement in the last days.

Early Pentecostals believed they were recovering aspects of New Testament Christianity that had been lost to the church—particularly the gifts of speaking in tongues, prophecy, and physical healing. Early Pentecostalism was theologically eclectic and threw up a number of teachings that were regarded as unacceptable by fellow Protestants and by many Pentecostals as well, including the "Jesus-only" doctrine, a Pentecostal version of unitarianism.[25] Several of its early key leaders also advocated British Israelite teachings that claimed that the British people (and by extension white America) constituted the ten lost tribes of Israel; and white-supremacist teachings of Anglo-Saxon superiority combined with apocalyptic speculation to reinforce the notion that its advocates were uniquely connected with the Jews, and, in fact, were Jews.[26]

---

[23]Paul W. Rood, "Early History of Biola's Teaching Position on Israel and the Millennial Kingdom," Paul Rood Academia.edu profile, 2017, https://paulrood.academia.edu/research.

[24]For a sketch of dispensationalism's impact on missions, see Pietsch, *Dispensational Modernism*, 205-9.

[25]The American Assemblies of God was founded in 1914 to bring together those who wanted to distance themselves from "Jesus Only" teaching and affirm a strong trinitarianism.

[26]Mormonism as it has developed since the nineteenth century has been fascinated with the return of the Jews to Palestine. See Yaakov Ariel, "Zionism in America," in *Oxford Research Encyclopedia of Religion* (Oxford: Oxford University Press, 2017), 10, https://doi.org/10.1093/acrefore/9780199340378.013.434, 8-9.

The Three Waves

The history of Pentecostals/charismatics is often divided into distinct periods, or "waves."[27] Classical Pentecostalism, or the "first wave," is linked to the renewal at Azusa Street in Los Angeles in 1906; the "second wave" refers to the emergence of the charismatic movement within the mainline Protestant churches (and Roman Catholicism) in the 1960s; and the "third wave," dated from the 1970s, refers to the "neo-charismatics" and is used to refer to independent denominations and ministries that do not easily fit within the two earlier movements.

Pentecostalism has expanded in the past century from a small and marginalized movement of the dispossessed into a global phenomenon. Since the crossover of Pentecostal concerns into Protestant mainline churches in America in the 1960s (second wave), charismatic expressions of the Christian faith have been birthed that have brought many Pentecostal distinctives (tongues-speaking, divine healing, enthusiastic worship) into both Protestantism and Roman Catholicism. In the 1970s the neo-charismatic movement (or third wave) took on a life of its own outside of established denominational structures with the emergence of new charismatic denominations and many independent megachurches, often with links to church networks in Africa and Latin America. By the 1980s renewalist churches began to grow very rapidly in the Global South, especially in South America and Africa, but also in parts of Europe and Asia.

First-wave Pentecostalism and Christian Zionism.

> *The American experience suggests that religious movements*
> *that denude themselves of an extensive past often compensate*
> *by providing themselves an extensive future. That certainly*
> *was the case for early Pentecostals.*[28]
>
> Grant Wacker

Pentecostalism's origins are often traced to a storefront church in Los Angeles where the Azusa Street revival occurred between 1906 and 1910.

---

[27]Westbrook traces its use to the 2005 edition of the *World Christian Encyclopedia*. Its use by the Pew researchers in 2006 brought it into academic discussion. Westbrook, "Christian Embassy," 11.

[28]Grant Wacker, *Heaven Below: Early Pentecostals and American Culture* (Cambridge, MA: Harvard University Press, 2001), 251.

Pentecostals generally had no need of a history, as one of its early apologists boasted: "The Pentecostal Movement has no such history, it leaps the intervening years crying, 'BACK TO PENTECOST!'"[29] As Grant Wacker comments, "The absence of roots, or at least of roots in the previous 1,800 years, left the revival free to imagine a future as vast in scope as it was glorious in complexity."[30]

What is often not realized is that from the beginning the Pentecostals' "extensive future" caused them to focus on Palestine and to strongly sympathize with Zionism;[31] three of the first five missionaries sent out from Azusa Street went to Jerusalem, which from 1908 served as the home base for its missionary work in the Middle East. The earliest American and British Pentecostal periodicals were suffused with Christian Zionist themes related to the Pentecostal mission in Palestine; the Pentecostal missionaries on the ground acted as the cultural brokers of Pentecostal Zionism.[32] Eric Newberg argues that "the pro-Zionist stance of the Pentecostal missionaries shaped Pentecostal attitudes toward the Arab-Zionist conflict in Israel/Palestine."[33] Unsuccessful in attempts to convert Jews and Muslims, Pentecostal missionaries turned their attention to Arab Christians, promoting philo-Semitism and Jewish "restoration" to the land. At a popular level the Pentecostals' acceptance of dispensational premillennialism was mediated through authors like William Blackstone, whose works they published.[34] The Pentecostals modified dispensational premillennialism to serve their interests, rejecting the dispensationalists' "cessationism"—the insistence that the gifts of the Holy Spirit ended with the apostolic age. Pentecostals renamed it the "Latter Rain covenant" and from its beginning often described Pentecostalism as "the Latter Rain movement." Three key adaptations to dispensationalism were made: first, they taught that "only Holy Spirit–baptized believers would be taken up in the Rapture."[35] Second, Christ would not return until the "*full* gospel"—that is, "the Pentecostal message of salvation, healing,

---

[29]Wacker, *Heaven Below*, 251.

[30]Wacker, *Heaven Below*, 251.

[31]Eric Nelson Newberg, *The Pentecostal Mission in Palestine: The Legacy of Pentecostal Zionism* (Eugene, OR: Pickwick, 2012), 154.

[32]Newberg, *Pentecostal Mission*, 2.

[33]For details on the Pentecostal mission see Newberg, *Pentecostal Mission*, 2.

[34]Newberg, *Pentecostal Mission*, 158.

[35]Wacker, *Heaven Below*, 253.

[Spirit] baptism (evidenced by tongues) and the Lord's return"—had been preached to the nations.[36] Third, and most important, they proposed a dramatically different understanding of the current age. Unlike Darby, the church age was not a parenthesis in God's dealings with humankind; it was the age of the Holy Spirit inaugurated on the day of Pentecost (the former or early rain) and was being consummated by the "latter rain" that had begun to fall at Azusa Street.[37] What they also retained of dispensationalism was its "Jewish restorationism": "Pentecostals agreed with the dispensational premise that the Jews were God's apocalyptic timepiece . . . [and] treated the War of Armageddon as a controlling motif of their eschatology."[38] Blackstone's belief that support of Zionism would enable believers "to hasten the day of God"—that is, bring closer the second coming of Christ—was eagerly embraced by the early Pentecostals.[39]

In 1909 David Wesley Myland developed a popular interpretation of Pentecostal history that linked it with the fledgling Zionist movement in Palestine. Fascinated with reports about increasing precipitation in Palestine between 1890 and 1900, Myland believed this was a sign of the end time indicating the return of Christ was at hand.[40] He argued from Joel 2:23, which reads, "Be glad then, ye children of Zion, and rejoice in the LORD your God: for he hath given you the former rain moderately, and he will cause to come down for you the rain, the former rain, and the latter rain in the first month" (KJV). In Pentecostal hands, this passage was linked with James 5:7-8: "Be patient therefore, brethren, unto the coming of the Lord. Behold, the husbandman waiteth for the precious fruit of the earth, and hath long patience for it, until he receive the early and latter rain. Be ye also patient; stablish your hearts: for the coming of the Lord draweth nigh" (KJV). This motif had been emphasized in the 1820s by the English historicist premillennialist Lewis Way, who developed his own emphasis on the "latter rain."

For Myland the literal latter rain was coming back to Palestine as the Jews returned; this phenomenon was now being matched by a spiritual latter rain.

---

[36]Wacker, *Heaven Below*, 253.

[37]Wacker, *Heaven Below*, 254-55.

[38]Newberg, *Pentecostal Mission*, 155.

[39]Charles F. Parham, whose influence on Pentecostalism predated Azusa Street, promoted Zionism in the 1890s. See Newberg, *Pentecostal Mission*, 159.

[40]Newberg, *Pentecostal Mission*, 22.

As God physically restored the rain to Palestine and brought the dispersed Jews back, he was also spiritually restoring the Holy Spirit to the church through the Pentecostal movement. "In his 'Latter Rain Covenant,' he brought together eschatological ideas on which most conservative evangelicals and Pentecostals could agree but then molded them into a creative synthesis of Christian Zionism and Pentecostal restorationism."[41] A great outpouring of the Holy Spirit was now occurring, one that was being validated by the restoration of charismatic gifts that Reformation Protestantism had wrongly taught had ceased with the apostolic age; for many Pentecostals this was a harbinger of the return of the Jewish people to Palestine.

The capture of Jerusalem in 1917 was greeted enthusiastically by Pentecostals and interpreted in light of this prophetic framework, as were instances of Arab resistance starting with the Arab uprising of 1929. Throughout the 1930s Pentecostal periodicals frequently cited the writings of the British Jewish Zionist Lord Melchett, who repeatedly devalued the rights of Palestinian Arabs and often demonized Arab perspectives,[42] creating a conspiratorial interpretation of these events that in their minds pitted the "true seed of Abraham" against the "seed of Ishmael who was cast out and is forever warring against God's purposes of victory for spirit over flesh."[43] Pentecostal eschatology therefore led them to oppose Lord Passfield's 1930 white paper, which proposed limiting Jewish migration and land purchases, openly siding with the Jewish Zionists and branding opponents as anti-Semitic.[44] Frequently Pentecostal publications called for the destruction of the Dome of the Rock in anticipation of the rebuilding of the temple in Jerusalem.[45] Throughout the Palestinian troubles of the 1930s, the Pentecostal missionaries on the ground—"the missionary brokers of Pentecostal Zionism"— repeatedly favored the Zionist cause and disparaged Palestinian aspirations. These missionary "brokers" "represented the events they reported so as to confirm the Pentecostal metanarrative. In so doing they only told half the story, the Zionist side, or, more precisely, the Pentecostal version of it."[46]

---

[41]Newberg, *Pentecostal Mission*, 163.
[42]Newberg, *Pentecostal Mission*, 175.
[43]Newberg, *Pentecostal Mission*, 174.
[44]Newberg, *Pentecostal Mission*, 176.
[45]Newberg, *Pentecostal Mission*, 177.
[46]Newberg, *Pentecostal Mission*, 182.

The founding of Israel in 1948 was greeted with rejoicing by the Pentecostal press, although after the initial event, some questions were raised by the fact that the Jews had not converted. But this could be fit into the larger Pentecostal metanarrative that served Pentecostal interests and legitimated the movement "by linking Pentecostalism and the restoration of the Jewish homeland in Palestine."[47] Pentecostal devotion to the study of the Bible, their focus on the imminent return of Christ, and the popularity of "blessing Israel" are all related to this theological framework. The legacy of this trajectory is clear in trends observable today in polling of Pentecostals and charismatics throughout the world.

The Sharon Movement or the Latter Rain Movement. Nineteen forty-eight was a momentous year for Pentecostals. The establishment of Israel was a boon for prophetic speculation. But the year saw the emergence of a new challenge for the emerging Pentecostal tradition. More than forty years had passed since the Azusa Street revival and the "routinization of charisma" observed by Max Weber was catching up with North American Pentecostals. In some Pentecostal circles, notably in the Assemblies of God, there had been an apparent decline in public charismatic expression, and some felt that the tradition was becoming more routine, and respectable. A spiritual dryness and aridity was said to characterize many churches. A revival began among students at the Sharon Orphanage and Schools in North Battleford, Saskatchewan, among people associated with the Pentecostal Assemblies of Canada—the sister denomination of the American Assemblies of God. It was known as the Sharon movement, or the Latter Rain movement—a phrase that had fallen out of use among Pentecostals by the 1930s. Similar in many ways to the Azusa Street revival in its manifestations in protracted prayer meetings (tongues, healings, holy laughter), the movement soon spread throughout North America. Several new practices were controversial, in particular the teaching that the New Testament offices of apostle and prophet were being renewed to the church (echoing the emphases of the Catholic Apostolic Church associated with Edward Irving in the 1830s). Those involved considered this new revival the harbinger of "an end-time 'latter rain' that would herald the imminent rapture

---

[47]Newberg, *Pentecostal Mission*, 181.

of the church."[48] For some this involved a peculiar teaching based on an understanding of the "manifest sons of God" reference in Romans 8:18-25, which asserted that the imminent outpouring of the Holy Spirit would result in the creation of a special group of "overcoming sons of God" who having achieved the "measure of the stature of the fullness of God" will "actually dethrone Satan, casting him out of the heavenlies, and finally binding him in the earthlies, bringing the hope of deliverance and life to all the families of the earth. This . . . great work of the Spirit shall usher a people into full redemption—free from the curse, sin, sickness, death and carnality."[49] Its detractors saw this as teaching a dangerously realized eschatology that was gnostic in tendency and elitist in spirit. The leaders self-described their movement the "New Order of the Latter Rain." The established Pentecostal denominations rejected these new teachings and the Assemblies of God publicly opposed it. By 1950 the movement had seemingly been isolated in independent churches, although it was embraced by well-known healing evangelists Thomas Wyatt and the controversial William Branham.[50] In the long term it exercised a profound influence on many renewalists by the end of the century who have come to embrace many of the movement's emphases.

The second wave. The emergence of charismatic expressions of Christian faith in mainline and independent Protestant churches in the early 1960s and their spread to American Catholicism beginning in 1967 (and from there to the Catholic Church globally) produced movements that distanced themselves from Pentecostal denominations even as they accepted the Pentecostal emphasis on the gifts of the Holy Spirit, without adopting Pentecostalism's general insistence on the gift of speaking in tongues as the evidence of Spirit baptism.[51]

---

[48]Vinson Synan, *The Holiness-Pentecostal Tradition: Charismatic Movements in the Twentieth Century*, rev. ed. (Grand Rapids, MI: Eerdmans, 1997), 213.

[49]J. Preston Eby, "The Day Is Upon Us," in *The Battle of Armageddon*, part 4 (1976), Kingdom Bible Studies, http://www.kingdombiblestudies.org/battle/battle-of-armageddon.htm.

[50]Synan, *Holiness-Pentecostal*, 213.

[51]Significant numbers of American Christians self-identified as charismatics by the turn of the century: 23 percent of evangelicals, 9 percent of mainline Protestants, 13 percent of American Catholics, and 36 percent of Black Protestants. Brad Christerson and Richard Flory, *The Rise of Network Christianity: How Independent Leaders Are Changing the Religious Landscape* (New York: Oxford University Press, 2017), 8.

The neo-charismatics or the third wave. The term *neo-charismatic* describes the emergence in the 1970s of new independent charismatic churches and ministries such as the Vineyard Christian Fellowship in Anaheim, California, Calvary Chapel in Costa Mesa, California, and Hope Chapel in Hermosa Beach, California. These movements were begun by gifted pioneers who then franchised their work and spun off new denominations, as the late John Wimber did with the Vineyard and the late Chuck Smith did with Calvary Chapel. However, these are American examples, and our primary concern is with renewalists beyond the West. Renewalism has become so intensely international and is no longer beholden to what happens in America. Westbrook has observed that "third-wave Renewalist Christians . . . are [now] by a good measure more internationally focused than perhaps all major Christian denominations (with the Assemblies of God not far behind)."[52] A few international examples of megachurches with Christian Zionist credentials include Sandor Nemeth's Church of the Faith in Hungary, which was strongly influenced by Derek Prince;[53] the Word of Life Church in Moscow with close ties to the International Christian Embassy Jerusalem;[54] Pastor Rene Terra Nova, the senior apostle of Ministerio Internacioal da Restaurcion, in Manaus, Brazil, who has a huge network of churches with about seven million members—again with close links to the International Christian Embassy Jerusalem;[55] and apostles Alberto and Gladys Mango of Primera Iglesia church in Santa Cruz De La Sierra in Bolivia, whose congregation boasts about ten thousand members.[56]

A fourth wave? Brad Christerson and Richard Flory have argued that there has emerged a new form of charismatic Christianity that is similar to the neo-charismatics but that differs in four distinct ways: (1) they eschew creating a franchise of churches or a movement; (2) they are not particularly interested in church-planting but rather seek to catalyze Christians from many backgrounds and denominations; (3) they are more interested in

---

[52]Matthew Westbrook, personal communication to author.

[53]See his church's website, www.nemethsandor.hu/eletrajz.

[54]See Howard Flower, "Moscow Pro-Israel Rally," International Christian Embassy Jerusalem, July 4, 2013, https://int.icej.org/news/special-reports/moscow-pro-israel-rally.

[55]See the home page of the International Coalition of Apostolic Leaders, www.icaleaders.com/.

[56]I am indebted to Matthew Westbrook for these examples.

social transformation than in traditional approaches to soul-saving[57] or church building; and (4) they reject formal organizational ties and emphasize personal connections in "networks of cooperation."[58]

To these four distinctives we might add the following: their leaders style themselves as modern-day apostles (both male and female) whose ministry is validated by their ability to perform modern-day miracles and affirmed by the informal recognition granted to them by other apostles in one of the transnational networks to which they belong.[59] Christerson and Flory call this "independent network charismatic" Christianity, which is a larger umbrella than the one proposed by C. Peter Wagner, one of the leading charismatic theorists who has written about a "New Apostolic Reformation."[60] Significantly, Wagner and even his critics have made the link between the Latter Rain movement of the 1940s and these new developments.[61] It would seem that while the Latter Rain movement of the late 1940s was short-lived in terms of its institutional expressions, its key distinctives have morphed and shaped these new "apostolic networks." Specific points of continuity with the Latter Rain movement include the following: renewalists often understand themselves as empowered to drive away Satan by their worship and through demonstrations of supernatural works of power; they believe in the restoration of the gifts of apostles and prophets in the life of the church; they often speak of being "manifest sons of God" (citing Romans 8:19); they tend to be very optimistic, emphasize overcoming the challenges facing the church, and focus on the Spirit and his power—particularly power over sickness, and even over natural phenomena such as the weather and natural disasters.[62] The latter are hallmarks of the Generals of Intercession (now Generals International), a group associated with Cindy Jacobs, who

---

[57]They are interested in seeing "souls saved," but they do not tend to engage in evangelism in ways typical of other evangelicals but expect people to be reached by observing modern-day demonstrations of power. I am indebted to Matthew Westbrook for this caveat.

[58]Christerson and Flory, *Network Christianity*, 34.

[59]One such network is known as the International Coalition of Apostolic Leaders. C. Peter Wagner of Fuller Seminary was the first presiding apostle of this network. See "The History of ICAL," International Coalition of Apostolic Leaders, 2019, www.icaleaders.com/about-ical /history-of-ica.

[60]Christerson and Flory, *Network Christianity*, 8, 10.

[61]Christerson and Flory, *Network Christianity*. 10.

[62]I am indebted to Matthew Westbrook for these observations.

had a close association with C. Peter Wagner;[63] Lou Engle of The Call, who organizes large prayer initiatives often focused on political causes;[64] and of Bill Johnson, senior pastor of Bethel Church in Redding, California.[65] All of the above names (save for Bill Johnson) are well known for strong advocacy of Christian Zionist beliefs.

Christerson and Flory point out that the independent network charismatic Christianity "is at its core simply a collection of strong leaders who know each other and combine and recombine for specific projects, but who are functionally independent of one another."[66] Their legitimacy is grounded not on academic achievement or degrees, or their preaching prowess or a position in a hierarchy, nor does it arise from their leadership of a congregation, or a role in a denomination. Like many early Pentecostals they "emphasize practice over belief, and those practices they deem most important are largely absent from traditional Protestantism. Specifically prophecy (receiving direct words from God), physical healing, and deliverance from evil spirits are the practices that define most Independent Network Charismatic practitioners."[67] Again, in many ways the independent network charismatics are the Latter Rain movement writ large, moving well beyond the original Pentecostal constituency of the earlier movement, and are much more international. They have become an important stream in the global underworld of renewalist Christianity.

Christian Zionism and the third and fourth waves. In the past several decades the basis of Christian Zionism has been shifting yet again. Dispensational premillennialism appears to be in decline beyond America, and new forms of prophecy interpretation are displacing it. Many scholars are unaware of this shift and keep on focusing on dispensationalism as the underlying dynamic, a tendency that is both ubiquitous and misleading, as it "tends to reify Christian Zionism as a single 'thing' in time and space, influencing in the present the global political definition of the situation in the Middle East in a monolithic and predictable manner. Such reification hinders understanding," Westbrook observes, "far more than it enlightens,

---

[63]See Generals International, "History of Generals International," www.generals.org/history.
[64]See The Call's website, https://www.thecall.com.
[65]See Bethel Redding's website, http://bethelredding.com.
[66]Christerson and Flory, *Network Christianity*, 11.
[67]Christerson and Flory, *Network Christianity*, 11-12.

and encourages readings of Christian Zionism in its renewalist and other forms that miss important theological, social, and political characteristics that those forms may manifest."[68]

Christerson and Flory assert that many of the Independent Network Christianity leaders are

> postmillennial in their theological orientation, meaning that they believe that the power of God is available now to usher in the "new kingdom of God," creating a heaven on earth in the here and now. This postmillennial utopianism is a break from classical Pentecostal theology, which is focused on building up the church and saving souls for the next life.[69]

However, as has been seen, optimistic utopianism is not the property of postmillennialists alone; it was characteristic of historicist premillennialism in the nineteenth century, which hoped in similar manner to see the kingdom of God ushered in. And postmillennialism has always been gradualist in expecting the kingdom of God to come in gradually, not cataclysmically.

What is being advocated might not be best characterized as postmillennialism but a very optimistic version of historic premillennialism that posits Christ's return before the millennium but after the tribulation. Their view is that the future is going to get worse and better at the same time, whereas postmillennialism has always posited a steady upward trajectory to the end of history as the kingdom of God is being realized, and with it a concomitant decline in societal distress. While the church will experience the tribulation, there will be such a massive revival that the majority of the world's population will experience salvation, asserts one of the leading writers, Dan Juster (discussed below), whose optimism regarding the breadth of those who will be saved is reminiscent of Jonathan Edwards's views (who was a postmillennialist). These prophetic understandings in renewalist Christianity are challenging more traditional expressions of dispensational premillennialism among those associated with the independent network charismatics whom Flory and Christerson study. They point to the International House of Prayer in Kansas City, Kansas, under the direction of Mike Bickle as a key example of the International Network, but Bickle clearly self-identifies with "historic

---

[68]Westbrook, "Christian Embassy," 37.
[69]Christerson and Flory, *Network Christianity*, 12.

premillennialism" and teaches that "the Church will be raptured after going through the tribulation in great victory."[70] So while Bickle's theology is very hopeful and emphasizes positive cultural engagement, it is clearly not a new version of postmillennialism.

Attention also needs to be given to two key spokesmen of the messianic Jewish movement who are important promoters of Christian Zionism among the renewalists. Prominent among them are Asher Intrater, who has influenced figures like Mike Bickle of the International House of Prayer.[71] The second is Dan Juster (b. 1947), the son of a Jewish father and Christian mother who serves as the director of Tikkun, "an apostolic network," and major writer in the messianic Jewish world, but whose writings and conference addresses are well known to many Christian Zionists.[72]

KEY FORMULATORS OF RENEWALIST ZIONISM:
DEREK PRINCE AND DAVID PAWSON

To understand the worldview of Christian renewalists, one has to appreciate their providentialist reading of history, which is centered on the Jews as a people. It draws on earlier Protestant readings of Jewish history, but in the twentieth century it became an integral part of the memory of untold millions of Christian Zionists across the world. Arguably the most important teller of this story has been Derek Prince (1915–2003), who was arguably the most influential Christian Zionist thinker, writer, and speaker in global Christian Zionist circles in the second half of the twentieth century. He is a household name in Christian Zionist circles as far afield as Hong Kong and Cape Town, London and Los Angeles.

Prince's background is remarkable. Born the son of a British army officer in India, at age thirteen he was elected a King's Scholar at Eton College and then was senior scholar of his year at King's College, Cambridge University. He achieved a first-class honors degree in both sections of the classical tripos (studying Latin and Greek language, culture, and history). For two years he was selected as the senior research student,

---

[70]Mike Bickle, "Historic Premillennialism and the Victorious Church," The Mike Bickle Library, April 18, 2017, mikebickle.org/resources/resource/3070.

[71]Many of Intrater's videos are available on the International House of Prayer website. See www.ihopkc.org/resources/asset/2016_05_14_1800_MSG_FCF/auto/true/. Accessed 21 January 2021.

[72]See Tikkun's website, https://tikkun.tv/.

pursuing a doctorate in classical philosophy at Cambridge. In March 1940 he was elected a fellow of King's College, Cambridge, having written a fellowship dissertation dealing with the evolution of Plato's philosophical method employing the understanding advanced by "the Cambridge school" of philosophy, and in particular the approach of his Cambridge teacher Ludwig Wittgenstein.[73] Shortly thereafter, Prince experienced a conversion to Christianity and embraced Pentecostalism. Prince enlisted in the British army in 1940 and served in North Africa in a noncombatant role in a medical corps from 1941 and was transferred to Palestine in 1944. After the war he resumed his doctoral studies at the Hebrew University in Jerusalem and was strengthened in his conviction that God was about to create a Jewish state in Palestine.[74] Before the end of the war, Prince married a Danish Pentecostal missionary, Lydia Christensen, who had worked closely with Laura Radford, one of the leading missionary brokers in Palestine of Pentecostal Zionism.[75] He wrote attacking supersessionist teaching and insisted on laying "the main responsibility for the violence done against the Jewish people, including the Holocaust, at the door of the Christian church."[76] He and his family were among missionaries evacuated during the fighting in Palestine in the summer of 1948. After pastoring in London and serving as a teacher in Kenya from 1957 to 1961, he moved to Canada, and then in 1963 to the United States, where he developed his international teaching ministry. Newberg views Derek Prince as the person most responsible for the "direct historical connection between the Pentecostal missionaries in Palestine, the charismatic movement, and the pro-Israel movement."[77] Prince was no dispensationalist, and his brief summary of his eschatological views has no place for a premillennial rapture of the saints. It would seem most appropriate to characterize his position as posttribulation premillennialism (that is, the historic premillennial position).[78]

---

[73]Brian Stanley, *Christianity in the Twentieth Century: A World History* (Princeton, NJ: Princeton University Press, 2018), 302.

[74]Newberg, *Pentecostal Mission*, 188.

[75]Newberg, *Pentecostal Mission*, 187. See also 184-85 on Radford.

[76]Newberg, *Pentecostal Mission*, 189.

[77]Newberg, *Pentecostal Mission*, 186.

[78]Derek Prince, "Epilogue: Drama in Three Acts," in Lydia Prince and Derek Prince, *Appointment in Jerusalem* (Grand Rapids, MI: Chosen Books, 1975), 176-88.

At the center of Prince's theology was his philo-Semitism, coupled with his attack on what he regarded as the Christian record of anti-Semitism, repeating themes that were current in nineteenth-century evangelicalism but put in very stark terms: his "chilling assessment was that the Jewish people were the innocent victims of false Christian theology,"[79] hence his forceful rejection of replacement theology and supersessionism. Its apex, he argued, was in the Holocaust: "We could sum up the outworking of the historical processes involved by saying that the Nazis merely reaped a harvest that the Church had sown."[80] The blame for anti-Semitism was no longer focused on Roman Catholicism in the way that it had been in both English Puritanism and in nineteenth-century evangelicalism. Prince's dropping of the anti-Catholic polemic in Christian Zionism is noteworthy. Several factors were likely at work here: first, Prince was not a Calvinist and as a Pentecostal/charismatic was not in tune with the older tradition and its blaming of the medieval Catholic "contempt of the Jews" tradition; second, guilt for the Holocaust fell largely on Lutheran Protestant shoulders, and therefore Protestant complicity in European anti-Semitism was being acknowledged; third, the charismatic movement in the late 1960s had come to include not only mainline Protestants but also Roman Catholics, some of whom were embracing Christian Zionism. The friendly talk at Vatican II in the 1960s about Protestants being "separated brethren" rather than "heretics" and the growth of secularism in Western culture both probably also contributed to the shift: Protestants increasingly needed Catholics as coworkers in dealing with a culture growing increasingly skeptical of received forms of Christianity. From the Roman Catholic side there has been considerable movement toward a more friendly attitude to the Israeli state.

Interestingly, Prince was certain that Jews were about to turn to Christ. Writing in *The Last Word on the Middle East* in 1982 he could aver, "The Jewish people are once again ready to receive and respond to God's Holy Spirit."[81] Christians could further this end by acknowledging their responsibility for the Holocaust and making amends by "blessing Israel," which involves fervent support for the Jewish state. Christians could thus help in

---

[79]Newberg, *Pentecostal Mission*, 188.
[80]Newberg, *Pentecostal Mission*, 189.
[81]Newberg, *Pentecostal Mission*, 189.

this special end-time ministry of "preparing the hearts of Israel for their Messiah." This agenda was to become the basis of a new Christian pro-Israel movement that emerged in the 1970s,[82] with its most public expression being the establishment of the International Christian Embassy Jerusalem. Related to these developments, yet distinct, was the emergence of messianic Judaism, which is strongly pro-Zionist and predominantly charismatic in orientation. There is tension between these two charismatic groups because while the ICEJ is cautious about proselytizing Jews, the messianic Jews (and many other charismatics) are not.

In his 1984 work *Our Debt To Israel*, Prince developed his providentialist reading of church history through the lens of Christian treatment of the Jews. This is not unique to Prince and has a long history in Christian Zionism and in particular in Pentecostalism since its beginning, and is similarly developed by other charismatic writers such as David Pawson. Prince sees the decline of Spain in the 1400 and 1500s as due to God's judgment on that nation for its expulsion of the Jews in 1492, and interprets the post–World War II decline of Great Britain's power to its lack of support for the new Jewish state and its handling of its responsibility as the mandatory power in Palestine in 1947–1948. Citing Isaiah 60:12—"For the nation and kingdom that will not serve thee shall perish; yea, those nations shall be utterly wasted" (KJV)—he comments, "God here promises Israel, and also warns all the Gentiles, that He will bring judgment on any nation that opposes His purposes of redemption and restoration for Israel."[83]

Convinced that the prayers of believing Christians can influence world events, he recounts his frustration with the senior British army officers when serving in North Africa whom he considered "selfish, irresponsible and undisciplined," concerned only with their own comfort.[84] They were sapping the morale of the two British armored divisions with which he worked. He was convinced that under such poor leadership British defeat was certain and that Nazi victory would bring about the fall of Palestine and a slaughter of its Jews. While the British army was in full retreat eastward to El Alamein,

---

[82]Newberg, *Pentecostal Mission*, 189.
[83]Shapiro, *Navigating*, 56.
[84]Derek Prince, *Shaping History Through Prayer and Fasting* (Old Tappan, NJ: Fleming H. Revell, 1973), 59.

just west of Cairo, to take its last stand against the Axis powers, Prince prayed daily for new leadership that would enable a victory to occur. A new commander, General Gott, was sent out to take command, but his plane was shot down and he was replaced by Bernard Montgomery, whom Prince says was the son of an evangelical Anglican bishop; he characterizes Montgomery as "*just* and *God-fearing*."[85] (Montgomery's father had been the Anglican bishop of Tasmania and later served as the head of the Society for the Propagation of the Gospel, a high-church society. Neither his credentials as an evangelical nor Field-Marshall Montgomery's being characterized as "God-fearing" seem justified.) However, Prince would claim,

> The British government chose Gott for their commander, but God set him aside and raised up Montgomery, the man of His own choosing. God did this to bring glory to His own name, and to answer a prayer which, by the Holy Spirit, He himself had first inspired me to pray. By this intervention God also preserved the Jews in Palestine from coming under the control of the Axis powers.[86]

This providentialist reading of history is then applied to the establishment of the state of Israel, the war of independence, and illustrated with frequent examples of answers to prayer on behalf of the fragile Jewish nation. Prince does not try, however, to account for the fact that Germany, whose record toward the Jews was infinitely worse than Britain's, had prospered spectacularly since World War II—something that is an ongoing problem, especially for German Christian Zionists.[87] Prince eventually moved to America and was associated with Christian Growth Ministries based in Fort Lauderdale, Florida.

Brian Stanley has argued that Prince's theological trajectory was shaped by Platonic influence, which he absorbed before his conversion to Christianity. Stanley notes that Prince, in one of his popular books, reproduces "the language of Plato's *Phaedo* almost verbatim": "The things that belong to the visible realm are transitory and impermanent. It is only in the invisible realm that we can find true and abiding reality. It is in this realm, too, that we discover the forces which will ultimately shape our destiny, even in the

---

[85]Prince, *Shaping History*, 61.

[86]Prince, *Shaping History*, 62.

[87]Contra to Shapiro, supersessionism is still a widely held belief among many English-speaking evangelicals who are the targets of Prince's arguments. Shapiro, *Navigating*, 76.

visible realm."[88] In a sense, Prince resacralized the world through his use of Platonism. This emphasis on the importance of the unseen world determining this-worldly realities later emerged in his teachings about spiritual warfare, and his insistence on the need of "deliverance ministries" in which he taught that even Spirit-filled Christians could be "demonized," by which he meant that they were "subject to demonic influence" and needed that influence expelled from their lives.[89] Such views were promoted by Prince in a daily radio program that was broadcast in thirteen languages throughout the world, through audio cassettes, through conference speaking (much of his teaching is still available on YouTube), and through his long list of books. His views on deliverance ministry were controversial in Pentecostal circles, but his influence in changing attitudes was enormous—especially in Africa, where his views meshed with the concerns of African traditional religion. Prince's teachings were important in the growth of a specific strain of prosperity-gospel teachings, especially in Africa.[90] He taught that "from the invisible realm of spiritual reality both blessings and curses flowed down the bloodline from up to four generations back, conveying good (evidenced in prosperity) or ill (manifested in poverty or hereditary sickness), a claim that meshed closely with African beliefs about ancestors."[91] His belief in ancestral blessings and cursings was reflective of Plato, who "shared with much Greek thought a belief in the polluting capacity of ancestral curses, and in his *Phaedrus* refers to families 'afflicted by horrendous illnesses and sufferings as a result of guilt incurred some time in the distant past.'"[92] For Prince, the historic Christian mistreatment of Jews was something from the past that needed to be repented of by Christendom, and should be replaced by "blessing Israel," in order on the one hand to mitigate the curse of God on

---

[88] Derek Prince, *Blessing or Curse: You Can Choose!* (Bletchley, UK: Authentic Media, 2015), 18-19. Quoted in Stanley, *Christianity in the Twentieth Century*, 303.

[89] Prince was careful to distinguish between "possession" and being "subject to demonic influence." He writes, "It is monstrous to suggest that such a person [a 'born-again Christian seeking to live for Christ'] belongs to the devil or is owned by the devil." Derek Prince, *They Shall Expel Demons: What You Need to Know About Demons—Your Invisible Enemies* (Grand Rapids, MI: Chosen Books, 1998), 16.

[90] For a summary of its key tenets see Katherine Attanasi, "Introduction: The Plurality of Prosperity Theologies and Pentecostalisms," in *Pentecostalism and Prosperity: The Socio-economics of the Global Charismatic Movement*, ed. Katherine Attanasi and Amos Yong (New York: Palgrave-MacMillan, 2012), 3-4.

[91] Stanley, *Christianity in the Twentieth Century*, 303.

[92] Stanley, *Christianity in the Twentieth Century*, 303.

those whose ancestors have cursed the Jews, and on the other to obtain the prosperity promised to those who follow God's command to bless Israel.

Another British figure who was enormously significant was David Pawson (1930–2020). Like Prince, Pawson had significant British military involvement in the Middle East early in life. In the 1950s he served as a Royal Air Force chaplain based in Aden "in the heartland of Islam," as he was later to characterize it.[93] By the 1970s he had become widely known as a Bible teacher with an international ministry in charismatic circles. As with Prince, in the 1970s audio-cassette recordings of his teachings were circulating around the globe. Longtime pastor of Guildford Baptist Church (southwest of London), he became a favorite speaker at renewalist conferences throughout the world and at events organized by the International Christian Embassy Jerusalem, particularly at its annual Feast of Tabernacles celebration. Among his many books is his *Defending Christian Zionism*,[94] in which he critiqued dispensational premillennialism and advocated his own version of historic premillennialism, arguing for a posttribulation rapture of the saints. He clearly believed that the prophecies concerning the nation of Israel are to be fulfilled during this age rather than understanding them as events that will occur after the rapture of the saints. In his 2003 *The Challenge of Islam to Christians*, he set out his conviction that, but for the grace of God, Britain will become Muslim and that this will be God's judgment on an apostate nation. However, he believed that God will use this judgment to bring about the purification of the Christian church.

In his study of popular renewalist literature, Newberg found six themes continually developed and asserted—and all of them are rooted in themes that Prince and Pawson have propounded: a strong Christian affinity for Zionism; a forceful assertion of Christian culpability for the Holocaust; a call for unambiguous denouncing of anti-Semitism (which often sees any form of anti-Zionism as a manifestation of anti-Semitism); a clear repudiation of replacement theology, which it holds responsible for anti-Semitism; an emphasis on the Jewish roots of Christianity, reflecting the influence of messianic Judaism; and an affirmation of philo-Semitism based not on prophetic speculation but rather on an unconditional covenant God

---

[93]David Pawson, *The Challenge of Islam to Christians* (London: Hodder & Stoughton, 2003), 4.
[94]David Pawson, *Defending Christian Zionism* (Bristol: Terra Nova Publications, 2008).

has made with the Jewish people. Significantly, much of renewalist literature now distances itself from dispensational premillennialism.[95]

This shift away from dispensationalism was one of the key facts that the Canadian-Israeli scholar Faydra Shapiro observed in her extensive study of contemporary Christian Zionism in Canada and Israel:

> Many Christian Zionists are eager to break the perceived connection between support for Israel and systems such as dispensationalism and the Bible prophecy movement, with its emphasis on showing that we are living in the final days before the end times.
>
> In my research it became clear very quickly that the connection between premillennial dispensationalism and Christian Zionism has been vastly overdrawn. Overwhelmingly my informants either did not consider themselves dispensationalists or—more often—did not know what dispensationalism meant.[96]

Shapiro's observation is confirmed by Stephen Spector: "Many [American] evangelicals do embrace these dispensational expectations, but, according to the best estimate, the vast majority do not."[97] The ICEJ has clearly repudiated dispensationalism, and many of its followers seem to be content with Pawson's posttribulation rapture position. But the general lack of interest in prophetic speculation that Newberg and Shapiro cite probably accounts for the fact that Pawson's views are uncontroversial among the renewalist Zionists. Westbrook has observed another factor influencing this trend:

> There exists a pragmatic and theological need within Christian Zionism, only now beginning to emerge in force, to play down connection to perceived instances of present and future prophecy fulfillment, given that language about prophecy does not have currency in the public sphere where political advocacy is conducted. Christian Zionists are beginning to realize that effective advocacy for Israel cannot find its roots in the fulfillment of prophecy.[98]

---

[95]This point is important and differs in the standard account of dispensationalism's importance reflected in several recent authors, including Stephen Sizer, *Christian Zionism: Roadmap to Armageddon?* (Downers Grove, IL: IVP Academic, 2006); Donald E. Wagner, *Anxious for Armageddon* (Scottdale, PA: Herald, 1995); Clifford A. Kiracofe, *Dark Crusade: Christian Zionism and US Foreign Policy* (London: L.B. Tauris, 2009); and Grace Halsell, *Prophecy and Politics* (Chicago: Lawrence Hill Books, 1986) and Halsell, *Forcing God's Hand: Why Millions Pray for a Quick Rapture—and Destruction of Planet Earth* (Beltsville, MD: Amana Publications, 2003).

[96]Shapiro, *Navigating*, 12.

[97]Stephen Spector, *Evangelicals and Israel: The Story of American Christian Zionism* (New York: Oxford University Press, 2009), 23.

[98]Westbrook, "Christian Embassy," 20.

But at the same time within the movement "the theme of revival of the past [as in the Feast of Tabernacles] as a harbinger of eschatological fulfillment is still a powerful motivator."[99]

RECENT DEVELOPMENTS

The global renewalist movement today has asserted itself with its own brand of Christian Zionist theologies, largely rejects dispensational premillennialism, and many now embrace historic premillennialism. Westbrook notes that "the ethos of classic dispensationalism, dominated as it was by a largely passive approach to prophecy fulfillment, which generally held that it was enough to merely watch what was happening in the world in order to understand what *God* was doing, has been jettisoned in favor of a more hands-on approach to prophecy fulfillment."[100] Westbrook has observed three interrelated themes consistently found in renewalist theology advocating for Christian Zionism: first, a "concern with Islamist violence against Christians, but also, in potential and actualized form for Americans, against the 'Judeo-Christian' West"; second, "the promotion of Christian Zionism as a central component of Renewalist theology"; and third, the promotion of "Israel-focused, Renewalist political advocacy."[101]

He points out that renewalist Zionism tends to tie the fates of Christians and Jews more closely together than previous forms of Christian Zionism and, together with their emphasis on supernatural triumphalism, provides the distinctive content of their Zionism versus earlier versions. Renewalist Zionism affirms both the spiritual and physical "restoration" of the Jewish people in history from a Christian perspective and is, in this way, much like the seventeenth-century Protestant restorationists. Renewalist Zionism has been actively distancing itself from dispensational premillennialism in the United States, and dispensationalism has rarely been embraced by renewalists outside of the United States.[102]

A key renewalist Zionist network is known as the New Apostolic Reformation, which is a loose coalition that is interdenominational and generally

---

[99]Westbrook, "Christian Embassy," 20.
[100]Matthew C. Westbrook, "Broadcasting Jesus' Return: Televangelism and the Appropriation of Israel Through Israeli-Granted Broadcasting Rights," in *Comprehending Christian Zionism: Perspectives in Comparison*, ed. Goran Gunner and Robert O. Smith (Minneapolis: Fortress, 2014), 71.
[101]Westbrook, "Christian Embassy," 87.
[102]I am particularly indebted to Matthew Westbrook for his insights on these matters.

postdenominational. Its leaders are the heads of their own networks of churches in various parts of the world, and recognize each other's leadership as modern apostles. Some see this as the end-time restoration of the gift of apostleship to the church—a view that we have seen was advocated in the Latter Rain movement of the late 1940s.[103] Many of them see Jerusalem as the international center of global Christianity, and are ardent supporters of the state of Israel. The renewalist Zionists are broader than the New Apostolic Reformation group, and include groups such as the International Christian Embassy Jerusalem.

Renewalist Christian Zionism Today

Mainstream renewalism today has largely abandoned British Israelite teachings; nevertheless, within renewalism there is currently a significant movement to nurture and symbolize connections between Jews and Christians. Many Pentecostals (and more recently the broader category of renewalists) have adopted Israel-themed ritual displays: the wearing of Jewish garb, the blowing of the shofar in worship, and celebrations of Jewish festivals, especially the Feast of Tabernacles in Jerusalem. For those who practice their faith in this way, this Hebrew Roots movement strongly reinforces symbolic connections with "God's chosen people." A fascination with all things Jewish came to characterize renewalists in America and throughout the world by the end of the twentieth century. Leading figures like David du Plessis and Derek Prince sought to configure Pentecostal/charismatic history around God's dealings with the state of Israel in the twentieth century and promoted strong support for Israel. These all have worked to place Israel, and symbolically Jerusalem, at the center of the renewalist imagination.[104] This fascination with the Jews has also spawned interesting Judaizing groups such as the Noahides, who have persuaded some evangelicals in the Philippines to forsake their Christian profession and become affiliated with Judaism as "Sons of Noah."[105]

---

[103]Joseph Williams, "The Pentecostalization of Christian Zionism," *Church History* 84, no. 1 (March 2015): 179-80.

[104]Williams, "Pentecostalization," 179.

[105]The Noahides, or Children of Noah, are Gentiles who follow "the Seven Laws of Noah," a Jewish moral code designed for Gentiles. Rachel Z. Feldman, "Field Notes: The Children of Noah; Has Messianic Zionism Created a New World Religion?," *Nova Religio: The Journal of Alternative and Emergent Religions* 22, no. 1 (2018): 117. See also Jeffrey Kaplan, *Radical Religion in America: Millenarian Movements from the Far Right to the Children of Noah* (Syracuse, NY: Syracuse University Press, 1997).

15

CHRISTIAN ZIONISM TODAY

A "New" Christian Zionism

From the nonrenewalist side of Christian Zionism, a new scholarly defense has recently been mounted under the leadership of Gerald R. McDermott, a distinguished scholar of Jonathan Edwards. The edited volume that he has produced offers an alternative vision differing from both traditional dispensationalism and the emergent renewalist strands of Christian Zionism. *The New Christian Zionism: Fresh Perspectives on Israel and the Land* (2017) brings together a number of leading evangelical academics to articulate an apology for Christian Zionism. The title invites the question: How new? It is novel in that the volume displays an unprecedented level of theological cooperation among Christian Zionists from different theological perspectives. The organizer and editor, Gerald McDermott, represents a Reformed covenantal position, while other contributors take quite different approaches.[1] What is also new is that several of the chapters reflect the shift in thinking among dispensational-premillennialist scholars that began in the 1970s and is now known as progressive dispensationalism.

In the 1980s some leading dispensationalists were beginning to rethink the whole dispensational system, and in 1986 they established the "Dispensationalism Study Group" within the Evangelical Theological Society.[2] The group was chaired by Darrell L. Bock and Craig A. Blaising, with significant involvement by Robert L. Saucy of Talbot Seminary. In the early 1990s a variant of dispensationalism was articulated by these three scholars in three

---

[1]McDermott offers a full explanation of his position in *Israel Matters: Why Christians Must Think Differently About the People and the Land* (Grand Rapids, MI: Brazos Press, 2017).
[2]See "Dispensational Study Group," Evangelical Theological Society, https://www.etsjets.org/puc/puc_dispensationalism.

different books: Craig A. Blaising and Darrell L. Bock, eds., *Dispensationalism, Israel and the Church: The Search for Definition* (1992); Robert L. Saucy, *The Case for Progressive Dispensationalism: The Interface Between Dispensational and Non-dispensational Theology* (1993); and Craig A. Blaising and Darrell L. Bock, eds., *Progressive Dispensationalism* (1993).

At the heart of their disagreement with traditional dispensationalism is Darby's insistence that biblical prophecy deals only with the Jews, and that the church age is a parenthesis between the sixty-ninth and seventieth weeks of the prophetic clock and is not referred to in biblical prophecy. Darby argued that God has put on hold his dealings with Israel during the church age. His insistence on such a radical discontinuity did not sit well with these biblical scholars, who argued that there are important links between the Old Testament and the New Testament that represent progress from the older dispensation to the new. Although the fulfillment of the promises regarding ethnic Israel remain to be fully realized in the future, they have been partially inaugurated in the New Testament (an "already-but-not-yet" stance). An emphasis on the material fulfilment of the promises remains.

At least two factors contributed to this rethinking. The first is that New Testament studies was coming to appreciate the inherent Jewishness of Jesus and of Paul and therefore the critical importance of understanding Jewish apocalyptic. These were important emphases of two prominent New Testament scholars, F. F. Bruce and G. B. Caird.[3] A second factor in the emergence of progressive dispensationalism was the rise of messianic Judaism. A number of progressive dispensationalism's leading proponents are Jewish converts to Christianity, including Darrell Bock of Dallas Theological Seminary, one of the earliest formulators of progressive dispensationalism. Bock and Blaising write two of the key theological chapters in

---

[3]F. F. Bruce (1910–1990) was Rylands Professor of Biblical Criticism at the University of Manchester and was raised in the Plymouth Brethren. Although he remained in the movement, he moved away from dispensationalism and influenced many both through his own writings and his numerous doctoral students. The other key scholar was G. B. Caird, Dean Ireland Professor of Scriptural Interpretation at Oxford, whose *Jesus and the Jewish Nation* (London: Athlone, 1965) emphasized understanding Jesus' Jewishness. His work on Paul's Jewishness was also seminal: notably his *Principalities and Powers: A Study in Pauline Theology* (Oxford: Clarendon, 1956) and *Paul's Letters from Prison* (London: Oxford University Press, 1976), although his influence was magnified many times through his doctoral students, including the well-known New Testament scholars E. P. Sanders and N. T. Wright.

The New Christian Zionism, and several of the other theological articles are written by messianic Jewish academics. Some prominent messianic believers, such as Arnold Fruchtenbuam, a graduate of Dallas Seminary in 1971, remain classic dispensationalists.[4]

In a manner very similar to the advocates of historicist premillennialism in the nineteenth century, progressive dispensationalists hold that the promises to Israel "according to the flesh" are to be realized in a very concrete way. Most notable is the physical return of the Jews to Palestine, which progressive dispensationalists often understand as having been fulfilled in 1948, although they are generally much more cautious about their claims in this regard than are the traditional dispensationalists. And unlike the historicists, they eschew date-setting. But clearly in their thinking, Scripture supports a strong Christian Zionist stance. Like the historicists and the traditional dispensationalists, they believe that Jesus will eventually reign over a Jewish realm based in Jerusalem.[5] Not surprisingly, some of their sharpest criticisms are of supersessionism, and, befitting a family feud, of traditional dispensationalism.

In his capstone chapter in *The New Christian Zionism*, Bock asks how Christian Zionism should move forward. For Bock, the Christian Zionist understanding grows out of a proper appreciation of God's character and his promises and reflects how one thinks about God: "Seeing Israel in the program of God says God keeps his promises to those he originally addressed. That story also is rooted in reconciliation, an important detail that gets lost when one dismisses the ongoing significance of Israel."[6] The clear implication is that non-Zionist Christians think wrongly about the character

---

[4]Fruchtenbaum is the founder and director of Ariel Ministries based in San Antonio, Texas. See "About Dr. Fruchtenbaum," Ariel Ministries, www.ariel.org/about/dr-fruchtenbaum. I am indebted to Daniel Hummel for this observation.

[5]Bock argues that "all of the covenants of promise are initially realized in the church. . . . To say that such realization occurs in the church is not to deny that these covenants were originally or ultimately for national, ethnic Israel. It is rather to note that because of the work of Christ, who is the key to fulfillment, initial fulfillment becomes possible in the context of the church. There awaits, in the age to come, an even more complete fulfillment of these promises in a period when Christ returns to reign on earth from Israel." Darrell Bock, "Covenants in Progressive Dispensationalism," in *Three Central Issues in Contemporary Dispensationalism*, ed. Herbert W. Bateman IV (Grand Rapids, MI: Kregel, 1999), 171.

[6]Darrell Bock, "How Should the New Christian Zionism Proceed?," in *The New Christian Zionism: Fresh Perspectives on Israel and the Land*, ed. Gerald McDermott (Downers Grove, IL: IVP Academic, 2017), 305.

of God, which of course they would contest. Evangelical critics of Christian Zionism like Bruce Waltke, Christopher Wright, and N. T. Wright would agree that God keeps his promises but that he fulfills them in unexpected ways that are far beyond the wildest dreams of the original hearers and that the promised reconciliation is far grander than "the land," but entails the whole universe.

Bock summarizes the various chapters of *The New Christian Zionism* that mount a biblical, historical, and theological defense of modern Israel without wholesale affirmation of all that the Israeli state does. He writes, "In one sense, all the term Christian Zionism means in the end is that Israel has a right to exist with the same human rights and security guarantees that other nations receive. But of course Christian Zionism is also more than that, for it makes a *theological* case for that right to exist, beyond a merely prudential one."[7] His definition of *Christian Zionism* is very close to the one that has been used in this book.

Bock makes several key distinctions about this "new" Christian Zionism. The first is that it emphasizes not "merely a hope for individual ethnic Jews" who will recognize Jesus as Messiah but "argues that Israel has a *corporate* future in God's plan and as a nation has a right to land in the Middle East. . . . That is the first key distinction the *New Christian Zionism* makes—the difference between individual hope for Jews and a corporate place for the nation."[8] Traditional dispensationalism was formulated well before Israel existed as a nation, and J. N. Darby, its formulator, did not expect that return of the Jews until after the rapture. This "new" Christian Zionism has been adapted to the political reality of the Israeli state.

A second crucial distinction he makes is between "national Israel" and "believing Israel":

> The existence of believing Israel . . . in distinction from national Israel does not mean exclusion of national or corporate Israel from God's program, or the hope that unbelieving Jews one day will come to faith in God's Messiah. Unbelieving Israel has a right to the land because God gave it to all the nation and seed of Abraham initially as an act of his grace when he called Abraham to form a nation even before the patriarch trusted God. This future for Jewish

[7]Bock, "How," 308.
[8]Bock, "How," 308.

people can be affirmed alongside the idea that Christ is also the heir of all promises, including promises about rule of the earth.[9]

National Israel's current state of unbelief does not abrogate the covenant made with her "but makes her subject to covenant discipline from the Messiah—even if she does not recognize it."[10] The implication of this is that Israel "is still responsible to God for how she responds to covenant blessings," and Christian Zionists should not be uncritical of how Israel behaves: Israel is bound to "govern and occupy" the land in a way that is both moral and responsible.[11] At the same time Jesus' own ministry "makes no sense of a dual track to salvation that argues that the Jews have one way of salvation and Gentiles have Jesus."[12]

Bock offers five theological emphases and one historical point that are needed to bring balance to Christian Zionism. The first is that "*inclusion should not become exclusion*" by which he intends that "if the land ultimately is Christ's and those who believe, whether Jew or Gentile, share in it because Jesus is their Messiah too, that does not exclude Israel's claim to the land and Israel's right to exist as a political people."[13] Bock acknowledges that more work is needed by Christian Zionists in putting into "proper relationship the following: fulfillment in Christ, current covenantal disciple for Israel, Israel's responsibility to be just and the nation's rights."[14] The second matter of "covenantal discipline" for Israel is bound to elicit cries of "anti-Semitism" from many in the Jewish community. As we have seen, David Wilson has argued that in the late 1930s and early 1940s American premillennialists, while not necessarily personally anti-Semitic, were conditioned by their interpretation of Scripture to expect anti-Semitism as a fact of life and inclined to lament but not openly oppose something they regarded as almost inevitable. Progressive dispensationalists' talk of "covenantal discipline" of the Jewish people would seem to leave its proponents open to similar lines of criticism. It is doubtful how popular talk of "covenantal discipline" would be received among many Christian Zionists who understand their own

---

[9]Bock, "How," 308.
[10]Bock, "How," 309.
[11]Bock, "How," 309.
[12]Bock, "How," 309.
[13]Bock, "How," 310.
[14]Bock, "How," 310.

identities as wrapped up in their obligation to "bless Israel." The third matter of Israel's responsibility to be just would necessarily involve Christian Zionists taking seriously the work that has been done by Israel's "New Historians," who freely acknowledge the ethical problems associated with the founding of the state of Israel but are unapologetic in defending these actions. There is little evidence that this proposal by Bock is likely to find much traction among Christian Zionists.

His second emphasis is on "the canon's repeated appeal to *God's faithfulness*,"[15] which is closely linked with his discussion of the character of God discussed above. Bock's third point is that "the case for Christian Zionism is *not as nationalistic* as some within the movement make it out to be and as some outside the movement perceive it to be."[16] Its advocates need to keep in mind that "the hope for life for Israel in the end as Scripture depicts it is not only for the land to be a haven of peace for Jews but also for it to be a place of peace and reconciliation that permeates all creation."[17] He addresses the question as to why the New Testament has little to say about the land and offers two responses: first, that when the New Testament was written the Jews were in the land and therefore there was no need to address the issue; and second, that the reconciliation of Jew and Gentile will relativize borders, and in this ultimate reconciliation "there can be unity and particularity without hostile rivalry. . . . With this vision of prospective peace, presence in the land is less nationalistic."[18] It would seem that the traditional dispensational distinction is coming through here— that even in the world to come, Jews and Gentiles will be treated separately, with Christ ruling the nations from Jerusalem. Darby, it will be recalled, taught that Jesus will rule over his physical people, the Jews, from Jerusalem, and over his spiritual people, Christians, from heaven. In Bock's view the bifurcation proposed by traditional dispensationalism is overcome in a reconciled one-people model.

Fourth, Bock concedes that "Christian Zionists need to put more emphasis on the *hope of reconciliation*."[19] He acknowledges the "legitimate

---

[15]Bock, "How," 311.
[16]Bock, "How," 312.
[17]Bock, "How," 312.
[18]Bock, "How," 313.
[19]Bock, "How," 313.

questions" that Palestinian Christians who live in the land are asking about how they fit into this vision. He acknowledges that "all the New Testament language about Gentiles as coheirs of promise mean that this question of justice needs to be addressed"[20] and calls for more reflection on the matter. This ties into the point above about the need for Christian Zionists to take seriously the perspectives of the Israeli New Historians as well as the experiences of Palestinian Christians who believe that Christian Zionism has been disastrous for them, both in the past and in their current lived experience, especially those in the disputed West Bank territories.

Bock's fifth point is that justice must be addressed in a "*non-discriminatory*" fashion. He argues that concern for injustice on the part of the Israelis needs to be balanced by concern for injustices on the part of her opponents. This, of course, is a fair point. He acknowledges that the hatred and mistrust that characterizes political groupings in the Middle East makes the pursuit of such a balance inherently difficult. His final point is the need for "the careful articulation of the *international and legitimate* right that Israel has to the land and to nationhood."[21] Again he is moving onto ground that has long been contested, and will undoubtedly remain contested by Israel's opponents.

CONTEMPORARY CHALLENGES TO CHRISTIAN ZIONISM

Christian Zionism has come under sustained criticism from at least three different directions in the recent past. The first major grouping of these critics are Palestinian Christian theologians, notably Naim Ateek and Mitri Raheb,[22] whose writings have found considerable support among Arab Christians and some mainline British and American churches. The organizational focus of this group is the Sabeel Ecumenical Liberation Theology Center in Jerusalem.

Naim Ateek, the former canon of St. George's Anglican Cathedral in Jerusalem, published his *Justice and Only Justice: A Palestinian Theology of Liberation* in 1989. His book begins with chronicling the tragedy of Ateek's family. Born in 1937, the son of an Anglican Palestinian businessman, he was

---

[20]Bock, "How," 313.

[21]Bock, "How," 314.

[22]Mitri Raheb (b. 1962) is the pastor of the Evangelical Lutheran Christmas Church in Bethlehem and a close associate of Ateek's. He is author of *I Am a Palestinian Christian* (Minneapolis: Fortress, 1995).

raised in the (largely Muslim) Arab village of Beisan (now Beit Shean), which the 1947 UN partition plan had allocated to the Jews. Three days before the Israeli declaration of independence in 1948, Israeli forces expelled all its villagers and forced them to relocate in Bethlehem. They were not allowed to visit their abandoned homes, nor did they receive any compensation. He chronicles the conditions of the Palestinian Arabs within the state of Israel over the next forty years, arguing that they moved through three stages: a period of shock (1948–1955), resignation (1956–1967), followed by a national awakening (1968–1988), which resulted in the formation of the Palestine Liberation Organization and the assertion of a desire for a self-governing Palestinian state alongside Israel. Although Ateek begins to develop his theology of the land in the book, a fuller and more mature account is to be found in chapter four of his *A Palestinian Christian Cry for Reconciliation* (2007) titled "The Bible and the Land." Central to his argument is that there are different theologies of the land found in the Old Testament, and while acknowledging them is helpful, it is more important to appreciate the trajectory away from an exclusivist understanding of them. Christians must consider them in light of the New Testament, filtering the Old Testament narratives "that reflect the inclusive and nonviolent message of Christ."[23] In doing so he favors the book of Jonah as "a standard against which Old Testament theology must be measured."[24] Texts like Isaiah 43:1-4, which emphasize the uniqueness of Jacob and Israel, and Isaiah 62:5-6, which he considers "narrow and racist,"[25] are to be set aside in an effort to "de-Zionize" these texts.[26]

Ateek develops his land theology in the midst of recognizing that the crucial issue at the center of the Palestinian-Israeli conflict is the issue of the land promises. He has been making his case since the early 1980s, and his argument is in line with liberal Protestant criticisms of Christian Zionism. But in his *A Palestinian Christian Cry for Reconciliation* he relies most on two English evangelical Anglican scholars for his exegesis: the Old Testament theologian Christopher J. H. Wright and N. T. Wright, a New Testament

---

[23]Naim Ateek, *A Palestinian Christian Cry for Reconciliation* (Maryknoll, NY: Orbis, 2007), 54.
[24]Ateek, *Cry*, 55.
[25]Ateek, *Cry*, 56.
[26]Ateek, *Cry*, 55.

scholar. Ateek particularly focuses on Jesus' words in Matthew 5:5—"Blessed are the meek, for they will inherit the earth"—and argues that Jesus is articulating a new understanding of the land whereby "the small land of Palestine becomes a prototype or a model for the earth. God had created the earth as a dwelling place for the meek."[27] In exegeting Jesus' encounter with Nathanael in John 1:43-51, he asserts that the point of Jesus' response is to indicate that "the angels of God were ascending and descending not on the land [as in Genesis 28:12-14], but on the Son of Man."[28] He observes, "Belonging to the kingdom of God, not the inheritance of a particular land, is what is important. From a Christian perspective the land no longer has any covenantal importance."[29] He develops his argument further from several references to passages in the Pauline epistles (Romans 4:13; Galatians 3:15-18; Ephesians 2:19-20).[30] From this basis he draws on the book of Jonah in particular to articulate a Palestinian Christian theology of liberation.[31]

The umbrella organization, Sabeel, which Ateek founded in 1989, has spearheaded activities aimed at countering Christian Zionism, including international conferences held in Jerusalem that have had considerable influence in mainline American Protestant circles, particularly its 2004 call for morally responsible investment, which sought to persuade Christian denominations to embrace the nonviolent option of divestment from "companies that work within the occupied territories (including the settlements) and that profit from the injustice and oppression of the Palestinians."[32] In 2004 it conducted a conference called "Challenging Christian Zionism" that drew in outspoken critics of Zionism, including Wagner, Burge, and Weber from the States, and Stephen Sizer and Colin Chapman (both evangelical Anglicans) from England, along with a wide assortment of non-evangelical critics of Christian Zionism. The conference resulted in a book: *Challenging Christian Zionism: Theology, Politics and the Israel-Palestine Conflict* (2005). Since 2010 Palestinian evangelicals have organized biennial meetings of their own at Bethlehem Bible College's "Christ at the

---

[27] Ateek, *Cry*, 59.
[28] Ateek, *Cry*, 60.
[29] Ateek, *Cry*, 60.
[30] Ateek, *Cry*, 63-64.
[31] Ateek, *Cry*, 67-77.
[32] Ateek, *Cry*, 139.

Checkpoint" conferences, which are more concerned to challenge American Christian Zionism (particularly in its dispensational forms) among fellow evangelicals than to influence the investment policies and the political stances of mainline churches.[33]

The second group of critics is made up of evangelical exegetes of Scripture who have been questioning the biblical basis of Christian Zionism. It is only possible to highlight a few of the most influential such scholars in this survey. As mentioned above, Ateek drew on Christopher J. H. Wright in his formulation of his theology of land. Wright did his doctorate at Cambridge on Old Testament economic ethics. His first book was based on his thesis: *God's People in God's Land: Family, Land and Property in the Old Testament* (1990). Wright has become a key influence leading many to rethink Christian Zionism. Wright was a close friend and associate of the late John R. W. Stott (arguably one of the most influential evangelicals in the world of the past half century). Wright became the International Ministries Director of the Langham Partnership International (founded by Stott) in 2001, which has given him a significant role in global evangelicalism. Both Stott and Wright are strongly against Christian Zionism.

A second British Anglican evangelical, the New Testament scholar Peter W. L. Walker, builds on the work of W. D. Davies, *The Gospel and the Land: Early Christianity and Jewish Territorial Doctrine* in his *Jesus and the Holy City: New Testament Perspectives on Jerusalem*.[34] Walker examines the entire New Testament regarding the issue of the land, the temple, and Jerusalem and like Davies cannot find support for Christian Zionist readings of these texts.

Arguably the best-known evangelical scholar who has questioned Christian Zionism is N. T. Wright (no relation to Christopher Wright), who prefers the term *transference theology* rather than supersessionism to describe his view. He has argued that Israel's covenant blessings have been transferred to the Christian church as a whole. Christ is himself the new

---

[33]It is perhaps the case that its organizers do not consider that dispensationalism may no longer be as important as it once was in Christian Zionist circles. I am indebted to Daniel Hummel for this observation.

[34]W. D. Davies, *The Gospel and the Land: Early Christianity and Jewish Territorial Doctrine* (Berkeley: University of California Press, 1974); Peter W. L. Walker, *Jesus and the Holy City: New Testament Perspectives on Jerusalem* (Grand Rapids, MI: Eerdmans, 1996).

Israel, and those who are "in Christ" constitute the new Israel. The old markers of Jewish identity have thus been erased, or universalized. He holds that through the Davidic King (Christ), the "whole world" promises of Psalm 2 and Psalm 72 have been universalized. For him this is affirmed in Paul's argument in Romans 4 that believers are to "inherit the world" and again in Romans 8, where what is to be inherited is no longer the "land" as such, but the entire renewed creation. As Wright has argued more pointedly,

> There can and must be no "Christian" theology of "holy places" (on the model or analogy of the "holy places" of a religion that has an essentially geographical base), any more than there can be a "Christian" theology of racial superiority on the model or analogy of a religion that has an essential racial base. To that extent, "Christian Zionism" is the geographical equivalent of a *soi-disant* "Christian" apartheid, and ought to be rejected as such.[35]

Christian Zionists are concerned that N. T. Wright's views are gaining more traction in evangelical circles and have targeted his views in their pushback against what they understand to be in line with classic supersessionism. David J. Rudolph and Mark S. Kinzer are but two of a number of scholars who have strongly critiqued Wright's position.[36]

Another such exegete is Bruce K. Waltke, who is probably better known in Christian Zionist circles than the British scholars mentioned above; his views are often considered more threatening because Waltke was once a leading figure in dispensationalist circles. Waltke is a former president of the Evangelical Theological Society and holds a ThD in New Testament from Dallas Theological Seminary and a PhD in Old Testament from Harvard. As a former professor of Old Testament at Dallas Theological Seminary, the key center of dispensationalist thinking, his move away from dispensationalism has been deeply problematic for many in the Christian Zionist community. In his writings he addresses the crucial issue of the relationship of the Old

---

[35]N. T. Wright, "Jerusalem in the New Testament," in *Jerusalem Past and Present in the Purposes of God*, ed. P. W. I. Walker (Cambridge: Tyndale House, 1992), 75. See also the debate between Kinzer and Wright at Samford University, September 19, 2019, titled "A Dialogue on the Meaning of Israel," YouTube, www.youtube.com/watch?v=qIBt64m-Py4.

[36]See David Rudolph, "Zionism in Pauline Literature," in McDermott, *New Christian Zionism*, 167-69, and especially Mark S. Kinzer, *Jerusalem Crucified, Jerusalem Risen: The Resurrected Messiah, the Jewish People, and the Land of Promise* (Portland, OR: Wipf and Stock, 2018), who also takes on Wright's views.

Testament promises to the Jews regarding the land, specifically the Abrahamic covenant. The word *'ereṣ* in Hebrew is one of the most frequently used words in the Old Testament and can mean either "land" or simply "earth." The crucial question arises as to the ongoing significance of the land promises in the New Testament. Have they been superseded by the new covenant, and are they now to be understood in reference to the church as the new Israel? Waltke has argued that what is striking about the New Testament is the Greek equivalent word for "land" is rarely used with reference to Israel, and—it should be noted—that when it is so used it occurs with reference to the history of Israel, never of a future prophecy for Israel. The land promises are never explicitly embraced or reiterate in the New.

Waltke argues that in the two New Testament passages pertaining to the land promises they have been interpreted to refer to the world. In Matthew 5:5, when Jesus quotes Psalm 37:11, "the meek shall inherit the land" (*'ereṣ*), many translators believe the term is to be interpreted as "earth": thus "Blessed are the meek, for they will inherit the earth." Waltke argues that the land promises have been universalized. So too in Romans 4:13, Paul says that God had promised Abraham and his offspring that he would inherit the world rather than the land. Again where one expects "the land" to be the promised inheritance, the promise is now deliberately much broader: the world, not the land. Waltke argues that the deliberate changing of focus indicates a theological shift from inheriting the land to inheriting the whole world. The promises are not abandoned, but they are now universalized, and no longer localized in Palestine.[37]

In 1992 in the first major book that outlined the progressive-dispensationalist approach, Waltke was invited to write a critical response, which was published in the volume *Dispensationalism, Israel and the Church: The Search for Definition* edited by Blaising and Bock. His detailed critique on exegetical grounds is a careful refutation of both traditional dispensationalism and progressive dispensationalism. In dealing with the key passage of Romans 9–11, Waltke summarizes his argument:

> If there be any passage where Paul should have singled out the land for special mention it is Romans 9–11. But nowhere, especially here . . . does Paul claim

---

[37]Bruce K. Waltke, "The Doctrine of the Land in the New Testament," *Crux* 53, no. 2 (Summer 2017): 2-9.

that the Jews will once again establish a nationalistic, territorial kingdom in the land. Dispensationalists put these words into the inspired apostle's mouth. In truth, none of the epistles—not those of Paul, of John, of Peter, or of the other Catholic Epistles of Hebrews and James—teach a future for national Israel in the land. The book of Hebrews denies it. The dispensationalist's case from the New Testament rests chiefly on the symbolic imagery of the Apocalypse, not on its clear letters and epistles.[38]

Scholars in a third group have written whole books critiquing Christian Zionism. For example, the evangelical New Testament scholar Gary Burge has written two books on the topic: *Whose Land, Whose Promise? What Christians Are Not Being Told About Israel and the Palestinians* (2003, rev. ed. 2013) and *Jesus and the Land: The New Testament Challenge to Holy Land Theology* (2010).[39] Timothy P. Weber, former professor at Denver Seminary and several other evangelical institutions, has written two significant works on the topic.[40] Two English evangelical Anglicans have also been important: Colin Chapman has written *Whose Promised Land? The Continuing Crisis over Israel and Palestine*,[41] and *Whose Holy City? Jerusalem and the Israeli-Palestinian conflict*;[42] and Stephen Sizer has written several books and maintains a virtual one-man crusade against Christian Zionism.[43]

DRAWING TOGETHER THE THREADS

This book has sought to trace the origins of Christian Zionism by first looking at the fifteen hundred years before the Reformation and examining Christian attitudes toward eschatology, the Jews, and the land. In doing so it found no evidence to support the claims that Christian Zionism existed as a political

---

[38]Bruce Waltke, "A Response," in *Dispensationalism, Israel and the Church: The Search for Definition*, ed. Craig A. Blaising and Darrell L. Bock (Grand Rapids, MI: Zondervan, 1992), 358.

[39]Gary Burge, *Whose Land, Whose Promise? What Christians Are Not Being Told About Israel and the Palestinians* (Cleveland: Pilgrim, 2003; rev. ed., 2013), and Burge, *Jesus and the Land: The New Testament Challenge to Holy Land Theology* (Grand Rapids, MI: Baker Academic, 2010).

[40]Timothy Weber's books include *Living in the Shadow of the Second Coming: American Premillennialism, 1875–1925* (New York: Oxford University Press, 1979; 2nd ed., Chicago: University of Chicago Press, 1987); and *On The Road to Armageddon: How Evangelicals Became Israel's Best Friends* (Grand Rapids, MI: Baker Academic, 2004).

[41]Colin Chapman, *Whose Promised Land? The Continuing Crisis over Israel and Palestine* (Leicester, UK: Inter-Varsity Press, 1995).

[42]Colin Chapman, *Whose Holy City? Jerusalem and the Israeli-Palestinian Conflict* (Oxford: Lion, 2004).

[43]Stephen Sizer, *Christian Zionism: Road Map to Armageddon* (Leicester, UK: Inter-Varsity Press, 2004), and Sizer, *Zion's Christian Soldiers* (Leicester, UK: Inter-Varsity Press, 2007).

movement seeking to return Jews to the Holy Land in this period. We then examined the movement known as "restorationism," which emerged in sixteenth-century Europe and came into its own in the Calvinistic wing of the Protestant reformation but did not find a home in Continental Lutheranism. Beginning with the Reformation, Luther's initial positive attitude toward the Jews turned sour as he grew increasingly unhappy with what he regarded as their continued obstinacy in refusing to convert to Christianity.

Restorationism was taken up by English Puritans, and by the mid-seventeenth century it began to shape English national identity. In the larger framework, restorationism was worked out in the conflict between Islam, Catholicism, and Protestantism, with the mission to the Jews being one of protecting them from Muslims and Catholics; working for their restoration to Palestine was understood to be a means of both blessing the Jews and of fulfilling biblical prophecy. These concerns influenced the readmission of Jews to England in the 1650s, some three and a half centuries after their expulsion in 1290. Many of its proponents promoted what I have termed a "teaching of love and esteem" toward the Jews, deliberately seeking to distance themselves from the "teaching of contempt," associated with late medieval Christendom. Most seventeenth-century Englishmen had never met a Jew but held on to the belief of an ongoing covenant with the Jews in spite of their unwillingness to embrace Christianity.

The belief spread to colonial America, where it became fused with Puritan hopes for the new land. At the same time as it was growing in the American colonies, a movement of renewal within German Lutheranism was emerging in the late seventeenth century that emphasized the central role that Jewish evangelism should play in Christian thinking, and it linked the fate of the church to the seriousness with which it took this task. The German Pietists devoted a great deal of energy devising practical ways to bring the much-despised Christian message to poor European Jews, pioneering evangelistic approaches that were adopted in the English-speaking world in the nineteenth century. The German Pietists profoundly affected Jewish-Christian relations through its philo-Semitism and its prioritizing of the evangelization of Jews.

Prophetic speculation was associated with the impact of the French Revolution, and in the late eighteenth and early nineteenth centuries the study

of prophecy did much to revive interest in Jewish restorationism. An incipient form of Christian Zionism emerged as a political force in England
in the 1830s under the guiding leadership of Anthony Ashley Cooper, the
seventh Earl of Shaftesbury, and the influence of historicist premillennialism
that was optimistic and reform-minded. Given Shaftesbury's important political connections with Lord Palmerston, the British foreign minister (and
later prime minister), important decisions were made that had long-term
impact: the establishment of a British diplomatic post in Jerusalem in 1838;
the setting up of a British-Prussian, Anglican-Lutheran bishopric in Jerusalem in 1841; and the building of an Anglican church there as well. These
actions helped to engender a scramble for power in Palestine and contributed to the modernization of the region.

American interest in prophecy increased dramatically in the nineteenth
century, being affected by historicist premillennialism from England.
Toward the end of the century another British product, dispensational
premillennialism, became an important influence in American Christianity.
Both movements were strongly restorationist, although often dispensationalism was sympathetic but generally much less engaged in politics.

The twentieth century saw a significant shift in the support base for
Christian Zionism from its Calvinist origins to the Pentecostal-Charismatic
movements that have engulfed both Protestant and Catholic Christianity
and created new, self-directed movements that have borrowed from earlier
Protestant teachings and created new global constituencies for Christian
Zionism. Even traditional dispensationalism has produced creative rethinking of the tradition that did so much from the late nineteenth century
to support Christian restorationism, and as it became a political concern,
Christian Zionism. These movements often configure their national identities around their support for Christian Zionism, embracing what they see
as their religious, philanthropic, and political duty to "bless Israel." The
appeal to Pentecostals and charismatics—as it was to seventeenth-century
Puritans, eighteenth-century American postmillennialists, and nineteenth-
century prophetic interpreters—is related to identity formation. By rooting
their movement in Jewish history and symbolically identifying with the Jews
as a people and Israel as a state, they find their roots going back centuries,
even millennia, in the faith of Abraham, Isaac, and Jacob and to what they

consider are eternal promises made to them regarding their homeland. But it is also an identity that is forward-looking, for Christian Zionists believe that they have the key to understanding the climax of history—that it is a grand, mysterious story involving God's dealings with his beloved people, the Jews, who are their "covenant brothers." Their identity is wrapped up in this narrative, and they believe that the best way that they can participate in the unfolding of history is by blessing Israel in whatever ways that are at hand to do so—whether by seeking to combat anti-Semitism or facilitating *aliyah* for Jews. In these ways they are expressing the identity that they have embraced, and are active participants in the final stage of human history.

Concluding Reflections

This book has touched on many complicated and controversial movements and perspectives that are difficult to track and understand. These movements have a strong popular appeal to many diverse constituencies across the globe and are of enormous importance, influencing Jewish-Christian relations, international politics, Muslim-Christian relations—the list goes on and on. In many ways Christian Zionism is a profoundly countercultural movement because it elevates religious concerns into the public square in ways that contradict the expected patterns of secular society. It often makes people uncomfortable—and not just Christians, but also Jews and secularists. And this book has argued that if it is to be taken seriously, one needs to pay attention to the theology and the cultural dynamics that both inform and inspire it.

Of the many things that I could reflect on at the end of this book, I will mention only three. The first is the uniqueness of the Jews. Anyone who studies Jewish history has to be perplexed at how a small group of people originating in the Middle East has survived as a distinct people for centuries in spite of exile, massive prejudice, misrepresentation, and murderous hatred. The very existence of an independent Jewish state is, perhaps, even more remarkable. In 1900 few would have taken seriously the idea that in the third decade of the twenty-first century one of the major fault lines in global politics would be a Jewish state in the Middle East, a strategic military power that punches well above its weight. In 1900 most Jews did not even want such a state, and though the Jewish religious tradition had for centuries longed for this Jewish return, it had been steadfastly opposed to human efforts to bring it about. Even in 1948 it is doubtful whether the majority of the Jews in the world supported the notion.

The second reflection is on the importance of the philo-Semitism of so many of the restorationists and Christian Zionists. While the professed love of the Jews continues to be met with suspicion and skepticism by many Jews, the "teaching of love and esteem" (and now "blessing") that this book has posited has been a major factor in both the rise of Christian Zionism and in shifting Christian attitudes toward the Jews on the part of many Christians. It is, of course, impossible to measure its impact, but the evidence is increasingly clear as to its historical importance. In spite of its being widely discounted by many Jews, it would appear to be a major factor shaping Jewish-Christian relations in the past several centuries, and to have played a significant role in Gentile support for the establishment and sustaining of the Israeli state.

My third reflection is that this "teaching of love, esteem, and blessing" that has arisen out of reflection on the Christian Scriptures should not neglect the obligations inherent in Judaism cited by Rabbi Hertz in his comments on the Balfour Declaration in 1917 cited above when he wrote,

> I welcome the reference to the civil and religious rights of the existing non-Jewish communities in Palestine. It is but a translation of the basic principles of the Mosaic legislation: "And if a stranger sojourn with thee in your land, ye shall not vex him. But the stranger that dwelleth with you shall be unto you as one born among you, and thou shalt love him as thyself." (Lev 19:33, 34.)[44]

The Old Testament has much to say about justice and mercy, and loving your neighbor as yourself is a key theme in the teaching of Jesus. Justice, mercy, and love need to be central in all Christian theology, including Christian Zionism.

As one reflects on Christian Zionism over five centuries, it is clear that it has no fixed theological home and is dependent on no single schema related to prophetic understandings of Scripture. Thus the history of Christian Zionism is one both of novelty in that it only arose in the sixteenth century and has morphed in a number of ways over time, and of profound instability in that it has no fixed theological address. As Aron Engberg has observed, it

---

[44]Christopher Sykes, *Two Studies in Virtue* (London: Collins, 1951), 222.

is now a global religious movement and must be understood dynamically as a movement, in the sense that it is "on the move."[45] Christian Zionism thus has a very convoluted history. Over the past five centuries it has been associated with very different theological frameworks and prophetic views. It is a movement that continues to morph in the multiple locations around the world where it is being embraced. There is evidence that it has at times contributed to the secularizing of evangelicalism and led toward a "dual-covenant" teaching, with a few of its leaders moving away from the apostle Paul's insistence on the gospel being offered "to the Jew first." Given evangelicals' commitment to the authority of Scripture, it is likely that future generations of evangelicals will subject its theology to intense scrutiny to see whether they consider it to be something that grows out of a fully orbed, biblical theology, or whether it has arisen in particular historical settings and through particular readings of Scripture, and no longer carries the persuasive power that it once did. The question of its validity is sure to generate ongoing debate among Christians.

---

[45] Aron Engberg, "'A Fool for Christ': Sense-Making and Negotiation of Identity in the Life Story of a Christian Soldier," in *Comprehending Christian Zionism: Perspectives in Comparison*, ed. Goran Gunner and Robert O. Smith (Minneapolis: Fortress, 2014), 30.

GENERAL INDEX

Abdul Hamid II, Sultan, 127
Abraham, 18-21, 70-1, 76, 109, 210, 216, 221, 244, 261, 307, 314, 327, 347, 355, 358
Abrahamic covenant, 19, 72, 136, 355
Abulafia, Anna Sapir, 32, 34-37
Aden, 340
Advent Testimony and Preparation Movement, 194
Adventism, 92-3, 96, 133
Adversus Iudeos, 38
Ahmadinejad, Mahmoud, 286
Al-Husseini, Mohammed Amin, 227, 230-32
Albright, William Foxwell, 253
Albury Conference, 94-95
Alexander II, Czar, 120-21
Alexander II, Pope, 34-35
Alexander, Michael Solomon, 114, 120, 130
Aliyah, 156, 165, 294-95
Allenby, Sir Edmund, 164, 190, 219
Allis, Oswald T., 251
Allon, General Yigal, 220
Alsted, Johann Heinrich, 69-70
Ambrose, Bishop of Milan, 31
American Board of Commissioners for Foreign Missions, 208
American Board of Missions to the Jews, 208
American Christian Palestine Committee, 224
American Council for Judaism, 213
American Institute of Holy Land Studies, 255, 264
American Israel Public Affairs Committee (AIPAC), 256
American Jewish Committee, 254, 256, 267-68, 270
American Palestine Council, 224

American Revolution, 86, 88, 90
American Zionist Committee on Public Affairs, 256
amillennial, 28, 31, 38, 45, 49, 64, 65, 146
Anabaptist, 49, 51
Anglican, 2, 58, 74, 89, 93-94, 97, 99, 104, 106, 117, 120, 122, 135, 142-43, 180-81, 212, 338, 350-53, 356, 358
Anglican Church in Jerusalem. *See* Christ Church, Jerusalem
Anglican-Lutheran bishopric, 117, 120, 358
Anglo-American Committee on Palestine, 228
Anglo-Catholicism, 129
anti-Arab, 210, 221, 308
anti-Catholicism, 5, 48, 54-55, 63, 130, 142, 187, 336
anti-Judaic, 25, 78, 115, 312
anti-Judaism, 45, 247, 312
anti-Semitism, 9-10, 12, 34-5, 37, 45, 108, 111-12, 122-23, 155, 162, 168, 170, 177, 179, 201-4, 206-9, 212-13, 234, 246-47, 253, 255, 271, 277, 281, 285, 290, 297, 310, 312, 314, 327, 336, 340, 348, 359
anti-Zionism (Jewish), 12, 167, 181, 184, 212, 213, 224-25, 256
anti-Zionism (non-Jewish), 231, 255, 271, 340
Antichrist, 46, 62, 89-90, 141-42, 148, 186-87, 194, 196, 209, 266, 278
apostles, modern-day, 330-31, 343
Apostles' Creed, 26
Arabs, 15, 40, 159, 166, 168-69, 170-71, 173, 176, 182-5, 210, 216, 217-55, 257-58, 260, 270-71, 274, 280, 285,

296-97, 302, 307-8, 319, 325, 327, 350-51
Christians, 325, 350
refugees, 237-38, 240
Arab Higher Committee, 230, 233
Arab Liberation Army, 230, 234, 236
Arab revolts, 168, 173, 183, 222, 227, 231
Arabic language, 35, 83
Ariel, Yaakov, 1, 6, 78, 151-52, 156, 190, 203-4, 208, 243, 257, 260, 263, 268, 280, 293, 298-99, 303
Arimathea, Joseph of, 54
Armageddon, 141, 163, 187, 288, 297, 326
Armstrong, Herbert W., 305
Ashley, Lord. *See* Shaftesbury, Lord
Asquith, Anthony, 171-72, 178
Assemblies of God, 323, 328-30
assimilationists (Jewish), 121, 158, 166-67, 176, 178, 181, 204, 224
Assyrians, 22
Ateek, Naim, 350-53
Attlee, Clement, 227
Augustine, 20, 28, 31-35, 41, 45-46, 49, 52, 57, 65, 68
Australia, 15, 143
Austro-Hungarian Empire, 172, 188
Aviner, Rabbi Shlomo, 302
Awad, Alex, 237
Azusa Street revival, 295, 324-26, 328
B'nai B'rith, 255
Babylon, 22, 49, 62, 89, 278-79
Babylonian Talmud, 9
Baillie, Robert, 55
Bakker, Jim and Tammy Faye, 275

Bale, John, 54
Balfour Declaration, 4, 11, 111,
118, 121, 131, 164-85, 188, 190,
200, 216, 242, 360
Balfour, James Arthur, 164,
165, 170-71, 174-75, 178,
180-82, 219
Balkans, 227
Baptists, 58, 75, 98, 133, 143,
174, 180, 189, 193, 197, 204,
207, 214, 251, 264, 276, 280,
340
Bar Kokhba Revolt, 23, 25,
300
Bar-Yosef, Eitan, 175
Barak, Ehud, 230, 283
Barbary Wars, 88
Barnes, George, 180-81
Barnhouse, Donald Grey, 240
Barrows, Cliff, 268
Barth, Karl, 211
Basel, 48, 84, 126
Basel Evangelical Mission, 124
Battle of Tours, 40
Baxter, Richard, 73
Bebbington, David, 96, 98-99
Begin, Menachem, 12, 228,
235, 268, 273, 301
Belorussia, 121
Ben-Gurion, David, 12, 14-15,
170, 230, 233, 236, 238,
250-51, 295
Ben-Yehuda, Eliezer, 170
Bengel, Johann Albrecht, 84
Berlin, 84, 158, 264
Bernadotte, Count, 237
Bernard of Clairvaux, 33, 37
Bethlehem, 233, 251
Bethlehem Bible College, 252
Beza, Theodore, 49, 52, 54-55,
64, 101-2
Bible Institute of Los Angeles,
144, 154, 161, 205, 210, 222
Bicheno, James, 93
Bickersteth, Edward, 93, 97,
99, 106-10, 113-15, 119,
128-29, 131, 133, 216
Bickle, Mike, 333-34
Billy Graham Evangelistic
Association, 264, 267
Biltmore Program, 225, 228
Blackstone, William E.,

153-60, 162, 188-90, 203-4,
207-8, 210-11, 214-15, 245,
266, 273, 304, 321-22,
325-26
Blackstone Memorial, 158, 159
Blaising, Craig A., 344-45,
355
Blessing Israel, 68, 267, 284,
289, 296, 298, 313-14, 318-19,
328, 336, 339, 357, 359-60
Bloch, Ruth, 90
Blumhardt, Johann Christian,
124
Bock, Darrell L., 344-50
Boettner, Loraine, 69
Bogue, David, 104
Bolshevik, 170, 183, 195, 206,
208
Bolsonaro, Jair, 319-20
Bonaparte, Napoleon, 95, 133
Bonar Law, Andrew, 178,
180-81
Borrhaus, Martin, 49-50
Boyer, Paul, 133, 143, 163,
201-3, 278, 307-8
Brandeis, Louis D., 159,
188-89, 213
Branham, William, 329
Brazil, 317-19, 330
Brethren movement. *See*
Plymouth Brethren
Brightman, Thomas, 61,
64-67, 87, 107, 136
British consulate in Jerusalem,
117
British Empire, 111, 114, 170
British Israelite, 323, 343
British Mandate, 12, 184
British national identity, 60,
116, 179
Brog, David, 227, 230-31, 235,
241, 283
Brookes, James H., 144-45,
147-49, 200, 205
Brown, David, 29
Bruce, F. F., 345
Bryan, William Jennings, 146,
196
Bucer, Martin, 49-50, 102
Buckingham, Jamie, 291
Bulgaria, 158, 172
Bunyan, John, 60

Burge, Gary, 352, 356
Burghley, Lord, 174
Bush, George H. W., 245, 277,
280
Bush, George W., 280, 287
Byron, Lord, 96
Byzantium, 33, 40-41
Caird, G. B., 345
Cairo, 226, 231, 318, 338
Callenberg, Johann Heinrich,
83
Calman, E. S., 130
Calvary Chapel, Coast Mesa,
California, 305, 330
Calvin, John, 48-52, 54,
101-2
Calvinism, Calvinist, 6, 45,
48-49, 52, 56, 58, 69, 75, 85,
99, 104, 116, 129, 143, 174,
180-81, 323, 336, 357-58
Cambridge, University of, 69,
73
Cameron, Robert, 158
Camp David, 271, 314
Canada, 143, 328, 335, 341
Cape Town, 263, 334
Capito, Wolfgang, 48, 55
Carenen, Caitlin, 211, 259, 314
Carpathia, Nicolae Jetty, 278
Carpenter, Joel, 203
Carson, Edward, 180
Carter, Jimmy, 271
Cartwright, Ebenezer and
Joanna, 71
Case, Shirley Jackson, 192
Catholic Apostolic Church,
97, 328
Celtic fringe, 104, 129, 180
Central Powers, 167, 172
Chafer, Lewis Sperry, 239
Chalmers, Thomas, 97
Chapman, Colin, 352, 356
Chapman, J. Wilbur, 147, 149
Charisma Magazine, 290
charismatic movement,
275-76, 294-95, 299, 316-17,
320-21, 323-24, 327-33,
335-37, 339, 340, 343, 358
Charles I (king of England),
61, 62, 64, 70
Charles II (king of England),
72-73

Chazan, Robert, 23-25, 33
Chesterton, G. K., 5
Chicago, 145, 152-57, 204, 208
Chicago Hebrew Mission in Behalf of Israel, 155
Chicago Sinai Congregation, 157
Chief Rabbinate, 15
Chiluba, Frederick, President of Zambia, 319
China, 118, 322
China Inland Mission, 118, 198, 322
Christ Church, Jerusalem, 117, 297
Christendom, 33-36 38-39, 42, 44-45, 47, 95, 150, 213, 339, 357
Christensen, Lydia, 335
Christerson, Brad, 330-33
Christian anti-internationalism, 193-94
Christian Broadcasting Network, 276
Christian Century, 192, 211-12, 248
Christian Coalition, 272, 277-78
Christian Council on Palestine, 224
Christian Growth Ministries, 338
Christian News from Israel, 252, 266
Christian Observer, 100
Christian Zionism definition, 2-3, 128
Christian-Jewish relations, 17, 24, 27, 84, 211, 260-61, 264-65, 357, 359-60
Christianity and Crisis, 258
Christians United for Israel, 6, 231, 281-85, 287, 289, 302, 310
Chrysostom, John, 31
church fathers, 23, 25-26, 28-30, 49
Church Missionary Society, 116, 124
Church of Scotland, 97-99
Church of the Holy Sepulchre, 297

Churchill, Winston, 218-19, 227
Cisling, Aahron, 241
Claphamite, 100, 106
Clark, Christopher, 82, 119
Clarke, Samuel, 73
Clinton, Bill, 280, 287
Cohen, Jeremy, 32
Cohn, Joseph, 208
Cold War, 195, 253, 270, 275, 278-79, 286
Coleridge, Samuel Taylor, 96
Collegium Orientale Theologicum, 83
Colley, Linda, 60
Colonial Bank, 160
Colonial Office, 219
Columbus, Christopher, 442
Communist, 15, 163, 194-95, 274, 307
concentration camps, 226
Congregationalist, 87-89, 197
Constantine, 31
Constantinople, 41, 173, 183
conversionist sermons, 39
Cook, Charles C., 205
Cotton, John, 87
Cousinhood, the, 166
Crimean War, 162
Criswell, W. A., 251
Crome, Andrew, 6, 7, 21, 59, 64, 65, 72-75, 108, 110-11, 113, 114, 116, 136, 261, 319
crusades, 34, 42, 47, 219, 280-81
Cumming, John, 162
Curzon, Lord, 180-81, 218
Cyrus Foundation, 294
Cyrus, 22, 156, 214
Czechoslovakia, 233
Dallas Theological Seminary, 239-40, 259, 269, 345-46, 354
Damascus Blood Libel Affair, 122, 165
Daniel, book of, 46, 62, 71, 95, 135, 137-38, 141-42, 162, 262
Darby, John Nelson, 4, 8, 118, 132, 134-46, 147-51, 153-55, 157, 160, 162, 202, 241, 244, 259, 284, 304, 321, 326, 345, 347, 349

Davies, W. D., 353
day-year theory, 71, 137, 142
day of Pentecost, 138, 190, 326
Dayan, Moshe, 220, 303
de Gaulle, Charles, 246
de Labadie, Jean, 48
Dearborn Independent, 206
Deir Yassin, 235-36, 250
deists, 74
Denver Seminary, 356
Dio Cassius, 23
Diocletian, 62
disabilities, Jewish, 107, 177
dispensational premillennialism, 4, 8, 86, 97-98, 112, 118-19, 132-63, 186, 188, 193-200, 203-4, 208-10, 220-21, 223-24, 229, 239, 244-46, 248, 251, 257, 259, 263, 267-69, 271-73, 276-79, 281, 284, 287, 297, 304, 306, 308, 310, 315, 321-23, 325-26, 332-33, 335, 340-42, 344-49, 353-56, 358
dispensations, 135-37, 139, 150
Dome of the Rock, 305, 327
Dominicans, 35, 37
dominion theology, 277
Draxe, Thomas, 68
Drummond, Henry, 94
du Plessis, David, 343
dual covenant theology, 254, 265, 311-12, 361
Dunant, Jean-Henri, 3
Durbin, Sean, 4, 6, 244, 281-82, 284, 286-87, 302
Dwight, Timothy, 90
Ebenezer Fund, 294
Eckstein, Rabbi Yichel, 277, 290
Edwards, Jonathan, 48, 82, 85, 87-90, 333, 344
Ehle, Carl, 30, 214-15
Eisenhower, Dwight, 225, 249-50, 252, 255, 257
El-Aqsa Mosque, 305
"elect nation" idea, 7-8, 11, 54, 58-59, 61, 87, 102, 114, 138, 156, 191, 214, 246, 261, 273, 318-19
Eliot, George, 3
Elizabeth, Charlotte, 115-16

Elliott, E. B., 94
England, 8, 34, 36, 44, 52-55,
    58-61, 64, 66-67, 69, 71-74,
    76-77, 85-87, 89, 90-91, 94,
    99, 107-8, 110-11, 114-16, 120,
    124-25, 132-33, 165, 167, 169,
    177, 180, 207, 222, 318, 352,
    357-58
Engle, Lou, 332
English Civil War, 64
Enlightenment, 83
Erdman, W. J., 146, 158
ethno-nationalism, 8, 91
Eusebius of Caesaria, 25, 28
Evangelical Alliance, 115
evangelical identity, 7, 112-13,
    128, 209, 310
Evangelical Theological
    Society, 344, 354
expulsions of Jews, 31, 37, 45,
    55, 72, 337, 357
Faber, George Stanley, 93
Faisal, Prince, 168-69
Falwell, Jerry, 243, 259, 265,
    271-76, 283, 291
Feast of Tabernacles, 265,
    291-93, 317, 340, 342-43
Federal Council of Churches,
    189, 193
Feinstein, Marnin, 159
Feldman, Rachel Z., 306
Ferdinand, King of Spain, 42
Finch, Sir Henry, 61, 66
Finn, Elizabeth, 105, 124
Finn, James, 124
First Zionist Conference, 3, 5,
    158, 160, 300
Foreign Office, British,
    166-68, 170, 219
Fourth Lateran Council, 1215,
    34-35, 39
Foxe, John, 54, 60, 63
Franciscans, 35, 37-39
Francke, August Hermann, 81,
    83
Frederick (king of Prussia),
    80
Frederick I (grand duke of
    Baden), 125-26, 214
Fremantle, William, 108
French Revolution, 74, 92-96,
    112, 129, 132, 257, 357

Frere, James Hadley, 93-94
Freston, Paul, 316-17, 319
Frey, Joseph, 103, 130
Friedman, Isaiah, 111
Fruchtenbaum, Arnold, 346
Fuller Seminary, 248, 251
fundamentalist movement,
    146, 161, 191-93, 195-98,
    200-203, 206-9, 211, 244,
    248, 259, 266, 272, 302
Fundamentals, The, 155, 161,
    322
futurist eschatology, 97, 118,
    132, 134, 135, 140-42, 148,
    154, 157, 162, 199, 245
Gaebelein, Arno C., 152-53,
    157-59, 160-62, 187, 191, 194,
    197, 206, 208, 241, 268
Gaebelein, Frank, 210
Garden Tomb, 291, 297
Gascoyne-Cecil, Lady
    Blanche, 297
Gawler, Lawrence, 3, 297
Gaza Strip, 258, 297, 301-2
Geneva Bible, 52-53, 102-3
George III (king of England),
    90
Gesenius, Wilhelm, 162
Gill, John, 75
Gillet, Lev, 5
Global South, 9, 316-17, 319,
    324
glocalization, 317-18
Gog, 46, 65, 66, 162, 196, 274,
    278
Golan Heights, 258
Goldfoot, Stanley, 305
Goldman, Samuel, 6, 91, 252,
    256, 261, 287
Goldman, Shalom, 1, 6, 9, 10,
    14, 126, 218
Goodwin, Thomas, 70
Goren, Rabbi Shlomo, 303
Gorenberg, Gershom, 300
Gottheil, Richard, 3
Gouge, William, 66-67
Graham, Billy, 248, 251, 254,
    256-57, 261, 267
Grand Sanhedrin, 10, 176
Great Schism of 1054, 40
Gregory IX (pope), 36
Gregory the Great (pope), 32

Gush Emunim, 301
Hadith, 42
Haganah, 218, 220, 222, 228,
    232-33
Hagar, 210
Hagee, John, 5-6, 244-45,
    264-66, 275-76, 282-85, 294,
    302, 309
Haldeman, Isaac H., 204-5
Halle, 80, 82-83
Halperin, Samuel, 214-15
Haman, 286
Har Herzl, 297
Hardinge, Lord, 185
Haredim, 14-15
Harrison, Benjamin, 158, 189,
    210
Hasidim, 300
Hatikvah, 14
Hebrew Roots movement, 291,
    310, 343
Hebrew University, 210, 319,
    335
Hechler, William, 124-28, 160,
    200, 214-15, 264, 266, 285,
    311
heeloni, 23
Henderson, Arthur, 180
Henry IV (Holy Roman
    Emperor), 34
Henry, Carl F., 248
Henry, Matthew, 102
Herschell, Ridley Haim, 130
Hertz, Joseph Herman, 217,
    242, 360
Hertzberg, Arthur, 260, 360
Herzl, Theodor, 2-3, 12, 120,
    126-28, 159, 165, 174, 188, 214
Hibbat Zion, 125
Hill, Christopher, 39
Hilsden, Wayne, 265
Hirsch, Emil G., 157-59
Hirshfeld, Philip, 130
historicist premillennialism,
    27, 69, 87, 92-99, 109, 113,
    118, 133-35, 138-39, 148-49,
    151, 199, 245, 276, 321, 326,
    333, 346, 358
Hitchin, Neil, 74
Hitler, Adolf, 12, 196-97,
    207-9, 225, 239
Hixson, Walter, 225, 250

Hodge, Cleveland H., 183
Holmes, Nathaniel, 70
Holocaust, 212-13, 227, 231,
 234-35, 239-40, 247, 255, 258,
 298, 310, 313, 317, 335-36
holy days, Jewish, 16
Hope of Israel Mission, 152, 159
Hovevei Zion, 300
Hovsha, Joshua, 301
Hummel, Daniel G., 6, 252,
 254-55, 257, 261, 263-64,
 267, 270, 273, 275, 277, 296,
 298, 314, 317
Hus, Jan, 39, 50
Hussein, Grand Sharif, 170,
 173, 183-85
Husseini clan, 223
 See also Al-Husseini,
 Mohammed Amin
Hyamson, Albert, 179
Ice, Thomas D., 30
Imber, Naphtali Herz, 14
Independent Network
 Charismatics, 320, 331-33
Innocent III (pope), 36, 39
Institutum Judaicum, 83
International Christian
 Embassy Jerusalem, 265,
 291-92, 317, 337, 340, 343
International Declaration of
 Human Rights, 5
International Fellowship of
 Christians and Jews, 277,
 283, 289-90, 294
International House of Prayer,
 333-34
Irgun, 226, 228, 231, 235, 273
Ironside, Harry A., 208
Irving, Edward, 93-94, 96-97,
 139, 328
Isabella (queen of Spain), 42
Islam, 11, 33, 40-42, 45, 47-48,
 63, 66, 70, 76
Israel Defense Forces, 15, 218,
 220, 241, 249-59, 270
Israel Emergency Fund, 260
Israel of God, 17, 19, 22, 52
Israeli independence, 4, 216,
 230, 239, 241, 244, 295, 304,
 313
Israeli Ministry of Tourism,
 296-97

Jabotinsky Award, 273
Jacobs, Cindy, 331
Jaffa, 124, 232, 234
James I (king of England),
 61-62, 64, 66, 74
Jenkins, Jerry B., 278
Jerusalem, 9, 14, 22-25, 27, 29,
 31, 41-42, 49, 65-66, 85, 98,
 111, 114, 117, 120, 124-27, 141,
 154, 156-57, 164, 187-88,
 190-91, 200, 218-19, 228, 230,
 232-35, 251, 255, 258-59,
 261-62, 264-65, 278, 282,
 284, 286, 291-92, 297, 303,
 305, 308, 314-15, 319-20, 325,
 327, 335, 337, 343, 346, 349,
 350, 352-53, 358
Jerusalem Post, 265
Jew Bill of 1753, 74
Jewish Agency in Palestine,
 226
Jewish converts, 103, 115, 117,
 130, 177, 201, 299, 310, 345
Jewish Era, The, 155
Jewish nation, 56, 65, 87,
 126-27, 161, 175-77, 185, 338
Jewish national identity, 130,
 177, 262
Jewish nationalism, 2, 10, 121,
 126-27, 130, 200, 226, 262,
 308
Jewish Readmission to
 England, 44, 71-72, 357
Jewish-Christian relations.
 See Christian-Jewish
 relations
Jews, American, 168, 189-90,
 201, 213, 215, 224-25, 250,
 252-53, 256, 258, 260-61,
 273-74, 277, 299, 309, 312
Jews, Russian, 10, 15, 120-25,
 127, 156-58, 162-63, 165-73,
 179, 202, 218, 290
Jews' Society. *See* LSJ
Joachim of Fiore, 38-39, 42,
 46, 49
Jocz, Jakob, 254
Johnson, Bill, 332
Johnson, Lyndon B., 255
Judeo-Christianity, 252-56,
 281, 285-86, 342
Julian (Roman emperor), 30

just war theory, 41
Juster, Dan, 333-34
Justin Martyr, 29
Justinian (Byzantine
 emperor), 95
Kashrut, 15
Kaunda, Kenneth, 319
Kennedy, John F., 225, 255
Keswick Holiness teaching,
 98, 118, 194, 188, 322
Kibbutzim, 233-35
Kibya. *See* Qibya massacre
King David Hotel bombing,
 228
King's Business, 187, 205, 210,
 222
Kinzer, Mark S., 354
Kishinev pogrom, 218
Kochav, Sarah, 175
Koestler, Arthur, 219, 225
Kollek, Teddy, 292
Kook, Rabbi Abraham Isaac,
 12, 301
Kook, Rabbi Zvi Yehuda, 301
Kromminga, D. H., 27
LaHaye, Tim, 278
Lambie, T. A., 229
land for peace, 271, 292
land promises, Old
 Testament, 18, 56, 262, 351,
 355
Langham Partnership
 International, 353
Lansdowne, Lord, 165
Late Great Planet Earth, 147,
 245, 268, 275, 278-79, 295,
 304
Latter Rain movement, 295,
 326-29, 331-32, 343
Lawrence, T. E., 184, 219
League of Nations, 149, 164,
 183-84, 193-94, 228, 279
Left Behind series, 278, 304
Lehi, 226, 228, 231, 233, 235,
 304
Leket, 293
Lewis, Bernard, 311
Liberty University, 273
Likud Party, 273, 301, 314
Lindsey, Hal, 147, 245, 268-69,
 275, 295
literalism, 101

Littell, Franklin H., 212
Lloyd George, David, 170-75, 178, 180-82, 218-19
London Missionary Society, 104
London Society for the Promotion of Christianity Amongst the Jews. *See* LSJ
Louise (grand duchess of Baden), 125
LSJ, 103-6, 109-11, 113-16, 121-25
Ludwig (prince of Baden), 125
Luther, Martin, 44-46, 48-52, 54, 62, 64, 81-82, 101-2, 107, 115, 310, 357
Lutheranism, 45, 48-49, 51, 55, 78-82, 117, 120, 125, 193, 204, 336, 357-58
Macintosh, C. H., 139
MacMichael, Sir Harold, 226
Magen David Adom, 293
Magnus, Laurie, 177
Magog, 46, 65, 66, 162, 278
Maimonides, Moses, 36
Malachy, Yona, 262
Mansion House, 123
Mapai, 238
Marian exiles, 52, 54
Maritain, Jacques, 5, 246
Marsden, George, 196
Marsh, Catherine, 116
Marshall, George, 213
Mary I (queen of England), 52
Masorti Judaism, 52
Massachusetts Bay Colony, 86
Matar, Nabil I., 29, 54, 57, 63
Mather, Cotton, 48, 88
Mather, Increase, 87-88, 108
Mathews, Shailer, 189, 192
Matthews, Mark, 194
McCaul, Alexander, 104-5, 123-24, 254
McDermott, Gerald R., 19, 344, 346
McGinn, Bernard, 46
McKinley, William, 159
McMahon, Henry, 185
McNeile, Hugh, 114, 129
Mede, Joseph, 61, 69-70, 88
Meir, Golda, 12, 267-68
Melanchton, Phillip, 49

Melchett, Lord, 327
Mendelssohn, Moses, 11
Meredith, John L., 240
Mesopotamia, 194
Messianic Jews, 103, 183, 299, 334, 337, 346
Messianic Judaism, 299, 337, 340, 345
Methodists, 143, 180, 212
Meyer, F. B., 194
Meyer, Louis, 161
Miles, Frederick J., 202
millenarian, 24, 26, 28, 30, 49, 51, 57, 61, 70, 73, 87, 90, 92, 94-95, 143, 146, 157, 175, 190, 197-200, 210
Miller, Perry, 88
Miller, William, 133
Millerites, 133-34, 199
Milner, Lord Alfred, 178, 180-81
Milton Stewart Evangelistic Fund, 76
Milton, John, 76
Minerbi, Sergio, 5
Mishmar Ha'emek, 236
Mishnah, 304
missionary, 39, 72, 80-84, 103-5, 109-10, 114, 116, 118, 121-22, 124, 146, 155, 159, 183, 197-98, 202, 220, 263-64, 299, 322, 325, 327, 335
Mitnagdim, 300
Mizrahi, 12
Mohammed, 154
Molodowsky, Kadya, 13
Montagu, Edwin Samuel, 178, 181
Montefiore, Claude, 177
Montgomery, Bernard, 338
Moody, Dwight L., 144, 146, 154, 204, 267
Moody Bible Institute, 144, 149, 154, 198, 206-7, 209-10, 251
Moody Church, Chicago, 208
Moody Monthly, 198, 208, 210
Moorehead, William G., 158
Moral Majority, 245, 271-72, 274-75, 277
Morales, Jimmy, 319
More, Henry, 73

Morgan, J. P., 159
Morgenstern, Ari, 283
Mormons, 272
Morris, Benny, 231, 234-38
Mosaic covenant, 19
Mosque of Omar, 309
Mount Scopus, 235
Moyne, Lord (Walter Guinness), 226
Munich Olympics, 271
Muntzer, Thomas, 51
Muslim, 5-6, 33-35, 40-42, 48, 51, 63, 88, 163, 180, 218-19, 223, 227-28, 255, 280-81, 292, 303, 305-6, 309, 311, 321, 325, 340, 351, 357, 359
Muslim Religious Council, Jerusalem, 303
Mussolini, Benito, 196
Myland, David Wesley, 326
mythical Zionists, 304
Nashashibis, 222
Nasser, Gamal Abdel, 250, 257-58
National Association of Evangelicals, 198, 252, 272, 275, 279
National Club, 123
National Council of Churches, 198
Naturalization Bill, 74
Nazi-Soviet Non-Aggression Pact, 197
Nebuchadnezzar, 22
Nefesh b'Nefesh, 294
Negev, 233
Nehemiah, 22
Nemeth, Sandor, 330
Netanyahu, Benjamin, 16, 220
Netanyahu, Benzion, 220
Netanyahu, Johnathan, 220, 282-83, 299
Netherlands, 71
New Apostolic Reformation, 331, 342-43
New Christian Right, 272
New Historians, 231, 241, 349-50
New World Order, 277, 279
New York City, 145, 159, 197, 204, 225, 246, 254, 270
New York State, 133, 214

New York Times, 3, 277
Newberg, Eric, 325, 335, 340-41
Newton, Benjamin Wills, 157
Newton, Bishop Thomas, 75
Newton, Isaac, 73
Niagara Bible Conference, 144, 158
Nicene-Constantinopolitan creed, 26
Nicholas I (czar), 121, 123
Nicholson, Sir Arthur, 166
Niebuhr, Reinhold, 211, 224, 258
Nigeria, 317, 321
Night Squad, 220
Nixon, Richard, 267-68, 270
Noahides, 343
Noll, Mark, 87, 90
Norris, J. Frank, 207
Nostra Aetate, 6, 247-48
Nyack College, 154
O'Brierne, Hugh James, 169
Obama, Barak, 281-82
October Revolution, 183
Oesterreicher, John M., 247-48
Oliphant, Laurence and Alice, 15
Olson, Jason, 256, 258
one-worldism, 277, 279
Onslow, Earl of, 166
Origen of Alexandria, 25, 28
Ottoman Empire, 11, 46, 63, 67, 83, 89, 108, 114-17, 127, 133, 158, 162-63, 166-68, 170, 172-73, 182-85, 187-88, 190, 263, 300
Oumansoff, Raissa, 246
Our Hope magazine, 159-60, 187, 206, 210
Owen, John, 66-67
Palestine Exploration Fund, 119
Palestine Liberation Organization, 351
Palestine Mandate, 164, 183, 210, 223, 228-29
Palmerston, Lord, 115, 358
papacy, 34, 36-37, 39, 45-46, 54, 60-63, 67, 70, 81, 95, 133, 142
Paradise Regained, 76

Parkes, James, 214, 247
Parr, Elnathan, 55
partition, 183, 217, 219, 223, 229, 230-34, 237-39, 351
Passfield White Paper, 219, 337
Patterson, John Henry, 220
Paul VI (pope), 247
Paul, Saint, 17-22, 24-25, 52-53, 62, 68, 79, 129, 138, 309-10, 345, 352, 354-55, 356, 361
Pawson, David, 334, 337, 340-41
Peasants' War of 1524–1525, 51
Peel Commission, 223
Pence, Mike, 282, 287
Pentecostal Assemblies of Canada, 328
Pentecostal Evangel, 222, 240
Pentecostalism, 192, 210, 251, 265, 275, 283, 295, 316-17, 319-21, 323-39, 343, 358
Perkins, William, 55
Perry, Yaron, 122
Persico, Tomer, 304
Pew Forum, 320
Philadelphia, 145, 190, 240
Philippines, 321, 343
philo-Semitism, 79, 92, 116, 128-29, 133, 201, 325, 336, 340, 357, 360
Pia Desideria, 79, 83
Picot, Francois Georges, 172, 183
Pieritz, G. W., 130
Pietism, 8, 77-85, 102-3, 110, 113, 116-17, 124-25, 130, 155, 201, 263, 266, 293, 298, 309-10, 357
Pietsch, Brendan, 144-45, 147, 151, 269, 322
pilgrims, Holy Land, 40-41
Pinsker, Judah Lieb, 125
Pius V (pope), 60
Plan D, 234
Platonism, 339
Plymouth Brethren / Christian Brethren, 4, 118, 134-35, 139, 142, 145, 146, 150, 157, 220, 345
pogroms, 10, 121, 156, 166, 218

Poland, 84, 105
Pompeo, Mike, 282
popery, 75, 129
population transfer, 241
postmillennialism, 28, 61, 63-65, 69-71, 79, 87, 89, 93-94, 96-98, 100, 112-13, 133, 135-36, 139, 146, 149, 151, 196, 199, 276, 333-34, 356
posttribulation rapture, 27, 157-58, 161, 276, 335, 340-41
Prayer Meeting Revival, 118, 142
premillennialism, historic/ historical/covenantal, 27, 333, 335, 340, 342
premillennialism, historicist, 27, 69, 87, 92-95, 97-99, 109, 113, 118, 133-35, 138-39, 148-49, 151, 199, 245, 276, 321, 326, 333, 346, 358
Presbyterian, 97, 99, 143-44, 146, 174, 180, 183, 189, 194, 197, 205, 211, 240
preterism, 27-28
Prince, Derek, 330, 334-40, 343
Princeton Seminary, 146
pro-Israel lobby in US, 188, 190, 213-14, 225, 229, 246, 250, 269-72, 274, 282, 285, 287, 289
Pro-Palestine Federation of America, 224
progressive dispensationalism, 343-46, 348, 355
Prophetic Bible Conferences, 143
prosperity gospel, 283-84, 319, 339
Protestant liberalism, 99
Protocols of the Elders of Zion, 206-8
Prussia, 80, 124-26, 358
Puritans, 8, 48, 52-53, 56-73, 75-77, 82, 84-93, 101-3, 107-8, 130, 156, 191, 310, 318, 336, 357-58
Qibya massacre, 249-50, 256
Quakers, 76
Qur'an, 11, 42
rabbinic Judaism, 9-10, 35-37, 43, 254

racial nationalism, 176-77
Radford, Laura, 335
Raheb, Mitri, 350
rapture, 4, 8, 87, 100, 118, 132, 134-35, 138, 140, 146-48, 150-52, 154-55, 158, 160, 163, 186-87, 189, 197, 199-200, 244-45, 259, 264, 269, 276, 278, 304, 325, 329, 334
Rausch, David, 201-2, 312-13
Reading, Lord, 171
Reagan, Ronald, 274-75
Reconquista, Spanish, 34
Reed, Ralph, 278
Reform Judaism, 105, 157, 213, 224, 277
Reformation, 4, 7, 8, 17, 19, 41, 46-47, 49, 50-51, 55, 58, 60, 62, 64, 82, 123, 142, 311, 321, 327, 356-57
Regent University, 276
Reines, Isaac Joseph, 12
Religious Roundtable, 272
Rembaum, Joel, 36
renewalist, 276, 316, 320-21, 323-24, 329-32, 334, 340-44
Rennie, Ian, 151
Renton, James, 176, 179
replacement theology. *See* supersessionism
Republican National Convention, 277
Resolution 181, United Nations, 229-30
restorationism, 2, 7, 28, 43, 44-45, 48, 59, 61, 69, 73, 75, 77, 85, 91, 92, 102, 108, 117, 128, 132, 221, 326-27, 357, 358
Richard, Cliff, 267
Ridolfi plot, 60
Riley, William Bell, 192, 207
Roberts, Oral, 251
Robertson, Pat, 245, 272, 275-79, 283, 290, 306
Rockefeller, John D., 159
Rohan, Dennis Michael, 305
Roman Catholic, 5, 26, 28, 47, 50, 59-60, 64, 74, 95, 129, 142, 169, 181, 246-47, 254, 256, 310-11, 320, 324, 336
Roman Empire, 22-23, 40, 62, 148, 186-88, 196

Romania, 15, 158, 278
Romanticism, 96-97
Roosevelt, Franklin D., 207, 227, 272
Rose, Jerry, 291
Rose, Norman, 130
Rothschild, Lord, 164
Ruderman, David, 104
Rudolph, David J., 354
Russia, 10, 108, 121-25, 158, 163, 169-73, 183, 187, 195-97, 218, 250, 255, 274-75, 278-79, 307
Russian Jews, 10, 15, 120-25, 127, 156-58, 162, 165, 168, 170, 179, 202, 218, 290
Russian Orthodox, 80
Russian Revolution, 183, 188, 274
Ryle, J. C., 143
Sabeel, 352
Sabeel Ecumenical Liberation Theology Center, 350
Sadat, Anwar, 271
Sadducean tradition, 35
Salisbury, Lord, 174
Samuel, Herbert, 171-72, 182, 218
Sandeen, Ernest, 92, 95, 135, 150, 197-98
Satan, 63, 89, 141, 285-86, 310, 329, 331
Saucy, Robert L., 344-45
Schaeffer, Francis, 253
Scheinberg, Aryeh, 265
Schick, Conrad, 297
Schneer, Jonathan, 166, 168, 171-72, 174, 184-85
Scofield Reference Bible, 112, 147, 157, 161, 245, 322
Scofield, Cyrus I., 136, 145, 149, 157, 161, 190, 198, 209
Scopes Monkey Trial, 272
Scotland, 52, 69, 76, 97-99, 104, 174, 180
Scott, Thomas, 93, 112-13, 128
Sea of Galilee, 67, 233
second coming, 27, 54, 65, 96, 110, 140-41, 144-45, 147, 221, 246, 267, 286, 326
Second Jewish Diaspora, 22
Second Vatican Council, 6

secret rapture, 135
secular state, Israel as a, 14
Segev, Tom, 171, 179
Seljuk Turks, 40
Seton Hall University, 247
settler movement, 301-2
Seventh-day Adventist Church, 133
Sevi, Sabbatai, 300
Shaftesbury, Lord (Anthony Ashley Cooper, Seventh Earl of Shaftesbury), 93, 109, 111, 114-17, 119-20, 122-25, 127-29, 131, 149, 168, 285, 358
Shah, Timothy H., 320-21
Shamir, Yitzhak, 226
Shannon, W. W., 209, 265
Shapiro, Faydra, 1, 293, 318, 341
Sharm El Sheikh, 257
Sharon movement. *See* Latter Rain movement
Shepherd, Naomi, 85
Shin Bet, 258
Sicut Iudeis, 32, 36
Simeon, Charles, 93, 106-7, 113, 128-29
Simpson, A. B., 154
Sinai, 250, 257-58, 271
Six-Day War, 4, 15, 245, 248, 252, 256-59, 261-52, 266, 295, 300, 303
Sizer, Stephen, 352, 356
slavery, 88
Smith, Al, 196
Smith, Chuck, 305, 330
Smith, Robert O., 4, 6, 54, 64, 89, 91, 132, 149
Smith, Wilbur T., 251, 308
Smuts, Jan Christian, 180
social gospel, 98, 192, 194-95
Society for the Investigation of Prophecy, 94
Society for the Propagation of the Gospel, 338
Sokolow, Nahum, 3, 83, 166, 169, 179
Southern Baptists, 193, 251, 254, 264, 280
Soviet Union, 229, 252, 257-58, 271, 275, 278-80, 286, 294

Spain, 33-34, 36, 40, 42, 169, 337
Spector, Stephen, 210, 244, 284, 307-11, 313-14, 341
Spence, Martin, 97-101, 139
Spener, Philipp Jakob, 79-83, 85, 107, 119
Spiritual Franciscans, 38
Spurgeon, Charles Haddon, 98
Saint Bartholomew's Day Massacre, 60
Stanislawski, Michael, 9
Stanley, Brian, 338
Stein, Leonard, 111, 179
Stern, Avraham, 226
Stewart, James Haldane, 93
Stewart, Lyman, 155, 322
Stewart, Milton, 155, 322
Stiffler, James M., 158
Stoecker, Adolf, 204
Stott, John R. W., 353
Straits of Tiran, 250, 257
Straus, Nathan, 188
Stroeter, Ernst F., 152, 160
Student Volunteer Movement, 146
Suez Canal, 170, 184, 219, 250, 258, 271
Sunday School Times, 187, 208, 229, 239
Sunday School Zionism, 219-20
Sunday, Billy, 147, 149, 192
supersessionism, 20-21, 68-69, 114, 212, 335-36, 346, 353-54
Sutton, Matthew Avery, 144, 149, 153-54, 192, 200-201, 245, 248, 272
Swaggart, Jimmy, 275
Sykes, Christopher, 11
Sykes, Sir Mark, 5, 168-69, 184
Sykes-Picot Agreement, 183
Syrian Colonisation Fund, 124
Tabor House, 297
Talbot Seminary, 344
Talmud, 9, 15, 35-36, 39, 42-43, 104
Tannenbaum, Marc, 254, 256, 262, 268, 270
Taylor, James Hudson, 118, 198, 322

teaching of contempt, 5, 44, 67, 76, 247, 357
teaching of esteem, 67-69, 76, 78-79, 84, 112-14, 136, 248, 313, 357
Tel Aviv, 232, 282
temple, 5, 9, 18, 25, 31, 141
rebuilding, 30, 161, 186, 278, 300-308, 327
Temple Mount, 278, 303-5
Temple Mount Faithful, 305
Temple Mount Foundation, 305
ten lost tribes of Israel, 22, 66, 323
Terra Nova, Rene, 330
Tertullian, 29, 70
Thering, Rose, 247
Third Temple, 300, 303-6
Thirty Years War, 64
Thompson, A. E., 190-91
time of Jacob's trouble, 141, 151, 203, 239-40
Times of London, The, 122-23
Toon, Peter, 46, 52, 62, 71
Torrey, Reuben A., 141, 147, 192
Tractarians, 142
transference theology. *See* supersessionism
Treaty of Berlin, 158
Trinity College, Dublin, 135
Trinity Evangelical Divinity School, 264
Trinity Theological Seminary, 264
Trump, Donald, 280, 282, 285, 287
Tuchman, Barbara, 171
Turk, the (a cipher for Islam), 142, 162-63, 191
Turkey, 158, 166, 169, 172-73, 182-83, 223
Turnbull, Charles G., 239
Tuveson, Ernest Lee, 26, 58, 149
Uganda, 165-66
Ukraine, 121
ultra-Orthodox, 14-15, 23, 293, 300
unitarianism, 323
United Jewish Appeal, 260

United Nations, 195, 224, 228-31, 233, 237-38, 249, 257, 278, 282, 292
United Nations Security Council, 282, 292
United Nations Special Committee on Palestine, 229
University of Chicago Divinity School, 189
Urban II (pope), 41
US Conference of Catholic Bishops, 6
van der Hoeven, Jan Willem, 291
Vatican, 5, 189, 246-47
Vatican II, 5-6, 247, 336
Vaught, W. O., 280
Vineyard Christian Fellowship, 330
Viorst, Milton, 9
Virgin Mary, 36
Wacker, Grant, 324-25
Wagner, C. Peter, 277, 331-32, 352
Walker, Peter W. L., 353
Walker, Robert, 291
Waltke, Bruce K., 347, 354-55
Walvoord, John F., 240-41, 259
War Cabinet, 169, 171, 178, 180-81, 217-18, 242
Warsaw, 104, 121, 263
Way, Lewis, 94, 96, 101, 104, 326
Weber, Max, 328
Weber, Timothy, 147, 150, 188, 269, 277, 306
Weizmann, Chaim, 167-68, 170, 174-77, 184
Weld, Angelina Grimke, 134
Werblowsky, R. J. Zwi, 262
Wesley, John, 84
West Bank, 257-58, 273, 282, 301, 350
West Jerusalem, 232-33
West, Nathaniel, 158
Westbrook, Matthew C., 2-3, 103, 153, 292, 321, 330, 332, 341-42
Westminster Theological Seminary, 251

Whalen, Robert K., 91, 133
Whiston, William, 73
Whitby, Daniel, 89
Whitehall conference, 72
Wilberforce, William, 106
Wilhelm I (kaiser), 125
Wilhelm II (kaiser), 126
Willmer, Haddon, 129
Wilson, Daniel, 106
Wilson, David, 202, 348
Wilson, Dwight, 162, 308
Wilson, Woodrow, 149, 182,
    188, 194
Wingate, Orde, 220
Winrod, Gerald, 207
Winthrop, John, 86
Wittgenstein, Ludwig, 335
Wolf, Lucien, 167, 177, 181, 184
Wolff, Joseph, 130
Wolffe, John, 322

Wollebius, Johannes, 48
Woodhead Commission, 223
World Conference of
    Pentecostal Churches, 251
World Congress of Zionists,
    126
World Jewish Conference, 293
World War I, 167, 186-88,
    192-93, 196, 213, 220
World War II, 202, 217, 219,
    227, 263, 279
World's Christian
    Fundamentals Association,
    191
World Zionist Organization,
    126, 213
Worldwide Church of God,
    305
Wright, Christopher J. H.,
    347, 351, 353

Wright, N. T., 347, 351, 353-54
Wyatt, Thomas, 329
Wycliffe, John, 39
Yardenit, 298
Yiddish language, 13, 83, 104,
    159
Yishuv, 210, 227, 232, 235,
    238-39
Yom Kippur War, 270
Young, G. Douglas, 255, 264,
    270
Zambia, 319
Zinzendorf, Nicholas von, 85
Zionism, definition of, 2
Zionism, Jewish, 9-16, 126-28,
    159-60, 165, 213, 260
Zionist Conference. *See*
    World Congress of Zionists
Zwingli, Ulrich, 49-50

SCRIPTURE INDEX

OLD TESTAMENT

Genesis
12, *18, 136*
12:1-8, *18*
12:3, *283*
22:17, *284*
28:12-14, *352*

Leviticus
19:33, *217, 242, 360*
19:34, *217, 242, 360*

Deuteronomy
28:8-9, *19*
32:10, *79*

Joshua
21:43-45, *19*

Psalms
2, *354*
17:8, *79*
37:11, *355*
59:11, *31*
72, *354*
114:3, *20*
122:6, *120, 308*

Proverbs
7:2, *79*

Isaiah
11:12-13, *66*
40:1, *291*
40:1-2, *308*
43:1-4, *351*
50:12, *114*
58, *290*
60:12, *337*
62:5-6, *351*
62:6, *286*

Jeremiah
3:12-14, *66*
30:7, *203, 240*
33:7-9, *106*

Ezekiel
4:4-6, *71*
37, *65*
37:16, *66*
37:19, *66*
38, *196*
38–39, *278*
38:6, *195*
38:15, *195*

Daniel
7, *95*
7:15-28, *95*
9:24-27, *137*

Hosea
1:11, *49, 66*
3:5, *49*

Joel
2:23, *326*

Zechariah
2:8, *78, 79, 309*
14:16, *291*

NEW TESTAMENT

Matthew
5:5, *352, 355*
5:14, *86*
24, *140*
24:2, *25*

Mark
13:2, *25*

Luke
19:44, *25*
21:24, *190, 259*

John
1:43-51, *352*
10:16, *20*

Acts
1:6, *303*
1:7, *303*
3, *101*
3:20, *100*

Romans
1:16, *79, 104*
2:10, *79*
2:28-29, *20*
4, *354*
4:13, *352, 355*
8, *354*
8:18-25, *329*
8:19, *331*
9–11, *355*
9:6, *21*
11, *48, 49, 52*
11:1, *21*
11:11, *32*
11:12, *107*
11:13, *254*
11:17-18, *18*
11:17-24, *21*
11:25, *53*
11:25-26, *48*
11:25-32, *21, 52*
11:26, *52*
11:28, *68, 76*
15, *309*
15:27, *309*

Galatians
3:15-18, *352*

3:29, *17, 19, 20*
6:15-16, *19*
6:16, *17, 52*

Ephesians
2:12, *138*
2:19-20, *352*

1 Thessalonians
4:13-18, *189*

2 Timothy
2:15, *136*

Titus
2:13, *138*

James
5:7-8, *326*

Revelation
6–20, *62*
7, *151*
11:1-3, *71, 142*
11:2, *71, 190*
13, *62, 95*
13:2, *142*
13:3, *142*
13:5, *71*
14:8, *62*
16, *95*
16:12, *64*
19:1-2, *62*
20, *26, 28, 69, 101*
20:1-7, *26*
20:2-7, *26*
20:3, *70*
20:8, *65*
20:9, *65*
20:11-12, *65*
21–22, *65*